Better Homes and Gardens.

the *ultimate*
cookie
book 2nd Edition

more than **500** best-ever treats plus
secrets for successful cookie baking

Hougthon Mifflin Harcourt
Boston • New York

Meredith Corporation

Editor: Jan Miller

Project Editor: Lisa Kingsley, Waterbury Publications, Inc.

Contributing Editors: Joy Taylor, Mary Williams,
Waterbury Publications, Inc.

Recipe Testing: Better Homes and Gardens® Test Kitchen

Better Homes and Gardens® Test Kitchen Product
Supervisor: Juliana Hale

Houghton Mifflin Harcourt

Publisher: Natalie Chapman

Editorial Director: Cindy Kitchel

Executive Editor: Anne Ficklen

Associate Editor: Heather Dabah

Editorial Associate: Molly Aronica

Managing Editor: Marina Padakis Lowry

Production Director: Tom Hyland

Design Director: Ken Carlson, Waterbury Publications, Inc.

Associate Design Director: Doug Samuelson,
Waterbury Publications, Inc.

Production Assistant: Mindy Samuelson, Waterbury
Publications, Inc.

Library of Congress Cataloging-in-Publication Data
The ultimate cookie book. — 2nd edition.
    pages cm
"Better Homes and Gardens."
Includes index.
ISBN 978-0-544-33929-3 (paperback); ISBN 978-0-544-33819-7 (ebk)
1. Cookies. I. Better Homes and Gardens Books (Firm) II. Title:
Better homes and gardens the ultimate cookie book.
TX772.U47 2014
641.86'54—dc23
2014026306

Book design by Waterbury Publications, Inc., Des Moines, Iowa.

SCP 10 9 8 7 6 5   4500677881

Printed in China

Our seal assures you that every recipe in *Better Homes
and Gardens*® *The Ultimate Cookie Book* has been tested in
the Better Homes and Gardens® Test Kitchen. This means
that each recipe is practical and reliable and meets
our high standards of taste appeal. We guarantee your
satisfaction with this book for as long as you own it.

Cover photos
Top row, from left: Salted Almond Brownies, page 281,
Filled Cherry Macarons, page 179, Giant Gingersnaps,
page 382; Middle row, from left: Bittersweet Chocolate
Biscotti, page 444, Cherry Pinwheels, page 67, Triple-
Peanut and Chocolate Chip Cookies, page 26; Bottom
row, from left: Caramel-Pecan Pumpkin Cheesecake
Bites, page 448, Holiday 7-Layer Bars, page 453, Lovely
Lemon Crinkles, page 435

table of
contents

cookies for every occasion!

No matter what your cookie mood—or cookie need—it's very likely you'll find the delicious solution in *Better Homes and Gardens® The Ultimate Cookie Book, Second Edition*. Looking for a chocolate fix? An after-school snack? Or perhaps an easy recipe for a potluck? They're all here.

* Large pans of brownies and bars to feed a crowd
* Brightly decorated cutouts and holiday favorites, many with international appeal
* Chill-ahead slice-and-bake cookies that save time
* Popular drop and sandwich cookies, many with flavorful twists
* Express ideas, some starting with a mix and others requiring no baking at all!

With 500 recipes to choose from, the hardest part will be picking which ones to make. So what are you waiting for?

Happy Baking!

cookie

bas

1

Making outstanding cookies requires just a few simple fundamentals. Using the right ingredients and measuring correctly is the first step. Having the proper baking utensils can help ensure perfect results. And for recipes to which you'd like to add decorative touches, be sure to follow the Test Kitchen tips for creating the prettiest cookies around.

ics

measuring primer

Baking success depends on how you measure ingredients. Wet ingredients go in one type of measuring cup, while dry products go in a different type. You lightly spoon flour, but pack brown sugar. To get the baking results achieved in our Test Kitchen, follow the easy guidelines on page 9 to measure ingredients.

get the scoop: Create uniform-size drop cookies by using cookie scoops or ice cream scoops to portion the dough. Scoops come in a variety of sizes, so you can create any size cookie (from a 1-tablespoon scoop for a small cookie to a ¼-cup scoop for a big cookie). Purchase a scoop with a release mechanism for easy dispensing of dough.

1 small amounts of ingredients: Scoop a dry ingredient—such as baking powder or salt—into a measuring spoon, then level it off with the edge of the container or a knife. To measure liquid ingredients—such as vanilla—pour up to the top edge of the measuring spoon.

2 liquids: Measure milk, oil, and other liquids in a liquid measuring cup (usually made of glass). Read the cup markings at eye level with the cup sitting on a flat surface. Looking at the cup from above gives a distorted view of the amount in the cup.

3 semisolid ingredients: Most shortening and butter comes in sticks with tablespoon measurements on the wrapping. If you use tub shortening, firmly press the shortening into a dry measuring cup with a silicone spatula to press out air bubbles. Level off excess with the flat edge of a knife. Use this same technique to measure peanut butter.

4 flour: There's no need to sift flour. Just stir the flour in the canister with a fork to lighten its volume. Gently spoon flour into a dry measuring cup. Use the flat edge of a knife to level flour even with the top of the cup.

5 brown sugar: Spoon brown sugar into a dry measuring cup. Use the back of a spoon to firmly pack sugar in the cup. Use the flat edge of a knife to level sugar even with the top of the cup.

granulated sugar: Scoop granulated sugar into a dry measuring cup (usually made of metal or plastic with stackable options for varying sizes). Use the flat edge of a knife to scrape the excess back into the canister, leaving the surface level with the top of the cup.

equipment

Stocking your kitchen with quality bakeware is just as important as using the best ingredients. Use these tips for foolproof baking.

baking sheets: Baking sheets come in many colors, textures, and sizes, but there's no reason to spend a fortune on them. Our Test Kitchen found that sheets—even inexpensive ones—with the following attributes yield the best, most evenly baked cookies:

> **Light to medium color:** Shiny and nonstick surfaces don't influence results.
>
> **Sturdy and heavy-duty:** Avoid lightweight pans.
>
> **One or two raised sides:** More than two raised sides prevents good air circulation.
>
> **Noninsulated:** Increases baking time and causes cookies to spread.
>
> **Nonperforated:** Crumbs stick in the holes of perforated pans/mats.

1 baking stones: Stones provide a nonstick surface and produce evenly baked cookies, but are heavy to work with. We've found that stones work better when heated prior to adding the cookie dough, but you must work quickly between batches to prevent dough from spreading.

2 parchment: We often call for cookie sheets lined with parchment paper. We usually do this if a cookie tends to stick to a pan (even when the pan is greased), is very delicate, or requires an ungreased pan. Parchment also makes transferring large cookies to a cooling rack much easier. Find parchment near the waxed paper in grocery stores and supercenters.

3 aluminum foil: Most of our bar recipes call for lining pans with foil. The pros in the Better Homes and Gardens Test Kitchen rely on this step for easy removal of bar cookies and even easier cleanup. Lining a pan with foil is particularly helpful when you bake sticky, sugary bars. Here's how to do it:

(2)

Mold a piece of foil around the back of an overturned pan, allowing overhang.

Flip pan upright. Place the foil shell into the pan. Press foil into pan to fit evenly.

ingredients

Sugar, flour, eggs—you know the fundamental ingredients for baking, but here's some expert insight on a few ingredients to you help master every recipe.

vanilla beans: Vanilla extract is a fine flavoring, but nothing compares to the essence imparted by seeds from a vanilla bean pod. Vanilla beans are available in the spice aisle of most grocery stores or at specialty spice stores. Here's how to use a vanilla bean: Cut a vanilla bean in half lengthwise (*right*). Use a small sharp knife to scrape the seeds from the bean. Use seeds as directed in your recipe. If desired, place the bean pod in a container of granulated sugar for 1 to 2 weeks to create vanilla sugar.

sour milk: When a recipe calls for buttermilk, and there's none in the fridge, you can generally use sour milk instead. To make 1 cup sour milk, place 1 tablespoon of lemon juice or white vinegar in a glass measuring cup. Add enough milk to equal 1 cup total. Let mixture stand about 5 minutes before using in a recipe.

butter vs. other fats: You just can't beat the wonderful flavor of real butter. That's why it's our number-one preference in baking. We decided to compare it to three other fats to see how they affect a cookie's quality. Although butter bakes up best and contributes the best taste and texture, we discovered that cookies

made with 100 percent margarine or 100 percent shortening both taste good, so those fats are acceptable substitutes. (Use a margarine with 100 calories per tablespoon). The cookies baked with vegetable oil, however, tasted, well, oily.

nutmeg: We always recommend freshly grated nutmeg because it yields a more intense, sweeter flavor than purchased ground nutmeg. Whole nutmeg seeds can be found in the spice section of most grocery stores. Rub the seeds briskly but carefully along a microplane grater to create piles of aromatic ground spice.

Vegetable Oil

Butter

Margarine

Shortening

white chocolate: True white chocolate contains cocoa butter extracted from the cocoa bean. Other white baking products—such as candy coating and white baking pieces—contain primarily milk, sugar, and hydrogenated oil. Easy-to-melt white baking products work for coating purposes, but true white chocolate is worth the fuss and cost for the flavor.

how to melt: The high amount of cocoa butter in true white chocolate makes it very sensitive to heat. When overheated, the milk proteins in white chocolate clump together (or seize). Once this happens, you must start over with new chocolate. For the best results, place chopped white chocolate in a small heavy saucepan (or in the top of a double boiler). Melt chocolate over low heat, stirring constantly. Or carefully melt the white chocolate in a microwave.

Place chopped white chocolate in a saucepan over low heat. Stir it to prevent scorching.

White chocolate clumps (seizes) when it gets too hot. If this happens, start over with new chocolate.

chopping nuts: A recipe might call for nuts to be chopped, finely chopped, or ground. Chop nuts with a chef's knife or pulse them in a food processor for the desired consistency. When grinding nuts in a food processor, be careful to halt the process before the mixture looks oily and turns into nut butter. Adding 1 tablespoon of sugar or flour from the recipe for each cup of nuts can help prevent overprocessing.

toasting nuts: In most of our recipes, we toast nuts to heighten their flavor. To toast whole nuts or large pieces, spread them in a single layer in a shallow baking pan. Bake in a 350°F oven for 5 to 10 minutes or until nuts are golden brown, stirring once or twice. Toast finely chopped nuts, sesame seeds, and pinenuts in a dry skillet over medium heat, stirring often.

Chopped

Finely chopped

Ground

determining doneness

Each type of cookie requires a different doneness test. Read your cookie recipe carefully to determine which test to use, then follow these tips for testing. Always check cookies after the mimimum recommended baking time; bake longer if needed.

1 firm or set edges: For some dark-color cookies, a common doneness test is when the cookie edges hold up to light pressure. Gently nudge the edge of a cookie with a spatula or your finger. (Be careful, the cookies and baking sheet are hot!)

2 tops appear dry or set: When some sugar cookies or other light-color cookies are done, the tops will no longer appear soft, melty, or doughy. You can very lightly touch the cookie tops with a spatula without causing indents.

3 bottoms are light brown: For some firm, sturdy cookies, you'll need to look at the bottom of the cookie to determine doneness. Lift the cookie with a spatula to see if the bottom is light brown.

4 clean toothpick: Some brownies or bars call for a toothpick test. Insert a toothpick into the center of the baked goods. If the toothpick comes out with wet batter on it, continue baking until the toothpick test comes out clean.

Using Cooling Racks: Our recipes often recommend placing a cookie sheet or baking pan on a cooling rack after baking. This helps air to circulate under the pan, speeding up the cooling process. Follow individual recipes to determine how long the cookies should rest on the rack.

freezing cookies or dough

Most baked cookies can be stored in the freezer for several months. And many cookie doughs can be made ahead and stashed in the freezer until you're ready to bake, letting you enjoy fresh-tasting cookies year-round.

1 baked sturdy cookies *(such as most drop cookies and sugar cookies):* Place baked, cooled, and unfrosted cookies in freezer bags labeled with the type of cookie and the date. Freeze the cookies up to 3 months. Thaw at room temperature before serving.

2 cookie dough: Most doughs can be frozen, but avoid freezing brownie batter and meringue mixtures. Place dough in a tightly sealed freezer container and freeze it up to 6 months. Thaw the dough in the fridge, then shape and bake as directed.

3 slice-and-bake cookie dough: Wrap dough logs in plastic wrap then in heavy-duty foil. Freeze the dough up to 6 months. Thaw dough logs in the refrigerator before slicing for baking.

4 shaped dough: For dough that is shaped into balls (such as Snickerdoodles, page 116), freeze balls on a cookie sheet. Place frozen balls in a freezer bag. Label bag with the type of cookie and date. (You might also include baking time and temp on the bag.) To bake dough balls from frozen, add 2 to 3 minutes to the baking time in the recipe.

Room Temperature Storage: Layer cookies between sheets of waxed paper in an airtight containter then cover. Store at room temperature up to 3 days. Throughout the book you'll also find some specific storage directions with some specialty cookies.

decorating techniques

Mixing the dough and baking is only half the fun. Adding decorative frosting to cutout cookies or garnishing a pan of bars will show your individual flair.

1 chocolate shards: To make chocolate shards to garnish the top of bar cookies, use a large, heavy chef's knife to cut very thin slices (almost shavings) from a thick bar or chunk of chocolate. Break pieces apart slightly to create long jagged pieces of chocolate.

2 stained-glass effect: You can use this technique for any cutout cookie (such as Sugar Cookies, page 417). Place cookie dough cutouts on a foil-lined cookie sheet. Cut out smaller shapes from inside each cutout. Sprinkle finely crushed fruit-flavor hard candies in each small cutout; bake for 5 minutes to melt the candies. Cool cookies on the cookie sheet so they continue baking on the hot pan.

3 shapes with sprinkles: To create a shape on a frosted cookie, place a cookie cutter on wet frosting. Fill inside the cutter with colored sugar or nonpareils. Carefully remove cutter. Allow cookie to dry.

using cookie stencils: Cookie stencils are available in an array of designs and for many cookie shapes and sizes. Choose stencils that fit a theme, such as ornaments for holiday cookies. Lay a stencil over the frosted cookie, and fill in with luster dust or edible glitter. Carefully remove stencil.

using cookie dough: For specialty dough shapes, such as arms and legs for the Roly-Poly Santas (page 436), form the main cookie shapes from dough, then use a small sharp knife to cut small pieces from the dough. Attach the small shapes to the main cookie shape on the cookie sheet. The pieces will join together as they bake. Pieces are very fragile once baked, so take care when moving and frosting the cookies.

1 **ombré effect:** Tint Royal Icing (page 18) three or four shades of the same color to create an ombré effect, (as shown on the Christmas tree cookies above). After adding each shade of icing and before it dries, drag a toothpick to swirl icings together where two colors meet.

2 **embedded designs:** Using Royal Icing (page 18) to decorate round sugar cookies (as shown below), frost each cookie with a base coat (such as green or white). For one version, pipe concentric circles in a different color onto the wet base coat, then drag a toothpick from center to edge and from edge to center to create a spiderweb design. For another version, pipe dots of a second color onto a wet base coat; use a toothpick to swirl the dots. Allow cookies to thoroughly dry. For a third idea, pipe two dots of the second color very close to one another onto the wet base coat; draw a toothpick between dots to create a heart shape.

3 **outlining with sugar:** To outline a cookie with colored sugar (as shown below), start by flooding a cookie with Royal Icing (page 18); let cookie stand until icing is dry. Using a pastry bag fitted with a plain round tip, pipe an outline of Royal Icing around the cookie edges. Sprinkle sugar on the wet icing, coating it completely. Tap the cookie gently to remove excess colored sugar.

chocolate-dipped cookie edges: Plain baked cookie cutouts can be dipped into dark chocolate then topped with finely chopped nuts or decorative sprinkles. Melt 6 ounces semisweet or bittersweet chocolate with 2 teaspoons shortening; cool slightly. Carefully dip each cookie about halfway into the chocolate, allowing excess to drip off. Place dipped cookies on a sheet of waxed paper and sprinkle with toppings. Let stand until set.

cookie basics

icing and frosting recipes

Our recipes frequently call for one of these basic icings or frostings. Many specialty frostings appear with specific recipes.

Royal Icing

start to finish: 15 minutes
makes: about 5 cups

1 16-ounce package powdered
   sugar (4 cups)
3 tablespoons meringue
   powder*
½ teaspoon cream of tartar
½ cup warm water
1 teaspoon vanilla

In a large bowl stir together powdered sugar, meringue powder, and cream of tartar. Add the water and vanilla. Beat with an electric mixer on low speed until combined. Beat on high speed for 7 minutes or until stiff. Cover bowl with damp paper towels and plastic wrap. Chill up to 48 hours.

nutrition facts per tablespoon: 22 cal., 0 g total fat, 0 mg chol., 0 mg sodium, 6 g carb., 0 g fiber, 0 g pro.

*tip: Look for meringue powder in the cake decorating aisle of hobby and crafts stores.

Powdered Sugar Icing

start to finish: 10 minutes
makes: ¼ cup

½ cup powdered sugar
½ teaspoon vanilla
   Milk

In a small bowl stir together the powdered sugar, vanilla, and enough milk (1 to 2 teaspoons) to make icing drizzling consistency.

nutrition facts per tablespoon: 60 cal., 0 g total fat, 0 mg chol., 1 mg sodium, 15 g carb., 0 g fiber, 0 g pro.

Creamy Frosting

start to finish: 25 minutes
makes: 3 cups

1   cup shortening
1½ teaspoons vanilla
½   teaspoon almond extract
1   16-ounce package (about
    4 cups) powdered sugar
3   to 4 tablespoons milk

In a large mixing bowl beat shortening, vanilla, and almond extract with an electric mixer on medium speed for 30 seconds. Gradually add about half of the powdered sugar, beating well. Beat in 2 tablespoons of the milk. Gradually beat in the remaining powdered sugar and enough of the remaining milk for frosting to reach spreading consistency.

nutrition facts per tablespoon: 75 cal., 4 g total fat (1 g sat. fat), 0 mg chol., 1 mg sodium, 9 g carb., 0 g fiber, 0 g pro.

Cream Cheese Frosting

start to finish: 20 minutes
makes: 3½ cups

1	8-ounce package cream cheese
½	cup butter
2	teaspoons vanilla
5½	to 6 cups powdered sugar

Allow cream cheese and butter to stand at room temperature for 30 minutes. In a large mixing bowl beat cream cheese, butter, and vanilla with an electric mixer on medium speed until light and fluffy. Gradually beat in powdered sugar until frosting reaches spreading consistency.

Cocoa-Cream Cheese Frosting: Prepare as above, except beat ½ cup unsweetened cocoa powder into the cream cheese mixture and reduce powdered sugar to 5 to 5½ cups.

nutrition facts per tablespoon plain or cocoa variation: 75 cal., 3 g total fat (2 g sat. fat), 9 mg chol., 28 mg sodium, 12 g carb., 0 g fiber, 0 g pro.

Butter Frosting

start to finish: 20 minutes
makes: 4½ cups

¾	cup butter
2	pounds powdered sugar (about 8 cups)
⅓	cup milk
2	teaspoons vanilla
	Milk
	Food coloring (optional)

Allow butter to stand at room temperature for 30 minutes. In a very large mixing bowl beat butter with an electric mixer on medium speed until smooth. Gradually add 2 cups of the powdered sugar, beating well. Slowly beat in the ⅓ cup milk and the vanilla. Gradually beat in the remaining powdered sugar. Beat in additional milk until frosting reaches spreading consistency. If desired, tint with food coloring.

nutrition facts per tablespoon: 67 cal., 2 g total fat (1 g sat. fat), 5 mg chol., 14 mg sodium, 13 g carb., 0 g fiber, 0 g pro.

Milk Chocolate Butter Frosting: Prepare as above, except melt 1 cup milk chocolate pieces; cool. Beat into the butter before adding the powdered sugar.

nutrition facts per tablespoon: 68 cal., 2 g total fat (1 g sat. fat), 5 mg chol., 16 mg sodium, 12 g carb., 0 g fiber, 0 g pro.

Chocolate Butter Frosting: Prepare as above, except substitute ½ cup unsweetened cocoa powder for ½ cup of the powdered sugar.

nutrition facts per tablespoon: 65 cal., 2 g total fat (1 g sat. fat), 5 mg chol., 14 mg sodium, 12 g carb., 0 g fiber, 0 g pro.

Strawberry Butter Frosting: Prepare as above, except beat ⅓ cup strawberry jam into butter before adding the powdered sugar.

nutrition facts per tablespoon: 67 cal., 2 g total fat (1 g sat. fat), 5 mg chol., 14 mg sodium, 13 g carb., 0 g fiber, 0 g pro.

Irish Cream Butter Frosting: Prepare as above, except substitute Irish cream liqueur for the milk.

nutrition facts per tablespoon: 70 cal., 2 g total fat (1 g sat. fat), 6 mg chol., 15 mg sodium, 13 g carb., 0 g fiber, 0 g pro.

Coffee Butter Frosting: Prepare as above, except add 1 tablespoon instant espresso powder or coffee crystals to the butter or substitute strong brewed coffee for the milk.

nutrition facts per tablespoon: 67 cal., 2 g total fat (1 g sat. fat), 5 mg chol., 14 mg sodium, 13 g carb., 0 g fiber, 0 g pro.

2

Looking for the absolute best chocolate chip or oatmeal cookie? This chapter is a collection of our best-ever classic recipes, plus dozens of jazzed-up variations. Of course you'll find all your favorite ingredients, including white chocolate, dark cocoa, bunches of nuts, peanut butter, caramel, and so much more. Which one will you try first?

delicious

drop

S

chocolate-hazelnut drops, page 38

A double whammy of chocolate spikes the dough. Buttery madacamia nuts take it over the top.

chocolate-macadamia dreams

prep: 35 minutes **bake:** 8 minutes at 350°F per batch
makes: 45 cookies

½   cup shortening
½   cup butter, softened
¾   cup granulated sugar
¾   cup packed brown
    sugar
½   teaspoon baking
    powder
¼   teaspoon baking soda
¼   teaspoon salt
2   eggs
1   teaspoon vanilla
1⅓ cups all-purpose flour
⅓   cup unsweetened
    cocoa powder
1½ cups rolled oats
1   cup semisweet
    chocolate pieces
1   cup white baking
    pieces or peanut
    butter-flavor pieces
1   cup chopped
    macadamia nuts

1 Preheat oven to 350°F. Line a cookie sheet with parchment paper; set aside. In an extra-large mixing bowl beat shortening and butter with an electric mixer on medium to high speed for 30 seconds. Add granulated sugar, brown sugar, baking powder, baking soda, and salt. Beat until combined, scraping sides of bowl occasionally. Beat in eggs and vanilla until combined. Beat in flour and cocoa powder on low speed just until combined. Using a wooden spoon, stir in oats, semisweet chocolate pieces, white baking pieces, and nuts.

2 Drop dough by rounded tablespoons 2 inches apart onto the prepared cookie sheet.

3 Bake for 8 to 10 minutes or just until edges are firm and centers are slightly soft. Cool on cookie sheet for 2 minutes. Transfer to a wire rack; cool.

nutrition facts per cookie: 169 cal., 10 g total fat (4 g sat. fat), 14 mg chol., 54 mg sodium, 20 g carb., 1 g fiber, 2 g pro.

Big flavors call for jumbo cookies. A glassful of ice-cold milk is the perfect go-along.

jumbo pistachio and milk chocolate chunk cookies

prep: 25 minutes **chill:** 1 hour **bake:** 10 minutes at 350°F per batch
makes: about 22 cookies

1 cup butter
1 cup packed brown sugar
¼ cup granulated sugar
1 egg
1 egg yolk
1 tablespoon milk
2 teaspoons vanilla
2½ cups bread flour or all-purpose flour
1 teaspoon salt
12 ounces milk chocolate, coarsely chopped
1½ cups pistachio nuts, coarsely chopped

1 In a small saucepan melt butter over low heat; cool slightly. Transfer melted butter to a large mixing bowl. Add sugars. Beat with an electric mixer on medium speed 2 minutes or until light.

2 In a small bowl whisk together the egg, egg yolk, milk, and vanilla. Add to butter mixture. Beat on low speed just until combined. Beat in flour and salt just until combined. Stir in chocolate chunks and nuts. Cover; chill dough for 1 hour.

3 Preheat oven to 350°F. Line cookie sheets with parchment paper. Using a ¼-cup measure or scoop, drop mounds of dough about 3 inches apart onto the prepared cookie sheets.

4 Bake for 10 to 12 minutes or until edges are lightly browned (centers may still appear moist). Cool on cookie sheets for 2 minutes. Transfer to wire racks; cool.

nutrition facts per cookie: 277 cal., 15 g total fat (8 g sat. fat), 38 mg chol., 175 mg sodium, 31 g carb., 2 g fiber, 5 g pro.

Generations never tire of this classic—and this is our best rendition ever!

chocolate chip cookies

prep: 40 minutes   **bake:** 8 minutes at 375°F per batch
makes: 60 cookies

½ cup butter, softened
½ cup shortening
1 cup packed brown sugar
½ cup granulated sugar
½ teaspoon baking soda
½ teaspoon salt
2 eggs
1 teaspoon vanilla
2¾ cups all-purpose flour
1 12-ounce package semisweet chocolate pieces or miniature candy-coated semisweet chocolate pieces (2 cups)
1½ cups chopped walnuts or pecans, toasted, if desired (optional)

1 Preheat oven to 375°F. In a large mixing bowl beat butter and shortening with an electric mixer on medium to high speed for 30 seconds. Add the brown sugar, granulated sugar, baking soda, and salt. Beat until mixture is combined, scraping sides of bowl occasionally. Beat in eggs and vanilla until combined. Beat in as much of the flour as you can with the mixer. Using a wooden spoon, stir in any remaining flour. Stir in chocolate pieces and, if desired, nuts.

2 Drop dough by rounded teaspoons 2 inches apart onto ungreased cookie sheets. (Or use a ¼-cup measure or scoop to drop mounds of dough 4 inches apart onto ungreased cookie sheets. If desired, flatten dough mounds to circles about ¾ inch thick.)

3 Bake for 8 to 9 minutes or until edges are just lightly browned. Cool on cookie sheet for 2 minutes. Transfer to wire racks; cool.

nutrition facts per cookie: 83 cal., 4 g total fat (2 g sat. fat), 9 mg chol., 37 mg sodium, 11 g carb., 0 g fiber, 1 g pro.

thin-and-crispy chocolate chip cookies:
Prepare as directed except increase butter to 1 cup and omit shortening; reduce brown sugar to ¾ cup and increase granulated sugar to ¾ cup; and reduce flour to 2 cups. Bake about 9 minutes or just until edges are lightly browned. Cool on cookie sheet for 1 minute. Transfer to wire rack; cool.
nutrition facts per cookie: 92 cal., 5 g total fat (3 g sat. fat), 15 mg chol., 55 mg sodium, 12 g carb., 0 g fiber, 1 g pro.

Use either light brown or dark brown sugar; however, the darker version adds more intense molasses flavor.

monster chocolate-toffee cookies

prep: 35 minutes **bake:** 10 minutes at 350°F per batch
makes: about 24 cookies

½ cup butter, softened
½ cup shortening
1 cup packed brown sugar
½ cup granulated sugar
½ teaspoon baking soda
½ teaspoon salt
2 eggs
1 teaspoon vanilla
2¾ cups all-purpose flour
2 cups candy-coated chocolate pieces
1 cup toffee pieces
⅔ cup pecans, coarsely chopped

1 Preheat oven to 350°F. In a large bowl combine butter and shortening. Beat with an electric mixer on medium to high speed for 30 seconds. Add brown sugar, granulated sugar, baking soda, and salt. Beat until combined, scraping sides of bowl occasionally. Beat in eggs and vanilla until combined. Beat in as much of the flour as you can with the mixer. Using a wooden spoon, stir in any remaining flour. Stir in chocolate pieces, toffee pieces, and pecans.

2 Drop dough by a cookie scoop or ¼-cup measure 4 inches apart onto ungreased cookie sheets.

3 Bake for 10 to 12 minutes or until edges are light brown. Cool on cookie sheet for 2 minutes. Transfer to a wire rack; cool.

nutrition facts per cookie: 316 cal., 18 g total fat (8 g sat. fat), 34 mg chol., 152 mg sodium, 38 g carb., 2 g fiber, 3 g pro.

These sturdy cookies travel well, making them an ideal treat to pack in tins for any gift-giving occasion.

triple-peanut and chocolate chip cookies

prep: 25 minutes **bake:** 10 minutes at 350°F per batch
makes: 72 cookies

½ cup butter, softened
½ cup shortening
½ cup creamy peanut butter
1 cup packed brown sugar
½ cup granulated sugar
1 teaspoon baking soda
2 eggs
1 teaspoon vanilla
3 cups all-purpose flour
½ cup bite-size miniature chocolate-covered peanut butter cups, unwrapped and cut up
½ cup semisweet chocolate pieces
½ cup milk chocolate pieces
½ cup honey-roasted peanuts

1 Preheat oven to 350°F. In a large mixing bowl beat butter, shortening, and peanut butter with an electric mixer on medium to high speed for 30 seconds. Add the brown sugar, granulated sugar, and baking soda. Beat until combined, scraping sides of bowl occasionally. Beat in eggs and vanilla until combined. Beat in as much of the flour as you can with the mixer. Using a wooden spoon, stir in any remaining flour, the peanut butter cups, chocolate pieces, and peanuts.

2 Drop dough by rounded teaspoons 2 inches apart onto ungreased cookie sheets.

3 Bake for 10 to 12 minutes or until golden brown. Transfer to a wire rack; cool.

nutrition facts per cookie: 97 cal., 5 g total fat (2 g sat. fat), 9 mg chol., 47 mg sodium, 11 g carb., 0 g fiber, 2 g pro.

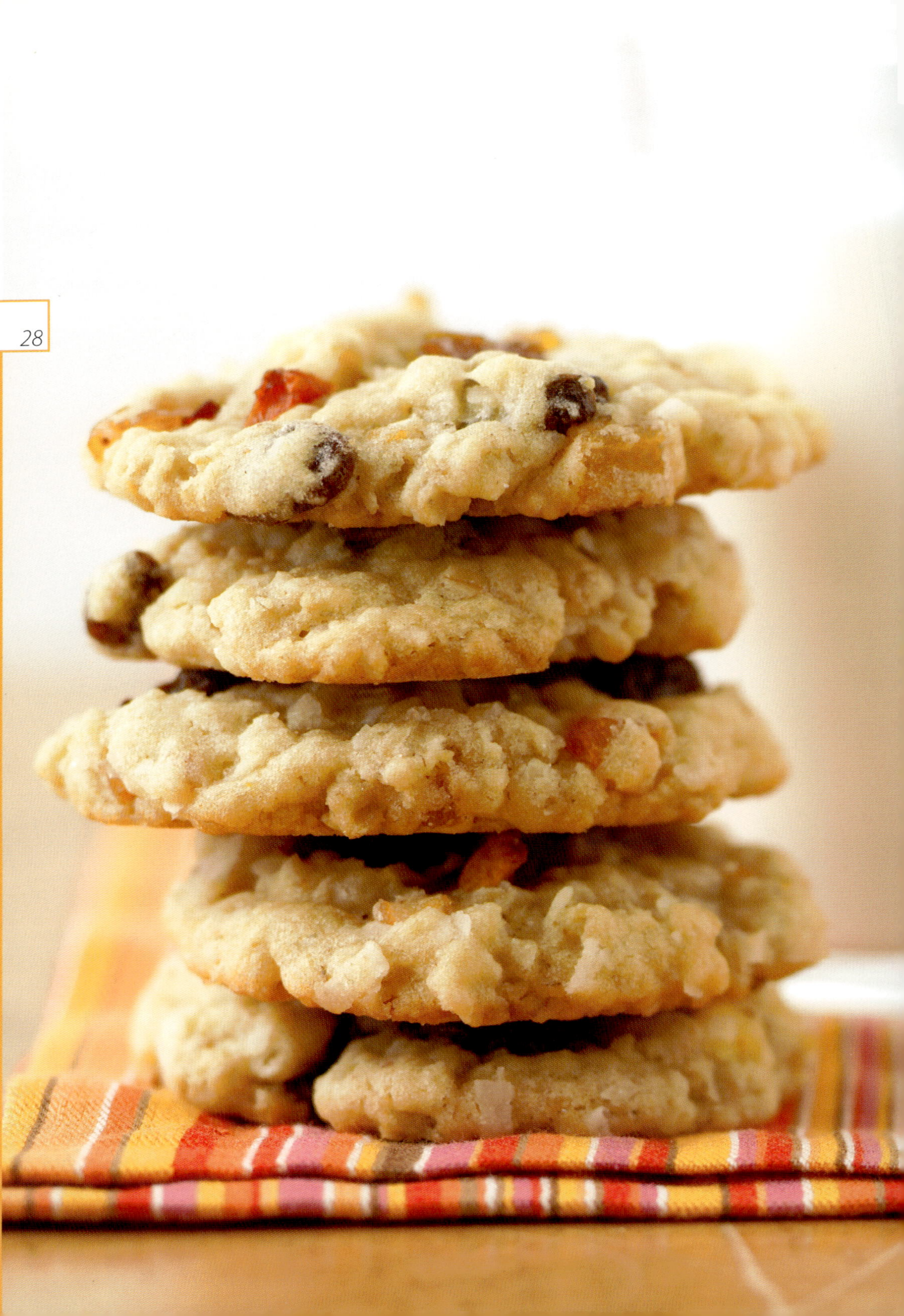

Oats, dried fruit, and coconut make these chewy morsels irresistible—and add a nutritional boost.

ranger cookies

½ cup butter, softened
½ cup granulated sugar
½ cup packed brown sugar
½ teaspoon baking powder
¼ teaspoon baking soda
1 egg
1 teaspoon vanilla
1¼ cups all-purpose flour
1 cup quick-cooking rolled oats
1 cup flaked coconut
1 cup raisins, dried cherries, dried cranberries, and/or mixed dried fruit bits

1 Preheat oven to 375°F. In a large mixing bowl beat butter with an electric mixer on medium to high speed for 30 seconds. Add granulated sugar, brown sugar, baking powder, and baking soda. Beat until combined, scraping sides of bowl occasionally. Beat in egg and vanilla until combined. Beat in as much of the flour as you can with the mixer. Using a wooden spoon, stir in any remaining flour, the oats, coconut, and dried fruit.

2 Drop dough by rounded teaspoons 2 inches apart onto an ungreased cookie sheet.

3 Bake for 8 to 10 minutes or until edges are golden and centers are set. Cool on cookie sheet for 1 minute. Transfer cookies to a wire rack; cool.

nutrition facts per cookie: 74 cal., 3 g total fat (2 g sat. fat), 10 mg chol., 34 mg sodium, 11 g carb., 1 g fiber, 1 g pro.

big ranger cookies: Prepare as directed through Step 1. Using a ⅓-cup measure or cookie scoop, drop dough in mounds about 4 inches apart onto an ungreased cookie sheet. Flatten each mound into a 3-inch circle. Bake for 10 to 12 minutes or until edges are golden and centers are set. Cool on cookie sheet for 1 minute. Transfer cookies to a wire rack; cool. Makes about 10 cookies.

nutrition facts per cookie: 355 cal., 14 g total fat (10 g sat. fat), 48 mg chol., 163 mg sodium, 53 g carb., 5 g fiber, 5 g pro,.

Substitute semisweet chocolate morsels if you prefer less intense chocolate flavor.

dark chocolate chip-granola cookies

prep: 20 minutes **bake:** 10 minutes at 350°F per batch
makes: 15 cookies

2⅔ cups all-purpose flour
1 teaspoon salt
1 teaspoon baking soda
1 cup butter, softened
1 cup packed brown sugar
1 cup granulated sugar
2 eggs
2 teaspoons vanilla
1½ cups dark chocolate pieces or bittersweet chocolate pieces
1 cup almond granola
½ cup rolled oats

1 Preheat oven to 350°F. Line cookie sheets with parchment paper; set aside. In a medium bowl stir together flour, salt, and baking soda; set aside. In a large mixing bowl beat butter with an electric mixer on medium to high speed for 30 seconds. Add brown sugar and granulated sugar. Beat until combined, scraping sides of bowl occasionally. Beat in eggs and vanilla until combined. Gradually add flour mixture, beating just until combined. Stir in chocolate pieces, granola, and oats. Drop dough by rounded tablespoons or small cookie scoop about 2 inches apart on prepared cookie sheets.

2 Bake for 10 to 14 minutes or until edges are lightly browned. Cool on cookie sheets for 1 minute. Transfer to wire racks; cool.

nutrition facts per cookie: 143 cal., 6 g total fat (4 g sat. fat), 19 mg chol., 108 mg sodium, 20 g carb., 1 g fiber, 2 g pro.

Tart apple varieties, such as Granny Smith or Rome Beauty, are good choices.

caramel apple cookies

prep: 45 minutes **bake:** 10 minutes at 350°F per batch
makes: 36 cookies

½ cup butter, softened
1¼ cups packed brown sugar
1 teaspoon baking soda
1 teaspoon apple pie spice
¼ teaspoon salt
1 egg
½ cup apple juice or milk
¼ cup whole wheat flour or all-purpose flour
2¼ cups all-purpose flour
1 large tart apple, peeled and coarsely shredded (about 1 cup)
½ cup packed brown sugar
3 tablespoons butter
3 tablespoons apple juice
2⅔ cups powdered sugar
½ cup finely chopped pecans, toasted (see tip, page 13)

1 Preheat oven to 350°F. Line a cookie sheet with parchment paper; set aside.

2 In a large mixing bowl beat the ½ cup butter with an electric mixer on medium speed for 30 seconds. Add the 1¼ cups brown sugar, the baking soda, apple pie spice, and salt. Beat until combined, scraping sides of bowl occasionally. Beat in egg. Add the ½ cup apple juice and the whole wheat flour, beating on low speed until combined. Beat in as much of the all-purpose flour as you can with the mixer. Stir in any remaining flour and the shredded apple. Drop dough by slightly rounded teaspoons 2 inches apart onto the prepared cookie sheet.

3 Bake about 10 minutes or until tops are light brown. Cool on cookie sheet for 2 minutes. Transfer cookies to a wire rack; cool.

4 For frosting, in a small saucepan heat and stir the ½ cup brown sugar, the 3 tablespoons butter, and the 3 tablespoons apple juice over medium heat until brown sugar is dissolved. Remove from heat. Gradually stir in powdered sugar until combined. Spread cookies with frosting and sprinkle with pecans. If frosting begins to harden, stir in a small amount of apple juice to reach spreading consistency.

nutrition facts per cookie: 154 cal., 5 g total fat (2 g sat. fat), 15 mg chol., 83 mg sodium, 27 g carb., 1 g fiber, 1 g pro.

With a cup of espresso on the side, you'll find cookie bliss!

blueberry lemon drops

prep: 20 minutes **bake:** 11 minutes at 375°F per batch
makes: 32 cookies

¼ cup butter, softened
¼ cup shortening
1 cup granulated sugar
1 teaspoon baking
    powder
1 teaspoon finely
    shredded lemon
    peel
½ teaspoon baking soda
½ teaspoon salt
2 eggs
1 tablespoon lemon
    juice
1½ cups all-purpose flour
½ cup flaked coconut
1 cup fresh blueberries
1 cup powdered sugar
1 tablespoon lemon
    juice
½ cup finely chopped
    pistachio nuts

1 Preheat oven to 375°F. Line a cookie sheet with parchment paper; set aside.

2 In a large mixing bowl beat butter and shortening with an electric mixer on medium to high speed for 30 seconds. Add granulated sugar, baking powder, lemon peel, baking soda, and salt. Beat until combined, scraping sides of bowl occasionally. Beat in eggs and 1 tablespoon lemon juice until combined. Beat in as much of the flour as you can with the mixer. Using a wooden spoon, stir in any remaining flour and the coconut. Drop dough by rounded teaspoons 3 inches apart onto the prepared cookie sheet. Place 3 or 4 blueberries in the center of each cookie.

3 Bake for 11 to 13 minutes or until edges are golden. Transfer to a wire rack; cool.

4 For icing, in a small bowl stir together powdered sugar and 1 tablespoon lemon juice. If necessary, stir in additional lemon juice, 1 teaspoon at a time, to reach thin spreading consistency. Gently spread icing on tops of cookies. Sprinkle with pistachios. Let stand until icing is set.

to store: Layer iced cookies between sheets of waxed paper in an airtight container; cover. Store at room temperature up to 3 days. To freeze; layer uniced cookies between sheets of waxed paper in an airtight container; freeze up to 3 months. To serve, thaw cookies and spread with icing.

nutrition facts per cookie: 108 cal., 5 g total fat (2 g sat. fat), 15 mg chol., 88 mg sodium, 16 g carb., 1 g fiber, 1 g pro.

Shop for white chocolate with cocoa butter. It's the creamiest, tastiest white chocolate for baking.

white chocolate-raspberry cookies

prep: 40 minutes **bake:** 7 minutes at 375°F per batch
makes: 48 cookies

11 ounces white baking chocolate with cocoa butter
½ cup butter, softened
1 cup granulated sugar
1 teaspoon baking soda
¼ teaspoon salt
2 eggs
2¾ cups all-purpose flour
½ cup seedless raspberry jam
½ teaspoon shortening

1 Chop 4 ounces of the white chocolate; set aside. In a small saucepan melt 4 ounces of the white chocolate over low heat until smooth; cool.

2 Preheat oven to 375°F. Grease a cookie sheet; set aside. In a large mixing bowl beat butter with an electric mixer on medium to high speed for 30 seconds. Add sugar, baking soda, and salt. Beat until combined, scraping sides of bowl occasionally. Beat in eggs and the melted white chocolate until combined. Beat in as much of the flour as you can with the mixer. Using a wooden spoon, stir in any remaining flour. Stir in the 4 ounces chopped white chocolate. Drop dough by rounded teaspoons 2 inches apart onto the prepared cookie sheet.

3 Bake for 7 to 9 minutes or until cookies are lightly browned around the edges. Cool on cookie sheet for 1 minute. Transfer to a wire rack; cool.

4 About 1 hour before serving, in a small saucepan heat and stir raspberry jam over low heat until melted. Spoon about ½ teaspoon of the jam onto the top of each cookie. In another small saucepan heat and stir the remaining 3 ounces white chocolate and the shortening over low heat until melted and smooth. Drizzle melted white chocolate mixture over cookies. If necessary, chill cookies about 15 minutes or until set.

to store: Prepare as directed through Step 3. Layer cookies between sheets of waxed paper in an airtight container; cover. Store at room temperature up to 3 days or freeze up to 1 month. To serve, thaw cookies, if frozen. Top as directed in Step 4.

nutrition facts per cookie: 109 cal., 4 g total fat (2 g sat. fat), 13 mg chol., 64 mg sodium, 16 g carb., 0 g fiber, 1 g pro.

For a timesaver, use canned sweet potatoes, drained well, then mashed.

sweet potato-pecan cookies

prep: 40 minutes   **bake:** 10 minutes at 350°F per batch
makes: 48 cookies

2¼ cups all-purpose flour
2   teaspoons baking powder
1   teaspoon baking soda
1   teaspoon ground cinnamon
½   teaspoon salt
½   cup butter, softened
½   cup granulated sugar
½   cup packed brown sugar
1   egg
1   teaspoon vanilla
1   cup mashed cooked sweet potato
1   recipe Maple Cream Cheese Frosting
48 pecan halves, toasted (see tip, page 13)

1 Preheat oven to 350°F. Line a cookie sheet with parchment paper; set aside. In a medium bowl stir together flour, baking powder, baking soda, cinnamon, and salt; set aside.

2 In a large mixing bowl beat butter with an electric mixer on medium speed for 30 seconds. Add granulated sugar and brown sugar. Beat until fluffy, scraping sides of bowl occasionally. Beat in egg and vanilla. Beat in mashed sweet potato. Add flour mixture to sweet potato mixture, beating until combined.

3 Drop dough by rounded teaspoons 2 inches apart onto the prepared cookie sheet.

4 Bake about 10 minutes or until edges start to brown. Transfer to a wire rack; cool. Frost cooled cookies with Maple Cream Cheese Frosting. Top each cookie with a pecan half.

to store: Layer cookies between sheets of waxed paper in an airtight container; cover. Store in the refrigerator up to 3 days or freeze unfrosted cookies up to 3 months. To serve, thaw cookies, if frozen. Frost cookies as directed. Top each cookie with a pecan half.

nutrition facts per cookie: 109 cal., 5 g total fat (2 g sat. fat), 15 mg chol., 111 mg sodium, 15 g carb., 0 g fiber, 1 g pro.

maple cream cheese frosting: In a mixing bowl beat 6 ounces cream cheese, softened, with an electric mixer on medium speed until smooth. Beat in 1½ cups powdered sugar, 3 tablespoons maple syrup, and 1½ teaspoons vanilla.

It's like carrot cake with extra goodies!

orange-carrot cookies with cream cheese frosting

prep: 45 minutes **bake:** 10 minutes at 350°F per batch
makes: 65 cookies

1   cup butter, softened
1   cup packed brown
      sugar
½   cup granulated sugar
1½ teaspoons baking
      powder
½   teaspoon baking soda
½   teaspoon salt
½   teaspoon ground
      cinnamon
2   eggs
1½ teaspoons finely
      shredded orange
      peel
1   teaspoon vanilla
2   cups all-purpose flour
2   cups quick-cooking
      rolled oats
1   cup shredded carrots
      (2 medium)
½   cup flaked coconut
½   cup chopped pecans,
      toasted (see tip,
      page 13) (optional)
½   recipe Cream Cheese
      Frosting (see
      page 19)

1 Preheat oven to 350°F. In an extra-large mixing bowl beat butter with an electric mixer on medium to high speed for 30 seconds. Add brown sugar, granulated sugar, baking powder, baking soda, salt, and cinnamon. Beat until combined, scraping sides of bowl occasionally. Beat in eggs, orange peel, and vanilla until combined. Beat in as much of the flour as you can with the mixer. Using a wooden spoon, stir in any remaining flour, the oats, carrots, coconut, and, if desired, pecans.

2 Drop dough by rounded teaspoons 2 inches apart onto an ungreased cookie sheet.

3 Bake for 10 to 12 minutes or until edges are golden and centers are set. Cool on cookie sheet for 2 minutes. Transfer to a wire rack; cool. Spread frosting on tops of cookies.

to store: Layer unfrosted cookies between sheets of waxed paper in an airtight container; cover. Store in the refrigerator up to 3 days or freeze up to 3 months. To serve, thaw cookies, if frozen. Frost as directed in Step 3.

nutrition facts per cookie: 103 cal., 5 g total fat (3 g sat. fat), 17 mg chol., 78 mg sodium, 14 g carb., 0 g fiber, 1 g pro.

delicious drops

Don't dare skip the scrumptious frosting!

pumpkin-pecan cookies

prep: 35 minutes **bake:** 10 minutes at 375°F per batch
makes: 40 cookies

2 cups all-purpose flour
1½ teaspoons baking powder
1 teaspoon ground cinnamon
¼ teaspoon baking soda
¼ teaspoon ground allspice
1 cup butter, softened
1 cup granulated sugar
1 cup canned pumpkin
1 egg
1 cup chopped pecans, toasted (see tip, page 13)
1 recipe Brown Sugar-Butter Frosting

1 Preheat oven to 375°F. In a medium bowl stir together flour, baking powder, cinnamon, baking soda, and allspice; set aside.

2 In a large mixing bowl beat butter with an electric mixer on medium to high speed for 30 seconds. Add sugar. Beat until combined, scraping sides of bowl occasionally. Beat in pumpkin and egg until combined. Using a wooden spoon, stir in flour mixture and pecans. Drop dough by rounded teaspoons 2 inches apart onto an ungreased cookie sheet.

3 Bake for 10 to 12 minutes or until bottoms are lightly browned. Transfer to a wire rack; cool. Spread cookies with Brown Sugar-Butter Frosting.

nutrition facts per cookie: 148 cal., 8 g total fat (4 g sat. fat), 21 mg chol., 80 mg sodium, 18 g carb., 1 g fiber, 1 g pro.

brown sugar-butter frosting: In a medium saucepan heat 6 tablespoons butter and ⅓ cup packed brown sugar over medium heat until butter is melted. Remove mixture from heat. Stir in 2 cups powdered sugar and 1 teaspoon vanilla. Add enough hot water (2 to 3 teaspoons) to make frosting spreadable. Frost cookies immediately after preparing frosting. If frosting becomes grainy, add a few more drops of hot water and stir frosting until smooth.

Serve these decadent morsels with a scoop of vanilla ice cream or orange sherbet for a simply elegant dessert.

chocolate and candied tangerine peel cookies

prep: 30 minutes **bake:** 10 minutes at 350°F per batch **stand:** 20 minutes
makes: 15 cookies

7   ounces bittersweet chocolate, chopped
5   ounces unsweetened chocolate, chopped
½   cup butter
⅓   cup all-purpose flour
¼   teaspoon baking powder
¼   teaspoon salt
1   cup granulated sugar
¾   cup packed brown sugar
4   eggs
¼   teaspoon orange extract
½   cup Candied Tangerine Peel (see recipe, page 327) or purchased candied orange peel, finely chopped

1 In a 2-quart saucepan combine bittersweet chocolate, unsweetened chocolate, and butter. Heat and stir over low heat until smooth. Remove from heat. Let stand at room temperature for 10 minutes. In a small bowl stir together flour, baking powder, and salt; set aside.

2 In a large mixing bowl beat granulated sugar, brown sugar, and eggs with an electric mixer on medium to high speed for 2 to 3 minutes or until color lightens slightly. Beat in orange extract and melted chocolate mixture until combined. Add flour mixture to chocolate mixture; beat until combined. Stir in finely chopped Candied Tangerine Peel. Cover surface of dough with plastic wrap. Let stand for 20 minutes (dough will thicken as it stands).

3 Preheat oven to 350°F. Line cookie sheets with parchment paper. Drop dough by rounded tablespoons 2 inches apart onto prepared cookie sheets. Bake for 10 to 12 minutes or just until tops are set. Cool on cookie sheets for 1 minute. Transfer to wire racks; cool.

nutrition facts per cookie: 194 cal., 11 g total fat (7 g sat. fat), 46 mg chol., 70 mg sodium, 26 g carb., 2 g fiber, 3 g pro.

Also called filberts, hazelnuts add a unique earthy flavor to this cookie. Toasted pecans make a good substitute. Pictured on page 21.

chocolate-hazelnut drops

prep: 30 minutes stand: 20 minutes bake: 8 minutes at 350°F per batch
makes: 60 cookies

6   ounces bittersweet chocolate, chopped
6   ounces unsweetened chocolate, chopped
½   cup butter
½   cup all-purpose flour
½   teaspoon ground cinnamon
¼   teaspoon baking powder
¼   teaspoon salt
1   cup granulated sugar
¾   cup packed brown sugar
4   eggs
2   teaspoons hazelnut liqueur
⅓   cup finely chopped toasted hazelnuts (filberts) (see tip, page 70)
1   cup powdered sugar
2   to 3 tablespoons hazelnut liqueur
2   tablespoons finely chopped toasted hazelnuts (filberts) (see tip, page 70) (optional)

1 In a medium saucepan combine bittersweet chocolate, unsweetened chocolate, and butter. Heat and stir over low heat until melted and smooth. Remove from heat. Cool for 10 minutes. In a small bowl stir together flour, cinnamon, baking powder, and salt; set aside.

2 In a large mixing bowl combine granulated sugar, brown sugar, eggs, and the 2 teaspoons hazelnut liqueur. Beat with an electric mixer on medium speed for 2 to 3 minutes or until color lightens slightly. Beat in melted chocolate mixture. Add flour mixture to chocolate mixture; beat until combined. Stir in the ⅓ cup hazelnuts. Cover dough; let stand for 20 minutes (dough will thicken as it stands).

3 Preheat oven to 350°F. Line cookie sheets with parchment paper. Drop dough by rounded teaspoons 2 inches apart onto the prepared cookie sheets.

4 Bake for 8 to 10 minutes or just until tops are set. Cool on cookie sheets for 1 minute. Transfer to a wire rack; cool.

5 For icing, in a small bowl stir together the powdered sugar and the 2 tablespoons hazelnut liqueur. Stir in additional liqueur, 1 teaspoon at a time, until icing reaches drizzling consistency. Drizzle over cooled cookies. If desired, sprinkle evenly with the 2 tablespoons hazelnuts. Let stand until set.

to store: Freeze uniced cookies up to 3 months; thaw and drizzle with icing.

nutrition facts per cookie: 88 cal., 5 g total fat (3 g sat. fat), 17 mg chol., 31 mg sodium, 12 g carb., 1 g fiber, 1 g pro.

triple-chocolate cookies

prep: 40 minutes stand: 20 minutes bake: 9 minutes at 350°F per batch
makes: 60 cookies

7   ounces bittersweet
     chocolate, coarsely
     chopped
5   ounces unsweetened
     chocolate, coarsely
     chopped
½   cup butter
⅓   cup all-purpose flour
¼   teaspoon baking
     powder
¼   teaspoon salt
4   eggs
1   cup granulated sugar
¾   cup packed brown
     sugar
¼   cup finely chopped
     pecans, toasted (see
     tip, page 13)
1   cup semisweet
     chocolate pieces
4   teaspoons shortening

1 In a medium saucepan heat and stir bittersweet chocolate, unsweetened chocolate, and butter over low heat until melted and smooth. Remove from heat; cool for 10 minutes.

2 Meanwhile, in a small bowl stir together flour, baking powder, and salt; set aside.

3 In a large mixing bowl beat eggs, granulated sugar, and brown sugar with an electric mixer on medium to high speed for 2 to 3 minutes or until light in color. Beat in chocolate mixture. Beat in flour mixture until combined. Stir in pecans. Cover surface of dough with plastic wrap. Let stand for 20 minutes (dough will thicken as it stands).

4 Preheat oven to 350°F. Line a cookie sheet with parchment paper or foil. Drop dough by rounded teaspoons 2 inches apart onto the prepared cookie sheet.

5 Bake about 9 minutes or just until tops are set. Cool on cookie sheet for 1 minute. Transfer cookies to a wire rack; cool.

6 In a small saucepan combine semisweet chocolate pieces and shortening. Heat and stir over low heat until melted and smooth. Remove from heat. Place cooled cookies on a cookie sheet lined with parchment or waxed paper. Drizzle melted chocolate mixture over cookies. Place in freezer for 4 to 5 minutes or until chocolate is set.

nutrition facts per cookie: 92 cal., 6 g total fat (3 g sat. fat), 18 mg chol., 19 mg sodium, 11 g carb., 1 g fiber, 1 g pro.

big triple-chocolate cookies: Prepare as directed, except for each cookie, drop 3-tablespoon-size mounds of dough 3 inches apart onto the prepared cookie sheet. Bake for 13 minutes. Makes about 18 cookies.
nutrition facts per cookie: 307 cal., 19 g total fat (2 g sat. fat), 61 mg chol., 63 mg sodium, 37 g carb., 3 g fiber, 4 g pro.

delicious drops

The perfect gift for coffee lovers!

devilish delights

prep: 25 minutes **bake:** 8 minutes at 350°F per batch
makes: 42 cookies

6   tablespoons all-purpose flour
½   teaspoon baking powder
⅛   teaspoon salt
2   eggs
½   cup granulated sugar
1   to 2 tablespoons coffee liqueur or strong brewed espresso
2   teaspoons vanilla
10   ounces bittersweet chocolate, chopped
2   tablespoons butter
1   teaspoon instant espresso coffee powder
12   ounces dark chocolate, chopped
     Powdered sugar (optional)

1 Preheat oven to 350°F. Lightly grease cookie sheets or line with parchment paper; set aside. In a small bowl combine flour, baking powder, and salt; set aside. In a large mixing bowl combine eggs, granulated sugar, liqueur, and vanilla. Beat with an electric mixer on medium speed until combined; set aside.

2 In a medium-sized heavy saucepan heat bittersweet chocolate, butter, and espresso coffee powder over medium-low heat until melted and smooth, stirring occasionally. Remove from heat. Whisk melted chocolate mixture into egg mixture until combined. Stir in flour mixture just until combined. Stir in dark chocolate (dough will resemble a thick brownie batter).

3 Drop dough by heaping teaspoons 2 inches apart onto prepared cookie sheets.

4 Bake for 8 to 9 minutes or until tops appear dry and centers remain soft. Cool on cookie sheets for 3 minutes. Transfer cookies to a wire rack; cool. If desired, dust with powdered sugar.

to store: Do not dust cookies with powdered sugar. Layer cookies between sheets of waxed paper in an airtight container; cover. Store at room temperature up to 3 days or freeze up to 3 months. If desired, dust with powdered sugar.

nutrition facts per cookie: 124 cal., 8 g total fat (5 g sat. fat), 14 mg chol., 24 mg sodium, 13 g carb., 2 g fiber, 2 g pro.

Flaxseed meal and dark chocolate add beneficial antioxidants for a guilt-free treat!

german chocolate cookies

prep: 25 minutes   bake: 8 minutes at 350°F per batch
makes: 35 cookies

¼ cup butter, softened
¾ cup packed brown sugar
½ teaspoon baking soda
⅛ teaspoon salt
1 egg
1 teaspoon vanilla
⅔ cup all-purpose flour
⅔ cup regular rolled oats
¼ cup flaxseed meal
¼ cup unsweetened cocoa powder
3 ounces special dark baking chocolate or sweet baking chocolate, chopped
⅓ cup flaked coconut
⅓ cup chopped pecans, toasted (see tip, page 13)
Flaked coconut (optional)
Coarsely chopped pecans (optional)

1 Preheat oven to 350°F. In a large mixing bowl beat butter with an electric mixer on medium to high speed for 30 seconds. Add brown sugar, baking soda, and salt. Beat until combined, scraping sides of bowl occasionally. Beat in egg and vanilla until combined. Beat in as much of the flour as you can with the mixer. Stir in any remaining flour, the rolled oats, flaxseed meal, and cocoa powder. Stir in chopped chocolate, the ⅓ cup coconut, and the ⅓ cup pecans (dough will be stiff).

2 Drop dough by rounded teaspoons 2 inches apart onto an ungreased cookie sheet. If desired, sprinkle with additional coconut and pecans.

3 Bake for 8 to 10 minutes or just until edges are firm and tops are set. Cool on cookie sheet for 1 minute. Transfer cookies to a wire rack; cool.

to store: Layer cookies between sheets of waxed paper in an airtight container; cover. Store at room temperature up to 2 days.

nutrition facts per cookie: 84 cal., 4 g total fat (2 g sat. fat), 10 mg chol., 45 mg sodium, 11 g carb., 1 g fiber, 2 g pro.

delicious drops

Dutch cocoa adds richer, darker flavor to the batter than the more commonplace cocoa powder.

double-chocolate-cranberry cookies

prep: 25 minutes bake: 8 minutes at 350°F per batch
makes: 42 cookies

1   cup whole wheat
    pastry flour
¼   cup unsweetened
    Dutch-process
    cocoa powder
½   cup butter, softened
½   cup packed brown
    sugar
¼   cup granulated sugar
½   teaspoon baking
    powder
1   egg
1   cup dark chocolate
    pieces
¾   cup dried cranberries

1 Preheat oven to 350°F. In a small bowl combine flour and cocoa powder; set side. In a large mixing bowl beat butter with an electric mixer on medium to high speed for 30 seconds. Add brown sugar, granulated sugar, and baking powder. Beat until combined, scraping sides of bowl occasionally. Beat in egg until combined. Beat in as much of the flour mixture as you can with the mixer. Using a wooden spoon, stir in any remaining flour mixture, the chocolate pieces, and cranberries.

2 Drop dough by rounded teaspoons 2 inches apart onto ungreased cookie sheets.

3 Bake for 8 to 10 minutes or until edges are set. Cool on cookie sheets for 2 minutes. Transfer to wire racks; cool.

nutrition facts per cookie: 107 cal., 5 g total fat (3 g sat. fat), 15 mg chol., 40 mg sodium, 15 g carb., 1 g fiber, 1 g pro.

Find sweet and tart dried cherries in the baking aisle at grocery stores. We think tart tastes best alongside the bittersweet chocolate.

chocolate gingerbread drops

prep: 30 minutes **bake:** 8 minutes at 375°F per batch
makes: 36 cookies

½ cup shortening
¾ cup packed brown sugar
¾ teaspoon baking soda
1 teaspoon ground ginger
1 teaspoon ground allspice
¼ teaspoon salt
¼ cup molasses
1 egg
2 cups all-purpose flour
½ cup dried tart red cherries
3 ounces bittersweet chocolate, coarsely chopped

1 Preheat oven to 375°F. In a large mixing bowl beat shortening with an electric mixer on medium to high speed for 30 seconds. Add brown sugar, baking soda, ginger, allspice, and salt; beat until combined. Beat in molasses and egg. Beat in as much flour as you can with the mixer. Using a wooden spoon, stir in any remaining flour, the cherries, and chocolate. Drop dough by rounded teaspoons onto ungreased cookie sheets.

2 Bake about 8 minutes or until bottoms are lightly browned. Transfer to wire racks; cool.

nutrition facts per cookie: 94 cal., 4 g total fat (1 g sat. fat), 6 mg chol., 48 mg sodium, 14 g carb., 0 g fiber, 1 g pro.

From peanut butter with whole wheat flour to jumbo butterscotch-molasses cookies, mix and match ingredients to make your favorite cookie.

make-it-mine oatmeal cookies

prep: 30 minutes **bake:** 8 to 12 minutes at 350°F per batch
makes: 72 teaspoon-size; 36 tablespoon-size, 24 cookie scoop-size; 18 ¼-cup-size

Fat
Sugar
1 teaspoon baking soda
Spice
½ teaspoon salt
2 eggs
Flavoring
Flour
3 cups regular or quick-cooking rolled oats
1 cup stir-in* (optional)

1 Preheat oven to 350°F. In a large mixing bowl beat fat with an electric mixer on medium to high speed for 30 seconds. Add sugar, baking soda, spice, and salt. Beat until combined, scraping sides of bowl. Beat in eggs and flavoring. Beat in as much of the flour as you can with the mixer. Stir in any remaining flour and the oats. If desired, add stir-in.*

2 Drop dough by rounded teaspoons or tablespoons or by a cookie scoop or ¼-cup measure 2 to 3 inches apart onto ungreased cookie sheets. Bake for 8 to 10 minutes for rounded teaspoons or tablespoons or 12 to 14 minutes for cookie-scoop or ¼ cup portions or until light brown and centers appear set. Cool on cookie sheets 2 minutes. Transfer to wire racks to cool completely.

*tip: Instead of using just one optional stir-in, use two or even three. Just be sure the total amount of stir-in equals 1 cup.

fat *(pick one)*
1 cup butter
½ cup butter plus ½ cup shortening
½ cup butter plus ½ cup peanut butter

sugar *(pick one)*
1 cup packed brown sugar plus ½ cup granulated sugar
1½ cups packed brown sugar
1 cup granulated sugar plus ½ cup molasses (add ¼ cup additional all-purpose flour)
1 cup granulated sugar plus ½ cup honey

spice *(pick one)*
1 teaspoon ground cinnamon, pumpkin pie spice, or apple pie spice
½ teaspoon ground allspice

flavoring *(pick one)*
1 teaspoon vanilla
½ teaspoon coconut flavoring
½ teaspoon maple flavoring

flour *(pick one)*
1½ cups all-purpose flour
¾ cup all-purpose flour plus ¾ cup whole wheat flour
1 cup all-purpose flour plus ½ cup oat bran
1¼ cups all-purpose flour plus ¼ cup toasted wheat germ

stir-in *(pick one)*
Raisins
Semisweet or milk chocolate pieces
Mixed dried fruit bits or dried tart red cherries
White baking pieces
Butterscotch-flavor baking pieces
Peanut butter-flavor baking pieces
Flaked coconut

Watch these cookies closely while they bake because the honey in the dough can cause the cookies to overbrown quickly.

honey-nut oatmeal drops

prep: 25 minutes **bake:** 8 minutes at 350°F per batch
makes: 48 cookies

2¼   cups all-purpose flour
1   teaspoon baking soda
½   teaspoon salt
1   cup butter, softened
1   cup packed brown
      sugar
½   cup honey
2   eggs
2   teaspoons vanilla
2½   cups quick-cooking
      rolled oats
¾   cup chopped honey-
      roasted peanuts
      Granulated sugar

1 Preheat oven to 350°F. Line cookie sheets with parchment paper; set aside. In a medium bowl combine flour, baking soda, and salt; set aside. In a large mixing bowl beat butter with an electric mixer on medium to high speed for 30 seconds. Add brown sugar. Beat until combined, scraping sides of bowl occasionally. Beat in honey, eggs, and vanilla until combined. Beat in as much of the flour mixture as you can with the mixer. Using a wooden spoon, stir in any remaining flour mixture, the oats, and peanuts.

2 Drop dough by rounded teaspoons 2 inches apart onto prepared cookie sheets. Lightly sprinkle tops with granulated sugar.

3 Bake for 8 to 10 minutes or until cookies are golden. Cool on cookie sheets for 2 minutes. Transfer cookies to wire racks; cool.

nutrition facts per cookie: 90 cal., 4 g total fat (2 g sat. fat), 14 mg chol., 76 mg sodium, 12 g carb., 1 g fiber, 1 g pro.

The old-fashioned oatmeal cookie gets a bolt of flavor, thanks to morsels of fruit, chocolate, coconut, and nuts.

coconut, cherry, and chocolate oatmeal cookies

prep: 30 minutes **bake:** 10 minutes at 350°F per batch
makes: 30 cookies

¼ cup butter, softened
½ cup packed brown
    sugar
⅓ cup granulated sugar
1 teaspoon ground
    cinnamon
½ teaspoon baking soda
⅛ teaspoon salt
1 egg
1 teaspoon vanilla
¾ cup all-purpose flour
¾ cup rolled oats
½ cup flaked coconut
2 ounces dark
    chocolate, finely
    chopped (⅓ cup)
¼ cup snipped dried
    cherries or
    cranberries
¼ cup chopped walnuts,
    toasted (see tip,
    page 13)

1 Preheat oven to 350°F. In a large mixing bowl beat butter with an electric mixer on medium to high speed for 30 seconds. Add brown sugar, granulated sugar, cinnamon, baking soda, and salt. Beat until combined, scraping sides of bowl occasionally. Beat in egg and vanilla until combined. Beat in flour just until combined. Using a wooden spoon, stir in oats, coconut, chocolate, dried cherries, and walnuts (dough may be crumbly). Drop dough by rounded teaspoons 2 inches apart onto an ungreased cookie sheet.

2 Bake about 10 minutes or just until edges are set. Cool on cookie sheet for 1 minute. Transfer to a wire rack; cool.

nutrition facts per cookie: 94 cal., 4 g total fat (2 g sat. fat), 10 mg chol., 52 mg sodium, 14 g carb., 1 g fiber, 2 g pro.

Try dried sweet cherries or cranberries in place of the raisins next time you bake these family pleasers.

oatmeal-raisin cookies

prep: 30 minutes **bake:** 8 minutes at 350 °F per batch
makes: 72 cookies (teaspoon-size)

1 cup butter, softened
1½ cups packed brown sugar
1 teaspoon baking soda
1 teaspoon ground cinnamon
½ teaspoon salt
2 eggs
1 teaspoon vanilla
1½ cups all-purpose flour
3 cups regular or quick-cooking rolled oats
1 cup raisins

1 Preheat oven to 350°F. In a large mixing bowl beat butter with an electric mixer on medium to high speed for 30 seconds. Add brown sugar, baking soda, cinnamon, and salt. Beat until combined, scraping sides of bowl occasionally. Beat in eggs and vanilla until combined. Beat in as much of the flour as you can with the mixer. Using a wooden spoon, stir in any remaining flour. Stir in oats and raisins.

2 Drop dough by rounded teaspoons or tablespoons 2 inches apart onto ungreased cookie sheets. (Or drop dough using a cookie scoop or ¼-cup measure 3 inches apart onto ungreased cookie sheets.)

3 Bake about 8 minutes (about 12 minutes for cookie-scoop portions), until edges are lightly browned and centers appear set. Cool on cookie sheet for 2 minutes. Transfer to a wire rack; cool.

nutrition facts per cookie: 83 cal., 3 g total fat (2 g sat. fat), 12 mg chol., 60 mg sodium, 12 g carb., 1 g fiber, 2 g pro.

loaded peanut butter and oatmeal cookies: Prepare as directed, except reduce butter to ½ cup and beat ½ cup creamy peanut butter and ¼ cup milk with butter. Omit raisins. Stir in ½ cup red and green candy-coated peanut butter pieces or white baking pieces and ½ cup dried cranberries or dried tart cherries.

nutrition facts per cookie: 35 cal., 1 g total fat (1 g sat. fat), 4 mg chol., 23 mg sodium, 5 g carb., 0 g fiber, 1 g pro.

The salty-sweet combo means your little cookie monsters will sneak their hands into the cookie jar again and again.

salty caramel and pecan oatmeal cookies

prep: 30 minutes **bake:** 11 minutes at 350°F per batch
makes: about 60 cookies

1 cup butter, softened
1 cup granulated sugar
1 cup packed dark
    brown sugar
1 teaspoon salt
1 teaspoon baking
    powder
1 teaspoon ground
    cinnamon
½ teaspoon baking soda
2 eggs
2 teaspoons vanilla
1½ cups all-purpose flour
3 cups rolled oats
1 11-ounce package
    caramel baking bits
1 cup pecans, toasted
    (see tip, page 13)
    and coarsely
    chopped
Coarse sea salt

1 Preheat oven to 350°F. LIne cookie sheets with parchment paper; set aside. In a large mixing bowl beat butter with an electric mixer on medium to high speed for 30 seconds. Add granulated sugar, brown sugar, the 1 teaspoon salt, the baking powder, cinnamon, and baking soda. Beat until combined, scraping sides of bowl occasionally. Beat in eggs and vanilla until combined. Beat in as much of the flour as you can with the mixer. Using a wooden spoon, stir in the remaining flour, oats, caramel baking bits, and pecans.

2 Using a small ice cream scoop or a tablespoon, drop 1½-inch mounds of dough 2 inches apart onto prepared cookie sheets.

3 Bake for 11 to 12 minutes or until the edges are light brown. (Centers will look undercooked.) Cool on cookie sheets for 3 to 4 minutes or until cookies can be easily removed. Transfer to a wire rack; cool.

nutrition facts per cookie: 145 cal., 7 g total fat (3 g sat. fat), 18 mg chol., 421 mg sodium, 21 g carb., 1 g fiber, 2 g pro.

Like potato chips, you'll find it hard to eat just one!

lacy cashew crisps

prep: 25 minutes **bake:** 6 minutes at 350°F per batch
makes: 48 cookies

⅔ cup all-purpose flour
½ cup dry-roasted, lightly salted cashews
⅓ cup butter
⅓ cup packed brown sugar
¼ cup light-color corn syrup
½ teaspoon vanilla

1 In a food processor combine flour and cashews. Cover and pulse with several on/off turns until mixture resembles fine crumbs; set aside.

2 In a medium-sized heavy saucepan combine butter, brown sugar, and corn syrup. Bring to boiling over medium heat, stirring to dissolve sugar. Remove from heat. Stir in the vanilla. Stir in the flour mixture until combined. Transfer dough to a medium bowl. Cool for 10 minutes.

3 Preheat oven to 350°F. Line cookie sheets with parchment paper. Using a measuring teaspoon, drop mounds of dough 3 inches apart on the prepared cookie sheets.

4 Bake for 6 to 7 minutes or until golden. Cool on cookie sheets for 5 minutes. Transfer to a wire rack; cool.

to store: Layer cookies between sheets of waxed paper in an airtight container; cover. Store at room temperature up to 2 days or freeze up to 1 month.

nutrition facts per cookie: 37 cal., 2 g total fat (1 g sat. fat), 3 mg chol., 22 mg sodium, 5 g carb., 0 g fiber, 0 g pro.

Brown the butter slowly and watch carefully to avoid overbrowning, which would taste burnt.

browned butter and oatmeal crisps

prep: 35 minutes bake: 10 minutes at 350°F per batch
makes: 42 servings

¾   cup butter
1¾ cups quick-cooking
      rolled oats
¾   cup sugar
¾   cup all-purpose flour
½   teaspoon baking
      powder
¼   cup dark-color corn
      syrup
¼   cup whipping cream

1 In a small saucepan heat and stir butter over medium heat until melted. Continue cooking until butter turns light golden brown, stirring occasionally. Remove from heat.

2 Preheat oven to 350°F. Line a large cookie sheet with foil; set aside. In a large bowl stir together oats, sugar, flour, and baking powder. In a small bowl combine the browned butter, corn syrup, and whipping cream. Add butter mixture to oat mixture, stirring to combine.

3 Drop dough by rounded teaspoons 3 inches apart onto the prepared cookie sheet. Bake about 10 minutes or until edges are golden and centers are bubbly. Cool cookies on cookie sheet. Carefully lift edges of cookies, then peel cookies off foil.

nutrition facts per cookie: 74 cal., 4 g total fat (2 g sat. fat), 11 mg chol., 38 mg sodium, 9 g carb., 0 g fiber, 1 g pro.

Drying the cookies in the oven leads to the crispy, chewy texture. Yields will vary depending on the size of cookie scoop you use.

giant coconut macaroons

prep: 30 minutes **bake:** 20 minutes at 325°F per batch **stand:** 30 minutes
makes: about 12 cookies

4   egg whites
1   teaspoon vanilla
¼   teaspoon cream of tartar
⅛   teaspoon salt
1⅓ cups granulated sugar
1   14-ounce package flaked coconut

1 Preheat oven to 325°F. Line two extra-large cookie sheets with parchment paper; set aside. In an extra-large mixing bowl beat egg whites, vanilla, cream of tartar, and salt with an electric mixer on high speed until soft peaks form (tips curl). Gradually add sugar, about 1 tablespoon at a time, beating until stiff peaks form (tips stand straight). Gently stir in coconut, half at a time.

2 Using a 2-inch-diameter ice cream scoop (#20 scoop or about 3 tablespoons),* drop batter into mounds on the prepared cookie sheets, leaving about 1 inch between mounds. Place cookie sheets on separate oven racks.

3 Bake for 20 minutes. Turn off oven; let cookies dry in oven for 30 minutes. Transfer cookies to a wire rack; cool.

*****tip:** If you do not have a #20 scoop, use a ¼-cup dry measure. Scoop a scant ¼ cup cookie batter for each mound. Use a spoon to form rounded mounds.

nutrition facts per cookie: 106 cal., 5 g total fat (4 g sat. fat), 0 mg chol., 56 mg sodium, 15 g carb., 1 g fiber, 1 g pro.

classic coconut macaroons: Preheat oven to 325°F. Drop batter from a teaspoon into small mounds on a baking sheet lined with parchment paper. Bake for 20 to 25 minutes or until cookies are lightly browned. Cool as above. Makes about 60 cookies.

nutrition facts per cookie: 21 cal., 1 g total fat (1 g sat. fat), 0 mg chol., 11 mg sodium, 3 g carb., 0 g fiber, 0 g pro.

Here's the perfect recipe for the dieter in the family who craves a bite of sweet.

chocolate-coconut macaroons

prep: 30 minutes **bake:** 15 minutes at 325°F per batch **stand:** 25 minutes
makes: 18 cookies

2   egg whites
½   teaspoon vanilla
⅛   teaspoon cream of
       tartar
       Dash salt
⅔   cup granulated sugar
¾   cup shredded coconut
2   ounces dark
       chocolate or
       semisweet
       chocolate, coarsely
       grated

1 Preheat oven to 325°F. Line two cookie sheets with parchment paper; set aside. In a large mixing bowl beat egg whites, vanilla, cream of tartar, and salt with an electric mixer on high speed until soft peaks form (tips curl). Gradually add sugar, about 1 tablespoon at a time, beating until stiff peaks form (tips stand straight). Gently fold in ½ cup of the coconut and the chocolate.

2 Drop 2 tablespoon-size mounds of batter on prepared cookie sheets leaving about 1 inch between mounds. Sprinkle with the remaining ¼ cup coconut.

3 Place cookie sheets on separate oven racks. Bake for 15 minutes. Rotate cookie sheets in oven by moving the top cookie sheet to the bottom rack and moving the bottom cookie sheet to the top rack. Turn off oven; let macaroons dry in oven for 25 minutes. Transfer to a wire rack; cool.

to store: Layer cookies between sheets of waxed paper in an airtight container; cover. Store in the refrigerator up to 2 days or freeze up to 3 months.

nutrition facts per cookie: 72 cal., 3 g total fat (2 g sat. fat), 0 mg chol., 28 mg sodium, 11 g carb., 1 g fiber, 1 g pro.

two-tone cinnamon
cookies, page 58

creative

cut

3

While cutout cookies may be on your must-bake list during the holidays, why limit yourself to the buttery goodness of cookie cutouts to just one time of year? From our best-ever sugar cookies to shortbread and sandwich cookies, these recipes will help you celebrate throughout the year.

outs

Use a food processor to finely grind the almonds. If the nuts are too chunky, you'll have difficulty cutting the dough.

almond-sour cream-sugar cookies

prep: 40 minutes **chill:** 1 hour **bake:** 7 minutes at 375°F per batch
makes: 30 cookies

⅔ cup butter, softened
1 cup granulated sugar
1 teaspoon baking powder
½ teaspoon salt
¼ teaspoon baking soda
1 egg
⅓ cup sour cream
2 teaspoons vanilla
½ to 1 teaspoon almond extract
⅓ cup finely ground blanched almonds
2¼ cups all-purpose flour
 White or silver luster dust (optional)
1 recipe Royal Icing (see recipe, page 18)

1 In a large mixing bowl beat butter with an electric mixer on medium to high speed for 30 seconds. Add sugar, baking powder, salt, and baking soda. Beat until combined, scraping sides of bowl occasionally. Beat in egg, sour cream, vanilla, and almond extract until combined. Beat in ground almonds. Beat in as much of the flour as you can with the mixer. Using a wooden spoon, stir in any remaining flour. Divide dough in half. Cover and chill for 1 to 2 hours or until dough is easy to handle.

2 Preheat oven to 375°F. On a well-floured surface, roll one dough portion at a time to ⅛-to ¼-inch thickness. Using 2½-inch cookie cutters, cut dough into desired shapes. Place cutouts 1 inch apart on an ungreased cookie sheet.

3 Bake for 7 to 8 minutes or until edges are firm and bottoms are very lightly browned. Transfer cookies to a wire rack; cool.

4 If desired, use a new small paintbrush to brush cookies with luster dust. Pipe Royal Icing on cookies in desired designs. Let stand until icing is set.

to store: Layer cookies between sheets of waxed paper in an airtight container; cover. Store at room temperature up to 3 days or freeze unfrosted cookies up to 3 months. To serve, thaw cookies, if frozen. Decorate as directed.

nutrition facts per cookie: 172 cal., 5 g total fat (3 g sat. fat), 18 mg chol., 106 mg sodium, 30 g carb., 0 g fiber, 1 g pro.

Look for dark molasses near the sugars at your grocery store.

fat molasses cookies

prep: 40 minutes **chill:** 1 hour **bake:** 10 minutes at 375°F per batch
makes: about 26 cookies

5 cups all-purpose flour
2 teaspoons baking soda
1 teaspoon ground ginger
1 teaspoon ground cinnamon
½ teaspoon salt
1 cup shortening
1 cup packed brown sugar
1 cup molasses
2 eggs
2 tablespoons water
2 tablespoons cider vinegar
 Coarse sugar or finely chopped crystallized ginger

1 In a large bowl combine flour, baking soda, ground ginger, cinnamon, and salt; set aside.

2 In an extra-large mixing bowl beat shortening with an electric mixer on medium to high speed for 30 seconds. Add brown sugar. Beat until combined, scraping sides of bowl occasionally. Add molasses, eggs, the water, and vinegar; beat until combined. Beat in as much of the flour mixture as you can with the mixer. Using a wooden spoon, stir in any remaining flour mixture. Divide dough in half. Cover and chill about 1 hour or until dough is easy to handle.

3 Preheat oven to 375°F. On a lightly floured surface, roll one dough portion at a time to ½-inch thickness. Using a 3-inch scalloped or round cookie cutter, cut out dough. Place cutouts 2½ inches apart on ungreased cookie sheets. Sprinkle with coarse sugar or crystallized ginger.

4 Bake about 10 minutes or until edges are firm. Transfer to a wire rack; cool.

nutrition facts per cookie: 239 cal., 8 g total fat (2 g sat. fat), 16 mg chol., 155 mg sodium, 39 g carb., 1 g fiber, 3 g pro.

fat maple cookies: Prepare as directed, except substitute 1½ teaspoons freshly grated nutmeg for ground ginger and cinnamon. Substitute ¾ cup pure maple syrup, ¼ cup dark-color corn syrup, and 1 teaspoon maple flavoring for the 1 cup molasses. Sprinkle with coarse sugar.
nutrition facts per cookie: 237 cal., 8 g total fat (2 g sat. fat), 16 mg chol., 156 mg sodium, 38 g carb., 1 g fiber, 3 g pro.

Two glazes swirled together over each cookie lend the two-tone effect. Pictured on page 54.

two-tone cinnamon cookies

prep: 35 minutes **chill:** 1 hour **bake:** 8 minutes at 375°F per batch
makes: 14 cookies

½ cup butter, softened
1 3-ounce package cream cheese, softened
1 cup powdered sugar
½ teaspoon baking powder
½ teaspoon salt
½ teaspoon ground cinnamon
1 egg
1½ teaspoons vanilla
2¼ cups all-purpose flour
1 recipe Cinnamon Glaze
1 recipe White Glaze

1 In a large mixing bowl beat butter and cream cheese with an electric mixer on medium to high speed for 30 seconds. Add powdered sugar, baking powder, salt, and cinnamon. Beat until combined, scraping sides of bowl occasionally. Beat in egg and vanilla until combined. Beat in as much of the flour as you can with the mixer. Using a wooden spoon, stir in any remaining flour. Cover and chill about 1 hour or until dough is easy to handle.

2 Preheat oven to 375°F. On a lightly floured surface, roll out dough to ¼-inch thickness. Using a fluted round 3½-inch cookie cutter, cut out dough. Place cutouts 1 inch apart on an ungreased cookie sheet.

3 Bake for 8 to 10 minutes or until edges are very lightly browned. Cool on cookie sheet for 1 minute. Transfer cookies to a wire rack; cool.

4 Fill a small resealable plastic bag with Cinnamon Glaze; snip off one small corner; set aside. Spoon White Glaze over tops of cookies, spreading almost to the edges. Place cookies on a wire rack set over waxed paper. Drizzle with Cinnamon Glaze. If desired, gently swirl a knife through glazes to marble. (Reheat either glaze in the microwave if necessary.) Let stand until glazes are set.

nutrition facts per cookie: 385 cal., 29 g total fat (12 g sat. fat), 39 mg chol., 231 mg sodium, 45 g carb., 1 g fiber, 4 g pro.

cinnamon glaze: In a small saucepan combine 1 cup cinnamon-flavor pieces, bittersweet chocolate pieces or semisweet chocolate pieces, and 2 teaspoons shortening. Heat and stir over low heat until melted.

white glaze: In a small saucepan combine 1 cup white baking pieces and 2 teaspoons shortening. Heat and stir over low heat until melted.

Add the cherry garnish at serving time.

triple-cherry cookies

prep: 35 minutes bake: 14 minutes at 325°F per batch
makes: 30 to 36 cookies

30 to 36 maraschino
      cherries with stems
¾ cup butter, softened
¼ cup cream cheese,
      softened (2 ounces)
½ cup granulated sugar
½ teaspoon almond
      extract
¼ teaspoon salt
2½ cups all-purpose flour
½ cup finely chopped
      candied cherries
1 recipe Cherry-
      Almond Frosting

1 Place maraschino cherries on paper towels to drain while preparing cookies. Preheat oven to 325°F. Line a cookie sheet with parchment paper; set aside.

2 In a large mixing bowl beat butter and cream cheese with an electric mixer on medium to high speed for 30 seconds. Add sugar, almond extract, and salt. Beat until combined, scraping sides of bowl occasionally. Beat in half the flour just until combined. Beat in candied cherries and the remaining flour.

3 On a lightly floured surface, roll dough to ½-inch thickness. Using a 1½- to 2-inch fluted round cutter, cut out dough. Place cutouts 1 inch apart on prepared cookie sheet.

4 Bake for 14 to 15 minutes or until bottoms are lightly browned. Cool on cookie sheet for 2 minutes. Transfer to a wire rack; cool. Pipe or spoon Cherry-Almond Frosting onto cookie centers. Top each cookie with a maraschino cherry.

to store: Layer unfrosted cookies between sheets of waxed paper in an airtight container; cover. Store at room temperature up to 3 days or freeze up to 3 months. To serve, thaw cookies, if frozen. Frost and top cookies as directed in Step 4.

nutrition facts per cookie: 179 cal., 8 g total fat (5 g sat. fat), 21 mg chol., 79 mg sodium, 26 g carb., 0 g fiber, 1 g pro.

cherry-almond frosting:
In a bowl beat 3 ounces cream cheese, softened, and ¼ cup butter, softened, with an electric mixer on low speed for 30 seconds. Gradually beat in 2 cups powdered sugar. Beat in 1 tablespoon cherry liqueur. Beat in ½ to 1 cup additional powdered sugar.

Use assorted colored sprinkles to decorate each cookie.

mocha wreaths with bittersweet chocolate glaze

prep: 40 minutes **chill:** 1 hour **bake:** 6 minutes at 350°F per batch
makes: 12 to 16 cookies

½ cup butter, softened
¾ cup packed brown sugar
1 egg
2 tablespoons unsweetened cocoa powder
1 tablespoon instant espresso coffee powder or instant coffee crystals
1 teaspoon vanilla
½ teaspoon baking powder
¼ teaspoon salt
1¾ cups all-purpose flour
6 ounces bittersweet chocolate, chopped
2 teaspoons shortening
¼ cup candy sprinkles

1 In a large mixing bowl beat butter with an electric mixer on medium to high speed for 30 seconds. Add the brown sugar. Beat until combined, scraping sides of bowl occasionally. Beat in egg, cocoa powder, espresso powder, vanilla, baking powder, and salt until combined. Beat in as much of the flour as you can with the mixer. Using a wooden spoon, stir in any remaining flour. Divide dough in half. Cover and chill dough for 1 hour or until easy to handle.

2 Preheat oven to 350°F. Line cookie sheets with parchment paper; set aside. On a lightly floured surface, roll one dough portion at a time to ¼-inch thickness. Using a 2- to 3-inch round cookie cutter, cut out dough. Place cutouts 1 inch apart on the prepared cookie sheets. Using a smaller round cookie cutter (at least 1 inch smaller than the larger cutter used), cut the center from each round. Reroll scraps once and cut out as directed. Discard any remaining scraps.

3 Bake for 6 to 8 minutes or just until edges are puffed and set (do not overbake). Cool on cookie sheet for 5 minutes. Transfer to a wire rack; cool.

4 In a small saucepan heat and stir bittersweet chocolate and shortening over low heat until melted and smooth. Carefully dip each cookie about halfway into the chocolate, allowing excess to drip off. Place dipped cookies on a sheet of waxed paper and sprinkle with candy sprinkles. Let stand until set.

nutrition facts per cookie: 294 cal., 15 g total fat (8 g sat. fat), 36 mg chol., 142 mg sodium, 39 g carb., 2 g fiber, 4 g pro.

Macadamia nuts and lime add a tropical note to these crisp treats.

lime lights

prep: 45 minutes **bake:** 11 minutes at 350°F per batch
makes: 42 cookies

1 cup butter, softened
½ cup granulated sugar
2 teaspoons finely shredded lime peel
¼ cup lime juice
1 teaspoon vanilla
2¼ cups all-purpose flour
¾ cup finely chopped macadamia nuts
1 recipe Lime-Cream Cheese Icing
Finely shredded lime peel (optional)

1 Preheat oven to 350°F. In a large mixing bowl beat butter with an electric mixer on medium to high speed for 30 seconds. Beat in granulated sugar until combined, scraping sides of bowl occasionally. Beat in the 2 teaspoons lime peel, the lime juice, and vanilla until combined. Beat in as much of the flour as you can with the mixer. Using a wooden spoon, stir in any remaining flour and the macadamia nuts. Divide dough in half.

2 On a lightly floured surface, roll one portion of dough at a time to ¼-inch thickness. Using a 2-inch cookie cutter, cut out dough. Place cutouts 1 inch apart on an ungreased cookie sheet.

3 Bake for 11 to 12 minutes or until edges are lightly browned. Transfer to a wire rack; cool. Spread or drizzle cookies with Lime-Cream Cheese Icing. If desired, sprinkle with lime peel.

to store: Layer cookies between sheets of waxed paper in an airtight container; cover. Store at room temperature up to 3 days or freeze uniced cookies up to 3 months. To serve, thaw cookies, if frozen. Ice as directed.

nutrition facts per cookie: 109 cal., 7 g total fat (3 g sat. fat), 14 mg chol., 46 mg sodium, 11 g carb., 0 g fiber, 1 g pro.

lime-cream cheese icing: Beat one 3-ounce package cream cheese, softened, with an electric mixer until smooth. Beat in 1 cup powdered sugar and 1 teaspoon vanilla. Beat in enough lime juice to make icing spreading or drizzling consistency.

For a tasty variation, flavor half the dough with orange extract instead of mint, then tint the dough orange.

spearmint dips

prep: 55 minutes   **chill:** 1 hour   **bake:** 7 minutes at 375°F per batch
makes: 96 cookies

1 cup butter, softened
1 cup granulated sugar
1 teaspoon baking powder
¼ teaspoon salt
1 egg
1 teaspoon vanilla
2¼ cups all-purpose flour
½ teaspoon mint extract
Green paste food coloring
9 ounces white baking chocolate with cocoa butter, chopped
2 teaspoons shortening
Green jimmies or nonpareils (optional)

1 In a large mixing bowl beat butter with an electric mixer on medium speed for 30 seconds. Add sugar, baking powder, and salt. Beat until combined, scraping sides of bowl occasionally. Beat in egg and vanilla. Beat in as much of the flour as you can with the mixer. Stir in any remaining flour.

2 Divide dough in half. Leave one portion plain. Stir mint extract into remaining portion and add enough food coloring to tint dough desired shade of green. Divide each portion of dough in half. Cover and chill about 1 hour or until dough is easy to handle.

3 Preheat oven to 375°F. On waxed paper, roll a plain portion of dough into a 9×6-inch rectangle. On a floured surface, roll a green portion into a 9×6-inch rectangle. Use waxed paper to invert plain dough rectangle on top of the green dough rectangle; peel off waxed paper. If necessary, press edges to align them. Cut each stacked rectangle into twenty-four 1½-inch squares. Cut each square in half diagonally to make 48 triangles. Repeat with remaining dough portions. Place triangles 1 inch apart on an ungreased cookie sheet.

4 Bake for 7 to 8 minutes or until edges are firm and bottoms are light brown. Transfer cookies to wire racks; cool.

5 In a small saucepan melt white chocolate and shortening over low heat. Dip half of each cookie into the white chocolate mixture, allowing excess to drip into saucepan. Place cookies on trays lined with waxed paper. If desired, immediately sprinkle dipped portions with jimmies. Chill until set.

nutrition facts per cookie: 52 cal., 3 g total fat (2 g sat. fat), 8 mg chol., 31 mg sodium, 6 g carb., 0 g fiber, 1 g pro.

A family of cookie cutouts is a fun decorating project for children. Or cut this spiced dough into simple rounds.

molasses cutouts

prep: 35 minutes   chill: 3 hours   bake: 5 minutes at 375°F per batch
makes: about 10 cookies

½   cup shortening
⅔   cup granulated sugar
2   teaspoons freshly
     grated nutmeg
     or 1½ teaspoons
     ground nutmeg
1   teaspoon baking
     powder
¼   teaspoon salt
½   cup mild-flavor
     molasses
1   egg
1   tablespoon cider
     vinegar
2½ cups all-purpose flour

1 In a large bowl beat shortening with an electric mixer on medium to high speed for 30 seconds. Add sugar, nutmeg, baking powder, and salt. Beat until combined, scraping sides of bowl occasionally. Beat in molasses, egg, and vinegar until combined. Beat in as much of the flour as you can with the mixer. Using a wooden spoon, stir in any remaining flour. Divide dough in half. Cover and chill about 3 hours or until dough is easy to handle.

2 Preheat oven to 375°F. Grease a cookie sheet; set aside. On a lightly floured surface, roll one dough portion at a time to ⅛-inch thickness. Using 2½- to 3-inch cookie cutters, cut dough into shapes. Place 1 inch apart on prepared cookie sheet.

3 Bake for 5 to 6 minutes or until bottoms are light brown. Cool on cookie sheet for 1 minute. Transfer cookies to a wire rack; cool.

nutrition facts per cookie: 86 cal., 3 g total fat (1 g sat. fat), 6 mg chol., 27 mg sodium, 14 g carb., 0 g fiber, 1 g pro.

Vanilla bean paste is another option for flavoring in this cookie. Use the same amount of paste as you would extract.

eggnog-frosted nutmeg sugar cookies

prep: 25 minutes **chill:** 1 hour **bake:** 8 minutes at 375°F per batch
makes: 24 cookies

½ of a vanilla bean, split in half lengthwise, or 2 teaspoons vanilla
1¼ cups butter, softened
1 cup granulated sugar
1½ teaspoons baking powder
1 teaspoon freshly grated nutmeg or ½ teaspoon ground nutmeg
½ teaspoon salt
1 egg
1 tablespoon dairy or canned eggnog
3¼ cups all-purpose flour
1 recipe Eggnog Icing Coarse sugar (optional)

1 Using the tip of a sharp knife, scrape pulp from vanilla bean (see page 12); set aside. In a large mixing bowl beat butter with an electric mixer on medium to high speed for 30 seconds. Add granulated sugar, baking powder, nutmeg, and salt. Beat until combined, scraping sides of bowl occasionally. Beat in egg, eggnog, and vanilla bean pulp or vanilla until combined. Beat in as much of the flour as you can with the mixer. Using a wooden spoon, stir in any remaining flour. Divide dough in half. Cover and chill about 1 hour or until dough is easy to handle.

2 Preheat oven to 375°F. On a lightly floured surface, roll one portion of dough at a time to ¼-inch thickness. Using a fluted round 3-inch cookie cutter, cut out dough. Place cutouts 1 inch apart on an ungreased cookie sheet.

3 Bake for 8 to 10 minutes or until edges are firm and bottoms are just lightly browned. Transfer cookies to a wire rack; cool. Spread cookies with Eggnog Icing. If desired, sprinkle with coarse sugar. Let icing dry.

nutrition facts per cookie: 235 cal., 10 g total fat (6 g sat. fat), 35 mg chol., 168 mg sodium, 34 g carb., 0 g fiber, 2 g pro.

eggnog icing: In a medium bowl stir together 3 cups powdered sugar and ½ teaspoon vanilla. Stir in enough dairy or canned eggnog or milk (3 to 4 tablespoons) to make icing spreading consistency.

Sunflower kernels add a pleasing crunch to the center of each windmill, including the cream cheese filling.

spice windmills

prep: 45 minutes **chill:** 4 hours **bake:** 8 minutes at 350°F per batch
makes: 32 cookies

⅓ cup butter, softened
⅓ cup shortening
¾ cup packed brown
 sugar
1 teaspoon baking
 powder
¾ teaspoon pumpkin pie
 spice
¼ teaspoon baking soda
¼ teaspoon salt
1 egg
2 teaspoons vanilla
2 cups all-purpose flour
1 3-ounce package
 cream cheese,
 softened
¼ cup packed brown
 sugar
1 teaspoon all-purpose
 flour
½ teaspoon vanilla
¾ cup salted dry- roasted
 sunflower kernels
1 tablespoon granulated
 sugar
½ teaspoon ground
 cinnamon
 Salted dry-roasted
 sunflower kernels

1 In a large mixing bowl beat butter and shortening with an electric mixer on medium speed for 30 seconds. Add the ¾ cup brown sugar, the baking powder, pumpkin pie spice, baking soda, and salt. Beat until combined, scraping sides of bowl occasionally. Beat in egg and the 2 teaspoons vanilla. Beat in as much of the 2 cups flour as you can with the mixer. If necessary, use a wooden spoon to stir in remaining flour. Divide dough in half. Cover and chill about 4 hours or until easy to handle.

2 Meanwhile, for cream cheese filling, in a medium mixing bowl combine cream cheese, the ¼ cup brown sugar, the 1 teaspoon flour, and the ½ teaspoon vanilla. Beat on medium speed until smooth. Stir in the ¾ cup sunflower kernels.

3 Preheat oven to 350°F. Lightly grease a cookie sheet; set aside. On a lightly floured surface, roll one portion of dough at a time into a 10-inch square. Using a pastry wheel, cut each dough square into sixteen 2½-inch squares.

4 Place squares 2 inches apart on prepared cookie sheet. Cut 1-inch slits from the corners toward the center of each square. Spoon about 1 teaspoon filling into the center of each square. Fold every other tip (one from each corner) to the center to form a windmill; pressing tips gently to seal. In a small bowl combine granulated sugar and cinnamon; sprinkle lightly over cookies. Press additional sunflower kernels in centers of cookies.

5 Bake for 8 to 10 minutes or until edges are lightly browned. Transfer cookies to a wire rack; cool.

to store: Place cookies in a single layer in an airtight container; cover. Store in the refrigerator up to 3 days.

nutrition facts per cookie: 125 cal., 7 g total fat (2 g sat. fat), 15 mg chol., 76 mg sodium, 14 g carb., 1 g fiber, 2 g pro.

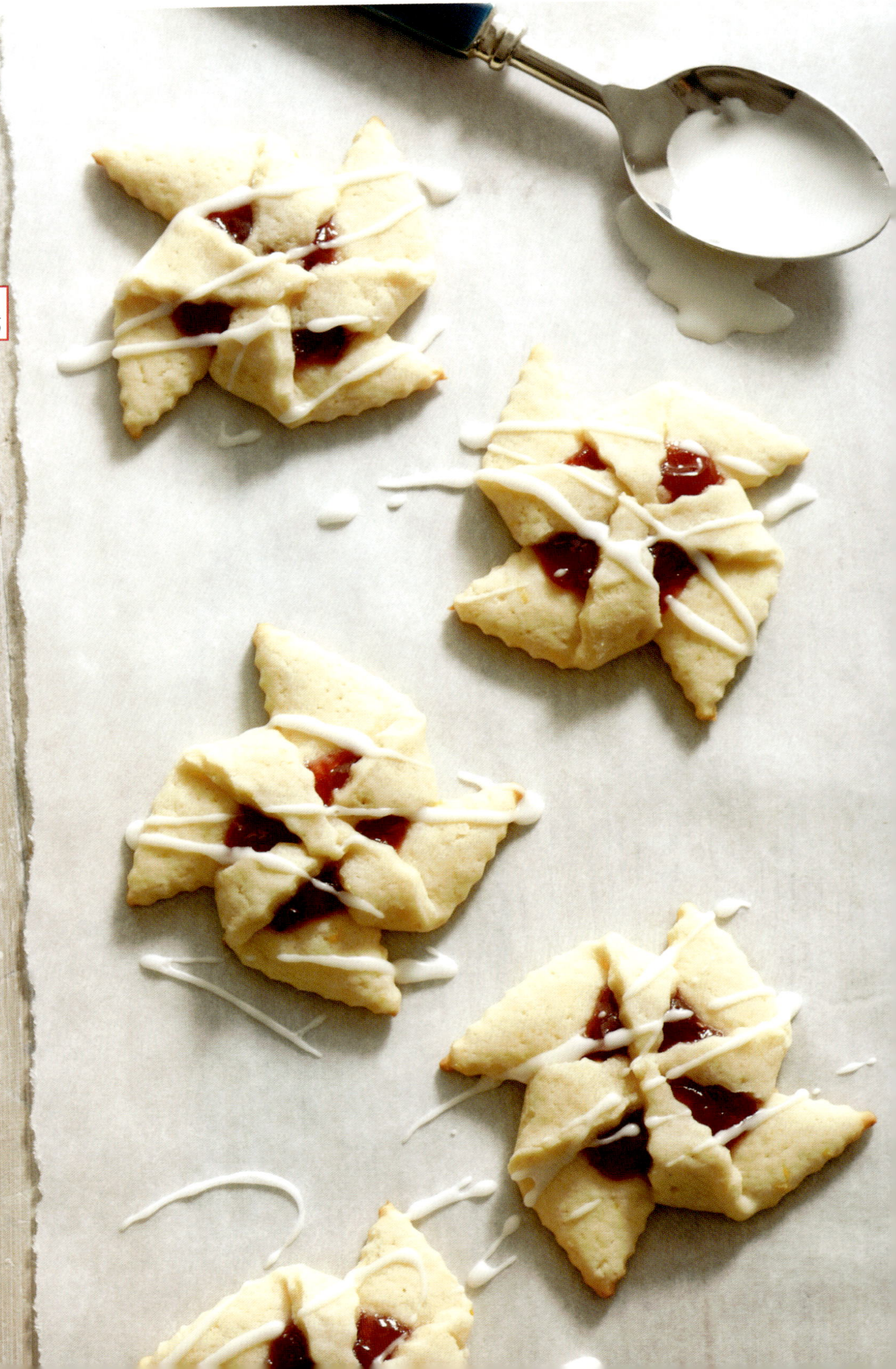

For extra flair, use a fluted pastry wheel to cut the dough.

cherry pinwheels

prep: 40 minutes chill: 2 hours bake: 8 minutes at 375°F per batch
makes: 36 cookies

½   cup butter, softened
1   cup granulated sugar
1   teaspoon baking
      powder
¼   teaspoon baking soda
      Dash salt
½   cup sour cream
1   egg
1   teaspoon finely
      shredded lemon
      peel
1   teaspoon vanilla
2¾ cups all-purpose flour
¾   cup cherry preserves
1   cup powdered sugar
¼   teaspoon almond
      extract
3   to 4 teaspoons milk

1 In a large mixing bowl beat butter with an electric mixer on medium speed for 30 seconds. Add granulated sugar, baking powder, baking soda, and salt. Beat until combined, scraping sides of bowl occasionally. Beat in sour cream, egg, lemon peel, and vanilla until combined. Beat in as much of the flour as you can with the mixer. Stir in any remaining flour. Divide dough into four equal portions. Cover and chill dough about 2 hours or until easy to handle.

2 Preheat oven to 375°F. Line cookie sheets with parchment paper; set aside. On a lightly floured surface, roll one portion of dough at a time into a 7½-inch square. Using a straight or fluted pastry wheel, cut the dough into 2½-inch squares. (Keep remaining dough chilled. If dough becomes too soft, return to refrigerator for a few minutes).

3 Place squares 2 inches apart on the prepared cookie sheets. Using the pastry wheel, cut 1-inch slits from the corners toward the center of each square. Snip any large pieces of fruit in the preserves. Spoon 1 level teaspoon of cherry preserves into the center of each square. Fold every other tip (one from each corner) into the center of each square to form a pinwheel. Press dough gently in the center to seal tips to filling.

4 Bake for 8 to 9 minutes or just until edges begin to brown. Cool on cookie sheet for 3 minutes. Transfer cookies to a wire rack; cool.

5 For icing, in a small bowl stir together powdered sugar, almond extract, and enough milk to make icing drizzling consistency. Drizzle over cooled cookies. Let stand until set.

nutrition facts per cookie: 118 cal., 3 g total fat (2 g sat. fat), 13 mg chol., 52 mg sodium, 21 g carb., 0 g fiber, 1 g pro.

Peach preserves or orange marmalade are suitable substitutes for apricot preserves.

apricot pinwheels

prep: 35 minutes **chill:** 1 hour **bake:** 9 minutes at 400°F per batch
makes: 27 cookies

1 8-ounce package cream cheese, softened
1 cup butter, softened
2½ cups all-purpose flour
¼ teaspoon salt
⅔ cup apricot preserves
1 egg, lightly beaten
   Coarse sanding sugar

1 In a large mixing bowl beat cream cheese and butter with an electric mixer on medium speed about 3 minutes or until light and fluffy, scraping sides of bowl occasionally. Gradually beat in flour and salt. Form dough into a ball; knead until smooth. Divide dough into thirds. Chill about 1 hour.

2 Preheat oven to 400°F. Line a cookie sheet with parchment paper; set aside. Remove dough, one portion at a time, from the refrigerator and place on a lightly floured surface. Roll dough into a 9-inch square. Cut square into nine 3-inch squares.

3 Place squares 1 inch apart on the prepared cookie sheet. Cut 1-inch slits from the corners toward the center of each square. Spoon about 1 teaspoon of the preserves into each center. Brush dough lightly with some of the beaten egg. Fold every other tip (one from each corner) to the center to form a pinwheel, pressing tips gently to seal. Brush lightly with remaining beaten egg and sprinkle with sanding sugar.

4 Bake for 9 to 10 minutes or just until golden and slightly puffed. Transfer cookies to a wire rack; cool.

nutrition facts per cookie: 157 cal., 10 g total fat (6 g sat. fat), 34 mg chol., 114 mg sodium, 15 g carb., 0 g fiber, 2 g pro.

Once considered a holiday specialty, shortbread is a year-round treat that can add a festive flair to wedding showers, Sunday brunches, and graduation parties.

vanilla-scented cornmeal shortbread

prep: 30 minutes **bake:** 15 minutes at 350°F
makes: 24 cookies

1   vanilla bean, split in
        half lengthwise
1   cup butter, softened
½   cup granulated sugar
¼   teaspoon salt
½   cup white cornmeal
2   tablespoons
        cornstarch
1⅔ cups all-purpose flour
        Sanding sugar or
        granulated sugar
        (optional)

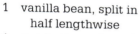 Preheat oven to 350°F. Using the tip of a small sharp knife, scrape seeds from vanilla bean (see page 12); set aside. In a large mixing bowl beat butter with an electric mixer on medium to high speed for 30 seconds. Add granulated sugar, salt, and vanilla bean seeds. Beat until combined, scraping sides of bowl occasionally. Beat in cornmeal and cornstarch until combined. Add flour, beating on low speed until dough starts to cling. Form dough into a ball and knead until smooth. Divide dough in half.

2 On each of two ungreased cookie sheets, roll or pat half the dough into an 8-inch circle. Using a fork, crimp edges of each circle. Prick dough with fork. Cut each circle into 12 wedges; do not separate wedges. If desired, sprinkle with sanding sugar.

3 Bake on separate oven racks about 15 minutes or just until edges begin to brown, rearranging cookie sheets halfway through baking. Recut circles into wedges while warm. Cool on cookie sheets for 5 minutes. Transfer wedges to wire racks; cool.

nutrition facts per cookie: 129 cal., 8 g total fat (5 g sat. fat), 20 mg chol., 92 mg sodium, 14 g carb., 0 g fiber, 1 g pro.

hazelnut-browned butter shortbread

prep: 35 minutes bake: 15 minutes at 325°F
makes: 16 cookies

1   cup butter, softened
¼   cup granulated sugar
¼   cup packed brown
      sugar
¼   teaspoon salt
1   teaspoon vanilla
2½ cups all-purpose flour
½   cup hazelnuts
      (filberts), toasted*
      and finely chopped
4   ounces bittersweet
      chocolate, chopped
½   teaspoon shortening
1   teaspoon fleur de sel
      (optional)

1 Preheat oven to 325°F. Lightly grease two cookie sheets; set aside.

2 In a small saucepan melt ¼ cup of the butter. Reduce heat to medium-low. Cook about 5 minutes or until golden; cool slightly.

3 In a large mixing bowl beat the remaining ¾ cup butter with an electric mixer on medium speed for 30 seconds. Add granulated sugar, brown sugar, and the ¼ teaspoon salt. Beat until combined. Beat in browned butter and vanilla. Beat in as much of the flour as you can with the mixer. Stir in any remaining flour and the hazelnuts. Divide dough in half.

4 On each cookie sheet, pat each dough half into an 8-inch circle; crimp edges. Prick every inch or so with a fork. Cut each circle into eight wedges; do not separate wedges.

5 Bake on separate oven racks about 15 minutes or until edges are lightly browned, rearranging cookie sheets halfway through baking. Recut circles into wedges while warm. Cool on cookie sheets for 5 minutes. Transfer wedges to wire racks; cool.

6 In a small saucepan melt and stir chocolate and shortening over low heat until smooth. Dip crimped edge of each wedge into chocolate, allowing excess chocolate to drip into saucepan. Return to wire rack. If desired, lightly sprinkle chocolate with fleur de sel. Let stand until set.

*tip: Spread hazelnuts In a shallow baking pan. Bake in a 350°F oven about 10 minutes or until toasted, stirring once. Place warm nuts in a clean kitchen towel and rub vigorously to remove skins.

nutrition facts per cookie: 262 cal., 17 g total fat (9 g sat. fat), 31 mg chol., 139 mg sodium, 26 g carb., 2 g fiber, 3 g pro.

Give into the temptation of nibbling one of these warm buttery nut rounds as they come out of the oven. The cream cheese drizzle makes 'em even more tempting.

iced walnut shortbread rounds

prep: 30 minutes **bake:** 18 minutes at 325°F
makes: 14 cookies

1¼ cups all-purpose flour
½ cup toasted walnuts
    (see tip, page 13),
    ground
¼ cup granulated sugar
⅛ teaspoon salt
½ cup butter
1 recipe Cream Cheese
   Drizzle
   Coarse sugar or
   granulated sugar
   (optional)

1 Preheat oven to 325°F. In a large bowl stir together flour, ground walnuts, sugar, and salt. Using a pastry blender, cut in butter until mixture resembles fine crumbs and starts to cling. Form dough into a ball and knead until smooth.

2 On a lightly floured surface, roll dough to ¼-inch thickness. Using a 2-inch scalloped round cookie cutter, cut out dough. Place cutouts on a large ungreased cookie sheet.

3 Bake for 18 to 22 minutes or just until edges start to brown. Transfer cookies to a wire rack; cool. Drizzle Cream Cheese Drizzle over cookies. If desired, sprinkle drizzled cookies with coarse sugar.

nutrition facts per cookie: 196 cal., 12 g total fat (6 g sat. fat), 26 mg chol., 105 mg sodium, 22 g carb., 0 g fiber, 2 g pro.

cream cheese drizzle: In a mixing bowl beat one 3-ounce package cream cheese, softened, and ¼ cup butter, softened, with an electric mixer on medium speed until smooth. Gradually beat in 2 to 3 cups powdered sugar, beating until combined. Beat in enough milk (1 tablespoon at a time) to make icing drizzling consistency.

Fans of red velvet cake will devour these morsels.

red velvet shortbread cookies

prep: 30 minutes **bake:** 20 minutes at 325°F per batch
makes: 24 cookies

1¼ cups all-purpose flour
⅓   cup granulated sugar
2   tablespoons
    unsweetened cocoa
    powder
¼   teaspoon salt
½   cup butter, cut up
1   tablespoon red food
    coloring
3   ounces white baking
    chocolate with
    cocoa butter,
    coarsely chopped
1½ teaspoons shortening

1 Preheat oven to 325°F. In a food processor combine flour, sugar, cocoa powder, and salt. Cover and process with on/off pulses until well mixed. Add butter and red food coloring. Cover and process with on/off pulses until dough starts to cling. Transfer to a large bowl. Form dough into a ball and knead until smooth.*

2 On a lightly floured surface, roll dough to ½-inch thickness. Using a 1½-inch scalloped round cookie cutter, cut out dough. Place cutouts 1 inch apart on an ungreased cookie sheet.

3 Bake for 20 to 25 minutes or until centers are set. Transfer cookies to a wire rack; cool.

4 In a small heavy saucepan heat and stir white chocolate and shortening over low heat until melted and smooth. Drizzle cookies with melted white chocolate. Let stand until white chocolate is set.

*tip: To mix by hand, in a medium bowl stir together flour, sugar, cocoa powder, and salt. Using a pastry blender, cut in butter and food coloring until dough resembles fine crumbs and starts to cling. Form dough into a ball and knead until smooth.

nutrition facts per cookie: 80 cal., 5 g total fat (3 g sat. fat), 9 mg chol., 47 mg sodium, 9 g carb., 0 g fiber, 1 g pro.

Love coconut? Add a few drops of coconut extract to the dough.

coconut-lime shortbread

prep: 30 minutes **bake:** 15 minutes at 325°F per batch
makes: 40 servings

½ cup granulated sugar
½ cup flaked coconut, toasted*
2 tablespoons finely shredded lime peel
1 teaspoon vanilla
2½ cups all-purpose flour
1 cup butter, cut up
1 recipe Lime Glaze (optional)
Finely shredded lime peel (optional)

lime glaze: In a small bowl stir together 2 cups powdered sugar, 2 tablespoons water, ½ teaspoon finely shredded lime peel, and 1 tablespoon lime juice. If necessary, stir in additional water, 1 teaspoon at a time, to make icing a thin spreading consistency.

1 Preheat oven to 325°F. In a food processor combine sugar, coconut, the 2 tablespoons lime peel, and vanilla. Cover and process until coconut is finely chopped. Add flour; cover and process with one on/off pulse just to combine. Add butter; cover and process until dough starts to cling. Transfer to an extra-large bowl. Form dough into a ball and knead until smooth. Divide dough in half.

2 On a lightly floured surface, roll half the dough at a time to ¼-inch thickness. Using 1½- to 2-inch cookie cutters, cut dough into shapes. Place cutouts 1 inch apart on an ungreased cookie sheet.

3 Bake for 15 to 17 minutes or just until bottoms start to brown. Transfer cookies to a wire rack; cool. If desired, spread cookies with Lime Glaze and sprinkle with additional lime peel.

***tip:** To toast coconut, spread desired amount in a shallow baking pan. Bake in a 350°F oven about 5 minutes stirring once or twice or just until coconut begins to turn golden brown, .

nutrition facts per cookie: 84 cal., 5 g total fat (3 g sat. fat), 12 mg chol., 37 mg sodium, 9 g carb., 0 g fiber, 1 g pro.

The universal love of chocolate combined with peanut butter won't dissapoint in these tender cookies.

chocolate-peanut butter shortbread bites

prep: 35 minutes **bake:** 20 minutes at 325°F per batch
makes: 32 cookies

1½ cups all-purpose flour
⅓ cup granulated sugar
¼ cup unsweetened
      cocoa powder
⅔ cup butter, cut up
¼ cup creamy peanut
      butter
½ cup semisweet
      chocolate pieces
1 tablespoon
      shortening
½ cup peanut butter-
      flavor pieces

1 Preheat oven to 325°F. In a food processor combine flour, sugar, and cocoa powder. Cover and process with on/off pulses until well mixed. Add butter and peanut butter. Cover and process with on/off pulses until dough starts to cling. Transfer to a large bowl. Form dough into a ball and knead until smooth.

2 On a lightly floured surface, roll dough to ½-inch thickness. Using 1- to 2-inch cookie cutters, cut dough into shapes. Place cutouts 1 inch apart on a large ungreased cookie sheet.

3 Bake for 20 to 25 minutes or until centers are set. Cool on cookie sheet for 5 minutes. Transfer cookies to a wire rack set over waxed paper; cool.

4 In a small microwave-safe bowl microwave chocolate pieces and 1½ teaspoons of the shortening on 50 percent power (medium) about 2 minutes or until melted, stirring once. In another small microwave-safe bowl microwave peanut butter pieces and the remaining 1½ teaspoons shortening on 50 percent power (medium) about 2 minutes or until melted, stirring once. Drizzle the cookies with melted peanut butter mixture and melted chocolate mixture. Let stand to set.

nutrition facts per cookie: 113 cal., 7 g total fat (4 g sat. fat), 10 mg chol., 51 mg sodium, 11 g carb., 1 g fiber, 2 g pro.

Turbinado sugar is a coarse-grained sugar that is less processed than white sugar. Look for it in the baking aisle.

rum-pecan praline shortbread bites

prep: 40 minutes **chill:** 4 hours **bake:** 18 minutes at 350°F + 10 minutes at 325°F per batch
makes: 140 cookies

1	cup pecan halves
¼	cup packed brown sugar
2	tablespoons whipping cream
2¼	cups all-purpose flour
1	teaspoon salt
½	teaspoon baking powder
1	cup butter, softened
⅔	cup powdered sugar
1	tablespoon dark rum
2	teaspoons vanilla
2	tablespoons turbinado (raw) sugar

1 Preheat oven to 350°F. Grease a 9-inch pie plate; set aside. In a medium bowl combine pecans, brown sugar, and whipping cream. Spread nuts in the prepared pie plate. Bake for 18 to 20 minutes or until coating is dry and crystallized, stirring once. Transfer nuts to a sheet of foil; cool completely.

2 In a food processor combine cooled nuts and ¼ cup of the flour. Cover and process with several on/off pulses until nuts are finely ground; set aside. In a medium bowl stir together the remaining 2 cups flour, salt, and baking powder; set aside.

3 In a large mixing bowl beat butter with an electric mixer on medium speed for 30 seconds. Add powdered sugar. Beat until smooth. Beat in rum and vanilla. Beat in flour mixture just until combined. Stir in ground nut mixture. Cover and chill for 4 hours.

4 Preheat oven to 325°F. Line a large cookie sheet with parchment paper; set aside. Roll dough between two sheets of waxed paper or parchment paper into a 14×10-inch rectangle. Sprinkle dough with turbinado sugar. Using a pizza cutter or sharp knife, cut dough into 1-inch squares. Place squares 1 inch apart on the prepared cookie sheet. Using the blunt end of a bamboo skewer, poke four holes into each cookie.

5 Bake for 10 to 12 minutes or until light golden. Transfer cookies to a wire rack; cool.

nutrition facts per cookie: 29 cal., 2 g total fat (1 g sat. fat), 4 mg chol., 30 mg sodium, 3 g carb., 0 g fiber, 0 g pro.

cherry shortbread cookies

prep: 45 minutes **freeze:** 1 hour **bake:** 10 minutes at 325°F per batch
makes: 60 cookies

¼ cup cherry preserves
1 cup butter, softened
½ teaspoon almond
     extract
2⅔ cups all-purpose flour
½ cup granulated sugar
⅛ teaspoon salt
2 tablespoons cherry
     preserves
2 cups powdered sugar
4 to 5 teaspoons milk
     Snipped dried
       cherries (optional)

strawberry shortbread cookies:
Prepare as directed except substitute
strawberry preserves for the cherry
preserves in the cookies and the glaze.

1 Snip any large pieces of fruit in the ¼ cup
cherry preserves. In a large mixing bowl beat
the ¼ cup preserves, the butter, and almond
extract with an electric mixer on medium speed
until combined. Transfer butter mixture to a sheet
of plastic wrap; shape into a 6-inch roll. Wrap and
freeze for 1 to 2 hours or just until firm.*

2 Preheat oven to 325°F. In a large bowl stir
together flour, granulated sugar, and salt. Add
frozen butter mixture, breaking or cutting roll if
necessary to fit into bowl. Using a pastry blender,
cut butter mixture into flour mixture until mixture
resembles fine crumbs and starts to cling. Form
dough into a ball and knead until smooth.

3 Divide dough in half. On a lightly floured
surface, roll each portion of dough to ¼-inch
thickness. Using a 1½- or 2-inch cookie cutter,
cut out dough. Place cutouts 1 inch apart on an
ungreased cookie sheet.

4 Bake for 10 to 12 minutes for 1½-inch cookies,
12 to 14 minutes for 2-inch cookies, or just
until edges start to brown. Transfer cookies to a
wire rack; cool.

5 For glaze, in a medium-size microwave-
safe bowl microwave 2 tablespoons cherry
preserves on 50 percent power (medium) about
30 seconds or until melted. Snip any large pieces
of fruit in preserves. Stir in powdered sugar until
smooth. Stir in enough of the milk to make glaze
spreading consistency. Spread glaze over tops of
cookies. If desired, sprinkle with dried cherries. Let
stand until glaze is set.

*tip: Freeze the butter mixture or it will be hard to
cut into flour mixture.

**nutrition facts per cherry or strawberry cookie
variation:** 75 cal., 3 g total fat (2 g sat. fat), 8 mg chol., 33 mg
sodium, 11 g carb., 0 g fiber, 1 g pro.

Cut the dough into rounds or squares—either way, these will go fast.

chocolaty shortbread bites

prep: 35 minutes **bake:** 12 minutes at 325°F per batch
makes: 80 cookies

2	cups all-purpose flour
⅔	cup packed brown sugar
⅓	cup unsweetened cocoa powder
½	teaspoon ground cinnamon
⅛	teaspoon salt
1	cup cold butter, cut into small pieces
2	ounces semisweet chocolate, melted and cooled
2	teaspoons vanilla Granulated sugar (optional)
4	ounces semisweet or white baking chocolate (optional)
2	teaspoons shortening (optional)

1 Preheat oven to 325°F. In a large bowl combine flour, brown sugar, cocoa powder, cinnamon, and salt. Using a pastry blender, cut in butter until mixture resembles fine crumbs. Stir the 2 ounces melted and cooled semisweet chocolate and the vanilla into butter mixture until combined. With hands, knead dough until it forms a ball and is smooth.

2 On a lightly floured surface, roll dough to ¼-inch thickness (18×8-inch rectangle). Using 2-inch cookie cutters, cut out dough. Reroll as necessary. (Or cut rectangle into 2-inch squares.) Place cutouts 1 inch apart on ungreased cookie sheets. Prick each shape three times with fork tines, all the way through the dough. If desired, sprinkle with sugar.

3 Bake for 12 to 15 minutes or until edges are set and tops appear dry. Cool on cookie sheet 2 minutes. Transfer to wire racks; cool. If desired, in a small saucepan melt 4 ounces semisweet or white chocolate and shortening until smooth. Dip some cookie edges in melted chocolate, or drizzle thin chocolate zigzags over tops of cookies.

nutrition facts per cookie: 96 cal., 6 g total fat (4 g sat. fat), 14 mg chol., 46 mg sodium, 11 g carb., 1 g fiber, 1 g pro.

Aromatic spices—cinnamon, ginger, and cardamom— replicate the flavors of India's spiced tea, chai.

chocolate-chai shortbread stars

prep: 25 minutes **bake:** 20 minutes at 325°F per batch
makes: 20 cookies

1¼ cups all-purpose flour
⅓ cup granulated sugar
¼ cup unsweetened cocoa powder
½ teaspoon ground cinnamon
½ teaspoon ground ginger
½ teaspoon ground cardamom
½ teaspoon salt
¼ teaspoon ground nutmeg
⅛ teaspoon ground cloves
½ cup butter
2 tablespoons dark chocolate pieces, melted (optional)
2 tablespoons white baking pieces, melted (optional)

1 Preheat oven to 325°F. In a medium bowl stir together flour, sugar, cocoa powder, cinnamon, ginger, cardamom, salt, nutmeg, and cloves. Using a pastry blender, cut in butter until mixture resembles fine crumbs and starts to cling. Form dough into a ball and knead until smooth.

2 On a lightly floured surface, roll dough to ½-inch thickness. Using a 1½- to 2-inch star-shape cookie cutter, cut out dough. Place cutouts 2 inches apart on an ungreased cookie sheet.

3 Bake about 20 minutes or just until cookies are firm in the center. Transfer to a wire rack; cool. If desired, drizzle cooled cookies with melted dark and/or white chocolate. Let stand until set.

to store: Layer undrizzled cookies between sheets of waxed paper in an airtight container; cover. Store at room temperature up to 3 days or freeze up to 3 months. If desired, drizzle with chocolate before serving.

nutrition facts per cookie: 85 cal., 5 g total fat (3 g sat. fat), 12 mg chol., 99 mg sodium, 10 g carb., 1 g fiber, 1 g pro.

Sift cocoa powder over the cookies right before serving.

coffee-and-cream sandwich cookies

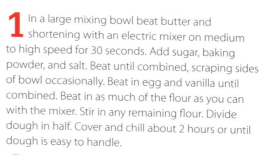

prep: 20 minutes **chill:** 2 hours **bake:** 8 minutes at 375°F per batch
makes: about 20 cookies

½ cup butter, softened
½ cup shortening
1 cup granulated sugar
1 teaspoon baking powder
¼ teaspoon salt
1 egg
1 teaspoon vanilla
2¼ cups all-purpose flour
1 recipe Coffee Filling
1 to 2 tablespoons unsweetened cocoa powder

1 In a large mixing bowl beat butter and shortening with an electric mixer on medium to high speed for 30 seconds. Add sugar, baking powder, and salt. Beat until combined, scraping sides of bowl occasionally. Beat in egg and vanilla until combined. Beat in as much of the flour as you can with the mixer. Stir in any remaining flour. Divide dough in half. Cover and chill about 2 hours or until dough is easy to handle.

2 Preheat oven to 375°F. On a lightly floured surface, roll one dough portion at a time to ⅛-inch thickness. Using a 1½-inch cookie cutter, cut out dough. Place cutouts 2 inches apart on an ungreased cookie sheet.

3 Bake for 8 to 10 minutes or until edges are lightly browned. Transfer to wire racks; cool.

4 Spread 1 teaspoon Coffee Filling on the bottom sides of half the cookies. Top with remaining cookies, bottom sides together. Sift cocoa powder through a fine-mesh sieve over cookies.

coffee filling: In a medium bowl stir together 2 cups powdered sugar; 2 tablespoons butter, softened; 2 teaspoons espresso powder; 1 teaspoon vanilla; and enough milk to make a filling of spreading consistency.

to store: Layer sandwich cookies between sheets of waxed paper in an airtight container; cover. Store at room temperature up to 3 days. Or layer unfilled cookies between sheets of waxed paper in an airtight container; cover. Store at room temperature up to 3 days or freeze up to 3 months. To serve, thaw cookies, if frozen, and assemble as directed in Step 4.

nutrition facts per sandwich cookie: 115 cal., 5 g total fat (2 g sat. fat), 12 mg chol., 54 mg sodium, 16 g carb., 0 g fiber, 1 g pro.

4

When life gets hectic, make homemade cookies in two stages. First mix the dough and chill it; hours or days later, slice the cookie dough and start baking. The recipes that follow are designed for busy bakers who don't want to sacrifice flavor.

slice & bak

e

milk chocolate mini cookies, page 96

Use a thin serrated knife to easily slice the chilled dough.

pistachio-cream cheese sugar cookies

prep: 35 minutes   **chill:** 1 hour   **bake:** 7 minutes at 375°F per batch
makes: 44 cookies

½   cup butter, softened
1   3-ounce package
     cream cheese,
     softened
1   cup powdered sugar
½   teaspoon baking
     powder
¼   teaspoon salt
1   egg
1   teaspoon vanilla
2½ cups all-purpose flour
2   teaspoons finely
     shredded orange
     or lemon peel
     (optional)
½   cup finely chopped
     lightly salted
     pistachio nuts

1 In a large mixing bowl beat butter and cream cheese with an electric mixer on medium to high speed for 30 seconds. Add powdered sugar, baking powder, and salt. Beat until combined, scraping sides of bowl occasionally. Beat in egg and vanilla until combined. Beat in as much of the flour as you can with the mixer. Using a wooden spoon, stir in any remaining flour and, if desired, the orange peel.

2 Divide dough in half. Shape each half into a 7½-inch log. Spread pistachios on waxed paper. Roll log in pistachios to coat. Wrap each log in plastic wrap or waxed paper. Chill about 1 hour or until dough is firm enough to slice.

3 Preheat oven to 375°F. Cut logs into ¼- to ⅜-inch slices. Place 1 inch apart on an ungreased cookie sheet.

4 Bake for 7 to 9 minutes or until edges are light brown. Transfer to a wire rack; cool.

nutrition facts per cookie: 72 cal., 4 g total fat (2 g sat. fat), 12 mg chol., 46 mg sodium, 9 g carb., 0 g fiber, 1 g pro.

Crystalized ginger adds a spicy, pungent note to these rounds.

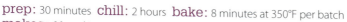

candied ginger and orange icebox cookies

prep: 30 minutes   **chill:** 2 hours   **bake:** 8 minutes at 350°F per batch
makes: 66 cookies

½   cup butter, softened
¾   cup granulated sugar
1½ teaspoons baking powder
⅛   teaspoon salt
1   egg
1   tablespoon milk
2   cups all-purpose flour
⅓   cup finely chopped crystallized ginger
2   teaspoons finely shredded orange peel
¼   cup coarse sugar
    Milk

1 In a large mixing bowl beat butter with an electric mixer on medium to high speed for 30 seconds. Add granulated sugar, baking powder, and salt. Beat until combined, scraping sides of bowl occasionally. Beat in egg and the 1 tablespoon milk until combined. Beat in as much of the flour as you can with the mixer. Using a wooden spoon, stir in any remaining flour, the crystallized ginger, and orange peel. If necessary, use your hands to knead dough until it comes together.

2 Divide dough into three portions. On a lightly floured surface, shape each portion into a 7-inch log. Spread coarse sugar on waxed paper. Roll each log in coarse sugar to coat, pressing lightly as you roll (you won't use all of the sugar). If necessary, reshape log. Wrap each log in waxed paper or plastic wrap. Chill for 2 to 3 hours.

3 Preheat oven to 350°F. Cut logs into ¼-inch slices. Place slices 1 inch apart on an ungreased cookie sheet. Brush lightly with additional milk and sprinkle with the remaining coarse sugar.

4 Bake about 8 minutes or until edges are lightly browned. Transfer cookies to a wire rack; cool.

nutrition facts per cookie: 43 cal., 2 g total fat (1 g sat. fat), 7 mg chol., 29 mg sodium, 7 g carb., 0 g fiber, 1 g pro.

Remember this popular treat for children's parties!

spiral cherry lollies

prep: 45 minutes **chill:** 2 hours **bake:** 10 minutes at 375°F per batch
makes: 36 cookies

¾   cup butter, softened
1   cup granulated sugar
½   teaspoon baking powder
1   egg
1   teaspoon cherry extract
2   cups all-purpose flour
½   cup finely chopped red candied cherries
Red paste food coloring
½   cup finely chopped green candied cherries
Green paste food coloring
¼   cup red and/or green nonpareils or sprinkles
Round paper lollipop sticks

1 In a large mixing bowl beat butter with an electric mixer on medium to high speed for 30 seconds. Add sugar and baking powder. Beat until combined, scraping sides of bowl occasionally. Beat in egg and cherry extract until combined. Beat in as much of the flour as you can with the mixer. Using a wooden spoon, stir in any remaining flour.

2 Divide dough in half. Stir red cherries into one dough portion; tint with red food coloring. Stir green cherries into remaining dough portion; tint with green food coloring. Divide each portion in half. Cover and chill dough about 1 hour or until easy to handle.

3 Between two pieces of waxed paper, roll one red dough portion into a 10×5-inch rectangle. Between two pieces of waxed paper, roll one green dough portion into a 10×5-inch rectangle. Remove the top layer of waxed paper from each rectangle. Invert the green rectangle on top of the red rectangle; remove top layer of waxed paper. Starting from a long side, roll up log. Pinch dough edges to seal. Roll in half of the nonpareils and wrap in plastic wrap. Repeat with remaining dough portions and nonpareils. Chill dough logs for 1 to 2 hours or until very firm.

4 Preheat oven to 375°F. Lightly grease cookie sheets; set aside. Unwrap logs; reshape, if necessary. Cut logs into ½-inch slices. Place slices 2 inches apart on the prepared cookie sheets. Push a lollypop stick into each slice, pressing dough around stick.

5 Bake about 10 minutes or until edges are firm and tops are set. Cool on cookie sheets for 1 minute. Transfer cookies to a wire rack; cool.

nutrition facts per cookie: 101 cal., 4 g total fat (2 g sat. fat), 15 mg chol., 41 mg sodium, 15 g carb., 0 g fiber, 1 g pro.

Toasting the sliced almonds that coat the dough isn't necessary because the nuts will brown as the cookies bake.

almond icebox rounds

prep: 30 minutes **chill:** 6 hours **bake:** 12 minutes at 350°F per batch
makes: 60 cookies

1 cup butter, softened
1 3-ounce package cream cheese, softened
⅔ cup granulated sugar
½ teaspoon salt
½ teaspoon vanilla
¼ teaspoon almond extract
2 cups all-purpose flour
¾ cup slivered almonds, toasted (see tip, page 13), and chopped
⅔ cup sliced almonds, chopped

1 In a large mixing bowl beat butter and cream cheese with an electric mixer on medium to high speed for 30 seconds. Add sugar, salt, vanilla, and almond extract. Beat until combined, scraping sides of bowl occasionally. Beat in as much of the flour as you can with the mixer. Using a wooden spoon, stir in any remaining flour and the ¾ cup toasted almonds.

2 Divide dough in half. Shape each half into a 7- to 8-inch log. Roll dough logs in the ⅔ cup sliced almonds, pressing lightly as you roll. Wrap each log in plastic wrap or waxed paper. Chill about 6 hours or until dough is firm enough to slice.

3 Preheat oven to 350°F. Line a cookie sheet with parchment paper. Cut logs into ¼-inch slices. Place slices 1 inch apart on the prepared cookie sheet.

4 Bake for 12 to 14 minutes or until edges are lightly browned. Transfer cookies to a wire rack; cool.

nutrition facts per cookie: 70 cal., 5 g total fat (2 g sat. fat), 10 mg chol., 51 mg sodium, 6 g carb., 0 g fiber, 1 g pro.

slice & bake

Look for the herbal tea, rooibos (pronounced "roy boss"), at a shop that specializes in teas. It sweetens the dough and glaze, adding a one-of-a-kind flavor.

vanilla rooibos tea meltaways

prep: 30 minutes **chill:** 2 hours **bake:** 9 minutes at 375°F per batch
makes: 36 cookies

¾ cup butter, softened
2 tablespoons vanilla rooibos tea leaves
1 cup powdered sugar
¾ teaspoon vanilla
1 cup all-purpose flour
½ cup cornstarch
1 tablespoon strong brewed vanilla rooibos tea

1 In a small saucepan heat and stir ¼ cup of the butter over medium heat until butter is melted and bubbly. Remove from heat. Stir in tea leaves. Allow tea to steep in butter for 4 minutes. Strain butter through a fine-mesh sieve; discard tea leaves.

2 In a large mixing bowl beat strained butter, the remaining ½ cup butter, and ½ cup of the powdered sugar with an electric mixer on medium to high speed until light and fluffy. Beat in vanilla. Beat in flour and cornstarch until combined.

3 Shape dough into a 10-inch log. Wrap log in plastic wrap or waxed paper. Chill about 2 hours or until dough is firm enough to slice.

4 Preheat oven to 375°F. Using a serrated knife, cut log into ¼-inch slices. Place slices 1 inch apart on an ungreased cookie sheet.

5 Bake for 9 to 11 minutes or until edges are lightly browned. Transfer cookies to a wire rack; cool for 10 minutes.

6 Meanwhile, for glaze, in a small bowl combine the remaining ½ cup powdered sugar and the brewed tea. Using a pastry brush, lightly coat cookies with glaze. Let stand on wire rack until glaze is set.

nutrition facts per cookie: 67 cal., 4 g total fat (2 g sat. fat), 10 mg chol., 34 mg sodium, 8 g carb., 0 g fiber, 1 g pro.

chocolate-mint checkerboard cookies

prep: 50 minutes **chill:** 3 hours **bake:** 9 minutes at 350°F per batch
makes: 50 cookies

1   cup butter, softened
1½   cups granulated sugar
1½   teaspoons baking
       powder
 ½   teaspoon salt
1   egg
1   teaspoon vanilla
2½   cups all-purpose flour
1   tablespoon
       unsweetened cocoa
       powder
1   ounce semisweet
       chocolate, grated
       (about ⅓ cup)
 ½   teaspoon mint extract
       Green paste food
       coloring

1 In a large mixing bowl beat butter with an electric mixer on medium speed for 30 seconds. Add sugar, baking powder, and salt. Beat until combined, scraping sides of bowl occasionally. Beat in egg and vanilla. Beat in as much of the flour as you can with the mixer. Stir in any remaining flour.

2 Divide dough in half. Stir cocoa powder and grated chocolate into one portion of dough. Stir mint extract into the remaining portion of dough; tint dough with green food coloring.

3 Shape each portion of dough into a 7×2×2-inch brick. Wrap each brick in plastic wrap or waxed paper. Chill about 2 hours or until dough is firm enough to slice. Using a long sharp knife, cut each brick lengthwise into four ½-inch slices. (You will have four 7×2-inch pieces from each color of dough.)

4 Stack four pieces of dough together, alternating colors. (You will have two bricks, each with four layers.) Gently press dough together to seal layers. Wrap each brick in plastic wrap or waxed paper and chill about 30 minutes or until dough is firm enough to slice.

5 Cut each brick lengthwise into four slices. (Each piece will have four layers in alternating colors.) Stack four slices of dough together, alternating colors, to create a checkerboard effect. Trim edges as needed to straighten sides and ends. If necessary, rewrap and chill about 30 minutes or until firm enough to slice.

6 Preheat oven to 350°F. Cut stacks crosswise into ¼-inch slices. Place slices 1 inch apart on an ungreased cookie sheet.

7 Bake for 9 to 11 minutes or just until edges are firm. Cool on cookie sheet for 1 minute. Transfer cookies to a wire rack; cool.

nutrition facts per cookie: 84 cal., 4 g total fat (2 g sat. fat), 14 mg chol., 72 mg sodium, 11 g carb., 0 g fiber, 1 g pro.

slice & bake

For an alcohol-free version, use milk in place of the liqueur, add a few drops of mint extract to the dough, and use food coloring to tint it pale green or pink.

white chocolate and crème de menthe shortbread

prep: 35 minutes **freeze:** 45 minutes **bake:** 10 minutes at 325°F per batch
makes: 40 cookies

2½   cups all-purpose flour
 ½   cup granulated sugar
 1   cup butter, cut up
 1   tablespoon green
       crème de menthe
 6   ounces white
       chocolate (with
       cocoa butter), cut
       up
 1   tablespoon
       shortening
 ¼   teaspoon mint extract

1 In a large bowl stir together flour and sugar. Using a pastry blender, cut in butter until dough resembles fine crumbs and starts to cling together. Using a fork, stir in crème de menthe. Knead until dough forms a ball (dough may seem crumbly at first, but will come together as you knead it). Divide dough in half.

2 Shape each half into a 6-inch-log, turning and flattening each side as you turn. Wrap each roll in plastic wrap or waxed paper. Freeze for 45 minutes to 1 hour or until firm (if dough gets too firm, let stand at room temperature for 10 minutes before slicing).

3 Preheat oven to 325°F. Cut logs into scant ¼-inch slices. Place slices 2 inches apart on ungreased cookie sheets. Bake for 10 to 12 minutes or until edges are lightly browned. Transfer to wire racks; cool.

4 In a small saucepan combine white chocolate and shortening; heat and stir over low heat until melted and smooth. Remove from heat; stir in mint extract. Drizzle over cookies.

to store: Layer drizzled cookies between sheets of waxed paper in an airtight container; cover. Store at room temperature up to 3 days. Or freeze undrizzled cookies up to 3 months. Thaw cookies at room temperature. Proceed with Step 4.

nutrition facts per cookie: 108 cal., 6 g total fat (4 g sat. fat), 13 mg chol., 37 mg sodium, 11 g carb., 0 g fiber, 1 g pro.

Cinnamon perfectly complements the java-chocolate combo.

chocolate-espresso coins

prep: 30 minutes **chill:** 2 hours **bake:** 5 minutes at 350°F per batch
makes: 144 cookies

½   cup butter, softened
¼   cup granulated sugar
¼   cup packed brown
       sugar
1   egg
1   tablespoon
       unsweetened cocoa
       powder
1½   teaspoons ground
       cinnamon
1   teaspoon instant
       espresso coffee
       powder or instant
       coffee crystals
½   teaspoon salt
1   cup all-purpose flour
3   ounces bittersweet
       chocolate, finely
       chopped
3   ounces bittersweet
       chocolate, melted

1 In a large mixing bowl beat butter with an electric mixer on medium to high speed for 30 seconds. Add granulated sugar and brown sugar. Beat until combined, scraping sides of bowl occasionally. Beat in egg, cocoa powder, cinnamon, coffee powder, and salt until combined. Beat in as much of the flour as you can with the mixer. Using a wooden spoon, stir in any remaining flour and the chopped chocolate.

2 Divide dough into three portions. Shape each portion into a 10- to 12-inch log. Wrap each roll in plastic wrap or waxed paper. Chill about 2 hours or until dough is firm enough to slice.

3 Preheat oven to 350°F. Lightly grease a cookie sheet or line with parchment paper. Cut logs into ¼-inch slices. Place slices ½ inch apart on the prepared cookie sheet.

4 Bake for 5 to 6 minutes or until lightly browned and set. Cool on cookie sheet for 1 minute. Transfer to a wire rack; cool. Drizzle cooled cookies with melted chocolate. Let stand until chocolate is set.

nutrition facts per cookie: 18 cal., 1 g total fat (1 g sat. fat), 3 mg chol., 14 mg sodium, 2 g carb., 0 g fiber, 0 g pro.

Pretty as a springtime bouquet of fresh flowers!

lemon-pistachio checkerboards

prep: 35 minutes **chill:** overnight **bake:** 11 minutes at 350°F per batch
makes: 36 cookies

slice & bake

2¼   cups all-purpose flour
½   teaspoon baking powder
¾   cup butter, softened
¾   cup granulated sugar
1   egg
2   teaspoons finely shredded lemon peel
2   drops yellow food coloring
¼   cup finely chopped pistachio nuts
⅛   teaspoon almond extract
3   drops green food coloring

1 In a medium bowl stir together flour and baking powder; set aside. In a large mixing bowl beat butter with an electric mixer on medium to high speed for 30 seconds. Add sugar. Beat until combined, scraping sides of bowl occasionally. Beat in egg until combined. Beat in as much of the flour mixture as you can with the mixer. Using a wooden spoon, stir in any remaining flour mixture.

2 Divide dough in half. Knead lemon peel and yellow food coloring into one portion of dough. Knead pistachios, almond extract, and green food coloring into the remaining portion of dough. Divide each portion in half and roll each portion into a 12-inch rope.

3 Place a yellow rope and a green rope side-by-side; press evenly into a 12×2-inch rectangle. Repeat with the remaining ropes to make a second 12×2-inch rectangle. Stack one rectangle on top of the other rectangle, alternating colors. Firmly press dough to seal layers; reshape stack. Cover and chill overnight.

4 Preheat oven to 350°F. Lightly grease a cookie sheet; set aside. Cut stack crosswise into ¼-inch slices. Place slices 1 inch apart on the prepared cookie sheet.

5 Bake for 11 to 13 minutes or just until golden. Transfer to a wire rack; cool.

nutrition facts per cookie: 87 cal., 5 g total fat (3 g sat. fat), 17 mg chol., 49 mg sodium, 11 g carb., 0 g fiber, 1 g pro.

"De-lish" even without the chocolate drizzle!

brown sugar icebox cookies

prep: 30 minutes **chill:** 4 hours **bake:** 10 minutes at 375°F per batch
makes: 72 cookies

½	cup shortening
½	cup butter, softened
1¼	cups packed brown sugar
½	teaspoon baking soda
¼	teaspoon salt
1	egg
1	teaspoon vanilla
2½	cups all-purpose flour
¾	cup ground toasted hazelnuts (filberts) or pecans (see tip, page 70)
⅔	cup finely chopped toasted hazelnuts (filberts) or pecans (see tip, page 70) (optional)
1	to 1½ cups semisweet or milk chocolate pieces (optional)
1	tablespoon shortening (optional)

1 In a large mixing bowl beat the ½ cup shortening and the butter with an electric mixer on medium speed for 30 seconds. Add brown sugar, baking soda, and salt. Beat until combined, scraping sides of bowl occasionally. Beat in egg and vanilla until combined. Beat in as much of the flour as you can with the mixer. Using a wooden spoon, stir in any remaining flour and the ¾ cup ground nuts. Divide dough in half.

2 On waxed paper, shape each portion of dough into a 10-inch-log. Lift and smooth the waxed paper to shape the logs. If desired, roll logs in the ⅔ cup finely chopped nuts. Wrap each log in plastic wrap or waxed paper. Chill about 4 hours or until firm enough to slice.

3 Preheat oven to 375°F. Cut logs into ¼-inch slices. Place slices 1 inch apart on an ungreased cookie sheet.

4 Bake for 10 to 12 minutes or until edges are firm. Transfer to a wire rack set over waxed paper; cool.

5 If desired, in a small saucepan combine chocolate pieces and the 1 tablespoon shortening. Heat and stir over low heat until smooth. Cool slightly. Transfer chocolate mixture to a small resealable plastic bag; seal bag. Snip off a tiny piece of one corner of the bag. Drizzle melted chocolate over cookies. Let stand until set.

nutrition facts per cookie: 65 cal., 4 g total fat (1 g sat. fat), 7 mg chol., 33 mg sodium, 7 g carb., 0 g fiber, 1 g pro.

If you're a fan of Dutch Letter pastries, you'll adore this recipe. Almond paste is the common denominator.

cinnamon-almond slices

prep: 25 minutes **chill:** 2 hours **bake:** 8 minutes at 350°F per batch
makes: 48 cookies

⅔ cup butter, softened
1 8-ounce can almond paste
¼ cup packed brown sugar
1 teaspoon baking powder
1 teaspoon ground cinnamon
½ teaspoon salt
1 egg
2 cups all-purpose flour
¼ cup almonds, toasted (see tip, page 13) and very finely chopped

1 In a large mixing bowl beat butter with an electric mixer on medium to high speed for 30 seconds. Add almond paste, brown sugar, baking powder, cinnamon, and salt. Beat until combined, scraping sides of bowl occasionally. Beat in egg until combined. Beat in as much of the flour as you can with the mixer. Using a wooden spoon, stir in any remaining flour and the almonds.

2 Divide dough in half. On a lightly floured surface, shape each half into an 8-inch log. Wrap each log in plastic wrap or waxed paper. Chill about 2 hours or until dough is firm enough to slice.

3 Preheat oven to 350°F. If necessary, reshape logs to make them round. Using a serrated knife, cut logs into ¼-inch slices. Place slices 1 inch apart on an ungreased cookie sheet.

4 Bake for 8 to 10 minutes or until edges are firm and centers are set. Transfer cookies to a wire rack; cool.

nutrition facts per cookie: 72 cal., 4 g total fat (2 g sat. fat), 11 mg chol., 59 mg sodium, 8 g carb., 0 g fiber, 1 g pro.

The juice of a Meyer lemon is sweeter than regular lemons and some even have a hint of orange.

meyer lemon-rosemary slices

prep: 40 minutes **chill:** 4 hours **bake:** 8 minutes at 350°F per batch
makes: 80 cookies

3　cups all-purpose flour
½　teaspoon baking soda
½　teaspoon salt
1½　cups granulated sugar
¾　cup butter, softened
1　egg
2　tablespoons finely shredded Meyer lemon peel or regular lemon peel
¼　cup freshly squeezed Meyer lemon juice or regular lemon juice
2　tablespoons finely snipped fresh rosemary
1　teaspoon lemon extract
½　cup powdered sugar

1 In a medium bowl stir together flour, baking soda, and salt. In a large mixing bowl beat granulated sugar and butter with an electric mixer on medium to high speed until fluffy, scraping sides of bowl occasionally. Beat in egg, lemon peel, lemon juice, rosemary, and lemon extract. Beat in as much of the flour mixture as you can with the mixer. Using a wooden spoon, stir in any remaining flour mixture.

2 Divide dough into four portions. Shape each dough portion into a 6-inch log. Wrap each log in plastic wrap or waxed paper. Chill about 4 hours or until dough is firm enough to slice.

3 Preheat oven to 350°F. Line cookie sheets with parchment paper; set aside. Cut logs into ¼-inch slices. Place slices about 1 inch apart on prepared cookie sheets.

4 Bake for 8 to 10 minutes or until edges are lightly browned. Cool on cookie sheets for 2 minutes. Place powdered sugar in a small bowl. Working in batches of two or three cookies, add warm cookies to the powdered sugar, turning to coat. Transfer to wire racks; cool.

nutrition facts per cookie: 51 cal., 2 g total fat (1 g sat. fat), 7 mg chol., 36 mg sodium, 8 g carb., 0 g fiber, 1 g pro.

Coating the cookies while they are still warm helps the powdered sugar adhere.

key lime coins

prep: 30 minutes **chill:** 3 hours **bake:** 15 minutes at 325°F
makes: 80 cookies

¾ cup butter, softened
⅓ cup powdered sugar
1 teaspoon finely shredded lime peel
2 tablespoons Key lime juice or lime juice
1 tablespoon water
1 teaspoon vanilla
1¾ cups all-purpose flour
2 tablespoons cornstarch
½ teaspoon salt
2 cups powdered sugar

1 In a large mixing bowl beat butter with an electric mixer on medium to high speed for 30 seconds. Add the ⅓ cup powdered sugar, the lime peel, lime juice, the water, and vanilla. Beat until combined, scraping sides of bowl occasionally. Beat in flour, cornstarch, and salt until combined.

2 Divide dough in half. Shape each half into a 10-inch log. Wrap each log in plastic wrap or waxed paper. Chill about 3 hours or until dough is firm enough to slice.

3 Preheat oven to 325° F. Line a cookie sheet with parchment paper. Cut logs into ¼-inch slices. Place slices 2 inches apart on the prepared cookie sheet.

4 Bake for 15 to 18 minutes or just until bottoms are golden. Cool on cookie sheet for 4 minutes. Place the 2 cups powdered sugar in a large bowl. Gently toss warm cookies, two or three at a time, in powdered sugar to coat. Transfer to a wire rack; cool.

nutrition facts per cookie: 40 cal., 2 g total fat (1 g sat. fat), 3 mg chol., 30 mg sodium, 6 g carb., 0 g fiber, 0 g pro.

to make ahead: Prepare as directed through Step 2, except freeze logs for up to 2 months. To serve, thaw logs slightly. Continue as directed in Step 3.

Wrap a stack of cookies for the ginger lovers on your Christmas list.

triple-ginger crisps

prep: 30 minutes **chill:** 4 hours 30 minutes **bake:** 8 minutes at 350°F per batch
makes: 96 cookies

4½	cups all-purpose flour
1	tablespoon ground ginger
1½	teaspoons baking powder
1½	teaspoons ground cinnamon
½	teaspoon baking soda
½	teaspoon salt
¼	teaspoon ground cloves
¼	teaspoon ground nutmeg
1½	cups butter, softened
1¾	cups granulated sugar
2	eggs
½	cup molasses
1	tablespoon grated fresh ginger
2	teaspoons lemon juice
¾	cup finely chopped crystallized ginger

1 In a medium bowl combine flour, ground ginger, baking powder, cinnamon, baking soda, salt, cloves, and nutmeg; set aside.

2 In an extra-large miximg bowl beat butter with an electric mixer on medium to high speed for 30 seconds. Beat in sugar until fluffy. Add eggs, molasses, fresh ginger, and lemon juice. Beat until well mixed, scraping sides of bowl occasionally. Beat in as much of the flour mixture as you can with the mixer. Using a wooden spoon, stir in any remaining flour mixture and the crystallized ginger. Divide dough into three portions. Cover and chill about 30 minutes or until dough is easy to handle.

3 Shape each portion into an 8-inch log. Wrap each log in plastic wrap or waxed paper. Chill for 4 hours or until dough is firm enough to slice.

4 Preheat oven to 350°F. Line cookie sheets with parchment paper; set aside. Cut logs into scant ¼-inch slices. Place slices about 1 inch apart on prepared cookie sheets.

5 Bake for 8 to 10 minutes or just until firm. Cool on cookie sheets for 2 minutes. Transfer to wire racks; cool.

nutrition facts per cookie: 72 cal., 3 g total fat (2 g sat. fat), 12 mg chol., 48 mg sodium, 11 g carb., 0 g fiber, 1 g pro.

slice & bake

In a hurry but still want to do the sandwich version? Use canned frosting for the cookie filling. Pictured on page 81.

milk chocolate mini cookies

prep: 45 minutes **chill:** 1 hour **bake:** 9 minutes at 350°F per batch
makes: 144 cookies

6   ounces milk chocolate, coarsely chopped
¾   cup all-purpose flour
¾   teaspoon baking powder
⅛   teaspoon salt
3   tablespoons butter, softened
½   cup granulated sugar
1   egg
¾   teaspoon vanilla
1   recipe Milk Chocolate-Sour Cream Frosting (optional)

1 In a small saucepan heat and stir chocolate over low heat until melted. Set aside.

2 In a medium bowl stir together flour, baking powder, and salt; set aside. In a medium mixing bowl beat butter with an electric mixer on medium to high speed for 30 seconds. Beat in sugar until light and fluffy. Beat in egg, vanilla, and melted chocolate until combined. Beat in flour mixture until combined.

3 Divide dough into four portions. Cover and chill about 1 hour or until dough is easy to handle.

4 Preheat oven to 350°F. Removing one portion of dough from the refrigerator at a time, shape each portion into a 10-inch log.* Cut each log into ¼-inch slices. Place 1 inch apart on an ungreased cookie sheet.

5 Bake for 9 to 10 minutes or until edges are set. Cool on cookie sheet for 2 minutes. Carefully transfer to a wire rack (cookies will be brittle); cool. If desired, spread ½ teaspoon of the Milk Chocolate-Sour Cream Frosting on bottoms of half the cookies. Top with the remaining cookies, bottom sides down. Serve filled cookies the same day.

milk chocolate-sour cream frosting:
In a medium saucepan melt 3 ounces milk chocolate, chopped, and 2 tablespoons butter over low heat, stirring frequently. Cool for 5 minutes. Stir in ¼ cup sour cream. Gradually add 1 to 1¼ cups powdered sugar until frosting is spreadable.

*tip: Place the dough on a sheet of waxed paper and use the paper to shape the log. If the dough becomes too sticky, place it in the freezer for a few minutes.

to store: Layer unfilled cookies between sheets of waxed paper in an airtight container; cover. Store at room temperature up to 3 days or freeze up to 3 months. To serve, thaw cookies, if frozen. If desired, fill as directed in Step 5.

nutrition facts per single mini cookie: 21 cal., 1 g total fat (1 g sat. fat), 3 mg chol., 9 mg sodium, 3 g carb., 0 g fiber, 0 g pro.

Bake with your favorite honey, such as clover or sage.

honey coins

prep: 30 minutes **chill:** 3 hours **bake:** 13 minutes at 325°F per batch
makes: 80 cookies

¾ cup butter, softened
⅓ cup powdered sugar
2 tablespoons honey
1 tablespoon water
1 teaspoon vanilla
1¾ cups all-purpose flour
2 tablespoons cornstarch
½ teaspoon salt
2 cups powdered sugar

1 In a large mixing bowl beat butter with an electric mixer on medium to high speed for 30 seconds. Add the ⅓ cup powdered sugar, honey, the water, and vanilla. Beat until combined, scraping sides of bowl occasionally. Beat in flour, cornstarch, and salt until combined.

2 Divide dough in half. Shape each portion into a 10-inch log. Wrap each log in plastic wrap or waxed paper. Chill about 3 hours or until dough is firm enough to slice.

3 Preheat oven to 325°F. Line a cookie sheet with parchment paper. Cut logs into ¼-inch slices. Place slices 2 inches apart on the prepared cookie sheet.

4 Bake for 13 to 15 minutes or just until bottoms are golden. Cool on cookie sheet for 4 minutes. Place the 2 cups powdered sugar in a large bowl. Add warm cookies, a few at a time, tossing gently to coat. Transfer to a wire rack; cool.

nutrition facts per cookie: 41 cal., 2 g total fat (1 g sat. fat), 5 mg chol., 30 mg sodium, 6 g carb., 0 g fiber, 0 g pro.

to make ahead: Prepare as directed through Step 2, except freeze logs for up to 2 months. To bake, thaw logs slightly. Continue as directed in Step 3.

These red-and-white sweets look especially festive on a Christmas cookie tray. Decorate the tray with candy canes.

peppermint sandwich crèmes

prep: 30 minutes *freeze:* 2 hours **bake:** 10 minutes at 350°F per batch
makes: 35 cookies

½   cup butter, softened
1   cup granulated sugar
¼   teaspoon baking soda
¼   teaspoon salt
1   egg
2   teaspoons vanilla
1   teaspoon peppermint extract
1¾ cups all-purpose flour
1   recipe Peppermint-Cream Cheese Filling
    Finely crushed peppermint candies or sprinkles

1 In a large mixing bowl beat butter with an electric mixer on medium to high speed for 30 seconds. Add sugar, baking soda, and salt. Beat until combined, scraping sides of bowl occasionally. Beat in egg, vanilla, and peppermint extract until combined. Beat in as much of the flour as you can with the mixer. Using a wooden spoon, stir in any remaining flour.

2 Divide dough into four portions. Shape each portion into an 8-inch log. Wrap each log in plastic wrap or waxed paper. Freeze for 2 to 3 hours or until dough is firm enough to slice.

3 Preheat oven to 350°F. Cut rolls into ⅜-inch slices. Place slices 1 inch apart on an ungreased cookie sheet.

4 Bake for 10 to 12 minutes or just until firm. Transfer cookies to a wire rack; cool. Spread Peppermint-Cream Cheese Filling on bottoms of half the cooled cookies, spreading filling to edges. Top with the remaining cookies, bottom sides down. Press lightly until filling just comes slightly over edges. Roll edges of cookies in crushed candies or sprinkles.

nutrition facts per sandwich cookie: 151 cal., 5 g total fat (3 g sat. fat), 19 mg chol., 66 mg sodium, 26 g carb., 0 g fiber, 1 g pro.

peppermint-cream cheese filling:
In a large mixing bowl beat one 3-ounce package cream cheese, softened, and ¼ cup butter, softened, with an electric mixer on medium speed until smooth. Beat in 1 teaspoon vanilla and ½ teaspoon peppermint extract. Gradually beat in 3 cups powdered sugar. If necessary, beat in enough milk, 1 teaspoon at a time, to make filling spreading consistency.

peppermint palmiers

prep: 45 minutes **chill:** 3 hours **freeze:** 4 hours **bake:** 10 minutes at 350°F per batch
makes: About 80 cookies

½ cup butter, softened
½ cup granulated sugar
½ cup packed brown sugar
½ teaspoon baking powder
¼ teaspoon salt
1 egg
2 tablespoons white crème
   de menthe
1 tablespoon milk
½ teaspoon vanilla
2¾ cups all-purpose flour
1 8-ounce package cream
   cheese, softened
½ cup powdered sugar
¼ cup all-purpose flour
1 tablespoon white crème
   de menthe
   Few drops red food
   coloring
½ cup finely crushed
   peppermint candies

1 In a large mixing bowl beat butter with an electric mixer on medium to high speed for 30 seconds. Add granulated sugar, brown sugar, baking powder, and salt. Beat until combined, scraping sides of bowl occasionally. Beat in egg, the 2 tablespoons crème de menthe, milk, and vanilla. Beat in as much of the 2¾ cups flour as you can with the mixer. Stir in any of the remaining 2¾ cups flour. Divide dough in half. Cover and chill about 3 hours or until dough is easy to handle.

2 Meanwhile, for filling, in a medium mixing bowl beat cream cheese, powdered sugar, the ¼ cup flour, and the 1 tablespoon crème de menthe on low speed until smooth. Stir in enough red food coloring to tint filling pale pink. Gently fold in crushed candies. Cover and chill up to 2 hours. (Chill no longer than 2 hours because the filling will become too soft and sticky.)

3 On a lightly floured surface, roll half the dough into a 12×8-inch rectangle. Spread half the filling on rectangle to within ½ inch of each long edge. Roll up both long edges, scroll fashion, to meet in the center. Brush seam with water where dough spirals meet. Lightly press together. Repeat with the remaining dough and filling. Wrap each scroll in plastic wrap; place on a tray or cookie sheet. Freeze for 4 to 24 hours or until firm.

4 Preheat oven to 350°F. Line a cookie sheet with parchment paper; set aside. Using a serrated knife, cut scrolls into ¼-inch slices. Place slices 2 inches apart on the prepared cookie sheet.

5 Bake about 10 minutes or until edges are firm and bottoms are lightly browned. Transfer cookies to a wire rack; cool.

to store: Layer cookies between sheets of waxed paper in an airtight container; cover. Store in the freezer up to 3 months. Thaw before serving.

nutrition facts per cookie: 53 cal., 2 g total fat (1 g sat. fat), 9 mg chol., 27 mg sodium, 8 g carb., 0 g fiber, 1 g pro.

Rolling the dough from the long sides to meet in the middle creates the double-spiral.

chocolate palmiers

prep: 35 minutes **chill:** 4 hours, 30 minutes **bake:** 8 minutes at 375°F per batch
makes: 72 cookies

1 8-ounce package cream cheese, softened
½ cup powdered sugar
¼ cup unsweetened cocoa powder
2 tablespoons all-purpose flour
2 tablespoons coffee liqueur or hazelnut liqueur
½ cup finely chopped pecans or hazelnuts, toasted (filberts) (see tip, page 13)
½ cup butter, softened
½ cup granulated sugar
½ cup packed brown sugar
½ teaspoon baking powder
½ teaspoon ground cinnamon
¼ teaspoon salt
1 egg
3 tablespoons milk
½ teaspoon vanilla
2¾ cups all-purpose flour

1 For filling, in a medium mixing bowl beat cream cheese, powdered sugar, cocoa powder, the 2 tablespoons flour, and the liqueur with an electric mixer on low to medium speed until smooth. Stir in nuts. Cover; set aside.

2 For dough, in a large mixing bowl beat butter with an electric mixer on medium to high speed for 30 seconds. Add granulated sugar, brown sugar, baking powder, cinnamon, and salt. Beat until combined, scraping sides of bowl occasionally. Beat in egg, milk, and vanilla until combined. Beat in as much of the 2¾ cups flour as you can with the mixer. Using a wooden spoon, stir in any remaining flour. Divide dough in half. If necessary, cover and chill about 30 minutes or until dough is easy to handle.

3 On a lightly floured surface, roll dough, one portion at a time, into a 12×8-inch rectangle. Spread each rectangle with half the filling, spreading to within ½ inch of the long edges. For each rectangle, roll up the two long edges to meet in the center. Brush the seam where the dough spirals meet with water and lightly press together. Wrap each roll in plastic wrap or waxed paper. Chill about 4 hours or until firm enough to slice.

4 Preheat oven to 375°F. Grease a cookie sheet; set aside. Using a sharp thin-blade knife, cut rolls into ¼-inch slices. Place slices, cut sides down, 2 inches apart on the prepared cookie sheet.

5 Bake 8 minutes or until bottoms are lightly browned. Transfer to racks; cool.

to store: Layer cookies between sheets of waxed paper in an airtight container; cover. Store in the refrigerator up to 3 days.

nutrition facts per cookie: 63 cal., 3 g total fat (2 g sat. fat), 9 mg chol., 34 mg sodium, 8 g carb., 0 g fiber, 1 g pro.

Two doughs, layered and rolled together, bake into delicious two-tone cookies that are simply irresistible.

brown sugar-hazelnut spirals

prep: 40 minutes **chill:** 1 hour **bake:** 8 minutes at 375°F per batch
makes: 72 cookies

1	cup butter, softened
¾	cup granulated sugar
¾	cup packed brown sugar
1½	teaspoons baking powder
½	teaspoon salt
1	egg
1	teaspoon vanilla
2½	cups all-purpose flour
⅓	cup purchased chocolate-hazelnut spread
¼	cup ground hazelnuts (filberts)

1 In a large mixing bowl beat butter with an electric mixer on medium to high speed for 30 seconds. Add granulated sugar, brown sugar, baking powder, and salt. Beat until combined, scraping sides of bowl occasionally. Beat in egg and vanilla until combined. Beat in as much of the flour as you can with the mixer. Using a wooden spoon, stir in any remaining flour.

2 Divide dough in half. Leave one half plain. Stir chocolate-hazelnut spread and hazelnuts onto the remaining half. Divide each portion in half again, making four portions total.

3 On waxed paper, roll each portion of dough into an 8×7-inch rectangle. Using the waxed paper, invert one chocolate dough rectangle on top of one plain dough rectangle. Roll dough together into a 10×8-inch rectangle. Peel off top sheet of waxed paper. Starting from a long side, tightly roll up dough into a spiral; seal edge. Repeat with remaining dough portions. Wrap each roll in plastic wrap. Chill for 1 to 2 hours or until dough is firm enough to slice.

4 Preheat oven to 375°F. Cut rolls into ¼-inch slices. Place slices 2 inches apart on an ungreased cookie sheet.

5 Bake for 8 to 10 minutes or until edges are firm and lightly browned. Cool on cookie sheet for 1 minute. Transfer cookies to a wire rack; cool.

nutrition facts per cookie: 66 cal., 3 g total fat (2 g sat. fat), 9 mg chol., 51 mg sodium, 9 g carb., 0 g fiber, 1 g pro.

These dainty bites have been a favorite in our test kitchen for decades.

linzer pinwheels

prep: 35 minutes **chill:** 5 hours **bake:** 10 minutes at 375°F per batch
makes: 72 cookies

1 cup butter, softened
1½ cups granulated sugar
½ teaspoon baking powder
½ teaspoon salt
2 eggs
1 teaspoon finely shredded lemon peel
3¼ cups all-purpose flour
⅔ cup seedless raspberry preserves

1 In a large mixing bowl beat butter with an electric mixer on medium to high speed for 30 seconds. Add sugar, baking powder, and salt. Beat until combined, scraping sides of bowl occasionally. Beat in eggs and lemon peel until combined. Beat in as much of the flour as you can with the mixer. Using a wooden spoon, stir in any remaining flour. Divide dough in half. Cover and chill about 1 hour or until dough is easy to handle.

2 Roll half the dough at a time between sheets of waxed paper into a 10-inch square. Remove top sheet of waxed paper. Spread dough with preserves to within ½ inch of the edges. Roll up dough using bottom sheet of waxed paper to help lift and guide the dough. Moisten edges; pinch to seal. Wrap each spiral log in waxed paper or plastic wrap. Chill for 4 to 24 hours or until dough is firm enough to slice.

3 Preheat oven to 375°F. Line a large cookie sheet with parchment paper. Quickly cut spiral logs into ¼-inch slices, rotating logs often to keep them from flattening. (If logs become too soft during cutting, place them in the freezer about 10 minutes or until they firm up.) Place slices 2 inches apart on the prepared cookie sheet.

4 Bake for 10 to 12 minutes or until edges are firm and bottoms are light brown. Cool on cookie sheet for 1 minute. Transfer cookies to a wire rack; cool.

to store: Layer cookies between sheets of waxed paper in an airtight container; cover. Store in the refrigerator up to 2 days or freeze up to 3 months.

nutrition facts per cookie: 70 cal., 3 g total fat (2 g sat. fat), 12 mg chol., 45 mg sodium, 11 g carb., 0 g fiber, 1 g pro.

Freeze any remaining almond meal, also called almond flour, for 3 months.

almond, cream cheese, and caramel swirls

prep: 45 minutes **chill:** 2 hours + 4 hours **bake:** 10 minutes at 350°F per batch
makes: 96 cookies

1   cup butter, softened
1   8-ounce package
        cream cheese,
        softened
1   cup packed brown
        sugar
1   egg yolk
1   teaspoon vanilla
½   teaspoon almond
        extract
½   cup almond meal
2¼   cups all-purpose flour
30   vanilla caramels,
        unwrapped
1   3-ounce package
        cream cheese,
        softened

1 In a large mixing bowl beat butter and 4 ounces of the cream cheese with an electric mixer on medium to high speed for 30 seconds. Add brown sugar. Beat on medium to high speed until light and fluffy, scraping sides of bowl occasionally. Beat in egg yolk, vanilla, and almond extract until combined. Beat in almond meal on low speed. Beat in as much of the flour as you can with the mixer. Using a wooden spoon, stir in any remaining flour. Divide dough in half. Cover and chill about 2 hours or until dough is easy to handle.

2 For filling, in a small saucepan heat and stir caramels over low heat until melted and smooth. Stir in the remaining 4 ounces cream cheese and the 3-ounce package of cream cheese. Heat and stir until smooth.

3 Roll half the dough at a time between sheets of waxed paper into a 14×8-inch rectangle. Remove top sheet of waxed paper. Spread dough with filling to within ½ inch of the edges. Starting from a long side, roll up dough using bottom sheet of waxed paper to help lift and guide the dough. Moisten edges; pinch to seal. Wrap each spiral log in plastic wrap or waxed paper. Chill for 4 to 24 hours or until dough is firm enough to slice.

4 Preheat oven to 350°F. Line a cookie sheet with parchment paper. Cut logs into ¼-inch slices. Place slices 2 inches apart on the prepared cookie sheet.

5 Bake for 10 to 12 minutes or until golden. Transfer cookies to a wire rack; cool.

nutrition facts per cookie: 64 cal., 4 g total fat (2 g sat. fat), 11 mg chol., 36 mg sodium, 7 g carb., 0 g fiber, 1 g pro.

Cinnamon rolls aren't just for breakfast anymore!

cinnamon-sugar roll cookies

prep: 40 minutes freeze: 2 hours bake: 8 minutes at 375°F per batch
makes: 60 cookies

¼ cup butter, softened
¼ cup shortening
2 ounces cream cheese, softened
1 cup packed brown sugar
½ teaspoon baking powder
½ teaspoon salt
½ teaspoon ground cinnamon
¼ teaspoon ground nutmeg
1 egg
2 teaspoons vanilla
2½ cups all-purpose flour
½ cup dry-roasted salted mixed nuts, finely chopped
¼ cup packed brown sugar
½ teaspoon ground cinnamon
2 tablespoons butter
1 recipe Vanilla Icing
    Dry-roasted salted mixed nuts, chopped (optional)

1 In a large mixing bowl beat butter, shortening, and cream cheese with an electric mixer on medium to high speed for 30 seconds. Add the 1 cup brown sugar, the baking powder, the salt, the ½ teaspoon cinnamon, and the nutmeg. Beat until combined, scraping sides of bowl occasionally. Beat in egg and vanilla until combined. Beat in as much of the flour as you can with the mixer. Using a wooden spoon, stir in any remaining flour.

2 For filling, in a medium bowl stir together the ½ cup mixed nuts, the ¼ cup brown sugar, and the ½ teaspoon cinnamon. Using a pastry blender, cut in the 2 tablespoons butter until mixture clings together.

3 Roll dough between sheets of lightly floured waxed paper into a 16×9-inch rectangle. Remove top sheet of waxed paper. Sprinkle dough with filling to within ½ inch of the edges. Starting from a long side, roll up dough using bottom sheet of waxed paper to help lift and guide the dough. Moisten edges; pinch to seal. Wrap log in plastic wrap or waxed paper. Freeze about 2 hours or until firm enough to slice.

4 Preheat oven to 375°F. Line a cookie sheet with parchment paper. Using a sharp knife, cut log into ¼-inch slices. Place slices 2 inches apart on the prepared cookie sheet.

5 Bake about 8 minutes or until edges are lightly browned. Cool on cookie sheet for 2 minutes. Transfer to a wire rack; cool. Drizzle cookies with Vanilla Icing. If desired, sprinkle with additional mixed nuts. Let stand until icing is set.

nutrition facts per cookie: 74 cal., 3 g total fat (1 g sat. fat), 7 mg chol., 43 mg sodium, 11 g carb., 0 g fiber, 1 g pro.

vanilla icing: Stir together 1 cup powdered sugar, 1 tablespoon milk, and 1 teaspoon vanilla. Add additional milk until icing is drizzling consistency.

A scaled-down recipe when you don't need dozens of cookies.

blueberry-walnut twirls

prep: 45 minutes **chill:** 5 hours **bake:** 10 minutes at 375°F per batch
makes: 42 cookies

1   cup butter, softened
1½   cups granulated
        sugar
 ½   teaspoon baking
        powder
 ½   teaspoon salt
2   eggs
1   teaspoon vanilla
3½   cups all-purpose flour
 ½   cup blueberry
        preserves or jam
1½   teaspoons cornstarch
 ½   cup very finely
        chopped walnuts,
        toasted (see tip,
        page 13)

1 In a large bowl beat butter with an electric mixer on medium to high speed for 30 seconds. Add sugar, baking powder, and salt. Beat until combined, scraping sides of bowl occasionally. Beat in eggs and vanilla until combined. Beat in as much of the flour as you can with the mixer. Using a wooden spoon, stir in any remaining flour. Divide dough in half. Cover and chill dough about 1 hour or until easy to handle.

2 Meanwhile, for filling, in a small saucepan combine blueberry preserves and cornstarch; heat and stir over medium heat until thickened and bubbly. Remove from heat. Stir in walnuts. Cover and set aside to cool.

3 Roll one portion of the dough between two sheets of waxed paper into an 11-inch square. Spread half of the filling over the square, leaving a ½-inch border along the edges. Roll up dough into a spiral. Moisten edges; pinch to seal. Wrap log in plastic wrap or waxed paper. Repeat with the remaining dough and the remaining filling. Chill for 4 hours or until dough is firm enough to slice.

4 Preheat oven to 375°F. Line cookie sheets with parchment paper; set aside. Cut roll into ¼-inch slices. Place slices about 1 inch apart on prepared cookie sheets.

5 Bake for 10 to 12 minutes or just until firm. Cool on cookie sheets for 2 minutes. Transfer to wire racks; cool.

nutrition facts per cookie: 128 cal., 6 g total fat (3 g sat. fat), 22 mg chol., 68 mg sodium, 18 g carb., 0 g fiber, 2 g pro.

Classic Italian biscotti are traditionally double-baked to create an extra-crisp dessert biscuit.

pecan crunch biscotti

prep: 40 minutes **bake:** 25 minutes at 350°F + 22 minutes at 325°F **cool:** 30 minutes
makes: 24 cookies

Nonstick cooking spray
1   tablespoon butter
1½   cups chopped pecans
¼   cup granulated sugar
⅓   cup butter, softened
½   cup packed brown sugar
2   teaspoons baking
        powder
1   teaspoon ground
        cinnamon
¼   teaspoon salt
2   eggs
2   tablespoons honey
1   teaspoon vanilla
2⅔   cups all-purpose flour
1   recipe Browned Butter
        Glaze

browned butter glaze:
In a saucepan melt ⅓ cup butter over low heat. Heat until butter turns a light brown. Remove from heat. In a bowl combine 3 cups powdered sugar, 2 tablespoons milk, and 1 teaspoon vanilla. Stir in butter until combined. If necessary, add additional milk, 1 teaspoon at a time, to make glaze a dipping consistency.

1 Line a cookie sheet with foil. Lightly coat foil with cooking spray; set aside. In a large nonstick skillet melt the 1 tablespoon butter over medium heat. Add pecans. Cook for 1 minute, stirring occasionally. Add granulated sugar; stir for 2 to 3 minutes or until sugar begins to melt and nuts are toasted. Transfer mixture to prepared cookie sheet; cool. When cool, place nuts in a sturdy resealable plastic bag; seal. Crush nut mixture in bag with a rolling pin; set aside.

2 Preheat oven to 350°F. Discard foil on cookie sheet. Lightly coat cookie sheet with cooking spray; set aside. In a large mixing bowl beat the ⅓ cup butter with an electric mixer on medium speed for 30 seconds. Add brown sugar, baking powder, cinnamon, and salt. Beat until combined, scraping sides of bowl occasionally. Beat in eggs, honey, and vanilla. Beat in as much of the flour as you can with the mixer. Stir in any remaining flour and the candied pecans. If necessary, knead with your hands until dough comes together.

3 Divide dough in half. Shape each portion into a 9-inch log. Place logs 4 inches apart on prepared cookie sheet; slightly flatten each log to 2½ inches wide.

4 Bake for 25 to 30 minutes or until a wooden toothpick inserted near centers comes out clean. Cool on cookie sheet for 30 minutes.

5 Preheat oven to 325°F. Using a serrated knife, cut each log diagonally into ½-inch slices. Place slices, cut sides down, on cookie sheet.

6 Bake for 10 minutes. Turn slices over; bake for 12 to 15 minutes more or until dry and crisp. Transfer to wire racks; cool. Dip top of each cookie into Browned Butter Glaze; let excess drip down cookie. Place cookies on waxed paper; let stand until set.

nutrition facts per cookie: 245 cal., 11 g total fat (4 g sat. fat), 30 mg chol., 123 mg sodium, 35 g carb., 1 g fiber, 3 g pro.

American flavors blend with Italian technique in this unique take on biscotti.

peanut butter-brownie biscotti

prep: 35 minutes **bake:** 20 minutes at 375°F + 20 minutes at 325°F **cool:** 1 hour
makes: 32 cookies

⅓ cup creamy peanut butter
¼ cup butter, softened
⅔ cup granulated sugar
⅓ cup unsweetened cocoa powder
1½ teaspoons baking powder
2 eggs
1 teaspoon vanilla
1¾ cups all-purpose flour
1 cup chopped bittersweet or semisweet chocolate (about 6 ounces)
1 recipe Peanut Butter Icing

peanut butter icing: In a small bowl stir together 1¼ cups powdered sugar, ⅓ cup creamy peanut butter, and ¼ cup milk until smooth.

1 Preheat oven to 375°F. In a large mixing bowl beat peanut butter and butter with an electric mixer on medium to high speed for 30 seconds. Add sugar, cocoa powder, and baking powder. Beat until combined, scraping sides of bowl occasionally. Beat in eggs and vanilla until combined. Beat in as much of the flour as you can with the mixer. Using a wooden spoon, stir in any remaining flour and the chopped chocolate. If necessary, knead with your hands until dough comes together.

2 Divide dough in half. Shape each half into a 9-inch log. Place log about 3 inches apart on a large ungreased large cookie sheet; flatten slightly to about 2 inches wide.

3 Bake for 20 to 25 minutes or until a wooden toothpick inserted near the centers comes out clean. Cool on cookie sheet on a wire rack for 1 hour.

4 Preheat oven to 325°F. Transfer logs to a cutting board. Using a serrated knife, cut into ½-inch slices. Place slices one cut side down on cookie sheet.

5 Bake for 10 minutes. Turn slices over; bake for 10 minutes more. Transfer to wire racks; cool. Dip tops of cooled cookies into Peanut Butter Icing, using a narrow metal spatula to smooth the icing. Let stand until icing is set.

nutrition facts per cookie: 138 cal., 7 g total fat (3 g sat. fat), 16 mg chol., 66 mg sodium, 19 g carb., 1 g fiber, 3 g pro.

white chocolate, cornmeal, and almond mini biscotti

prep: 35 minutes **bake:** 20 minutes at 375°F + 16 minutes at 325°F **cool:** 2 hours
makes: 42 cookies

¾ cup butter, softened
½ cup granulated sugar
1 teaspoon baking powder
1 egg
1 teaspoon vanilla
1 cup cornmeal
1½ cups all-purpose flour
½ cup slivered almonds, chopped
3 ounces white baking chocolate with cocoa butter, chopped
2 teaspoons finely shredded orange peel
5 ounces white baking chocolate with cocoa butter, coarsely chopped
1 tablespoon shortening
½ cup white jimmies or coarse sugar (optional)

1 Preheat oven to 375°F. In a large mixing bowl beat butter with an electric mixer on medium to high speed for 30 seconds. Add granulated sugar and baking powder. Beat until combined, scraping sides of bowl occasionally. Beat in egg and vanilla until combined. Beat in cornmeal. Beat in as much of the flour as you can with the mixer. Using a wooden spoon, stir in any remaining flour, the almonds, 3 ounces chopped white chocolate, and orange peel.

2 Divide dough into three portions. Shape each portion into an 8-inch log. Place logs about 4 inches apart on a large ungreased cookie sheet; flatten slightly. Bake about 20 minutes or until a wooden toothpick inserted near the centers comes out clean. Cool on cookie sheet for 1 hour.

3 Preheat oven to 325°F. Using a serrated knife, cut each log diagonally into ½-inch slices. Place slices one cut side down on an ungreased cookie sheet. Bake for 8 minutes. Carefully turn slices over and bake for 8 to 10 minutes more or until lightly browned. Transfer to wire racks; cool for 1 hour.

4 In a small heavy saucepan heat and stir 5 ounces white chocolate and shortening over low heat until melted and smooth. Dip tops of cookies in melted white chocolate and sprinkle immediately with white jimmies. Place cookies on waxed paper; let stand until white chocolate is set.

nutrition facts per cookie: 108 cal., 6 g total fat (3 g sat. fat), 14 mg chol., 47 mg sodium, 12 g carb., 0 g fiber, 1 g pro.

Finely snip the dried cherries or pulse them in a food processor, because small bits of fruit will make slicing the dough easier.

cherry-almond biscotti

prep: 25 minutes **bake:** 25 minutes at 325°F + 20 minutes at 325°F
makes: 48 cookies

2¾ cups all-purpose flour
1½ cups granulated sugar
1½ teaspoons baking powder
1 teaspoon salt
2 eggs
2 egg yolks
6 tablespoons butter, melted
1 cup coarsely chopped almonds
½ cup snipped dried cherries
1 tablespoon granulated sugar
1 recipe Almond-Cream Cheese Icing

1 Preheat oven to 325°F. Line two large cookie sheets with parchment paper; set aside.

2 In a large bowl combine flour, the 1½ cups sugar, the baking powder, and salt. Make a well in the center of the flour mixture, set aside. In a small bowl lightly beat eggs and egg yolks. Stir the melted butter into beaten eggs. Place egg mixture in the well in flour mixture; stir flour mixture until the dough starts to form a ball. Stir in almonds and dried cherries (dough will be crumbly). Using your hands, knead the dough until it comes together.

3 On a lightly floured surface, divide dough into three equal portions. Shape each portion into a 14-inch log. Place logs about 3 inches apart on prepared cookie sheets; flatten rolls to about 1½ inches wide. Sprinkle with 1 tablespoon sugar.

4 Bake for 25 to 30 minutes or until rolls are firm and light brown. Remove from oven. Place cookie sheets on wire racks; cool for 15 minutes.

5 Transfer logs to cutting board. Using a serrated knife, cut each log diagonally into ½-inch slices. Place slices, cut sides down, on cookie sheets.

6 Bake for 10 minutes. Turn slices over; bake for 10 to 15 minutes more or until crisp and golden brown.

7 Transfer biscotti to wire racks placed over sheets of waxed paper. Drizzle Almond-Cream Cheese Icing over biscotti. Let stand until set.

almond-cream cheese icing: In a medium bowl beat 3 ounces cream cheese, softened, and ¼ teaspoon almond extract with an electric mixer on medium to high speed until creamy. Beat in 1 cup powdered sugar, adding milk as necessary to make icing drizzling consistency.

to store: Layer undrizzled biscotti between sheets of waxed paper in an airtight container; cover. Store at room temperature up to 3 days or freeze up to 1 month. To serve, thaw cookies, if frozen. Drizzle cookies as directed in Step 7.

nutrition facts per cookie: 101 cal., 3 g total fat (1 g sat. fat), 23 mg chol., 79 mg sodium, 16 g carb., 1 g fiber, 2 g pro.

Adults and kids alike will go for this candy-infused version.

chocolate-malted milk biscotti

prep: 30 minutes **bake:** 25 minutes at 325°F + 16 minutes at 325°F **cool:** 1 hour
makes: 36 cookies

1¾ cups all-purpose flour
¾   cup unsweetened
     cocoa powder
¼   cup malted milk
     powder
1   teaspoon baking soda
½   teaspoon salt
3   eggs
1   cup granulated sugar
¼   cup butter, melted
1   teaspoon vanilla
1   cup coarsely chopped
     malted milk balls
½   cup milk chocolate
     pieces

1 Preheat oven to 325° F. Line a large cookie sheet with parchment paper; set aside.

2 In a large bowl stir together flour, cocoa powder, malted milk powder, baking soda, and salt. Make a well in the center of the flour mixture; set aside. In a medium bowl whisk together eggs, sugar, melted butter, and vanilla. Add egg mixture to the flour mixture; stir until dough starts to form a ball. Stir in malted milk balls and chocolate pieces (dough will be crumbly). Knead the dough until it comes together.

3 Turn the dough out onto a lightly floured surface. Divide dough in half. Shape each half into a 10-inch-log Place log about 3 inches apart on the prepared cookie sheet; flatten slightly to about 2 inches wide.

4 Bake for 25 minutes. Cool on cookie sheet on a wire rack for at least 1 hour.

5 Transfer logs to a cutting board. Using a serrated knife, cut each log diagonally into ½-inch slices. Place slices, cut sides down, on cookie sheet.

6 Bake for 8 minutes. Turn slices over; bake for 8 minutes more. Transfer to a wire rack; cool. (Cookies will crisp as they cool.)

nutrition facts per cookie: 100 cal., 3 g total fat (2 g sat. fat), 20 mg chol., 99 mg sodium, 16 g carb., 1 g fiber, 2 g pro.

A light brushing of warm honey accentuates the lemon flavor.

pistachio biscotti

prep: 30 minutes **bake:** 30 minutes at 325°F + 20 minutes at 325°F **cool:** 30 minutes
makes: 24 cookies

3	cups all-purpose flour
2	teaspoons baking powder
¼	teaspoon salt
¾	cup butter, softened
¾	cup granulated sugar
2	eggs
1	teaspoon finely shredded lemon peel
1¼	cups pistachio nuts, coarsely chopped
¼	cup honey, warmed
⅓	cup finely chopped pistachio nuts

1 Preheat oven to 325°F. In a medium bowl stir together flour, baking powder, and salt; set aside.

2 In a large mixing bowl beat butter and sugar with an electric mixer on medium to high speed until light and fluffy. Beat in eggs and lemon peel until combined. Beat in as much of the flour mixture as you can with the mixer. Using a wooden spoon, stir in any remaining flour mixture and the 1¼ cups coarsely chopped pistachios (dough will be stiff).

3 Divide dough in half. Shape each portion into an 8-inch log. Place logs about 3 inches apart on a large ungreased cookie sheet; flatten each log to about 3 inches wide.

4 Bake for 30 to 35 minutes or until firm and lightly browned. Cool on cookie sheet for 15 minutes. Using a serrated knife, cut each log diagonally into ¾-inch slices. Place slices on an ungreased cookie sheet.

5 Bake for 10 minutes. Carefully turn slices over and bake about 10 minutes more or until biscotti are golden and crisp. Transfer to wire racks; cool.

6 Lightly brush warmed honey on one side of each biscotti and sprinkle with some of the finely chopped pistachios on top. Place on waxed paper; let stand until honey is no longer sticky.

nutrition facts per cookie: 197 cal., 10 g total fat (4 g sat. fat), 31 mg chol., 158 mg sodium, 24 g carb., 1 g fiber, 4 g pro.

chocolate blooms,
page 117

scrumptious

sha

5

Thumbprint cookies filled with jam, buttery spritz, elegant madeleines, and nut-coated delights are a few of the special shapes in this chapter. Best of all, shaped cookies are super easy, and an ideal choice for baking with children.

pes

Our recipe for this perennial favorite is foolproof, plus we offer two tasty variations, with the saffron version pictured below.

snickerdoodles

prep: 35 minutes   **chill:** 1 hour   **bake:** 10 minutes at 375°F per batch
makes: 48 cookies

1   cup butter, softened
1½   cups granulated
      sugar
1   teaspoon baking soda
1   teaspoon cream of
      tartar
¼   teaspoon salt
2   eggs
1   teaspoon vanilla
3   cups all-purpose flour
¼   cup sugar
2   teaspoons ground
      cinnamon

1 In a large mixing bowl beat butter with an electric mixer on medium to high speed for 30 seconds. Add the 1½ cups sugar, the baking soda, cream of tartar, and salt. Beat until combined, scraping sides of bowl occasionally. Beat in eggs and vanilla until combined. Beat in as much of the flour as you can with the mixer. Using a wooden spoon, stir in any remaining flour. Cover and chill about 1 hour or until dough is easy to handle.

2 Preheat oven to 375°F. In a small bowl combine the ¼ cup sugar and the cinnamon. Shape dough into 1¼-inch balls. Roll balls in cinnamon-sugar to coat. Place balls 2 inches apart on an ungreased cookie sheet.

3 Bake for 10 to 12 minutes or until bottoms are lightly browned. Transfer cookies to a wire rack; cool.

nutrition facts per cookie: 94 cal., 4 g total fat (3 g sat. fat), 19 mg chol., 69 mg sodium, 13 g carb., 0 g fiber, 1 g pro.

praline snickerdoodles: Prepare as directed, except stir 1 cup toffee pieces and ½ cup chopped pecans into the dough before chilling.

nutrition facts per cookie: 126 cal., 6 g total fat (3 g sat. fat), 22 mg chol., 89 mg sodium, 16 g carbo., 0 g fiber, 1 g pro.

saffron snickerdoodles: Prepare dough as directed except add a dash of ground saffron with the sugar. In a small bowl combine the ¼ cup sugar and a dash of ground saffron or 2 teaspoons chai spice blend. Proceed as directed in step 2.

nutrition facts per cookie: 94 cal., 4 g total fat (3 g sat. fat), 18 mg chol., 75 mg sodium, 13 g carb., 0 g fiber, 1 g pro.

Decadant chocolate ganache spiked with raspberry liqueur fills the center of each cookie. Pictured on page 114.

chocolate blooms

prep: 40 minutes **bake:** 8 minutes at 350°F per batch
makes: 56 cookies

1½ cups all-purpose flour
¾ cup unsweetened Dutch-process cocoa powder
½ cup shortening
¼ cup butter, softened
1 cup packed brown sugar
½ teaspoon baking powder
¼ teaspoon salt
1 egg
1 teaspoon vanilla
1 cup miniature semisweet chocolate pieces
¾ cup finely chopped almonds (optional)
1 recipe Raspberry Ganache
 Small fresh raspberries (optional)

1 Preheat oven to 350°F. In a small bowl stir together flour and cocoa powder; set aside.

2 In a large mixing bowl beat shortening and butter with an electric mixer on medium to high speed for 30 seconds. Add brown sugar, baking powder, and salt. Beat until combined, scraping sides of bowl occasionally. Beat in egg and vanilla until combined. Beat in as much of the flour mixture as you can with the mixer. Using a wooden spoon, stir in any remaining flour mixture and the chocolate pieces.

3 Shape dough into 1-inch balls. If desired, roll balls in chopped almonds to coat. Place balls 1½ inches apart on an ungreased cookie sheet. Press your thumb into the center of each ball.

4 Bake for 8 to 10 minutes or until edges are set. If cookie centers puff during baking, gently indent centers with the back of a measuring teaspoon. Transfer cookies to a wire rack; cool.

5 Spoon Raspberry Ganache into the indentation of each cookie. Let stand at room temperature or in the refrigerator until ganache is set. If desired, garnish each cookie with a raspberry.

to store: Layer unfilled cookies between sheets of waxed paper in an airtight container; cover. Store at room temperature up to 3 days or freeze up to 3 months. To serve, thaw cookies, if frozen. Fill as directed. Or store filled cookies in an airtight container in the refrigerator up to 2 days.

nutrition facts per cookie: 101 cal., 6 g total fat (3 g sat. fat), 8 mg chol., 26 mg sodium, 11 g carb., 1 g fiber, 1 g pro.

raspberry ganache: In a small microwave-safe bowl combine 6 ounces chopped dark chocolate (70 percent cocoa), ⅓ cup whipping cream, and, if desired, 1 tablespoon seedless raspberry jam. Microwave on 100 percent power (high) for 1 minute. Stir until melted. If desired, add 1 tablespoon raspberry liqueur; stir until smooth. Let stand until slightly thickened (about 15 minutes).

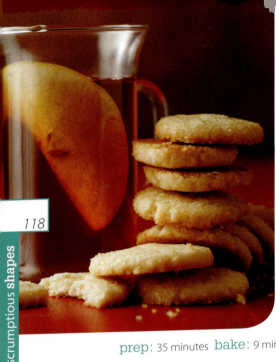

Before baking, roll the balls of dough in turbinado sugar, a raw, coarse molasses-flavor sweetener.

apple cider buttons

prep: 35 minutes   **bake:** 9 minutes at 375°F per batch   **makes:** 60 cookies

1 cup butter, softened
6 tablespoons granulated sugar
1 tablespoon instant hot apple cider mix
1 teaspoon vanilla
¼ teaspoon salt
2 cups all-purpose flour
1 tablespoon milk
½ cup turbinado (raw) sugar

1 Preheat oven to 375°F. In a large mixing bowl beat butter with an electric mixer on medium to high speed for 30 seconds. Add granulated sugar, apple cider mix, vanilla, and salt. Beat until combined, scraping sides of bowl occasionally. Beat in flour until combined. Add milk; beat just until combined.

2 Place turbinado sugar in a small bowl. Shape dough into ¾-inch balls. Roll balls in turbinado sugar to coat. Place balls 2 inches apart on an ungreased cookie sheet. Using the bottom of a glass or the palm of your hand, press balls to ¼-inch thickness.

3 Bake for 9 to 11 minutes or until edges are firm and bottoms are lightly browned. Transfer cookies to a wire rack; cool.

nutrition facts per cookie: 55 cal., 3 g total fat (2 g sat. fat), 8 mg chol., 37 mg sodium, 6 g carb., 0 g fiber, 1 g pro.

The subtle licorice flavor in this aromatic cookie comes from the five-spice powder, an Asian blend of star anise and other sweet spices.

vanilla-star anise crescents

prep: 30 minutes **chill:** 1 hour **bake:** 8 minutes at 350°F per batch
makes: 48 cookies

1   vanilla bean, split lengthwise
2   cups powdered sugar
⅛   teaspoon five-spice powder
1½ cups butter, softened
½   cup granulated sugar
2   cups slivered almonds, finely ground
½   teaspoon salt
3   cups all-purpose flour

1 Using the tip of a small sharp knife, scrape out the seeds from the vanilla bean. In a food processor process the powdered sugar, five-spice powder, and seeds until seeds are well incorporated. Set aside.

2 In a large mixing bowl beat butter with an electric mixer on medium to high speed for 30 seconds. Add the granulated sugar, almonds, and salt. Beat until combined, scraping sides of bowl occasionally. Beat in as much of the flour as you can with the mixer. Using a wooden spoon, stir in any remaining flour. Cover and chill dough about 1 hour or until easy to handle.

3 Preheat oven to 350°F. Lightly grease cookie sheets. Shape dough into 1-inch balls then mold into a crescent shape. Place crescents 2 inches apart on the prepared cookie sheets.

4 Bake for 8 to 10 minutes or until set and edges are golden. Cool on cookie sheets for 5 minutes. While warm, roll cookies in powdered sugar mixture. Transfer to a wire rack; cool. Roll cooled cookies in the sugar mixture again.

nutrition facts per cookie: 133 cal., 8 g total fat (4 g sat. fat), 15 mg chol., 75 mg sodium, 14 g carb., 1 g fiber, 2 g pro.

make-ahead directions:
Prepare and shape dough. Place crescents on parchment- or foil-lined cookie sheets; freeze. Transfer frozen crescents to an airtight container; cover. Freeze up to 3 months. To bake, arrange frozen crescents on cookie sheets. Let stand at room temperature while the oven preheats. Bake for 10 to 12 minutes or until cookies are set and edges are golden.

Glistening jelly brightens the appearance and taste of these sweet bites.

red currant-poppy seed thumbprints

prep: 25 minutes **bake:** 10 minutes at 350°F per batch
makes: 36 cookies

1	cup butter, softened
½	cup granulated sugar
2	egg yolks
1	tablespoon orange liqueur or orange juice
2⅔	cups all-purpose flour
2	tablespoons poppy seeds
2	teaspoons finely shredded orange peel
½	teaspoon salt
⅓	to ½ cup red currant jelly, melted and cooled

1 Preheat oven to 350°F. In a large mixing bowl beat butter with an electric mixer on medium to high speed for 30 seconds. Add sugar. Beat until combined, scraping sides of bowl occasionally. Beat in egg yolks and liqueur until combined. In a small bowl stir together flour, poppy seeds, orange peel, and salt. Gradually add flour mixture to butter mixture, beating on low speed just until combined.

2 Shape dough into 1-inch balls. Place balls 1 inch apart on an ungreased cookie sheet. Press your thumb into the center of each ball.

3 Bake for 10 to 12 minutes or until edges are lightly browned. If cookie centers puff during baking, gently indent with the back of a measuring teaspoon.

4 Transfer cookies to a wire rack; cool. Spoon about ½ teaspoon of the melted jelly into the indentation of each cookie.

nutrition facts per cookie: 105 cal., 6 g total fat (3 g sat. fat), 24 mg chol., 79 mg sodium, 12 g carb., 0 g fiber, 1 g pro.

Love the pucker of lemon? This citrus filling will please.

sugared lemon-fennel cookies

prep: 30 minutes chill: 4 hours bake: 10 minutes at 375°F per batch
makes: 42 cookies

⅔ cup butter, softened
½ cup granulated sugar
2 eggs
2 teaspoons finely shredded lemon peel
2 tablespoons lemon juice
1 teaspoon fennel seeds, crushed
1 teaspoon vanilla
2 cups all-purpose flour
   Coarse sugar
   Lemon curd (optional)
   Finely crushed fennel seeds (optional)

1 In a large mixing bowl beat butter with an electric mixer on medium to high speed for 30 seconds. Add granulated sugar. Beat until combined, scraping sides of bowl occasionally. Beat in eggs, lemon peel, lemon juice, the 1 teaspoon fennel seeds, and vanilla until combined. Beat in as much of the flour as you can with the mixer. Using a wooden spoon, stir in any remaining flour. Cover and chill about 4 hours or until dough is easy to handle.

2 Preheat oven to 375°F. Place coarse sugar in a small bowl. Shape dough into 1-inch balls. Roll balls in coarse sugar to coat. Place 1 inch apart on an ungreased cookie sheet. Using your thumb, make an indentation in the center of each cookie. (Or use the bottom of a glass to slightly flatten balls.)

3 Bake for 10 to 12 minutes or until edges are very lightly browned. Transfer to a wire rack; cool. Before serving, if you made indentations in the cookies, spoon lemon curd into the centers. If desired, sprinkle with additional crushed fennel seeds.

nutrition facts per cookie: 63 cal., 3 g total fat (2 g sat. fat), 17 mg chol., 29 mg sodium, 8 g carb., 0 g fiber, 1 g pro.

Use real milk chocolate, not imitation chocolate pieces, for the best flavor.

milk chocolate and cherry cookies

prep: 30 minutes **bake:** 10 minutes at 350°F per batch
makes: 42 cookies

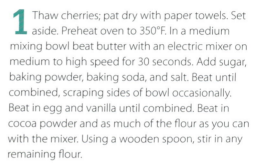

2 cups frozen pitted dark sweet cherries (about 42)
½ cup butter, softened
1 cup granulated sugar
¼ teaspoon baking powder
¼ teaspoon baking soda
¼ teaspoon salt
1 egg
1½ teaspoons vanilla
½ cup unsweetened cocoa powder
1½ cups all-purpose flour
1 cup milk chocolate pieces
½ cup sweetened condensed milk
4 teaspoons cherry liqueur or milk

1 Thaw cherries; pat dry with paper towels. Set aside. Preheat oven to 350°F. In a medium mixing bowl beat butter with an electric mixer on medium to high speed for 30 seconds. Add sugar, baking powder, baking soda, and salt. Beat until combined, scraping sides of bowl occasionally. Beat in egg and vanilla until combined. Beat in cocoa powder and as much of the flour as you can with the mixer. Using a wooden spoon, stir in any remaining flour.

2 Shape dough into 1-inch balls. Place balls about 2 inches apart on an ungreased cookie sheet. Press your thumb into the center of each ball. Place a cherry in each indentation.

3 For frosting, in a small saucepan heat and stir chocolate pieces and sweetened condensed milk over low heat until chocolate is melted. Stir in cherry liqueur. Spoon about 1 teaspoon of the frosting over each cherry.

4 Bake about 10 minutes or until edges are firm. Cool on cookie sheet for 1 minute. Transfer cookies to a wire rack; cool.

nutrition facts per cookie: 103 cal., 5 g total fat (3 g sat. fat), 13 mg chol., 54 mg sodium, 15 g carb., 1 g fiber, 2 g pro.

Cornmeal plus sugar coating add to the crispy finish of these morsels.

caramel corn cookies

prep: 35 minutes **bake:** 8 minutes at 350°F per batch
makes: 48 cookies

½   cup shortening
¼   cup butter, softened
½   cup granulated sugar
½   cup packed brown sugar
½   cup yellow cornmeal
1   teaspoon baking soda
½   teaspoon salt
1   egg
¼   cup honey
1   tablespoon vanilla
1¾ cups all-purpose flour
1   cup miniature round caramel bits or butterscotch-flavor pieces
½   cup chopped honey-roasted peanuts
    Coarse sugar or turbinado sugar

1 Preheat oven to 350°F. Line a cookie sheet with parchment paper or lightly grease cookie sheet; set aside.

2 In a large mixing bowl beat shortening and butter with an electric mixer on medium to high speed for 30 seconds. Add granulated sugar, brown sugar, cornmeal, baking soda, and salt. Beat until combined, scraping sides of bowl occasionally. Beat in egg, honey, and vanilla until combined. Beat in as much of the flour as you can with the mixer. Using a wooden spoon, stir in any remaining flour, the caramel bits, and peanuts.

3 Place coarse sugar in a small bowl. Shape dough into 1¼-inch balls. Roll balls in coarse sugar to coat. Place 2 inches apart on the prepared cookie sheet.

4 Bake for 8 to 10 minutes or until tops are golden and edges are firm. Cool on cookie sheet for 2 minutes. Transfer cookies to a wire rack; cool.

nutrition facts per cookie: 98 cal., 4 g total fat (1 g sat. fat), 7 mg chol., 74 mg sodium, 15 g carb., 0 g fiber, 1 g pro.

Kids have craved this basic recipe for generations. The adult version, Salted Peanut Blossoms, is pictured.

peanut butter blossoms

prep: 25 minutes bake: 10 minutes at 350°F per batch
makes: 54 cookies

½	cup shortening
½	cup peanut butter
¾	cup granulated sugar
½	cup packed brown sugar
1	teaspoon baking powder
⅛	teaspoon baking soda
1	egg
2	tablespoons milk
1	teaspoon vanilla
1¾	cups all-purpose flour
54	milk chocolate kisses, unwrapped, or milk chocolate stars

1 Preheat oven to 350°F. In a large mixing bowl beat shortening and peanut butter with an electric mixer on medium to high speed for 30 seconds. Add ½ cup of the granulated sugar, the brown sugar, baking powder, and baking soda. Beat until combined, scraping sides of bowl occasionally. Beat in egg, milk, and vanilla until combined. Beat in as much of the flour as you can with the mixer. Using a wooden spoon, stir in any remaining flour.

2 Shape dough into 1-inch balls. Roll balls in the remaining ¼ cup granulated sugar to coat. Place 2 inches apart on an ungreased cookie sheet.

3 Bake for 10 to 12 minutes or until edges are firm and bottoms are lightly browned. Immediately press a chocolate kiss into each cookie center. Transfer to a wire rack; cool.

nutrition facts per cookie: 96 cal., 5 g total fat (2 g sat. fat), 5 mg chol., 27 mg sodium, 11 g carb., 0 g fiber, 2 g pro.

salted peanut blossoms: Prepare as directed except omit chocolate candy. Cut two 2.2-ounce salted peanut-coated caramel-topped nougat bars (such as salted nut rolls) into 26 slices each (54 total). Immediately after removing cookies from oven, press nougat bar slices into cookie centers.
nutrition facts per cookie: 87 cal., 4 g total fat (1 g sat. fat), 4 mg chol., 36 mg sodium, 11 g carb., 0 g fiber, 2 g pro.

butter pecan blossoms: Prepare as directed, except substitute ½ cup softened butter for the ½ cup peanut butter. Increase flour to 2¼ cups and add ½ teaspoon ground cinnamon. If desired, substitute 2 tablespoons melted butter pecan ice cream for the 2 tablespoons milk. Omit the ¼ cup granulated sugar for rolling. In a food processor process ⅔ cup pecans until finely ground. Transfer pecans to a bowl; stir in 2 tablespoons packed brown sugar. In a small bowl lightly beat 2 egg whites. Roll balls in egg whites, then in pecan-sugar mixture to coat. Bake as directed. If desired, substitute chocolate kisses filled with caramel for milk chocolate kisses.
nutrition facts per cookie: 99 cal., 5 g total fat (2 g sat. fat), 8 mg chol., 38 mg sodium, 12 g carbo., 0 g fiber, 1 g pro.

chocolate and cherry thumbprints

prep: 40 minutes bake: 8 minutes at 350°F per batch
makes: 36 cookies

1¼ cups semisweet chocolate pieces

2 tablespoons shortening

2 cups all-purpose flour

1 tablespoon unsweetened cocoa powder

1 teaspoon baking powder

¼ teaspoon salt

¼ teaspoon instant espresso coffee powder

½ cup unsalted butter, softened

¾ cup granulated sugar

1 egg

1 tablespoon milk

1 teaspoon vanilla

½ cup finely chopped walnuts, toasted (see tip, page 13)

¾ cup cherry pie filling (with 36 to 40 cherries)

1 Preheat oven to 350°F. Line a cookie sheet with parchment paper; set aside. In a small saucepan heat and stir ½ cup of the chocolate pieces and 1 tablespoon of the shortening over low heat until melted; cool slightly. In a medium bowl stir together flour, cocoa powder, baking powder, salt, and coffee powder; set aside.

2 In a large mixing bowl beat butter with an electric mixer on medium to high speed for 30 seconds. Add sugar. Beat until light and fluffy, scraping sides of bowl occasionally. Beat in melted chocolate. Beat in egg, milk, and vanilla until combined. Beat in flour mixture on low speed just until combined.

3 Place chopped walnuts in a small bowl. Shape dough into 1-inch balls. Roll balls in walnuts to coat. Place balls 1 inch apart on the prepared cookie sheet. Press your thumb into the center of each ball.

4 Bake for 8 to 10 minutes or until edges are firm. If cookie centers puff during baking, indent centers with the back of a measuring teaspoon. Transfer cookies to a wire rack; cool.

5 Spoon pie filling into indentations, placing one cherry in each cookie. Melt the remaining ¾ cup chocolate pieces and the remaining 1 tablespoon shortening over low heat; cool slightly. Drizzle melted chocolate over tops of cookies. Let stand until chocolate is set.

to store: Layer unfilled cookies between sheets of waxed paper in an airtight container; cover. Store at room temperature or in the refrigerator up to 3 days or freeze up to 3 months. To serve, thaw cookies, if frozen. Fill with pie filling and drizzle with chocolate as directed.

nutrition facts per cookie: 119 cal., 6 g total fat (3 g sat. fat), 12 mg chol., 34 mg sodium, 15 g carb., 1 g fiber, 1 g pro.

frosted blood orange cookies

prep: 1 hour chill: 1 hour bake: 10 minutes at 350°F per batch
makes: 48 cookies

1   cup butter, softened
¾   cup granulated sugar
1   tablespoon baking
      powder
¼   teaspoon salt
1   egg
2   teaspoons finely
      shredded blood
      orange peel or
      orange peel
1   tablespoon blood
      orange juice or
      orange juice
¼   teaspoon anise
      extract
3   cups all-purpose flour
1   recipe Blood Orange
      Frosting
1   recipe Candied Citrus
      Threads

1 In a large mixing bowl beat butter with an electric mixer on medium to high speed for 30 seconds. Add sugar, baking powder, and salt. Beat until combined, scraping sides of bowl occasionally. Beat in egg, orange peel, orange juice, and anise extract until combined. Beat in as much of the flour as you can with the mixer. Using a wooden spoon, stir in any remaining flour. Cover and chill about 1 hour or until dough is easy to handle.

2 Preheat oven to 350°F. Line a cookie sheet with parchment paper. Shape dough into 1-inch balls. Place balls 1 inch apart on the prepared cookie sheet. If desired, flatten balls to about ½-inch thickness.

3 Bake about 10 minutes or until bottoms are lightly browned. Transfer cookies to a wire rack; cool. Spread tops of cookies with Blood Orange Frosting. Sprinkle with Candied Citrus Threads.

nutrition facts per cookie: 119 cal., 5 g total fat (3 g sat. fat), 17 mg chol., 87 mg sodium, 18 g carb., 0 g fiber, 1 g pro.

blood orange frosting: In a medium mixing bowl beat ¼ cup butter, softened, with an electric mixer on medium speed until smooth. Gradually add 1½ cups powdered sugar, beating well. Beat in 3 tablespoons milk, 1 tablespoon finely shredded blood orange peel or orange peel, and ½ teaspoon vanilla. Beat in an additional 1½ cups powdered sugar. If necessary, beat in 1 tablespoon milk, 1 teaspoon at a time, to reach spreading consistency.

candied citrus threads: Using a citrus zester, remove peel from 2 blood oranges or oranges in threadlike pieces. In a small saucepan combine orange peel and enough water to cover. Bring just to boiling over medium-high heat; reduce heat. Simmer for 5 minutes; drain. In the same saucepan combine 1½ cups granulated sugar and 1½ cups water. Bring just to boiling over medium-high heat, stirring to dissolve sugar. Stir in orange peel; reduce heat. Simmer for 8 to 10 minutes or until peel is tender; drain well. Sprinkle a large shallow pan with enough sugar to cover lightly. Sprinkle orange peel evenly over sugar. Let stand until dry and brittle.

Nutmeg and rum replicate the holiday flavors of fresh eggnog.

eggnog-nut thumbprints

prep: 50 minutes **bake:** 12 minutes at 375°F per batch
makes: 40 cookies

¾ cup butter, softened
½ cup granulated sugar
⅛ teaspoon ground
    nutmeg
2 egg yolks
1 teaspoon vanilla
1½ cups all-purpose flour
2 egg whites, lightly
    beaten
1½ cups finely chopped
    walnuts
1 recipe Rum Filling
    Grated whole nutmeg
    or ground nutmeg
    (optional)

1 In a large mixing bowl beat butter with an electric mixer on medium to high speed for 30 seconds. Add sugar and the ⅛ teaspoon nutmeg. Beat until combined, scraping sides of bowl occasionally. Beat in egg yolks and vanilla until combined. Beat in as much of the flour as you can with the mixer. Using a wooden spoon, stir in any remaining flour. If necessary, cover and chill about 1 hour or until dough is easy to handle.

2 Preheat oven to 375°F. Grease a cookie sheet; set aside. Place egg whites and walnuts in separate small bowls. Shape dough into 1-inch balls. Roll balls in egg whites, then in walnuts to coat. Place balls 1 inch apart on the prepared cookie sheet. Press your thumb into the center of each ball.

3 Bake for 12 to 15 minutes or until edges are lightly browned. If cookie centers puff during baking, indent centers with the back of a measuring teaspoon. Transfer cookies to a wire rack; cool.

4 Pipe or spoon about ½ teaspoon of the Rum Filling into the indentation of each cookie. If desired, sprinkle with additional nutmeg.

rum filling: In a medium mixing bowl beat ¼ cup butter, softened, with an electric mixer on medium to high speed for 30 seconds. Add 1 cup powdered sugar. Beat until fluffy, scraping sides of bowl occasionally. Beat in 1 teaspoon rum or ¼ teaspoon rum extract and enough milk (1 to 2 teaspoons) to make filling spreading consistency.

nutrition facts per cookie: 96 cal., 6 g total fat (3 g sat. fat), 22 mg chol., 46 mg sodium, 9 g carb., 0 g fiber, 1 g pro.

Almond extract complements the sweet cherries.

cherry-walnut balls

prep: 40 minutes bake: 18 minutes at 325°F per batch
makes: 48 cookies

¼ cup coarsely chopped maraschino cherries
1 cup butter, softened
½ cup powdered sugar
½ teaspoon almond extract
½ teaspoon vanilla
2 cups all-purpose flour
¾ cup chopped walnuts, toasted (see tip, page 13)
   Red edible glitter (optional)
   Powdered sugar

1 Preheat oven to 325°F. Drain chopped maraschino cherries on paper towels; pat dry to remove any excess liquid. Set cherries aside.

2 In a large mixing bowl beat butter with an electric mixer on medium to high speed for 30 seconds. Add the ½ cup powdered sugar, almond extract, and vanilla. Beat until combined, scraping sides of bowl occasionally. Beat in as much of the flour as you can with the mixer. Using a wooden spoon, stir in any remaining flour, the walnuts, and maraschino cherries. Shape dough into 1-inch balls. Place balls 2 inches apart on an ungreased cookie sheet.

3 Bake for 18 to 20 minutes or until bottoms are lightly browned. Cool on cookie sheets for 5 minutes.

4 If desired, stir some red edible glitter into additional powdered sugar. Roll warm cookies in the powdered sugar mixture to coat. Place cookies on wire racks; cool. If desired, roll cooled cookies in the powdered sugar mixture again before serving.

nutrition facts per cookie: 74 cal., 5 g total fat (3 g sat. fat), 10 mg chol., 34 mg sodium, 6 g carb., 0 g fiber, 1 g pro.

After baking, you have the option of finishing these chewy morsels with a coffee glaze. Then immediately top with finely chopped nuts so they adhere.

coffee-toffee walnut sandies

prep: 35 minutes chill: 30 minutes bake: 15 minutes at 325°F per batch
makes: 48 cookies

1	cup butter, softened
2¼	cups powdered sugar
¼	cup packed brown sugar
1	tablespoon strong brewed coffee
1	teaspoon vanilla
2	cups all-purpose flour
1	cup finely chopped walnuts, toasted (see tip, page 13)
½	cup toffee pieces
¼	cup strong brewed coffee
¼	teaspoon coffee extract (optional)
⅓	cup finely chopped walnuts, toasted (see tip, page 13) (optional)

1 In a large mixing bowl beat butter with an electric mixer on medium to high speed for 30 seconds. Add ¼ cup of the powdered sugar and the brown sugar. Beat until combined, scraping sides of bowl occasionally. Beat in the 1 tablespoon coffee and the vanilla until combined. Beat in as much of the flour as you can with the mixer. Using a wooden spoon, stir in any remaining flour, the 1 cup walnuts, and the toffee pieces. Cover and chill for 30 to 60 minutes or until dough is easy to handle.

2 Preheat oven to 325°F. Shape dough into 1-inch balls. Place balls 1 inch apart on an ungreased cookie sheet.

3 Bake for 15 to 17 minutes or until bottoms are lightly browned. Transfer to a wire rack; cool.

4 For glaze, in a medium bowl combine the remaining 2 cups powdered sugar, the ¼ cup coffee, and, if desired, coffee extract. Dip tops of cookies into the glaze, letting excess drip back into bowl. Sprinkle cookies with ⅓ cup walnuts. Let stand until glaze is set.

nutrition facts per cookie: 122 cal., 8 g total fat (3 g sat. fat), 11 mg chol., 45 mg sodium, 13 g carb., 0 g fiber, 1 g pro.

These two-bite treats are a fun way to use leftover candy canes.

peppermint sandies with white chocolate glaze

prep: 25 minutes bake: 15 minutes at 325°F per batch stand: 48 minutes
makes: 48 cookies

1	cup butter, softened
⅓	cup powdered sugar
¼	cup finely crushed striped round peppermint candies
1	tablespoon water
½	teaspoon vanilla
½	teaspoon peppermint extract
2	cups all-purpose flour
½	cup whipping cream
6	ounces white baking chocolate with cocoa butter
	Crushed striped round peppermint candies or candy canes

1 Preheat oven to 325°F. In a large mixing bowl beat butter with an electric mixer on medium to high speed for 30 seconds. Add powdered sugar and the ¼ cup crushed peppermint candies. Beat until combined, scraping sides of bowl occasionally. Beat in the water, vanilla, and peppermint extract until combined. Beat in as much of the flour as you can with the mixer. Stir in any remaining flour. Shape dough into 1-inch balls. Place 1 inch apart on an ungreased cookie sheet.

2 Bake about 15 minutes or until bottoms are lightly browned. Transfer cookies to a wire rack; cool.

3 Meanwhile, for glaze, in a medium saucepan bring whipping cream just to simmering. Remove from heat. Add white chocolate; let stand for 3 minutes. Stir until smooth. Let stand about 45 minutes or until glaze starts to thicken.

4 Spoon about 1 teaspoon of the glaze over each cooled cookie. Sprinkle with additional crushed peppermint candies. Let stand until glaze is set.

nutrition facts per cookie: 102 cal., 7 g total fat (4 g sat. fat), 18 mg chol., 34 mg sodium, 9 g carb., 0 g fiber, 1 g pro.

A hint of fresh herb makes these tender bites memorable.

rosemary-kissed orange thumbprint cookies

prep: 30 minutes **chill:** 1 hour **bake:** 14 minutes at 325°F per batch
makes: 24 cookies

1 cup all-purpose flour
½ cup cornstarch
1 teaspoon snipped
    fresh rosemary
¼ teaspoon salt
¾ cup butter, softened
⅓ cup powdered sugar
    Few drops almond
    extract
¼ cup orange
    marmalade
    Powdered sugar
    (optional)

1 In a small bowl stir together flour, cornstarch, rosemary, and salt; set aside. In a medium mixing bowl beat butter with an electric mixer on medium to high speed for 30 seconds. Add the ⅓ cup powdered sugar and the almond extract. Beat until combined, scraping sides of bowl occasionally. Beat in as much of the flour mixture as you can with the mixer. Using a wooden spoon, stir in any remaining flour mixture. Cover and chill about 1 hour or until dough is easy to handle.

2 Preheat oven to 325°F. Line a cookie sheet with parchment paper; set aside. Shape dough into 1¼-inch balls. Place balls 2 inches apart on the prepared cookie sheet. Press your thumb into the center of each ball. Spoon about ½ teaspoon of the marmalade into the indentation of each cookie.

3 Bake about 14 minutes or until edges are lightly browned. Cool on cookie sheet for 1 minute. Transfer to a wire rack; cool. If desired, sprinkle cookies with additional powdered sugar.

nutrition facts per cookie: 105 cal., 6 g total fat (4 g sat. fat), 15 mg chol., 67 mg sodium, 13 g carb., 0 g fiber, 1 g pro.

Chocolate, salt, and caramel is irresistible. Dare to eat just one!

salted caramel thumbprint cookies

prep: 40 minutes bake: 12 minutes at 350°F per batch
makes: 32 cookies

2 cups all-purpose flour
⅔ cup granulated sugar
1 cup butter
½ teaspoon vanilla
16 vanilla caramels, unwrapped
⅓ cup whipping cream*
3 ounces bittersweet chocolate, coarsely chopped (optional)
½ teaspoon shortening (optional)
Fleur de sel or other coarse gourmet salt

1 Preheat oven to 350°F. Line cookie sheets with parchment paper; set aside. In a large bowl combine flour and sugar. Using a pastry blender, cut in butter and vanilla until mixture resembles fine crumbs and starts to cling. Form dough into a ball, kneading until smooth.

2 Shape dough into 1-inch balls. Place balls 2 inches apart on prepared cookie sheets. Using your thumb, make an indentation in each dough ball.

3 Bake for 12 to 14 minutes or until edges are lightly browned. If cookie centers puff during baking, indent centers with a measuring teaspoon. Cool on cookie sheets for 5 minutes. Transfer to a wire rack; cool.

4 In a small heavy saucepan combine caramels and whipping cream. Heat and stir over very low heat until caramels are melted and smooth. Spoon a scant teaspoon caramel mixture into each indentation.

5 If desired, in a small saucepan heat and stir chocolate and shortening over low heat until melted and smooth. Drizzle over cooled cookies. Sprinkle each cooled cookie with several grains of salt.

*tip: Do not substitute milk for whipping cream, because it would casuse the texture of caramel to be too thin.

nutrition facts per cookie: 124 cal., 7 g total fat (5 g sat. fat), 19 mg chol., 89 mg sodium, 14 g carb., 0 g fiber, 1 g pro.

Sugar coating amplifies the signature cracking of these spiced cookies.

giant ginger cookies

prep: 30 minutes **bake:** 12 minutes at 350°F per batch
makes: 24 cookies

4½ cups all-purpose flour
4 teaspoons ground ginger
2 teaspoons baking soda
1½ teaspoons ground cinnamon
1 teaspoon ground cloves
¼ teaspoon salt
1½ cups shortening
2 cups granulated sugar
2 eggs
½ cup molasses
¾ cup granulated sugar or coarse sugar

1 Preheat oven to 350°F. In a large bowl stir together flour, ginger, baking soda, cinnamon, cloves, and salt; set aside.

2 In a large mixing bowl beat shortening with an electric mixer on medium to high speed for 30 seconds. Add the 2 cups sugar. Beat until combined, scraping sides of bowl occasionally. Beat in eggs and molasses until combined. Beat in as much of the flour mixture as you can with the mixer. Using a wooden spoon, stir in any remaining flour mixture.

3 Using a ¼-cup measure or cookie scoop, shape dough into 2-inch balls. Roll the balls in the ¾ cup sugar to coat. Place balls 2½ inches apart on an ungreased cookie sheet.

4 Bake for 12 to 14 minutes or until cookies are lightly browned and puffed. (Do not overbake or cookies will not be chewy.) Cool on cookie sheet for 2 minutes. Transfer cookies to a wire rack; cool.

nutrition facts per ginger or nutmeg cookie variation: 303 cal., 14 g total fat (4 g sat. fat), 16 mg chol., 139 mg sodium, 43 g carb., 1 g fiber, 3 g pro.

giant nutmeg cookies: Prepare as directed in Step 1 except omit ginger and cloves and decrease cinnamon to 1 teaspoon. Add 2 tablespoons freshly grated nutmeg or 1 tablespoon ground nutmeg to flour mixture. In Step 3, roll balls in a mixture of ¾ cup granulated sugar and 1 teaspoon freshly grated nutmeg or ½ teaspoon ground nutmeg.

The patterned bottom of a glass can replace a cookie stamp.

orange-pecan shortbread cookies

prep: 25 minutes **bake:** 18 minutes at 325°F per batch
makes: 20 cookies

1¼	cups all-purpose flour
3	tablespoons granulated sugar
2	tablespoons finely chopped pecans
1	tablespoon finely shredded orange peel
½	cup butter
	Granulated sugar (optional)
4	ounces white baking chocolate with cocoa butter, coarsely chopped
1	teaspoon shortening

1 Preheat oven to 325°F. Lightly grease a cookie sheet; set aside. In a medium bowl stir together flour, the 3 tablespoons sugar, pecans, and the orange peel. Using a pastry blender, cut in butter until mixture resembles fine crumbs and starts to cling (dough will still be crumbly). Form dough into a ball and knead until smooth.

2 Shape dough into 1-inch balls. Place 2 inches apart on the prepared cookie sheet. Using a cookie stamp, press each ball to ½-inch thickness. If desired, sprinkle with additional sugar.

3 Bake for 18 to 20 minutes or until bottoms start to brown and centers are set. Transfer cookies to a wire rack; cool.

4 In a small saucepan heat and stir white chocolate and shortening over low heat until melted and smooth. Dip the bottom of each cookie into melted white chocolate mixture, letting excess drip back into saucepan. Return cookie, upside down, to wire rack. Let cookies stand until white chocolate is set.

nutrition facts per cookie: 57 cal., 4 g total fat (2 g sat. fat), 7 mg chol., 23 mg sodium, 6 g carb., 0 g fiber, 1 g pro.

Cardamom, often used in Scandinavian baked goods, adds a sweet-spicy taste.

browned butter-cardamom cookies

prep: 35 minutes   **chill:** 1 hour   **bake:** 12 minutes at 300°F per batch
makes: 46 cookies

½   cup butter
½   cup shortening
2   cups granulated sugar
1   teaspoon baking soda
1   teaspoon cream of tartar
½   teaspoon ground cardamom
⅛   teaspoon salt
3   eggs
½   teaspoon vanilla
2¼ cups all-purpose flour
1   recipe Browned Butter Glaze

1 In a small saucepan melt butter over medium heat. Cook until butter turns light golden brown, stirring occasionally. Transfer to a small bowl. Cover and chill until slightly firm.

2 In a large mixing bowl beat browned butter and shortening with an electric mixer on medium to high speed for 30 seconds. Add sugar, baking soda, cream of tartar, cardamom, and salt. Beat until combined, scraping sides of bowl occasionally. Beat in eggs and vanilla. Beat in as much of the flour as you can with the mixer. Stir in any remaining flour. Cover and chill for 1 to 2 hours or until dough is easy to handle.

3 Preheat oven to 300°F. Shape dough into 1-inch balls. Place balls 2 inches apart on an ungreased cookie sheet.

4 Bake for 12 to 14 minutes or until edges are set (do not let edges brown). Cool on cookie sheet for 2 minutes. Transfer to a wire rack; cool. Drizzle cookies with Browned Butter Glaze. Let stand until glaze is set.

nutrition facts per cookie: 118 cal., 6 g total fat (3 g sat. fat), 20 mg chol., 72 mg sodium, 16 g carb., 0 g fiber, 1 g pro.

browned butter glaze: In a small saucepan cook and stir ¼ cup butter over medium heat until melted. Cook until butter turns a light golden brown, stirring occasionally. Transfer to a small mixing bowl. Add 2¼ cups powdered sugar, 1 tablespoon milk, and ⅛ teaspoon salt, beating with an electric mixer on low speed until smooth. If necessary, beat in additional milk until glaze reaches drizzling consistency. Use immediately.

The mix of cayenne and chocolate is a classic Mexican flavor.

mexican chocolate snickerdoodles

prep: 25 minutes **bake:** 10 minutes at 350°F per batch
makes: 30 cookies

½ cup butter, softened
¾ cup granulated sugar
¾ cup packed brown
    sugar
1 teaspoon cream of
    tartar
½ teaspoon baking soda
½ teaspoon salt
¼ teaspoon cayenne
    pepper (optional)
2 eggs
2 teaspoons vanilla
½ cup unsweetened
    cocoa powder
2¼ cups all-purpose flour
¼ cup granulated sugar
2 teaspoons ground
    cinnamon

1 In a large mixing bowl beat butter with an electric mixer on medium to high speed for 30 seconds. Beat in the ¾ cup sugar, the brown sugar, cream of tartar, baking soda, salt, and, if desired, cayenne pepper, scraping sides of bowl occasionally. Beat in eggs and vanilla until combined. Beat in cocoa powder and as much of the flour as you can with the mixer. Using a wooden spoon, stir in any remaining flour. If necessary, cover and chill dough about 1 hour or until easy to handle.

2 Preheat oven to 350°F. In a small bowl stir together the ¼ cup sugar and the. Shape dough into 1¼-inch balls. Roll balls in cinnamon-sugar to coat. Place balls 2 inches apart on ungreased cookie sheets.

3 Bake for 10 to 12 minutes or until edges are set and tops are cracked. Cool on cookie sheet for 1 minute. Transfer to a wire rack; cool.

nutrition facts per cookie: 118 cal., 4 g total fat (2 g sat. fat), 21 mg chol., 94 mg sodium, 20 g carb., 1 g fiber, 2 g pro.

make-ahead directions:
Prepare dough as directed, shape into balls, and roll in cinnamon-sugar mixture. Place on parchment- or foil-lined cookie sheets and freeze. When frozen, transfer balls to an airtight container; cover. Store in the freezer. When ready to bake, arrange frozen balls on cookie sheets and bake as directed for 13 to 15 minutes.

Closely watch each batch during baking to prevent overbrowning.

honey-basil cookies

prep: 20 minutes **bake:** 6 minutes at 375°F per batch
makes: 48 cookies

1   cup butter, softened
⅔   cup granulated sugar
1   egg
2   tablespoons honey
1   tablespoon snipped
     fresh basil or
     1 teaspoon dried
     basil, crushed
2   teaspoons finely
     shredded orange
     peel
1   teaspoon vanilla
¼   teaspoon almond
     extract (optional)
3   cups all-purpose flour
     Granulated sugar

1 Preheat oven to 375°F. In a large mixing bowl beat butter with an electric mixer on medium to high speed for 30 seconds. Add the ⅔ cup sugar. Beat until combined, scraping sides of bowl occasionally. Beat in egg, honey, basil, orange peel, vanilla, and, if desired, almond extract. Beat in as much of the flour as you can with the mixer. Using a wooden spoon, stir in any remaining flour.

2 Place additional sugar in a shallow bowl. Shape dough into 1- to 1½-inch balls. Place balls 2 inches apart on ungreased cookie sheets. Dip the patterned bottom of a glass or a cookie stamp into sugar; flatten balls to ¼-inch thickness.

3 Bake for 6 to 8 minutes or until bottoms are lightly browned. Cool on cookie sheets on wire racks for 1 minute. Transfer to wire racks; cool.

nutrition facts per cookie: 79 cal., 4 g total fat (2 g sat. fat), 14 mg chol., 36 mg sodium, 10 g carb., 0 g fiber, 1 g pro.

Maple-flavor pancake syrup—a less expensive ingredient option—can be substituted for the real deal.

soft maple sugar cookies

prep: 30 minutes **bake:** 12 minutes at 300°F per batch
makes: 48 cookies

½   cup butter, softened
½   cup shortening
1½   cups granulated
       sugar
¼   cup packed brown
       sugar
¼   cup pure maple syrup
1   teaspoon baking soda
1   teaspoon cream of
       tartar
⅛   teaspoon salt
3   egg yolks
½   teaspoon vanilla
1¾   cups all-purpose flour
1   recipe Maple Icing

1 Preheat oven to 300°F. In a large mixing bowl combine butter and shortening. Beat with an electric mixer on medium to high speed for 30 seconds. Add granulated sugar, brown sugar, maple syrup, baking soda, cream of tartar, and salt. Beat until combined, scraping sides of bowl occasionally. Beat in egg yolks and vanilla until combined. Beat in as much of the flour as you can with the mixer. Using a wooden spoon, stir in any remaining flour.

2 Shape dough into 1-inch balls. Place 2 inches apart on an ungreased cookie sheet.

3 Bake for 12 to 14 minutes or until edges are lightly browned. Cool on cookie sheet for 2 minutes. Transfer to a wire rack; cool. Centers will dip as cookies cool. Drizzle with Maple Icing.

nutrition facts per cookie: 134 cal., 6 g total fat (3 g sat. fat), 22 mg chol., 54 mg sodium, 20 g carb., 0 g fiber, 1 g pro.

maple icing: In a medium bowl stir together ¼ cup whipping cream or milk; ¼ cup butter, melted; and 3 tablespoons pure maple syrup. Whisk in 3 to 4 cups powdered sugar to make icing drizzling consistency.

Cashew lovers will dive into the honey-cashew variation, pictured below.

peanut butter cookies

prep: 35 minutes **chill:** 1 hour **bake:** 7 minutes at 375°F per batch
makes: 50 cookies

1	cup peanut butter
½	cup butter, softened
½	cup shortening
1	cup granulated sugar
1	cup packed brown sugar
1	teaspoon baking soda
1	teaspoon baking powder
2	eggs
1	teaspoon vanilla
2½	cups all-purpose flour
1	cup peanuts, chopped (optional)
	Granulated sugar

1 In a large mixing bowl beat peanut butter, butter, and shortening with an electric mixer on medium speed for 30 seconds. Add the 1 cup granulated sugar, the brown sugar, baking soda, and baking powder. Beat until combined, scraping sides of bowl occasionally. Beat in eggs and vanilla until combined. Beat in as much of the flour as you can with the mixer. Stir in any remaining flour and, if desired, peanuts. Cover and chill about 1 hour or until dough is easy to handle.

2 Preheat oven to 375°F. Place additional granulated sugar in a small bowl. Shape dough into 1¼-inch balls. Roll balls in granulated sugar to coat. Place balls 2 inches apart on an ungreased cookie sheet. Flatten by making crisscross marks with the tines of a fork.

3 Bake for 7 to 9 minutes or until bottoms are lightly browned. Cool on cookie sheet for 1 minute. Transfer cookies to a wire rack; cool.

nutrition facts per cookie: 126 cal., 7 g total fat (2 g sat. fat), 13 mg chol., 71 mg sodium, 15 g carb., 0 g fiber, 2 g pro.

honey-cashew cookies: Prepare as directed, except substitute 1 cup roasted cashew butter for the peanut butter, ½ cup honey for the brown sugar, and, if desired, 1 cup chopped roasted cashews for the peanuts.

nutrition facts per cookie: 120 cal., 7 g total fat (2 g sat. fat), 13 mg chol, 78 mg sodium, 14 g carb., 0 g fiber, 2 g pro.

Crunchy toffee pieces—yum! Look for a bag near the chocolate chips at your grocery store.

toffee crackle cookies

prep: 25 minutes **bake:** 20 minutes at 300°F per batch
makes: 48 cookies

1 cup butter, softened
1 cup packed brown
    sugar
1 teaspoon baking
    powder
¼ teaspoon salt
1 egg
1 teaspoon vanilla
2¼ cups all-purpose flour
1 cup chocolate-covered
    toffee pieces
    Granulated sugar

1 Preheat oven to 300°F. In a large mixing bowl beat butter with an electric mixer on medium to high speed for 30 seconds. Add brown sugar, baking powder, and salt. Beat until combined, scraping sides of bowl occasionally. Beat in egg and vanilla until combined. Beat in as much of the flour as you can with the mixer. Using a wooden spoon, stir in any remaining flour. Stir in toffee pieces.

2 Shape dough into 1¼-inch balls. Place 2 inches apart on an ungreased cookie sheet. Dip the bottom of a glass in granulated sugar and flatten each ball to about ¼-inch thickness.

3 Bake about 20 minutes or until edges are firm but not brown. Transfer cookies to a wire rack; cool.

nutrition facts per cookie: 109 cal., 5 g total fat (3 g sat. fat), 16 mg chol., 76 mg sodium, 14 g carb., 0 g fiber, 1 g pro.

Don't let the long list of ingredients deter you. The method is quite easy and the results irresistible.

chocolate, hazelnut, and caramel thumbprint cookies

prep: 40 minutes **chill:** 1 hour **bake:** 10 minutes at 350°F per batch
makes: 36 cookies

1   cup all-purpose flour
⅓   cup unsweetened Dutch-process cocoa powder
½   cup butter, softened
⅔   cup granulated sugar
¼   teaspoon salt
1   egg yolk
2   tablespoons milk
1   teaspoon vanilla
1   egg white, lightly beaten
1   cup finely chopped hazelnuts (filberts)
14   vanilla caramels, unwrapped
3   tablespoons whipping cream
½   cup semisweet chocolate pieces
1   teaspoon shortening
     Whole hazelnuts (filberts), toasted (see tip, page 70)

1 In a small bowl stir together flour and cocoa powder; set aside. In a medium mixing bowl beat butter with an electric mixer on medium to high speed for 30 seconds. Add sugar and salt. Beat until combined, scraping sides of bowl occasionally. Beat in egg yolk, milk, and vanilla until combined. Beat in as much of the flour mixture as you can with the mixer. Using a wooden spoon, stir in any remaining flour mixture. Cover and chill about 1 hour or until dough is easy to handle.

2 Preheat oven to 350°F. Grease a cookie sheet; set aside. Place egg white and the 1 cup chopped hazelnuts in separate small bowls. Shape dough into 1-inch balls. Roll balls in egg white, then in hazelnuts to coat. Place balls 1 inch apart on the prepared cookie sheet. Press your thumb into the center of each ball.

3 Bake for 10 to 12 minutes or until edges are firm. If cookie centers puff during baking, indent with the back of a measuring teaspoon. Transfer cookies to a wire rack; cool.

4 For filling, in a small heavy saucepan heat and stir caramels and whipping cream over low heat until smooth. Spoon about 1 teaspoon of the filling into the indentation of each cookie.

5 In a small microwave-safe bowl microwave chocolate pieces and shortening on 100 percent power (high) for 30 to 45 seconds or until melted, stirring once or twice. Spoon melted chocolate onto each cookie and top with a whole hazelnut. Let stand until chocolate is set.

nutrition facts per cookie: 115 cal., 7 g total fat (3 g sat. fat), 14 mg chol., 51 mg sodium, 12 g carb., 1 g fiber, 2 g pro.

Search the grocery store candy aisle to find chocolate-coated caramels.

salted chocolate-caramel rounds

prep: 30 minutes **bake:** 8 minutes at 375°F per batch
makes: 36 cookies

2¾ cups all-purpose flour
¾ cup unsweetened cocoa powder
1 teaspoon baking soda
¼ teaspoon salt
1 cup butter, softened
1 cup granulated sugar
1 cup packed brown sugar
2 eggs
2 teaspoons vanilla
36 milk chocolate-covered round caramels
12 vanilla caramels, unwrapped
1 tablespoon whipping cream, half-and-half, or light cream
Coarse salt

1 In a medium bowl stir together flour, cocoa powder, baking soda, and salt; set aside.

2 In a large mixing bowl beat butter with an electric mixer on medium to high speed for 30 seconds. Add granulated sugar and brown sugar. Beat until combined, scraping sides of bowl occasionally. Beat in eggs and vanilla until combined. Beat in as much of the flour mixture as you can with the mixer. Using a wooden spoon, stir in any remaining flour mixture. If necessary, cover and chill for 1 hour or until dough is easy to handle.

3 Preheat oven to 375°F. Shape dough into 1½-inch balls. Press a chocolate-covered caramel into each ball and shape dough around caramel to enclose. Place cookies 2 inches apart on an ungreased cookie sheet.

4 Bake for 8 to 10 minutes or until edges are firm. Transfer cookies to a wire rack; cool.

5 To decorate, in a small saucepan combine vanilla caramels and whipping cream. Heat over medium-low heat until caramels melt and mixture is smooth. Drizzle melted caramel mixture over cookies; sprinkle cookies with coarse salt. Let stand until set.

to store: Layer undecorated cookies between sheets of waxed paper in an airtight container; cover. Store at room temperature up to 3 days or freeze up to 3 months. To serve, thaw cookies, if frozen. Frost and top cookies as directed in Step 5.

nutrition facts per cookie: 177 cal., 8 g total fat (5 g sat. fat), 27 mg chol., 140 mg sodium, 26 g carb., 1 g fiber, 2 g pro.

Use a mini food processor to quickly grind the nuts.

almond-cinnamon cookies

prep: 30 minutes **bake:** 13 minutes at 375°F per batch
makes: 42 cookies

¾   cup butter, softened
1½ cups granulated sugar
½   teaspoon baking soda
½   teaspoon cream of tartar
½   teaspoon ground cinnamon
1   egg
1   teaspoon vanilla
½   cup blanched almonds, ground
2   cups all-purpose flour
1   recipe Browned Butter Drizzle

1 Preheat oven to 375°F. In a large mixing bowl beat butter with an electric mixer on medium to high speed for 30 seconds. Add sugar, baking soda, cream of tarter, and cinnamon. Beat until combined, scraping sides of bowl occasionally. Beat in egg and vanilla until combined. Beat in ground almonds. Beat in as much of the flour as you can with the mixer. Using a wooden spoon, stir in any remaining flour.

2 Shape dough into 1-inch balls, or scoop dough with a 1-inch cookie scoop. Place balls 2 inches apart on an ungreased cookie sheet.

3 Bake about 13 minutes or until cookies are light brown. Transfer to a wire rack; cool. Drizzle cookies with Browned Butter Drizzle.

nutrition facts per cookie: 109 cal., 5 g total fat (3 g sat. fat), 15 mg chol., 44 mg sodium, 16 g carb., 0 g fiber, 1 g pro.

browned butter drizzle: In a small saucepan heat 2 tablespoons butter over medium heat until butter turns the color of light brown sugar, stirring frequently. Remove from heat. Slowly stir in 1½ cups powdered sugar, 1 teaspoon vanilla, and enough milk (about 2 tablespoons) to make icing drizzling consistency.

If centers puff up during baking, press with the back of a measuring spoon immediately after removing from the oven.

chocolate-pecan thumbprints

prep: 20 minutes **chill:** 1 hour **bake:** 10 minutes at 350°F per batch
makes: 54 cookies

2   cups all-purpose flour
1   cup finely ground
      pecans
¼   teaspoon salt
¾   cup unsalted butter,
      softened
½   cup granulated sugar
½   cup powdered sugar
2   eggs
2   teaspoons vanilla
4   ounces semisweet
      chocolate, finely
      chopped
⅓   cup whipping cream
      Pecan halves
      (optional)

1 In a medium bowl stir together flour, ground pecans, and salt; set aside.

2 In a large mixing bowl beat butter with an electric mixer on medium to high speed for 30 seconds. Add granulated sugar and powdered sugar. Beat until light and fluffy, scraping sides of bowl occasionally. Beat in eggs and vanilla until combined. Beat in as much of the flour mixture as you can with the mixer. Using a wooden spoon, stir in any remaining flour mixture. Cover and chill about 1 hour or until dough is easy to handle.

3 Preheat oven to 350°F. Using 2 teaspoons of the dough for each cookie, shape dough into balls. Place balls 1½ inches apart on an ungreased cookie sheet. Press your thumb into the center of each ball.

4 Bake for 10 to 11 minutes or until lightly browned. If cookie centers puff during baking, immediatley indent with the back of a measuring teaspoon. Cool on cookie sheet for 1 minute. Transfer cookies to a wire rack; cool.

5 For filling, place chocolate in a small bowl; set aside. In a small saucepan heat whipping cream over medium heat just until small bubbles appear around the edges. Pour whipping cream over chocolate, stirring until melted. Cool slightly.

6 Spoon filling into the indentation of each cookie. If desired, top each cookie with a pecan half. Let stand at room temperature or in the refrigerator until filling is set.

nutrition facts per cookie: 80 cal., 5 g total fat (2 g sat. fat), 17 mg chol., 14 mg sodium, 8 g carb., 0 g fiber, 1 g pro.

Perfect pretzel shapes take some practice, but the imperfect ones taste just as good!

chocolate pretzels

prep: 45 minutes chill: 1 hour bake: 8 minutes at 350°F per batch
makes: 24 cookies

1¾   cups all-purpose flour
 ¼   cup unsweetened
        cocoa powder
        Dash salt
 ¾   cup unsalted butter,
        softened
 ¾   cup packed light
        brown sugar
  1   egg
  1   teaspoon vanilla
        Unsweetened cocoa
        powder (optional)
  1   egg white
  1   tablespoon water
  4   teaspoons coarse
        sugar

1 In a small bowl stir together flour, the ¼ cup cocoa powder, and salt; set aside.

2 In a large mixing bowl beat butter with an electric mixer on medium to high speed for 30 seconds. Add brown sugar. Beat until fluffy, scraping sides of bowl occasionally. Beat in egg and vanilla until combined. Beat in as much of the flour mixture as you can with the mixer. Stir in any remaining flour mixture. Cover and chill about 1 hour or until dough is easy to handle.

3 Preheat oven to 350°F. Line a cookie sheet with parchment paper; set aside. Divide dough into 24 portions. Roll each dough portion into a 9-inch rope. If desired, lightly roll ropes in cocoa powder. Shape each rope by crossing one end over the other to form a loop, overlapping about 2 inches from each end. Take one end of dough in each hand and twist once at the point where the dough overlaps. Carefully lift each end across loop to opposite edge of loop. Place twisted loops 1 inch apart on the prepared cookie sheet.

4 In a small bowl whisk together egg white and the water. Brush dough with egg white mixture; sprinkle with coarse sugar. Bake for 8 to 9 minutes or just until firm. Cool on cookie sheet for 1 minute. Transfer to a wire rack; cool.

nutrition facts per cookie: 119 cal., 6 g total fat (4 g sat. fat), 23 mg chol., 14 mg sodium, 15 g carb., 1 g fiber, 2 g pro.

Raspberry jam marries with spice and lemon to re-create the flavors of Austria's famous tart.

linzertorte thumbprint cookies

prep: 30 minutes   bake: 14 minutes at 325°F per batch
makes: 16 cookies

⅓   cup hazelnuts
     (filberts), toasted
     (see tip, page 70)
¼   cup powdered sugar
1   cup all-purpose flour
1½ teaspoons
     unsweetened cocoa
     powder
½   teaspoon ground
     cinnamon
⅛   teaspoon ground
     cloves
½   cup butter, softened
2   teaspoons finely
     shredded lemon
     peel
⅓   cup seedless red
     raspberry jam
     and/or orange
     marmalade
     Semisweet chocolate,
     melted

1 Preheat oven to 325°F. Line a cookie sheet with parchment paper; set aside.

2 In a food processor combine hazelnuts and the ¼ cup powdered sugar. Cover; process until finely ground. In a bowl stir together flour, cocoa powder, cinnamon, and cloves; set aside.

3 In a medium mixing bowl beat butter and lemon peel with an electric mixer on medium to high speed for 30 seconds. Add nut mixture. Beat until combined, scraping sides of bowl occasionally. Beat in flour mixture until combined.

4 Shape dough into 1-inch balls. Place balls 1 inch apart on the prepared cookie sheet. Press your thumb into the center of each ball.

5 Bake for 8 minutes. If cookie centers puff during baking, indent with the back of a measuring teaspoon. Spoon jam into the indentation of each cookie. Bake for 6 to 8 minutes more or until bottoms are lightly browned. Transfer cookies to a wire rack; cool. If desired, drizzle with melted chocolate.

nutrition facts per cookie: 122 cal., 7 g total fat (4 g sat. fat), 15 mg chol., 53 mg sodium, 13 g carb., 1 g fiber, 1 g pro.

Even better, use a tablespoon of snipped fresh sage instead of the dried herb.

berry-sage thumbprints

prep: 25 minutes bake: 10 minutes at 350°F per batch
makes: 60 cookies

2 cups all-purpose flour
⅔ cup yellow cornmeal
1½ teaspoons dried sage, crushed
¼ teaspoon baking powder
1 cup butter, softened
1 cup packed brown sugar
2 egg yolks
2 teaspoons finely shredded lemon peel
1½ teaspoons vanilla
¾ cup blackberry preserves

1 Preheat oven to 350°F. In a medium bowl stir together flour, cornmeal, dried sage, and baking powder; set aside.

2 In a large mixing bowl beat butter with an electric mixer on medium speed for 30 seconds. Add brown sugar. Beat until combined, scraping sides of bowl occasionally. Beat in egg yolks, lemon peel, and vanilla. Beat in as much of the flour mixture as you can with the mixer. Stir in any remaining flour mixture.

3 Shape dough into ¾-inch balls. Place balls 1 inch apart on an ungreased cookie sheet. Press your thumb into the center of each ball. Spoon about ½ teaspoon of the blackberry preserves into the indentation of each cookie.

4 Bake about 10 minutes or until bottoms are lightly browned. Cool on cookie sheet for 1 minute. Transfer cookies to a wire rack; cool.

to store: Place cookies in a single layer in an airtight container; cover. Store in the refrigerator up to 2 days.

nutrition facts per cookie: 115 cal., 5 g total fat (3 g sat. fat), 24 mg chol., 57 mg sodium, 16 g carb., 0 g fiber, 1 g pro.

scrumptious **shapes**

The classic powdered sugar-coated cookie goes tropical with the addition of unsweetened coconut.

coconut-pecan sandies

prep: 45 minutes **chill:** 30 minutes **bake:** 15 minutes at 325°F per batch
makes: 40 cookies

1	cup butter, softened
½	cup powdered sugar
1	tablespoon water
1	teaspoon vanilla
2	cups all-purpose flour
¾	cup finely chopped pecans, toasted (see tip, page 13)
¾	cup finely chopped coconut
¾	cup powdered sugar

1 In a large mixing bowl beat butter with an electric mixer on medium to high speed for 30 seconds. Add the ½ cup powdered sugar. Beat until combined, scraping sides of bowl occasionally. Beat in the water and vanilla until combined. Beat in as much of the flour as you can with the mixer. Using a wooden spoon, stir in any remaining flour, the pecans, and coconut. Cover and chill for 30 to 60 minutes or until dough is easy to handle.

2 Preheat oven to 325°F. Shape dough into 1-inch balls or 2×½-inch logs. Place balls or logs 1 inch apart on an ungreased cookie sheet. Bake about 15 minutes or until bottoms are lightly browned. Transfer cookies to a wire rack; cool.

3 Place the ¾ cup powdered sugar in a large resealable plastic bag. Add cooled cookies, a few at a time, shaking gently to coat.

to store: Layer cookies between sheets of waxed paper in an airtight container; cover. Store at room temperature up to 3 days or freeze uncoated cookies up to 3 months. To serve, thaw cookies, if frozen. Shake cookies in powdered sugar as directed.

nutrition facts per coconut-pecan or cocoa-covered cookie variation: 99 cal., 7 g total fat (3 g sat. fat), 12 mg chol., 45 mg sodium, 10 g carb., 1 g fiber, 1 g pro.

cocoa-covered sandies Prepare as directed, except in Step 3 reduce the powdered sugar to ½ cup and stir in 3 tablespoons unsweetened cocoa powder. Shake cooled cookies in the powdered sugar-cocoa mixture.

Look for canned dulce de leche, a sweet caramelized milk product used in Latin American cuisine, in the baking aisle near canned milk products.

dulce de leche snappers

prep: 30 minutes **bake:** 8 minutes at 350°F per batch
makes: 36 cookies

½ cup butter, softened
½ cup granulated sugar
½ cup packed brown sugar
½ teaspoon baking powder
¼ teaspoon salt
1 egg
1½ teaspoons vanilla
2 cups all-purpose flour
2 cups pecan halves, walnut halves, and/or whole almonds
¾ cup dulce de leche
Sea salt (optional)

1 Preheat oven to 350°F. In a medium mixing bowl beat butter with an electric mixer on medium to high speed for 30 seconds. Add granulated sugar, brown sugar, baking powder, and the ¼ teaspoon salt. Beat until combined, scraping sides of bowl occasionally. Beat in egg and vanilla until combined. Beat in as much of the flour as you can with the mixer. Using a wooden spoon, stir in any remaining flour.

2 Shape dough into 1-inch balls. On an ungreased cookie sheet, arrange nuts in groups of three, with groups 2 inches apart. Place each ball of dough on a nut cluster, with nuts peeking out from under ball. Flatten dough slightly.

3 Bake for 8 to 10 minutes or just until edges are firm. Cool on cookie sheet for 1 minute. While cookies are warm, spread each cookie with 1 teaspoon of the dulce de leche. If desired, sprinkle with sea salt. Transfer cookies to a wire rack; cool.

nutrition facts per cookie: 131 cal., 7 g total fat (2 g sat. fat), 14 mg chol., 55 mg sodium, 15 g carb., 1 g fiber, 2 g pro.

Call on a cookie press to make these pretty gems.

mocha and apricot jam bites

prep: 30 minutes **bake:** 8 minutes at 375°F per batch
makes: 84 cookies

1½ cups butter, softened
½ 8-ounce package
    cream cheese,
    softened
1 cup granulated sugar
¼ cup unsweetened
    cocoa powder
4 teaspoons instant
    espresso powder
1 teaspoon baking
    powder
¼ teaspoon salt
1 egg
1 teaspoon vanilla
3½ cups all-purpose flour
½ cup apricot jam or
    preserves*
    Powdered sugar

1 Preheat oven to 375°F. In a large mixing bowl beat butter and cream cheese with an electric mixer on medium to high speed for 30 seconds. Add sugar, cocoa powder, espresso powder, baking powder, and salt. Beat until combined, scraping sides of bowl occasionally. Beat in egg and vanilla. Beat in as much of the flour as you can with the mixer. Using a wooden spoon, stir in any remaining flour.

2 Pack dough into a cookie press fitted with a star or flower plate. Force dough through press 1 inch apart onto ungreased cookie sheets.

3 Bake for 8 to 10 minutes or until edges are firm. Transfer cookies to a wire rack; cool.

4 Just before serving, spoon about ¼ teaspoon of the apricot jam into the center of each cookie. Sprinkle with powdered sugar.

*tip: Use kitchen scissors to cut up any large pieces of fruit in the jam or preserves.

to store: Layer unfilled cookies between sheets of waxed paper in an airtight container; cover. Store at room temperature up to 3 days or freeze up to 3 months. Thaw cookies, if frozen. Fill as directed in Step 4.

nutrition facts per cookie: 69 cal., 4 g total fat (2 g sat. fat), 12 mg chol., 48 mg sodium, 8 g carb., 0 g fiber, 1 g pro

Commonly known as an ingredient in hummus, thick tahini tenderizes these cookies while adding sesame flavor.

chocolate-sesame cookies

prep: 30 minutes   chill: 30 minutes   bake: 10 minutes at 350°F per batch
makes: 42 cookies

8   ounces semisweet
    chocolate, coarsely
    chopped
2   tablespoons butter
3   tablespoons tahini
    (sesame seed paste)
⅔   cup all-purpose flour
½   teaspoon baking
    powder
½   teaspoon salt
2   eggs
¾   cup packed brown
    sugar
1   teaspoon vanilla
½   cup sesame seeds,
    toasted (see tip,
    page 13)

1 In a small saucepan heat and stir chocolate and butter over low heat until melted. Remove from heat; stir in tahini. Set aside. In a small bowl stir together flour, baking powder, and salt; set aside.

2 In a large mixing bowl beat eggs with an electric mixer until frothy. Add brown sugar and vanilla. Beat until combined, scraping sides of bowl occasionally. Beat in melted chocolate mixture. Beat in flour mixture on low speed until combined. Cover and chill about 30 minutes or until dough is easy to handle.

3 Preheat oven to 350°F. Place sesame seeds in a small bowl. Shape dough into 1-inch balls. Roll balls in sesame seeds to coat. Place balls 2 inches apart on an ungreased cookie sheet.

4 Bake for 10 to 12 minutes or until cookies are puffed and bottoms are set. Transfer cookies to a wire rack; cool.

nutrition facts per cookie: 73 cal., 4 g total fat (2 g sat. fat), 12 mg chol., 41 mg sodium, 9 g carb., 1 g fiber, 1 g pro.

Like other herbs, lavender adds a sweet note, but more is not necessarily better. Use only the one teaspoon called for.

lavender-vanilla pillows

prep: 35 minutes bake: 20 minutes at 325°F per batch
makes: 36 cookies

1   teaspoon dried
     lavender
1   tablespoon water
1   cup butter, softened
½   cup powdered sugar
1   vanilla bean, split in
     half and scraped or
     1 teaspoon vanilla
2   cups all-purpose flour
     Powdered sugar

1 Preheat oven to 325°F. Using a mortar and pestle, grind and crush the dried lavender. In a small bowl combine lavender and the water. Set aside for 10 minutes.

2 In a medium mixing bowl beat butter with an electric mixer on medium speed for 30 seconds. Add the ½ cup powdered sugar. Beat until combined, scraping sides of bowl occasionally. Beat in lavender mixture and vanilla bean seeds. Gradually add flour, beating on low speed until combined.

3 Divide dough into 36 equal portions (about 1 tablespoon each). With lightly floured fingers, evenly press each portion into bottom of an ungreased 1¾-inch muffin cup.

4 Bake about 20 minutes or until edges lightly brown and toothpick inserted in center comes out clean. Cool in muffin cups on a wire rack for 10 minutes. Using a thin knife, loosen edges of cookies and remove. Cool on rack.

5 Sprinkle cookies with powdered sugar just before serving.

nutrition facts per cookie: 79 cal., 5 g total fat (3 g sat. fat), 14 mg chol., 37 mg sodium, 7 g carb., 0 g fiber, 1 g pro.

Bake the dough in batches if you don't have 24 madeleine molds. These cakelike cookies are famous throughout France.

lemony madeleines with raspberry ganache

prep: 35 minutes **bake:** 10 minutes at 375°F per batch
makes: 24 cookies

2   egg yolks
½   cup granulated sugar
½   cup butter, melted and cooled
½   teaspoon finely shredded lemon peel
1   tablespoon lemon juice
½   teaspoon vanilla
½   cup all-purpose flour
½   teaspoon baking powder
⅛   teaspoon baking soda
⅛   teaspoon salt
2   egg whites, lightly beaten
¼   cup finely chopped pecans, toasted (see tip, page 13)
1   recipe White Chocolate-Raspberry Ganache

1 Preheat oven to 375°F. Grease and flour twenty-four 3-inch madeleine molds; set aside.

2 In a medium mixing bowl combine egg yolks and sugar. Beat with an electric mixer on medium to high speed for 30 seconds. Add melted butter, lemon peel, lemon juice, and vanilla. Beat on low speed until combined.

3 In a small bowl stir together flour, baking powder, baking soda, and salt. Sprinkle flour mixture over egg yolk mixture; stir in gently. Gently stir in egg whites and pecans. Spoon batter into the prepared molds, filling each about half full.

4 Bake for 10 to 12 minutes or until edges are golden and tops spring back when lightly touched. Let stand for 1 minute in molds. Using the tip of a knife, loosen cookies from molds; invert onto a wire rack. Remove molds; cool cookies on wire rack.

5 Using a soft brush, brush excess crumbs from cookies. Holding each cookie at an angle, dip halfway into White Chocolate-Raspberry Ganache; let excess drip back into pan. Let stand until ganache is set.

nutrition facts per cookie: 113 cal., 8 g total fat (4 g sat. fat), 30 mg chol., 73mg sodium, 10 g carb., 0 g fiber, 1 g pro.

white chocolate-raspberry ganache: In a small saucepan heat ⅓ cup whipping cream over low heat just until boiling. Remove from heat. Add 4 raspberry-flavor tea bags. Let steep for 15 minutes. Meanwhile, finely chop 4 ounces white baking chocolate with cocoa butter. Remove tea bags from cream; discard. Return cream to boiling. Remove from heat. Immediately add white chocolate, stirring until melted. Tint with red paste food coloring. Cool slightly.

6

What's more fun to eat than creamy filling sandwiched between two buttery cookies? You'll find oodles of cookie sandwich ideas, including whoopie pies and crescents stuffed with nuts, candies, and jam.

stuffed &

fille

d

mascarpone-filled brownie
sandwiches, page 176

Roll up each dough wedge like crescent roll dough.

poppy seed croissant cookies

prep: 40 minutes **chill:** 1 hour 45 minutes **bake:** 15 minutes at 350°F per batch
makes: 48 cookies

1   8-ounce package cream cheese, softened
1   cup butter, softened
¼   cup granulated sugar
2   teaspoons finely shredded lemon peel
1   teaspoon vanilla
¼   teaspoon salt
2   cups all-purpose flour
1   12.5-ounce can poppy seed pastry and dessert filling
2   tablespoons granulated sugar
1   egg
1   tablespoon milk
1   to 2 tablespoons powdered sugar

1 In a large mixing bowl beat cream cheese, butter, and the ¼ cup granulated sugar with an electric mixer on medium to high speed until light and fluffy. Beat in 1 teaspoon of the lemon peel, the vanilla, and salt. Add flour; beat on low speed just until combined.

2 Turn dough out onto a lightly floured surface; divide into four equal portions. Shape each portion into a ball. Cover and chill dough about 1 hour or until easy to handle.

3 Meanwhile, for filling, in a medium bowl stir together poppy seed filling, the 2 tablespoons sugar, and the remaining 1 teaspoon lemon peel.

4 Line cookie sheets with parchment paper; set aside. On a lightly floured surface roll one portion of dough at a time into a 9-inch circle. Spoon about ¼ cup of the filling onto the circle; spread to ½ inch from the edge. Using a sharp knife, cut circle into 12 wedges. Starting at the wide edge, roll up each wedge. Place 2 inches apart on prepared cookie sheets, point sides down. Repeat with remaining dough and filling. Cover and chill for 45 minutes.

5 Preheat oven to 350°F. In a small bowl whisk together egg and milk until frothy. Brush lightly on cookies.

6 Bake for 15 to 18 minutes or until tops are light golden brown. Transfer to a wire rack; cool. Sprinkle cooled cookies lightly with powdered sugar.

nutrition facts per cookie: 102 cal., 6 g total fat (3 g sat. fat), 19 mg chol., 68 mg sodium, 10 g carb., 0 g fiber, 1 g pro.

A chocolatey center is the surprise kiss of flavor.

cherry surprise crinkles

prep: 30 minutes bake: 10 minutes at 350°F per batch
makes: 36 cookies

½   cup butter, softened
1   cup granulated sugar
½   teaspoon baking powder
¼   teaspoon baking soda
¼   teaspoon salt
1   egg
1   teaspoon almond extract
2   cups all-purpose flour
½   cup chopped maraschino cherries, well drained and patted dry with paper towels
36   Kisses cherry cordials or Kisses dark chocolates

1 Preheat oven to 350°F. In a medium mixing bowl beat butter with an electric mixer on medium to high speed for 30 seconds. Add granulated sugar, baking powder, baking soda, and salt. Beat until combined, scraping sides of bowl occasionally. Beat in egg and almond extract until combined. Beat in as much of the flour as you can with the mixer. Using a wooden spoon, stir in any remaining flour and the cherries.

2 Divide dough into 36 equal portions.* Shape each portion into a ball around a Kiss. Place balls 2 inches apart on ungreased cookie sheets.

3 Bake for 10 to 12 minutes or until bottoms are light golden brown. Transfer cookies to a wire rack; cool.

*tip: To divide dough equally, pat dough into a rectangle on a lightly floured surface. Using a sharp knife, cut dough into 6 equal rows then cut each row into 6 equal portions.

nutrition facts per cookie: 97 cal., 4 g total fat (3 g sat. fat), 12 mg chol., 56 mg sodium, 15 g carb., 1 g fiber, 1 g pro.

Plenty of melted butter crisps the pastries.

caramel-apple triangle treats

prep: 30 minutes **bake:** 15 minutes at 350°F per batch
makes: 16 cookies

1 cup caramel baking bits, snipped in half
3 tablespoons snipped dried apples
3 tablespoons chopped walnuts, toasted (see tip, page 13)
½ cup butter, melted
1 0.74-ounce package spiced apple cider mix (2 tablespoons)
16 sheets frozen phyllo dough (9×14-inch rectangles), thawed
1 tablespoon powdered sugar

1 Preheat oven to 350°F. Line a large cookie sheet with parchment paper; set aside. For filing, in a small bowl combine caramel bits, dried apples, and walnuts; set aside.

2 In a small bowl stir together melted butter and apple cider mix. Unroll phyllo dough; cover with plastic wrap. (As you work, keep phyllo covered to prevent it from drying out, removing sheets as you need them.) Place one sheet of phyllo dough on a flat surface. Lightly brush sheet with some of the butter mixture. Place another sheet of phyllo on top; brush with butter mixture. Repeat, adding two more sheets of phyllo.

3 Using a sharp knife, cut the layered sheets lengthwise into four equal strips. Spoon a heaping tablespoon of filling 1 inch from an end of a dough strip. To fold strip into a triangle, bring a corner over filling so the short edge lines up with the side edge. Continue folding the triangular shape along the entire length of the strip. Place filled triangle on the prepared baking sheet. Repeat with remaining 3 strips, then repeat using remaining phyllo, butter mixture, and filling. Brush triangles with remaining butter mixture.

4 Bake about 15 minutes or until crisp and golden brown. Cool slightly on baking sheet; dust with powdered sugar.

to store: Layer triangles between sheets of waxed paper in an airtight container; cover. Store at room temperature up to 24 hours.

nutrition facts per cookie: 177 cal., 9 g total fat (5 g sat. fat), 15 mg chol., 186 mg sodium, 23 g carb., 1 g fiber, 2 g pro.

Chill the mint filling as you prepare the cookie dough.

peppermint munchies

prep: 35 minutes **chill:** 30 minutes **bake:** 9 minutes at 375°F per batch
makes: 32 cookies

1 recipe Peppermint
   Filling
¾ cup butter, softened
1 cup granulated sugar
1 teaspoon baking
   powder
1 egg
1 tablespoon milk
1 teaspoon vanilla
2 cups all-purpose flour
2 tablespoons coarse
   white and/or red
   sugar

1 Prepare Peppermint Filling. Cover and chill for 30 minutes.

2 Preheat oven to 375°F. In a large mixing bowl beat butter with an electric mixer on medium speed for 30 seconds. Add sugar and baking powder. Beat until combined, scraping sides of bowl occasionally. Beat in egg, milk, and vanilla until combined. Beat in as much of the flour as you can with the mixer. Stir in any remaining flour.

3 Shape dough into 1¼-inch balls. Make an indentation in the center of each ball; place ½ teaspoon of the Peppermint Filling in indentation. Shape dough around filling to enclose; roll dough gently in hands until smooth. Place balls 2 inches apart on an ungreased cookie sheet. Dip the bottom of a glass in coarse sugar and flatten each ball to ½-inch thickness.

4 Bake for 9 to 12 minutes or until lightly browned. Cool on cookie sheet for 1 minute. Transfer cookies to a wire rack; cool.

nutrition facts per cookie: 110 cal., 5 g total fat (3 g sat. fat), 20 mg chol., 65 mg sodium, 14 g carb., 0 g fiber, 1 g pro.

peppermint filling: In a small mixing bowl combine one 3-ounce package cream cheese, softened; 2 tablespoons powdered sugar; 2 tablespoons finely crushed peppermint candies; and ¼ teaspoon peppermint extract. Beat with an electric mixer on low speed until smooth.

Just as our photo shows, the cherry filling easily leaks out, but do press the dough edges together with a fork to minimize the runout.

cherry-almond half moons

prep: 45 minutes **chill:** 1 hour 30 minutes **bake:** 12 minutes at 375°F per batch
makes: 32 cookies

1   cup butter, softened
1   8-ounce package cream cheese, softened
1   teaspoon almond extract
2   cups all-purpose flour
½   cup cherry preserves
2   egg whites
1   recipe Almond Icing

1 In a large mixing bowl beat the butter and cream cheese with an electric mixer on medium to high speed for 30 seconds. Beat in almond extract until combined. Beat in the flour until dough comes together. Divide dough in half. Cover and chill dough about 1½ hours or until easy to handle.

2 Preheat oven to 375°F. Line cookie sheets with parchment paper; set aside. On a lightly floured surface roll half the dough at a time to ⅛- inch thick. Using a 3-inch round scalloped-edge cookie cutter, cut out dough. Place rounds 1 inch apart on prepared cookie sheets.

3 Spoon ½ teaspoon cherry preserves onto one side of each round; spread to ¼ inch from the edge. Fold dough rounds in half, enclosing preserves; press edges with the tines of a fork to seal. Whisk egg whites until frothy; brush cookies lightly with egg whites.

4 Bake for 12 to 15 minutes or until cookies are lightly browned. Transfer cookies to a wire rack; cool. Drizzle cookies with Almond Icing. Sprinkle with almonds. Let stand until icing is set.

nutrition facts per cookie: 134 cal., 9 g total fat (5 g sat. fat), 23 mg chol., 79 mg sodium, 13 g carb., 0 g fiber, 2 g pro.

almond icing: In a small bowl stir together ¾ cup powdered sugar, ¼ teaspoon almond extract, and enough water (1 to 2 tablespoons) to make icing drizzling consistency.

Each cookie is a tiny bite of hardened meringue—an ideal treat for gluten-free snacking.

raspberry almond meringues

prep: 45 minutes **bake:** 20 minutes at 300°F per batch **stand:** 1 hour
makes: 40 cookies

3   egg whites
4   ounces blanched
     almonds (¾ cup)
2   tablespoons
     granulated sugar
¼   teaspoon almond
     extract
⅛   teaspoon salt
⅓   cup granulated sugar
¼   to ⅓ cup raspberry
     preserves or jam
     Powdered sugar

1 Allow egg whites to stand at room temperature for 30 minutes. Preheat oven to 300°F. Line two large cookie sheets with foil or parchment paper.

2 Meanwhile, place almonds and the 2 tablespoons sugar in a food processor. Cover and process until almonds are finely ground (you should have about 1⅓ cups). (Or, if you have a coffee grinder or nut grinder, work in small batches to grind the nuts and sugar.)

3 In a large mixing bowl combine egg whites, almond extract, and salt. Beat with an electric mixer on medium speed until soft peaks form (tips curl). Gradually add ⅓ cup sugar, 1 tablespoon at a time, beating on high speed until stiff peaks form (tips stand straight). Fold in almond mixture.

4 Spoon meringue into a decorating bag fitted with a small open star tip or a round tip with a large opening. Pipe into 1½-inch circles 1 inch apart on prepared cookie sheets, building up the edges. If the tip gets clogged, use a toothpick to unclog.

5 Bake on separate racks in the oven for 20 minutes. Turn off oven and let cookies dry in oven with door closed for 1 hour. Transfer cookies to a wire rack; cool completely. Just before serving, spoon about ¼ to ½ teaspoon of the raspberry preserves into the center of each cookie. Sift powdered sugar lightly over filled cookies.

nutrition facts per cookie: 32 cal., 1 g total fat (0 g sat. fat), 0 mg chol., 13 mg sodium, 4 g carb., 0 g fiber, 1 g pro.

The gooey caramel center contrasts with the tender cake, making for one splendid taste experience.

chocolate-caramel cupcake bites

prep: 20 minutes **bake:** 12 minutes at 350°F per batch
makes: 20 cup cake bites

1	cup butter, softened
1	cup packed brown sugar
½	cup granulated sugar
½	teaspoon baking soda
½	teaspoon salt
3	eggs
2	teaspoons vanilla
⅓	cup unsweetened cocoa powder
2¼	cups all-purpose flour
1	12-ounce package chocolate-covered caramel candies, unwrapped
2	tablespoons whipping cream or milk

1 Preheat oven to 350°F. Line twenty 2½-inch muffin cups with paper bake cups; set aside.

2 In a large mixing bowl beat butter with an electric mixer on medium to high speed for 30 seconds. Add the brown sugar, granulated sugar, baking soda, and salt. Beat until combined, scraping sides of bowl occasionally. Beat in eggs, one at a time, and vanilla until combined. Beat in cocoa powder until combined. Beat in as much of the flour as you can with the mixer. Using a wooden spoon, stir in any remaining flour.

3 Spoon about 3 tablespoons of batter into each paper bake cup. Gently press 1 unwrapped chocolate-covered caramel candy into the center of each muffin cup until top of candy is slightly below the batter.

4 Bake for 12 to 15 minutes or until set. Cool in muffin cups on a wire rack for 2 minutes. Transfer to a wire rack; cool. Centers will fall slightly as cakes cool.

5 Meanwhile, in a small heavy saucepan, heat and stir the remaining chocolate-covered caramel candies and the whipping cream over medium-low heat until candies are melted and mixture is smooth. Drizzle some of the mixture over the top of each cooled cupcake cookie.

nutrition facts per cupcake bite: 295 cal., 14 g total fat (9 g sat. fat), 56 mg chol., 218 mg sodium, 39 g carb., 1 g fiber, 4 g pro.

mexican chocolate-dulce de leche sandwich cookies

prep: 30 minutes **chill:** 2 hours **bake:** 8 minutes at 325°F per batch
makes: 26 sandwich cookies

3 cups all-purpose flour
½ cup unsweetened dark cocoa powder
1 teaspoon ground cinnamon
1 teaspoon baking powder
1 teaspoon baking soda
½ teaspoon salt
1 cup butter, softened
1 cup granulated sugar
½ cup packed brown sugar
2 eggs
1 tablespoon vanilla
1 13.4-ounce can dulce de leche

1 In a medium bowl stir together flour, cocoa powder, cinnamon, baking powder, baking soda, and salt; set aside. In a large mixing bowl combine butter, granulated sugar, and brown sugar. Beat with an electric mixer on medium speed until light and fluffy. Add eggs and vanilla; beat until combined, scraping sides of bowl occasionally. Beat in as much of the flour mixture as you can with the mixer. Using a wooden spoon, stir in any remaining flour mixture. Divide dough in half. Cover and chill about 2 hours or until dough is easy to handle.

2 Preheat oven to 325°F. Line cookie sheets with parchment paper; set aside. On a lightly floured surface, roll one portion of the dough at a time to ¼-inch thickness. Using a 3-inch round scalloped-edge cookie cutter, cut out dough. Place cutouts 1 inch apart on prepared cookie sheets. Using a 1-inch round scalloped-edge cookie cutter, cut out the center of half the cutouts.

3 Bake for 8 to 10 minutes or until firm when lightly pressed with a finger. Cool on cookie sheets for 2 minutes. Transfer to a wire rack; cool.

4 Spread about 2 teaspoons dulce de leche on the flat side of each cookie with center intact. Top with a cookie with cutout center, bottom side down..

nutrition facts per sandwich cookie: 219 cal., 9 g total fat (5 g sat. fat), 37 mg chol., 200 mg sodium, 32 g carb., 1 g fiber, 3 g pro.

Ground cumin is the surprise spice in the nutty-marshmallow center.

peanut butter cream sandwich cookies

prep: 50 minutes bake: 7 minutes at 350°F per batch
makes: 96 sandwich cookies

½ cup chunky peanut butter
½ cup shortening
1 cup packed brown sugar
1 teaspoon baking soda
⅛ teaspoon salt
1 egg
1 teaspoon vanilla
1¼ cups all-purpose flour
   Granulated sugar
1 recipe Peanut Cream Filling

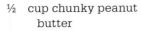

1 Preheat oven to 350°F. In a large mixing bowl beat peanut butter and shortening with an electric mixer on medium to high speed for 30 seconds. Add brown sugar, baking soda, and salt. Beat until combined, scraping sides of bowl occasionally. Beat in egg and vanilla until combined. Beat in as much of the flour as you can with the mixer. Using a wooden spoon, stir in any remaining flour.

2 For each cookie, shape 1 level teaspoon of the dough into a ball. Place balls 1½ inches apart on an ungreased cookie sheet. Flatten by making crisscross marks with the tines of a fork dipped in granulated sugar.

3 Bake for 7 to 8 minutes or until edges are lightly browned. Cool on cookie sheet for 1 minute. Transfer cookies to a wire rack; cool.

4 Spread Peanut Cream Filling onto bottoms of half the cookies. Top with the remaining cookies, bottom sides down.

nutrition facts per sandwich cookie: 98 cal., 6 g total fat (1 g sat. fat), 4 mg chol., 69 mg sodium, 11 g carb., 1 g fiber, 2 g pro.

peanut cream filling: In a medium bowl whisk together ¾ cup chunky peanut butter, ¾ cup marshmallow creme, 3 tablespoons milk, ¾ teaspoon ground cinnamon, and ¼ teaspoon ground cumin. Gradually whisk in 3 tablespoons powdered sugar until combined.

After trying this nutty variation with a lemon cream filling, you may never bake plain sugar cookies again!

lemon buttercream sugar cookies
lemon buttercream sandwich cookies

prep: 40 minutes chill: 30 minutes bake: 8 minutes at 350°F per batch
makes: 32 sandwich cookies

1	cup butter, softened
½	cup granulated sugar
2	teaspoons finely shredded lemon peel
¼	cup lemon juice
1	teaspoon vanilla
2¼	cups all-purpose flour
¾	cup finely chopped Brazil nuts or hazelnuts (filberts)
1	recipe Lemon Buttercream

1 In a large mixing bowl beat butter with an electric mixer on medium to high speed for 30 seconds. Add granulated sugar. Beat until combined, scraping sides of bowl occasionally. Beat in lemon peel, lemon juice, and vanilla until combined. Beat in as much of the flour as you can with the mixer. Using a wooden spoon, stir in any remaining flour and the nuts. Divide dough in half. Cover and chill for 30 to 60 minutes or until dough is easy to handle.

2 Preheat oven to 350°F. On a lightly floured surface, roll half the dough at a time to slightly less than ¼-inch thickness. Using a 2-inch round scalloped-edge cookie cutter, cut out dough. Place cutouts 1 inch apart on an ungreased cookie sheet.

3 Bake for 8 to 10 minutes or until edges are lightly browned. Transfer cookies to a wire rack; cool.

4 To assemble, spread Lemon Buttercream on the bottoms of half the cookies. Top with the remaining cookies, bottom sides down.

lemon buttercream: In a medium mixing bowl beat 3 tablespoons butter, softened, with an electric mixer on medium to high speed for 30 seconds. Gradually add 2 cups powdered sugar, beating well. Beat in 1 teaspoon finely shredded lemon peel and 2 tablespoons lemon juice. Beat in 1 cup additional powdered sugar. Beat in enough whipping cream (1 to 2 tablespoons) to make frosting spreading consistency.

to store: Layer unfilled cookies between sheets of waxed paper in an airtight container; cover. Store at room temperature up to 3 days or freeze up to 3 months. To serve, thaw cookies if frozen. Assemble as directed.

nutrition facts per sandwich cookie: 172 cal., 9 g total fat (5 g sat. fat), 19 mg chol., 61 mg sodium, 22 g carb., 0 g fiber, 1 g pro.

The cookie part of this recipe can be used when you're making any dessert that calls for ladyfingers, such as charlotte or tiramisu.

lemon ladyfinger sandwich cookies

prep: 45 minutes **bake:** 5 minutes at 425°F per batch
makes: 20 sandwich cookies

6 egg whites
⅔ cup granulated sugar
5 egg yolks
2 tablespoons granulated sugar
1 teaspoon vanilla
1 cup all-purpose flour
2 teaspoons finely shredded lemon peel
2 tablespoons powdered sugar
1 recipe Lemon Cheesecake Filling

lemon cheesecake filling: In a medium mixing bowl beat one 8-ounce package cream cheese, softened, with an electric mixer on medium to high speed for 30 seconds. Beat in ½ cup lemon curd until combined. Beat in about 5 cups powdered sugar so filling reaches piping consistency.

1 Preheat oven to 425°F. Line three large cookie sheets with parchment paper; set aside. In a large mixing bowl beat egg whites with an electric mixer on medium speed until soft peaks form (tips curl). Gradually add the ⅔ cup granulated sugar, about 1 tablespoon at a time, beating on high speed until stiff peaks form (tips stand straight). Set aside.

2 In a medium mixing bowl beat egg yolks and the 2 tablespoons granulated sugar on high speed about 5 minutes or until thick. Beat in vanilla.

3 Fold egg yolk mixture into beaten egg whites just until combined. Sprinkle ⅓ cup of the flour over egg mixture; fold in gently just until combined. Repeat with the remaining flour, ⅓ cup at a time, being careful not to overmix. Fold in lemon peel.

4 Spoon about one-third of the batter into a decorating bag fitted with a ½-inch round tip. Pipe batter into 3×1-inch logs, 1 inch apart, onto one of the prepared cookie sheets. Sprinkle logs lightly with some of the 2 tablespoons powdered sugar. (Wait to pipe the remaining batter until just before baking so the batter does not deflate while standing.)

5 Bake for 5 to 6 minutes or until lightly browned. Cool on cookie sheet for 10 minutes. Transfer cookies to a wire rack; cool.

6 Spoon filling into a decorating bag fitted with a small tip. Pipe filling onto bottoms of half the cookies. Top with the remaining cookies, bottom sides down.

to store: Layer unfilled cookies between sheets of waxed paper in an airtight container; cover. Store in the refrigerator up to 2 days. Fill as directed.

nutrition facts per sandwich cookie: 258 cal., 5 g total fat (3 g sat. fat), 65 mg chol., 62 mg sodium, 50 g carb., 1 g fiber, 3 g pro.

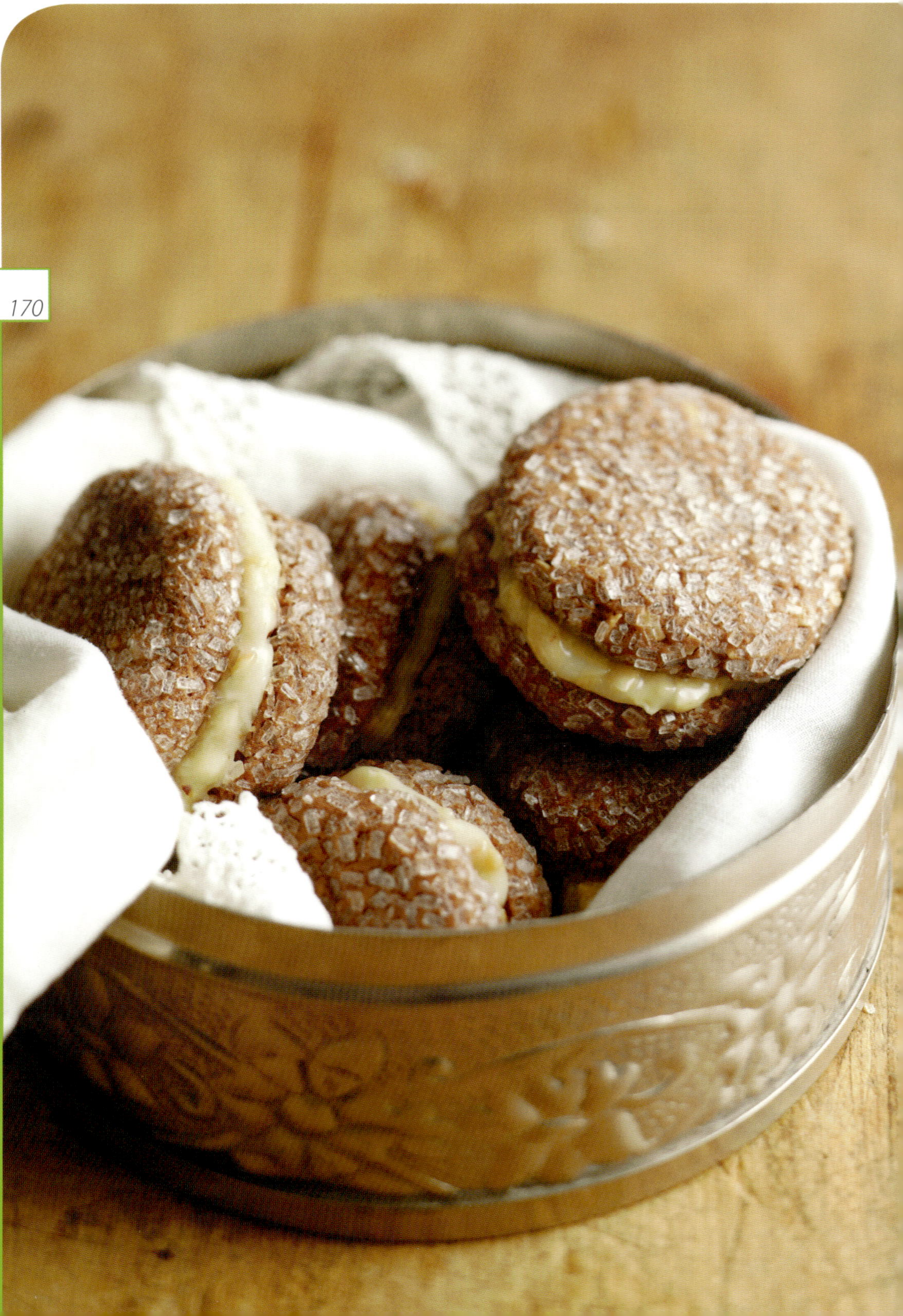

You could fill these sandwich cookies with your favorite frosting, homemade or canned.

little hazelnut-chocolate cookie sandwiches

prep: 30 minutes **chill:** 1 hour **bake:** 6 minutes at 350°F per batch
makes: 48 sandwich cookies

1⅓ cups all-purpose flour
¼ cup unsweetened cocoa powder
¼ teaspoon salt
¾ cup butter, softened
½ cup powdered sugar
1 teaspoon vanilla
1 egg
½ cup finely chopped hazelnuts (filberts), toasted (see tip, page 70)
    Coarse sugar
1 recipe White Chocolate-Hazelnut Filling

1 In a medium bowl stir together flour, cocoa powder, and salt; set aside. In a large mixing bowl beat butter with an electric mixer on medium to high speed for 30 seconds. Add powdered sugar and vanilla. Beat until combined, scraping sides of bowl occasionally. Beat in egg until combined. Beat in as much of the flour mixture as you can with the mixer. Using a wooden spoon, stir in any remaining flour mixture and the hazelnuts. Cover and chill about 1 hour or until dough is easy to handle.

2 Preheat oven to 350°F. Place coarse sugar in a small bowl. Shape dough into ¾-inch balls. Roll balls in coarse sugar to coat. Place balls 1½ inches apart on an ungreased cookie sheet. Using the bottom of a glass, flatten balls into circles, about 1¼ inches in diameter.

3 Bake for 6 to 8 minutes or just until tops are firm. Transfer cookies to a wire rack; cool.

4 Spread a rounded ½ teaspoon of the White Chocolate-Hazelnut Filling onto bottoms of half the cookies. Top with the remaining cookies, bottom sides down.

nutrition facts per sandwich cookie: 87 cal., 6 g total fat (3 g sat. fat), 14 mg chol., 39 mg sodium, 6 g carb., 0 g fiber, 1 g pro.

white chocolate-hazelnut filling: In a small saucepan heat and stir 6 ounces white chocolate, chopped, and 3 tablespoons whipping cream over low heat just until melted. Remove from heat. Stir in ½ cup finely chopped hazelnuts (filberts), toasted (see tip, page 70).

When shopping for vanilla beans, look for moist plump beans, not pods that are brittle or dry. And you should be able to detect a deep vanilla aroma.

vanilla bean shortbread sandwiches with vanilla bean buttercream

prep: 35 minutes bake: 16 minutes at 325°F per batch
makes: 24 sandwich cookies

½   split vanilla bean
      (see page 12) or
      1 teaspoon vanilla
1¼ cups all-purpose flour
3   tablespoons
      granulated sugar
½   cup butter
1   recipe Vanilla Bean
      Buttercream

vanilla bean buttercream:
Scrape seeds from one-fourth split vanilla bean with the tip of a small sharp knife; set aside. (Or substitute ½ teaspoon vanilla for the vanilla seeds.) In a small mixing bowl beat 2 tablespoons butter, softened, with an electric mixer on medium speed until smooth. Add ½ cup powdered sugar, 2 teaspoons milk, and the vanilla seeds or vanilla; beat until smooth. Beat in an additional ½ cup powdered sugar and, if necessary, enough milk (1 teaspoon) to reach piping consistency.

1 Preheat oven to 325°F. If using vanilla bean, scrape seeds from vanilla bean with the tip of a small sharp knife. Set aside.

2 In a large bowl stir together flour and sugar. Using a pastry blender, cut in the butter and the vanilla seeds or vanilla until mixture resembles fine crumbs and starts to cling (dough will appear dry). Form dough into a ball and knead until smooth.

3 On a lightly floured surface, roll dough into an 8×6-inch. Using a fluted pastry wheel or a knife, cut dough into forty-eight 1-inch squares. Place squares 1 inch apart on an ungreased cookie sheet. If desired, prick tops of squares with a fork.

4 Bake for 16 to 18 minutes or until edges are firm. Cool on cookie sheet for 5 minutes. Transfer cookies to a wire rack; cool.

5 Spoon Vanilla Bean Buttercream into a decorating bag fitted with a small star tip. Pipe buttercream on bottoms of half the cookies. Top with the remaining cookies, bottom sides down.

to store: Layer filled cookies between sheets of waxed paper in an airtight container; cover. Store in the refrigerator up to 3 days or freeze up to 3 months. Let stand at room temperature for 30 minutes before serving.

nutrition facts per sandwich cookie: 93 cal., 5 g total fat (3 g sat. fat), 13 mg chol., 43 mg sodium, 12 g carb., 0 g fiber, 1 g pro.

Ground chipotle is made from smoked jalapeño peppers, so the minuscle amount used here adds a touch of heat to the cookie batter.

mexican chipotle-chocolate bites

prep: 30 minutes **chill:** 1 hour **bake:** 6 minutes at 350°F per batch
makes: 25 sandwich cookies

9 ounces Mexican-style sweet chocolate or semisweet chocolate, chopped
2 tablespoons whipping cream
1 tablespoon butter
¼ cup butter, softened
¼ cup shortening
2 ounces cream cheese, softened
1 cup packed brown sugar
½ to 1 teaspoon ground chipotle chile pepper
½ teaspoon baking powder
½ teaspoon salt
½ teaspoon ground cinnamon
¼ teaspoon ground nutmeg
1 egg
2 teaspoons vanilla
2½ cups all-purpose flour
Ground chipotle chile pepper (optional)

1 For filling, in a small heavy saucepan heat and stir 6 ounces of the chocolate, the whipping cream, and the 1 tablespoon butter over low heat until chocolate is melted. Transfer to a medium mixing bowl. Cover and chill about 1 hour or until nearly firm. Beat with an electric mixer on medium to high speed until light and fluffy.

2 Preheat oven to 350°F. Line a cookie sheet with parchment paper; set aside. In a large mixing bowl beat the ¼ cup softened butter, the shortening, and cream cheese on medium to high speed for 30 seconds. Add brown sugar, the ½ to 1 teaspoon ground chipotle pepper, the baking powder, salt, cinnamon, and nutmeg. Beat until combined, scraping sides of bowl occasionally. Beat in egg and vanilla until combined. Beat in as much of the flour as you can with the mixer. Using a wooden spoon, stir in any remaining flour and the remaining 3 ounces chocolate.

3 Shape dough into 1-inch balls. Place balls 1 inch apart on the prepared cookie sheet. Using the bottom of a glass, flatten balls to ¼-inchness thick. If desired, sprinkle with additional ground chipotle pepper.

4 Bake for 6 to 8 minutes or until edges are set. Cool on cookie sheet for 2 minutes. Transfer cookies to a wire rack; cool.

5 Spread filling onto bottoms of half the cookies. Top with the remaining cookies, bottom sides down.

nutrition facts per sandwich cookie: 177 cal., 7 g total fat (4 g sat. fat), 18 mg chol., 90 mg sodium, 26 g carb., 1 g fiber, 2 g pro.

hazelnut shortbread sandwich cookies

prep: 30 minutes **freeze:** 30 minutes **bake:** 12 minutes at 350°F per batch
makes: 25 sandwich cookies

2   cups all-purpose flour
1   cup hazelnuts
      (filberts), coarsely
      chopped
½   teaspoon salt
1   cup unsalted butter,
      softened
¾   cup powdered sugar
½   cup purchased
      chocolate-hazelnut
      spread
2   to 4 tablespoons
      whipping cream

1 In a food processor combine flour, ½ cup of the coarsely chopped hazelnuts, and the salt. Cover and process about 1 minute or until nuts are finely ground. Transfer flour mixture to a medium bowl. In the processor combine butter and powdered sugar. Cover and process until smooth. Add flour mixture. Cover and process with on/off pulses just until a dough forms, scraping down sides of bowl as necessary. Add the remaining ½ cup coarsely chopped hazelnuts. Cover and process with on/off pulses until combined. Divide dough in half. Shape each half into an 8-inch log. Wrap each log in plastic wrap or waxed paper. Freeze about 30 minutes or until firm.

2 Preheat oven to 350° F. Line a large cookie sheet with parchment paper. Cut log into ¼-inch slices. Place slices 1 inch apart on the prepared cookie sheet.

3 Bake for 12 to 15 minutes or just until edges are golden. Cool on cookie sheet on a wire rack.

4 For ganache, in a small microwave-safe bowl microwave the chocolate-hazelnut spread on 100 percent power (high) about 1 minute or until warm, stirring once. Stir 2 tablespoons of the whipping cream into the chocolate-hazelnut spread. If necessary, stir in additional whipping cream, a small amount at a time, to reach spreading consistency.

5 Spread 1 teaspoon of the ganache onto bottoms of half the cookies. Top with the remaining cookies, bottom sides down.

nutrition facts per sandwich cookie: 188 cal., 13 g total fat (6 g sat. fat), 21 mg chol., 51 mg sodium, 16 g carb., 1 g fiber, 2 g pro.

Mascarpone lends a mild butteriness taste to the citrus filling.

rosemary-lemon sandwich cookies

prep: 30 minutes **bake:** 8 minutes at 400°F per batch
makes: 20 sandwich cookies

1   cup unsalted butter, softened
¾   cup granulated sugar
2   teaspoons snipped fresh rosemary
2   teaspoons finely shredded lemon peel
½   teaspoon baking powder
¼   teaspoon salt
1   teaspoon vanilla
2¼ cups all-purpose flour
      Granulated sugar
½   cup lemon curd
½   cup mascarpone
1   tablespoon powdered sugar (optional)

1 Preheat oven to 400°F. Line a cookie sheet with parchment paper; set aside. In a large mixing bowl beat butter with an electric mixer on medium to high speed for 30 seconds. Add the ¾ cup granulated sugar, the rosemary, lemon peel, baking powder, and salt. Beat until combined, scraping sides of bowl occasionally. Beat in vanilla. Beat in as much of the flour as you can with the mixer. Using a wooden spoon, stir in any remaining flour.

2 Shape dough into 1-inch balls. Place balls 2 inches apart on the prepared cookie sheet. Using the bottom of a glass dipped in additional granulated sugar, flatten each ball to ½-inch thickness.

3 Bake about 8 minutes or until bottoms are lightly browned. Cool on cookie sheet for 1 minute. Transfer cookies to a wire rack; cool.

4 For filling, in a small bowl combine lemon curd and mascarpone. Spread filling onto bottoms of half the cookies. Top with the remaining cookies, bottom sides down. If desired, sprinkle with powdered sugar.

to store: Layer sandwich cookies between sheets of waxed paper in an airtight container; cover. Store in the refrigerator up to 24 hours. Let stand at room temperature for 30 minutes before serving.

nutrition facts per sandwich cookie: 215 cal., 12 g total fat (8 g sat. fat), 38 mg chol., 49 mg sodium, 25 g carb., 1 g fiber, 2 g pro.

For adult brownie lovers, this is the one! Pictured on page 157.

mascarpone-filled brownie sandwiches

prep: 30 minutes   **bake:** 8 minutes at 375°F per batch
makes: 12 sandwich cookies

5 ounces semisweet chocolate, chopped
2 ounces unsweetened chocolate, chopped
2 tablespoons butter
¼ cup all-purpose flour
¼ teaspoon baking powder
¼ teaspoon salt
¼ teaspoon instant espresso coffee powder or instant coffee crystals
2 eggs
⅔ cup granulated sugar
1½ teaspoons vanilla
¾ cup miniature semisweet chocolate pieces
1 8-ounce carton mascarpone cheese
2 tablespoons powdered sugar
1 tablespoon whipping cream

1 In a small heavy saucepan heat and stir semisweet chocolate, unsweetened chocolate, and butter over low heat until melted and smooth; cool slightly. In a small bowl stir together flour, baking powder, salt, and coffee powder; set aside.

2 In a medium mixing bowl beat eggs, granulated sugar, and 1 teaspoon of vanilla with an electric mixer on high speed about 4 minutes or until thickened and light yellow. Fold in melted chocolate mixture. Fold in flour mixture until combined. Fold in semisweet chocolate pieces. Let stand for 10 minutes (batter will thicken as it stands).

3 Preheat oven to 375°F. Line a cookie sheet with parchment paper. Drop batter by slightly rounded tablespoons 2 inches apart onto the prepared cookie sheet. Bake about 8 minutes or until cookies are set and tops are crackled. Cool on cookie sheet for 1 minute. Transfer cookies to a wire rack; cool.

4 For filling, in a small bowl stir together mascarpone, powdered sugar, whipping cream, and the remaining ½ teaspoon vanilla until smooth. Spread about 1 tablespoon of filling onto bottoms of half the cookies. Top with the remaining cookies, bottom sides down

to store: Layer sandwich cookies between sheets of waxed paper in an airtight container; cover. Store in the refrigerator up to 3 days or freeze up to 1 month.

nutrition facts per sandwich cookie: 328 cal., 21 g total fat (13 g sat. fat), 62 mg chol., 101 mg sodium, 34 g carb., 2 g fiber, 7 g pro.

lemon curd linzer stars

prep: 45 minutes   **chill:** 2 hours   **bake:** 8 minutes at 350°F per batch
makes: 20 sandwich cookies

1   cup coarsely chopped pecans or almonds, toasted (see tip, page 13)
2½   cups all-purpose flour
¼   teaspoon salt
1   cup butter, softened
¾   cup granulated sugar
1   egg
1   teaspoon vanilla
½   teaspoon finely shredded lemon peel
1   recipe Powdered Sugar Icing or powdered sugar Jimmies, nonpareils, yellow sugar, and/ or edible glitter (optional)
½   cup lemon curd

powdered sugar icing:
In a small bowl combine 2 cups powdered sugar, 2 tablespoons milk, and 1 tablespoon light-color corn syrup. Stir in enough additional milk, 1 teaspoon at a time, to reach thick drizzling consistency.

1 Place nuts in a food processor. Cover and process with on/off pulses until finely ground. Transfer ground nuts to a small bowl. Stir in flour and salt; set aside.

2 In a large mixing bowl beat butter and granulated sugar with an electric mixer on medium speed until light and fluffy. Add egg, vanilla, and lemon peel. Beat until combined, scraping sides of bowl occasionally. Beat in as much of the flour mixture as you can with the mixer. Using a wooden spoon, stir in any remaining flour mixture. Divide dough in half. Cover and chill about 2 hours or until dough is easy to handle.

3 Preheat oven to 350°F. On a lightly floured surface roll one portion of the dough at a time tp ¼-inch thickness. Using a 2½- to 3-inch star-shape cookie cutter, cut out dough. Using a 1-inch star-shape cookie cutter, cut a star from the center of half the cookies.* Place cookies 1 inch apart on an ungreased cookie sheet.

4 Bake for 8 to 12 minutes or until edges are lightly browned and centers are set. Cool on cookie sheet for 1 minute. Transfer to a wire rack; cool.

5 Dip the tops of half the cutout star cookies in Powdered Sugar Icing and, if desired, sprinkle with jimmies, nonpareils, yellow sugar, and/ or edible glitter. (Or sprinkle tops of cutout cookies with powdered sugar.) Let stand on a wire rack set over waxed paper until icing is set. Spread about 1 teaspoon of the lemon curd on bottoms of the whole cookies (without icing). Top with the iced cutout cookies, bottom sides down.

*tip: Bake the small star cutouts separately or reroll with the remaining dough.

nutrition facts per sandwich cookie: 286 cal., 14 g total fat (6 g sat. fat), 40 mg chol., 122 mg sodium, 39 g carb., 2 g fiber, 3 g pro.

Ricotta cheese is a traditional ingredient in Italy's cannoli.

pistachio macarons with cannoli cream

prep: 35 minutes **stand:** 30 minutes **bake:** 9 minutes at 325°F per batch
makes: 30 sandwich cookies

1½   cups finely ground pistachio nuts
1¼   cups powdered sugar
 3   egg whites
 ½   teaspoon vanilla
     Salt
 ¼   cup granulated sugar
 2   to 4 green drops food coloring (optional)
 1   recipe Cannoli Cream

1 Line three large cookie sheets with parchment paper; set aside. In a medium bowl stir together pistachio nuts and powdered sugar; set aside.

2 In a large mixing bowl combine egg whites, vanilla, and salt. Beat with an electric mixer on medium speed until frothy. Gradually add granulated sugar, about 1 tablespoon at a time, beating on high speed just until soft peaks form (tips curl). Stir in nut mixture and, if desired, food coloring.

3 Spoon batter into a large pastry bag fitted with a large (about ½ inch) round tip.* Pipe 1½-inch circles 1 inch apart onto the prepared cookie sheets. Let stand for 30 minutes.

4 Preheat oven to 325°F. Bake for 9 to 10 minutes or until set. Cool cookies on cookie sheets on wire racks. Carefully peel cookies off parchment paper. Spread Cannoli Cream on bottoms of half the cookies. Top with the remaining cookies, bottom sides down.

cannoli cream: In a medium mixing bowl combine 4 ounces cream cheese, softened, and ¼ cup granulated sugar. Beat with an electric mixer on medium speed until combined. Beat in ½ cup ricotta cheese until combined. Stir in ¼ cup miniature semisweet chocolate pieces.

*tip: If you don't have a pastry bag, spoon batter into a large resealable plastic bag and snip off ½-inch from one corner of the bag.

to store: Layer unfilled cookies between sheets of waxed paper in an airtight container; cover. Store in the refrigerator up to 3 days or freeze up to 3 months. Thaw cookies, if frozen. Fill as directed in Step 4.

nutrition facts per sandwich cookie: 100 cal., 5 g total fat (2 g sat. fat), 6 mg chol., 27 mg sodium, 12 g carb., 1 g fiber, 2 g pro.

Like meringue cookies, macarons are a good choice for gluten-free desserts.

filled cherry macarons

prep: 35 minutes **stand:** 30 minutes **bake:** 11 minutes at 325°F per batch
makes: 22 sandwich cookies

1½ cups finely ground almonds (about 6 ounces)
1¼ cups powdered sugar
3 egg whites
½ teaspoon vanilla
¼ teaspoon salt
¼ cup granulated sugar
4 to 5 drops red food coloring
1 recipe Cherry Buttercream Filling

1 Line cookie sheets with parchment paper. Draw 1½-inch circles about 1½ inches apart on the parchment paper. Turn paper over; set cookie sheets aside.

2 In a medium bowl stir together the almonds and powdered sugar. In a large mixing bowl combine egg whites, vanilla, and salt. Beat with an electric mixer on medium speed until frothy. Gradually add the granulated sugar, 1 tablespoon at a time, beating on high speed until soft peaks form (tips curl). Gently stir in food coloring. Fold in nut mixture.

3 Transfer meringue to a large pastry bag fitted with a ½-inch round tip. Pipe 1½-inch flat circles into drawn circles on parchment paper. Let stand for 30 minutes before baking (meringue should feel dry to the touch).

4 Preheat oven to 325°F. Bake for 11 to 12 minutes or until set. Using parchment paper, lift and transfer macaros to a wire rack; cool. Carefully peel cooled macarons off parchment paper.

5 Spread Cherry Buttercream Filling on flat sides (bottoms) of half the cooled macarons. Gently press the flat sides of the remaining macarons against the filling.

to store: Place unfilled macarons between sheets of waxed paper in an airtight container; cover. Store at room temperature up to 1 week or freeze up to 3 months. Fill cookies just before serving.

nutrition facts per sandwich cookie: 140 cal., 5 g total fat (1 g sat. fat), 4 mg chol., 48 mg sodium, 23 g carb., 1 g fiber, 2 g pro.

cherry buttercream filling: In a medium mixing bowl combine ½ cup cream cheese, softened; 2 tablespoons butter, softened; and 1 tablespoon honey. Beat with an electric mixer on medium speed until combined. Gradually beat in 2 cups powdered sugar. Using paper towels, pat dry ¼ cup finely snipped maraschino cherries. Stir in cherries and 1 to 2 tablespoons maraschino cherry juice (1 teaspoon at a time) to make a spreadable filling.

Because a medley of cinnamon, allspice, ginger, and nutmeg is in both pumpkin pie spice and apple pie spice, they are interchangable here.

pumpkin spice macarons

prep: 45 minutes **stand:** 30 minutes **bake:** 9 minutes at 325°F per batch
makes: 30 sandwich cookies

1½ cups finely ground almonds
1¼ cups powdered sugar
1 teaspoon pumpkin pie spice or apple pie spice
3 egg whites
½ teaspoon vanilla
Dash salt
¼ cup granulated sugar
8 drops yellow food coloring
2 drops red food coloring
½ cup pumpkin butter or apple butter

1 Line three large cookie sheets with parchment paper; set aside. In a medium bowl stir together almonds, powdered sugar, and pumpkin pie spice; set aside.

2 In a large mixing bowl combine egg whites, vanilla, and salt. Beat with an electric mixer on medium speed until frothy. Gradually add granulated sugar, about 1 tablespoon at a time, beating on high speed just until soft peaks form (tips curl). Stir in nut mixture and food coloring.

3 Spoon batter into a large decorating bag fitted with a large (about ½-inch) round tip.* Pipe 1½-inch circles 1 inch apart onto the prepared cookie sheets. Let stand for 30 minutes before baking.

4 Preheat oven to 325°F. Bake for 9 to 10 minutes or until set. Cool on cookie sheets on wire racks. Carefully peel macarons off parchment paper.

5 Spread pumpkin butter on bottoms of half the macarons. Top with the remaining macarons, bottom sides down.

*tip: If you don't have a decorating bag, spoon batter into a large resealable plastic bag; snip off ½-inch from one corner of the bag.

to store: Layer unfilled macarons between sheets of waxed paper in an airtight container; cover. Store in the refrigerator up to 3 days or freeze up to 3 months. To serve, thaw macarons if frozen. Fill as directed in Step 5.

nutrition facts per sandwich cookie: 65 cal., 2 g total fat (0 g sat fat), 0 mg chol., 17 mg sodium, 11 g carb., 1 g fiber, 1 g pro.

lemon macarons with cranberry-mascarpone filling

prep: 40 minutes stand: 30 minutes bake: 9 minutes at 325°F per batch
makes: 12 sandwich cookies

1½ cups finely ground almonds
1¼ cups powdered sugar
3   egg whites
½   teaspoon vanilla
¼   teaspoon salt
¼   cup granulated sugar
1   teaspoon finely shredded lemon peel
1   recipe Cranberry-Mascarpone Filling

1 Line three large cookie sheets with parchment paper; set aside. In a medium bowl stir together almonds and powdered sugar; set aside.

2 In a large mixing bowl combine egg whites, vanilla, and salt. Beat with an electric mixer on medium speed until frothy. Gradually add granulated sugar, about 1 tablespoon at a time, beating on high speed just until soft peaks form (tips curl). Stir in almond mixture and lemon peel.

3 Using a large pastry bag fitted with a ½-inch round tip, pipe batter into 2-inch flat circles onto prepared cookie sheets, leaving 1 inch between circles. Let stand for 30 minutes before baking.

4 Preheat oven to 325°F. Bake, one sheet at a time, for 9 to 10 minutes or until set. Cool on cookie sheet on a wire rack. Carefully peel cookies off parchment paper.

5 Spread Cranberry-Mascarpone Filling on bottoms of half the macarons. Top with remaining macarons, bottom sides down.

to store: Layer unfilled macarons between waxed paper in an airtight container; cover. Store at room temperature up to 3 days or freeze up to 3 months. To serve, thaw cookies if frozen. Fill macarons as directed in Step 5. (You may store leftover filled macarons in the refrigerator, but they will be less crisp.)

nutrition facts per sandwich cookie: 216 cal., 9 g total fat (2 g sat. fat), 9 mg chol., 74 mg sodium, 32 g carb., 2 g fiber, 4 g pro.

cranberry-mascarpone filling: In a medium mixing bowl beat ¼ cup mascarpone or cream cheese, softened; 1 tablespoon butter, softened; and 1 tablespoon honey with an electric mixer on medium speed until smooth. Gradually add 1 cup powdered sugar, beating well. Stir in 2 tablespoons finely snipped dried cranberries or cherries, and ½ teaspoon finely shredded lemon peel. Stir in enough food coloring to tint the filling pink. Stir in enough lemon juice (2 to 4 teaspoons) to make filling spreading consistency.

spearmint whoopie pies with white chocolate-mascarpone filling

prep: 40 minutes **bake:** 7 minutes at 375°F per batch
makes: 36 sandwich cookies

1   recipe White
    Chocolate-
    Mascarpone
    Filling (see recipe,
    page 185)
½   cup butter, softened
1   cup granulated sugar
½   teaspoon baking soda
¼   teaspoon salt
1   egg
1   teaspoon vanilla
½   teaspoon mint extract
2   cups all-purpose flour
½   cup buttermilk or
    sour milk (see tip,
    page 12)
    Green food coloring
    Round striped
    spearmint candies,
    crushed (optional)

1 Prepare and chill White Chocolate-Mascarpone Filling.

2 In a large mixing bowl beat butter with an electric mixer on medium to high speed for 30 seconds. Add sugar, baking soda, and salt. Beat until combined, scraping sides of bowl occasionally. Beat in egg, vanilla, and mint extract until combined. Alternately add flour and buttermilk to butter mixture, beating on low speed after each addition just until combined. Stir in desired amount of green food coloring. If necessary, cover and chill for 1 to 2 hours or until dough is easy to handle.

3 Preheat oven to 375°F. Line a cookie sheet with parchment paper. Drop dough by rounded teaspoons 2 inches apart onto the prepared cookie sheet.

4 Bake for 7 to 8 minutes or until edges are set. Cool on cookie sheet for 2 minutes. Transfer cookies to a wire rack; cool.

5 Pipe or spread a thick layer of filling on bottoms of half the cookies. Top with the remaining cookies, bottom sides down. If desired, roll edges of whoopie pies in crushed candies.

to store: Layer sandwich cookies between sheets of waxed paper in an airtight container; cover. Store in the refrigerator up to 3 days. Let stand at room temperature for 15 minutes before serving.

nutrition facts per sandwich cookie: 169 cal., 7 g total fat (4 g sat. fat), 22 mg chol., 78 mg sodium, 26 g carb., 0 g fiber, 1 g pro.

Marshmallow creme is the key ingredient in these delightful treats.

classic whoopie pies

prep: 20 minutes   bake: 10 minutes at 350°F per batch
makes: 16 whoopie pies

1   recipe Creamy Filling
2¼   cups all-purpose flour
⅔   cup unsweetened cocoa powder
½   cup shortening
1   cup granulated sugar
1   teaspoon baking soda
⅛   teaspoon salt
1   egg
1¼   cups buttermilk or sour milk (see tip, page 12)
1   teaspoon vanilla

1 Prepare Creamy Filling. Cover and chill as directed.

2 Preheat oven to 350°F. In a medium bowl stir together flour and cocoa powder; set aside. In a large mixing bowl beat shortening with an electric mixer on medium to high speed for 30 seconds. Add sugar, baking soda, and salt. Beat until combined, scraping sides of bowl occasionally. Beat in egg, buttermilk, and vanilla until combined. Beat in as much of the flour mixture as you can with the mixer. Using a wooden spoon, stir in any remaining flour mixture.

3 Drop dough by rounded tablespoons 2½ inches apart onto an ungreased cookie sheet.* Bake about 10 minutes or until edges are firm. Cool on cookie sheet for 2 minutes. Transfer cookies to a wire rack; cool.

4 Spread 1 rounded tablespoon of the filling on bottoms of half the cookies. Top with the remaining cookies, bottom sides down.

*tip: Try to keep mounds of dough nicely rounded.

to store: Place whoopie pies in a single layer in an airtight container; cover. Store in the refrigerator up to 1 week.

nutrition facts per whoopie pie: 329 cal., 13 g total fat (6 g sat. fat), 28 mg chol., 174 mg sodium, 52 g carb., 2 g fiber, 4 g pro.

creamy filling: In a large mixing bowl combine ½ cup butter, softened; 1¾ cups powdered sugar; one 7-ounce jar marshmallow creme; and 1 teaspoon vanilla. Beat with an electric mixer on medium speed for 2 minutes or until smooth. Cover; chill until firm.

stuffed & filled

Purchase smooth applesauce, not chunky, for this fall snack.

apple whoopie pies

prep: 45 minutes **bake:** 10 minutes at 350°F per batch
makes: 36 whoopie pies

2   cups packed light brown sugar
¾   cup unsalted butter, softened
2   eggs
1   teaspoon vanilla
1½ cups unsweetened applesauce
¾   cup whipping cream
2¾ cups all-purpose flour
1   tablespoon ground cinnamon
1   teaspoon baking powder
1   teaspoon baking soda
1   teaspoon salt
1   recipe Fluffy Filling
    Apple peel ribbons (optional)

1 Preheat oven to 350°F. Line a large cookie sheet with parchment paper; set aside. In a large mixing bowl beat brown sugar and butter with an electric mixer on medium speed until fluffy. Add eggs and vanilla; beat until combined. Add applesauce and whipping cream; beat well. In a medium bowl combine flour, cinnamon, baking powder, baking soda, and salt. Gradually add flour mixture to the beaten mixture, beating until well mixed. Drop batter by spoonfuls about 2 inches apart onto prepared cookie sheet.

2 Bake for 10 to 12 minutes or until edges are lightly browned. Transfer to a wire rack; cool.

3 Spread Fluffy Filling on bottoms of half of the cooled cookies. Top with the remaining cookies, bottom sides down. Serve immediately or store in the refrigerator and serve within 24 hours.

nutrition facts per whoopie pie: 267 cal., 11 g total fat (7 g sat. fat), 43 mg chol., 160 mg sodium, 41 g carb., 1 g fiber, 2 g pro.

fluffy filling: In a medium bowl combine 1 cup butter, softened; ½ cup marshmallow creme; ¼ cup whole milk; ¼ cup all-purpose flour; and 1 teaspoon vanilla. Beat with an electric mixer on medium speed until well mixed. Gradually add 4 cups powdered sugar, 1 cup at a time, beating until well mixed and fluffy. Makes about 2⅔ cups.

This sophisticated version gives new meaning to the whimsical whoopie pie.

mini raspberry and white chocolate whoopie pies

prep: 1 hour bake: 7 minutes at 375°F per batch chill: 30 minutes
makes: 72 mini whoopie pies

½ cup butter, softened
1 cup granulated sugar
½ teaspoon baking soda
¼ teaspoon salt
1 egg
1 teaspoon vanilla
2 cups all-purpose flour
½ cup buttermilk or
    sour milk (see tip,
    page 12)
1 recipe White
    Chocolate and
    Mascarpone Filling
½ cup seedless
    raspberry preserves

1 Prepare and chill White Chocolate and Mascarpone Filling.

2 Preheat oven to 375°F. Line a cookie sheet with parchment paper; set aside.

3 In a large mixing bowl beat butter with an electric mixer on medium to high speed for 30 seconds. Add sugar, baking soda, and salt. Beat until combined, scraping sides of bowl occasionally. Beat in egg and vanilla until combined. Alternately add flour and buttermilk to butter mixture, beating on low speed after each addition just until combined. Drop dough by rounded teaspoons 1 inch apart onto the prepared cookie sheet.

4 Bake for 7 to 8 minutes or until tops are set. Cool on cookie sheet on a wire rack.

5 Spoon White Chocolate and Mascarpone Filling into a large decorating bag fitted with a small star tip. Peel cooled cookies off parchment paper. Spread about ¼ teaspoon of the raspberry preserves onto bottoms of half of the cookies; pipe filling onto preserves. Top with the remaining cookies, bottom sides down. Chill for 30 minutes before serving.

nutrition facts per whoopie pie: 91 cal., 3 g total fat (2 g sat. fat), 11 mg chol., 39 mg sodium, 15 g carb., 0 g fiber, 1 g pro.

white chocolate and mascarpone filling: In a heavy small saucepan combine 3 ounces white baking chocolate with cocoa butter, chopped, and ¼ cup whipping cream. Cook and stir over low heat until chocolate nearly melts. Remove from heat; stir until smooth. Cool for 15 minutes. Meanwhile, in a large mixing bowl beat ½ cup mascarpone cheese or cream cheese, softened, and ¼ cup butter, softened with an electric mixer on medium to high speed until smooth. Beat in ½ teaspoon vanilla. Gradually add 4 cups powdered sugar, beating well. Beat in the cooled white chocolate mixture. Chill about 30 minutes or until firm enough to pipe.

A tassie is like a ultra-mini version of your favorite pie, ready to eat in just one bite.

ultimate tassies

prep: 40 minutes **chill:** 1 hour **bake:** 6 minutes at 375°F per batch
makes: 24 cookies

½ cup butter, softened
1 3-ounce package cream cheese, softened
3 tablespoons unsweetened cocoa powder
1 tablespoon granulated sugar
1 cup all-purpose flour
½ cup peanut butter
⅓ cup butter, softened
1 teaspoon vanilla
2 cups powdered sugar
1 to 2 tablespoons milk
2 tablespoons unsweetened cocoa powder

1 In a medium mixing bowl beat ½ cup butter and cream cheese with an electric mixer on medium to high speed for 30 seconds. Add 3 tablespoons cocoa powder and granulated sugar. Beat until combined, scraping sides of bowl occasionally. Beat in as much of the flour as you can with the mixer. Using a wooden spoon, stir in any remaining flour (mixture will be crumbly). Form mixture into a ball. Cover and chill dough for 1 hour.

2 Preheat oven to 375°F. For pastry shells, divide dough into 24 pieces; shape each piece into a ball. Press a ball evenly onto the bottom and up the sides of each of 24 ungreased 1¾-inch muffin cups. Gently prick dough with a fork. Bake for 6 to 8 minutes or until pastry shells are set and dry (shells will puff during baking). Cool in muffin cups on wire racks for 5 minutes. Gently remove from cups; cool completely on racks.

3 For fillings, in a large mixing bowl combine peanut butter, ⅓ cup butter, and vanilla. Beat on medium speed for 30 seconds. Gradually beat in powdered sugar. Beat in enough of the milk to make a mixture of piping consistency.

4 Divide peanut butter mixture in half and place in separate bowls. Add 2 tablespoons cocoa powder to one portion; beat until combined. If necessary, beat in additional milk to make the cocoa mixture piping consistency.

5 In a large decorating bag fitted with a star tip, spread the cocoa filling down one half of the bag. Spread the peanut butter filling down the other half of the bag. Pipe swirls of the fillings into pastry shells.

nutrition facts per tassie: 163 cal., 11 g total fat (5 g sat. fat), 21 mg chol., 93 mg sodium, 16 g carb., 1 g fiber, 2 g pro.

Tangerine or orange peel could be used in place of the clementine.

almond-clementine lace cookies

prep: 30 minutes **bake:** 7 minutes at 350°F per batch
makes: 20 cookies

⅓ cup granulated sugar
2 tablespoons butter, melted
2 tablespoons light-color corn syrup
1 teaspoon finely shredded clementine peel
1 tablespoon clementine juice or orange juice
½ cup finely chopped almonds
⅓ cup all-purpose flour
1 cup whipping cream
1 8-ounce carton sour cream
¾ cup powdered sugar
1 teaspoon finely shredded clementine peel
Finely shredded clementine peel (optional)

1 Preheat oven to 350°F. Line a cookie sheet with parchment paper; set aside.

2 In a small bowl combine granulated sugar, melted butter, corn syrup, 1 teaspoon clementine peel, and clementine juice. Stir in almonds and flour. Drop batter by rounded measuring teaspoons 3 inches apart onto the prepared cookie sheet. Bake only 3 or 4 cookies at a time. Bake for 7 to 8 minutes or until cookies are bubbly and deep golden brown.

3 Cool on cookie sheet for 1 to 2 minutes or just until set. Using a metal spatula, quickly remove cookies, one at a time, and drape over a greased wooden spoon handle. When the cookie is firm, slide the cookie off the spoon handle and place it on a wire rack to cool. (If cookies harden before you shape them, reheat them in the 350°F oven about 1 minute or until softened.)

4 Before serving, in a medium mixing bowl beat whipping cream, sour cream, powdered sugar, and 1 teaspoon clementine peel with an electric mixer on medium to high speed until soft peaks form (tips curl). Spoon mixture into a decorating bag fitted with a large star tip. Pipe mixture into cookies. If desired, sprinkle with additional clementine peel. Serve immediately.

to store: Layer unfilled cookies between sheets of waxed paper in an airtight container; cover. Store at room temperature up to 3 days or freeze up to 3 months. To serve, thaw cookies if frozen. Fill as directed.

nutrition facts per cookie: 134 cal., 9 g total fat (5 g sat. fat), 25 mg chol., 25 mg sodium, 13 g carb., 0 g fiber, 1 g pro.

Mexican chocolate flavored with cinnamon, almonds, and vanilla, is available at Latin markets and some supermarkets.

mexican-chocolate truffle tartlets

prep: 45 minutes   chill: 4 hours 30 minutes   bake: 6 minutes at 375°F per batch
stand: 30 minutes   makes: 24 tarlets

16   ounces Mexican-style sweet chocolate, coarsely chopped
½   cup whipping cream
6   tablespoons butter
2   tablespoons granulated sugar
     Nonstick cooking spray
⅔   cup all-purpose flour
¼   cup butter
1   egg yolk
     Unsweetened cocoa powder

1 Set aside ⅓ cup of the chocolate for pastry. For filling, in a small heavy saucepan heat and stir the remaining chocolate, the whipping cream, the 6 tablespoons butter, and the sugar over low heat just until chocolate is melted and sugar is dissolved. Transfer chocolate mixture to a medium mixing bowl. Cover and chill for 2½ to 3 hours or until firm.

2 Preheat oven to 375°F. Generously coat twenty-four 1¾-inch muffin cups with cooking spray; set aside. For pastry, place the reserved ⅓ cup chocolate in a small saucepan. Cook and stir over low heat just until melted (chocolate will be thick and grainy). Cool slightly.

3 Place flour in a medium bowl. Using a pastry blender, cut in the ¼ cup butter until pieces are pea size. In a small bowl combine egg yolk and melted chocolate. Stir egg yolk mixture into flour mixture (mixture will be crumbly). Knead just until smooth.

4 Divide pastry into 24 portions; shape into balls. Press balls onto the bottoms and up the sides of the prepared muffin cups. Bake for 6 to 8 minutes or until pastry is set. Cool in muffin cups on a wire rack for 5 minutes. Remove pastry shells from muffin cups. Cool completely on wire rack.

5 Beat filling with an electric mixer on medium speed about 2 minutes or until fluffy and lightened in color. Pipe or spoon filling into pastry shells. Cover and chill for at least 2 hours or until completely chilled. Let stand at room temperature for 30 minutes before serving. Lightly sprinkle tartlets lightly with cocoa powder.

nutrition facts per tartlet: 162 cal., 10 g total fat (6 g sat. fat), 28 mg chol., 37 mg sodium, 19 g carb., 1 g fiber, 1 g pro.

When fresh pomegranates aren't available, look for frozen pomegranate seeds in specialty markets.

pomegranate cream thimbles

prep: 45 minutes bake: 7 minutes at 350°F per batch
makes: 15 thimbles.

Nonstick cooking spray
4   sheets frozen phyllo
    dough (14×9-inch
    rectangles), thawed
2   tablespoons butter,
    melted
¼   cup whipped cream
    cheese
¼   cup pomegranate jelly
    or 2 tablespoons
    pomegranate
    molasses
2   tablespoons frozen
    whipped dessert
    topping, thawed
2   tablespoons
    pomegranate seeds
    Finely shredded lemon
    peel or diced candied
    lemon peel (optional)
1   recipe Pomegranate
    Syrup

1 For phyllo cups, preheat oven to 350°F. Coat fifteen 1¾-inch muffin cups with cooking spray; set aside. Keep phyllo dough covered with plastic wrap to prevent it from drying out. Lay one sheet of phyllo on a flat work surface. Lightly brush phyllo dough with some of the melted butter. Top with another phyllo sheet, brushing top with melted butter. Repeat with remaining phyllo sheets. Cut phyllo stack lengthwise into three 14-inch long strips. Cut each strip crosswise into five rectangles. Press each rectangle into a prepared cup, pleating as needed to fit. Bake for 7 to 9 minutes or until cups are golden brown. Carefully transfer cups to a wire rack to cool completely. (If you do not have 15 muffin cups, bake phyllo cups in batches. Cool muffin pan between batches.)

2 For filling, in a small bowl combine cream cheese and pomegranate jelly until smooth. Fold in whipped topping.

3 Spoon filling into phyllo cups. Garnish with pomegranate seeds and, if desired, lemon peel. Before serving, drizzle with Pomegranate Syrup.

nutrition facts per thimble: 85 cal., 3 g total fat (2 g sat. fat), 7 mg chol., 54 mg sodium, 15 g carb., 0 g fiber, 1 g pro.

make-ahead directions:
Place unfilled phyllo cups in a single layer in an airtight container; cover. Store at room temperature up to 2 days. Cover and store syrup and filling separately in the refrigerator up to 2 days. Before serving, fill and garnish phyllo cups as directed.

pomegranate syrup: In a small saucepan combine 1½ cups pomegranate juice, ¼ cup honey, and 1 tablespoon lemon juice. Bring to boiling over medium heat; reduce heat. Boil gently, uncovered, for 30 to 40 minutes or until syrup is reduced to ½ cup. Transfer syrup to a small bowl; cool. Cover and chill any remaining syrup up to 1 week.

Instead of making the dough from scratch, save time by buying 30 store-bought miniature phyllo dough shells.

browned butter-toffee tartlets

prep: 30 minutes **bake:** 15 minutes at 350°F per batch
makes: 24 tarlets

Nonstick cooking
    spray
12   sheets frozen phyllo
      dough (14×9-inch
      rectangles), thawed
¼   cup butter, melted
2   eggs, lightly beaten
½   cup granulated sugar
⅓   cup all-purpose flour
1½   teaspoons vanilla
¼   teaspoon salt
½   cup butter
¾   cup toffee pieces
    Chocolate-covered
      English toffee bars,
      chopped

1 Preheat oven to 350°F. Lightly coat twenty-four 1¾-inch muffin cups with cooking spray; set aside.

2 Unroll phyllo dough. Place one sheet of phyllo on a work surface. (While you work, keep the remaining phyllo covered with plastic wrap to prevent it from drying out.) Brush phyllo sheet with some of the ¼ cup melted butter. Top with three more phyllo sheets, brushing each sheet with melted butter. Trim edges to form a 12×8-inch rectangle. Cut phyllo stack into eight 4×3-inch rectangles. Repeat with the remaining phyllo and melted butter to make 24 rectangles total. Gently press rectangles into the prepared muffin cups, pleating as necessary to fit.

3 In a medium bowl whisk together eggs, sugar, flour, vanilla, and salt until combined; set aside.

4 In a small saucepan melt the ½ cup butter over medium heat. Reduce heat to medium-low. Cook, without stirring, for 5 to 6 minutes or until butter turns a light golden brown; cool slightly. Whisk browned butter into egg mixture. Spoon egg mixture into phyllo-lined muffin cups. Sprinkle with the ¾ cup toffee pieces.

5 Bake for 15 to 18 minutes or until tops are golden. Cool in muffin cups on a wire rack for 5 minutes. Carefully remove tartlets from muffin cups. Cool completely on wire rack.

6 Top with chopped toffee bars. Cover and chill within 2 hours.

nutrition facts per tartlet: 170 cal., 11 g total fat (6 g sat. fat), 40 mg chol., 167 mg sodium, 17 g carb., 0 g fiber, 1 g pro.

Making homemade lemon curd for the filling is worth the extra effort.

lemon tassies

prep: 40 minutes **bake:** 10 minutes at 375°F per batch **cool:** 10 minutes **chill:** 1 hour
makes: 36 tassies

1¼ cups all-purpose flour
1 cup granulated sugar
4 teaspoons finely
   shredded lemon peel
½ cup butter
1 egg yolk, lightly beaten
2 tablespoons water
1 tablespoon cornstarch
½ cup lemon juice
¼ cup water
2 tablespoons butter
3 egg yolks, lightly beaten
   Lemon peel strips
   (optional)

1 For pastry, in a medium bowl stir together flour, ⅓ cup of the sugar, and 2 teaspoons of the lemon peel. Using a pastry blender, cut in the ½ cup butter until mixture resembles coarse crumbs. In a small bowl combine 1 egg yolk and the 2 tablespoons water. Gradually stir egg yolk mixture into flour mixture. Knead gently to form a ball. If necessary, cover and chill for 30 to 60 minutes or until dough is easy to handle.

2 For filling, in a medium saucepan stir together the remaining ⅔ cup sugar and the cornstarch. Stir in the remaining 2 teaspoons lemon peel, the lemon juice, the ¼ cup water, and the 2 tablespoons butter. Cook and stir over medium heat until thickened and bubbly. Gradually stir about half the hot mixture into the 3 egg yolks. Return egg yolk mixture to saucepan. Bring to a gentle boil over medium heat; reduce heat. Cook and stir for 2 minutes. Transfer to a small bowl. Cover surface with plastic wrap and chill until needed.

3 Preheat oven to 375°F. Divide pastry into 36 portions; shape into balls. Press balls into the bottoms and up the sides of 36 ungreased 1¾-inch muffin cups. Bake about 10 minutes or until pastry is golden. Cool in muffin cups on wire racks for 10 minutes. Remove pastry shells from muffin cups.

4 Spoon 1 rounded teaspoon of the filling into each pastry shell. Cover and chill for 1 to 2 hours before serving. If desired, garnish with lemon peel strips.

to store: Place tassies in a single layer in an airtight container; cover. Store in refrigerator up to 3 days or freeze up to 3 months.

nutrition facts per tassie: 74 cal., 4 g total fat (2 g sat. fat), 32 mg chol., 24 mg sodium, 10 g carb., 0 g fiber, 0 g pro

Delicate almond pastry encases a cheesecake -filling and a burst of berry preserves.

almond and raspberry blossoms

prep: 35 minutes **chill:** 30 minutes **bake:** 25 minutes at 325°F per batch
makes: 24 cookies

1   cup all-purpose flour
½   cup ground slivered
      almonds
¼   cup granulated sugar
½   cup butter
1   egg yolk, lightly
      beaten
1   teaspoon water
1   3-ounce package
      cream cheese,
      softened
¼   cup butter, softened
2   tablespoons
      granulated sugar
1   egg
¼   teaspoon finely
      shredded orange
      peel
1   tablespoon orange
      juice
      Nonstick cooking
      spray
¼   cup seedless
      red raspberry
      or blackberry
      preserves
      Powdered sugar
24 raspberries or
      blackberries
      (optional)

1 In a medium bowl stir together flour, ¼ cup of the ground almonds, and the ¼ cup granulated sugar. Using a pastry blender, cut in the ½ cup butter until pieces are pea-size. In a small bowl combine egg yolk and 1 teaspoon water. Gradually stir yolk mixture into flour mixture, adding 1 to 2 teaspoons additional water if necessary, to make dough cling. Gently knead dough just until a ball forms. Wrap dough in plastic wrap and chill for 30 to 60 minutes or until dough is easy to handle.

2 Meanwhile, for filling, in a small mixing bowl beat cream cheese, the ¼ cup softened butter, and the 2 tablespoons granulated sugar with an electric mixer on medium speed until light and fluffy. Add egg, orange peel, and orange juice. Beat until combined, scraping sides of bowl occasionally. Stir in the remaining ¼ cup ground almonds.

3 Preheat oven to 325°F. Coat twenty-four 1¾-inch muffin cups with cooking spray. Divide dough into 24 portions; shape each portion into a ball. Press balls onto the bottoms and up the sides of the prepared muffin cups.

4 Spoon ½ teaspoon of the preserves into each pastry-lined muffin cup. Spoon filling over preserves. Bake about 25 minutes or until filling is set. Cool in muffin cups on a wire rack for 5 minutes. Remove cookies from muffin cups; cool on wire rack.

5 Before serving, sprinkle cookies lightly with powdered sugar. If desired, top each cookie with a raspberry.

nutrition facts per cookie: 121 cal., 8 g total fat (5 g sat. fat), 35 mg chol., 67 mg sodium, 10 g carb., 0 g fiber, 2 g pro.

Candied orange peel, homemade or purchased, adds a sweet contrast to the chocolate filling.

orange truffle cups

prep: 40 minutes chill: 30 minutes + 2 hours bake: 12 minutes at 375°F per batch
makes: 24 cookies

5 ounces sweet baking chocolate, chopped
½ cup whipping cream
2 tablespoons orange liqueur or orange juice
1 teaspoon vanilla
1½ cups all-purpose flour
¼ cup granulated sugar
1 teaspoon finely shredded orange peel
½ cup butter, cut up
2 egg yolks
1 recipe Candied Orange Peel and/or dark chocolate curls (optional)

1 For filling, in a medium microwave-safe bowl microwave sweet baking chocolate, whipping cream, and 1 tablespoon of the liqueur on 100 percent power (high) for 1 to 2 minutes or until chocolate is melted, stirring every 30 seconds. Stir in vanilla. Cover and chill for 30 to 60 minutes or until mixture is slightly thickened, stirring occasionally.

2 Meanwhile, preheat oven to 375°F. For pastry, in a food processor combine flour, sugar, and orange peel. Cover and process just until combined. Add butter; cover and process with on/off pulses until pieces are pea size. Add egg yolks and the remaining 1 tablespoon liqueur; cover and process just until combined. Divide pastry into 24 portions; shape into balls. Press balls onto the bottoms and up the sides of 24 ungreased 1¾-inch muffin cups.

3 Bake for 12 to 15 minutes or until pastry is light brown. Cool completely in muffin cups on a wire rack. Remove pastry shells from muffin cups.

4 Spoon filling into pastry shells. Cover and chill for at least 2 hours or until completely chilled. If desired, garnish with Candied Orange Peel and/or dark chocolate curls.

to store: Place tartlets in a single layer in an airtight container; cover. Store in the refrigerator up to 3 days or freeze up to 1 month.

nutrition facts per cookie: 122 cal., 8 g total fat (5 g sat. fat), 35 mg chol., 30 mg sodium, 12 g carb., 1 g fiber, 2 g pro.

candied orange peel: Score 1 medium orange into four lengthwise quarters, cutting just through the pulp to the surface of the fruit. Pry back the quartered peel with a spoon. Scrape off the soft, white bitter portions inside the peel. Cut orange peels into ⅛-inch strips. (Wrap and store peeled fruit in the refrigerator for another use.) Coat orange strips with ¼ cup granulated sugar. Heat a large skillet over medium-high heat. Add orange peel and cook until sugar is melted, stirring occasionally. Transfer orange peel to a sheet of parchment paper. Let stand to cool and set. If desired, roll orange peel in additional sugar.

This dessert will remind you of summer pie anytime of the year. Crumble any leftovers over vanilla ice cream.

cherry pie bites

prep: 30 minutes **bake:** 25 minutes at 325°F per batch
makes: 24 cookies

½ cup butter, softened
1 3-ounce package cream cheese, softened
1 cup all-purpose flour
2 tablespoons chopped walnuts or pecans, toasted (see tip, page 13)
2 tablespoons packed brown sugar
2 tablespoons all-purpose flour
⅛ teaspoon ground nutmeg
1½ tablespoons butter
2 cups fresh or frozen unsweetened pitted tart red cherries, thawed
⅓ cup granulated sugar
2 teaspoons cornstarch

1 Preheat oven to 325°F. In a medium mixing bowl beat the ½ cup butter and the cream cheese with an electric mixer on medium to high speed until combined. Stir in the 1 cup flour. Shape dough into 24 balls. Evenly press the balls into the bottoms and up the sides of 24 ungreased 1¾-inch muffin cups.

2 For streusel, stir together nuts, brown sugar, 2 tablespoons flour, and nutmeg. Using a pastry blender, cut in the 1½ tablespoons butter until mixture is crumbly. Set aside.

3 For filling, in a small saucepan combine the cherries, granulated sugar, and cornstarch. Cook over medium heat until cherries release juices, stirring occasionally. Continue to cook, stirring constantly, over medium heat until thickened and bubbly. Spoon about 1 heaping teaspoon of the filling into each pastry-lined cup. Evenly sprinkle filled cups with streusel.

4 Bake for 25 to 30 minutes or until edges are golden brown. Cool bites in pan on a wire rack for 5 minutes. Carefully transfer to a wire rack; cool.

to store: Place bites in a single layer in an airtight container; cover. Store in the refrigerator up to 2 days or freeze up to 2 months.

nutrition facts per cookie: 100 cal., 6 g total fat (4 g sat. fat), 16 mg chol., 52 mg sodium, 10 g carb., 0 g fiber, 1 g pro.

chewy chocolate-caramel
bars, page 210

express

trea

When you crave a home-baked sweet or are asked to show up with a tray of cookies, these streamlined recipes will save the day, without hours of work. Just doctor up purchased cookie dough or a dry mix, then pop the treats in the oven. Go ahead, call it homemade—the enticing aroma in the kitchen is proof!

Also try with frozen unsweetened blueberries.

cherry crumb bars

prep: 20 minutes **bake:** 45 minutes at 350°F
makes: 16 bars

Nonstick cooking
    spray
1 17.5-ounce package
    oatmeal cookie mix
½ cup butter
1 egg, lightly beaten
1 teaspoon vanilla
½ teaspoon almond
    extract
1 16-ounce package
    frozen unsweetened
    pitted tart red
    cherries, thawed
    and drained
¼ cup granulated sugar
1 recipe Powdered
    Sugar Icing

1 Preheat oven to 350°F. Line a 9×9×2-inch baking pan with foil, extending the foil over edges of pan. Lightly coat foil with cooking spray; set pan aside.

2 For crust, place cookie mix in a large bowl. Using a pastry blender, cut in butter until mixture resembles coarse crumbs. Remove 1 cup of the crumb mixture for topping. Stir egg, vanilla, and almond extract into the remaining crumb mixture until combined. Press evenly onto the bottom of the prepared baking pan.

3 In a medium bowl stir together cherries and sugar; spoon evenly over layer in pan. Sprinkle with the reserved crumb mixture.

4 Bake about 45 minutes or until topping is golden. Cool in pan on a wire rack. Drizzle with Powdered Sugar Icing. Let stand until icing is set. Using the edges of the foil, lift uncut bars out of pan. Cut into bars.

to store: Place bars in a single layer in an airtight container; cover. Store in the refrigerator up to 3 days or freeze up to 3 months.

nutrition facts per bar: 240 cal., 12 g total fat (5 g sat. fat), 27 mg chol., 202 mg sodium, 31 g carb., 0 g fiber, 3 g pro.

powdered sugar icing: In a small bowl stir together ½ cup powdered sugar, ½ teaspoon vanilla, and enough milk (1 to 2 teaspoons) to make icing drizzling consistency.

Discriminating dessert lovers will never guess you got a head start with a cookie mix.

viennese almond bars

prep: 25 minutes   bake: 40 minutes at 350°F
makes: 30 bars

1   17.5-ounce package sugar cookie mix
½   8-ounce package cream cheese
¼   cup butter
½   cup sliced almonds, toasted (see tip, page 13) and finely chopped
1   8-ounce can almond paste
¼   cup granulated sugar
1   egg
2   to 3 tablespoons milk
⅔   cup seedless raspberry preserves
¼   cup sliced almonds, toasted (see tip, page 13)

1 Preheat oven to 350°F. Line a 13×9×2-inch baking pan with foil, extending the foil over edges of pan. Lightly grease foil; set pan aside.

2 Place cookie mix in a large bowl. Using a pastry blender, cut in cream cheese and butter until mixture resembles coarse crumbs. Stir in ½ cup chopped almonds. Remove about 1 cup of the crumb mixture for topping. Press the remaining crumb mixture evenly onto the bottom of the prepared baking pan. Bake 15 minutes or until set.

3 Meanwhile, in a large mixing bowl beat almond paste, sugar, and egg with an electric mixer on medium speed until combined. Beat in enough milk, 1 tablespoon at a time, to reach spreading consistency. Carefully spread almond mixture over crust to within ¼ inch of the edges. Stir preserves; carefully spread over almond mixture. Sprinkle with the reserved crumb mixture and the ¼ cup almonds.

4 Bake for 25 to 30 minutes or until topping is lightly browned. Cool in pan on a wire rack. Using the edges of the foil, lift uncut bars out of pan. Cut into diamond-shape or square bars.

nutrition facts per bar: 174 cal., 8 g total fat (2 g sat. fat), 15 mg chol., 70 mg sodium, 24 g carb., 1 g fiber, 2 g pro.

Kneading sweet spices into refrigerated dough gives the pastry a homemade taste.

cranberry-nut sticks

prep: 25 minutes bake: 38 minutes at 350°F
makes: 30 bars

1 16.5-ounce package refrigerated sugar cookie dough
1 teaspoon ground ginger
½ teaspoon ground cinnamon
¼ teaspoon ground cloves
2 eggs
1 cup walnuts, chopped
½ cup packed brown sugar
½ cup molasses
½ cup fresh cranberries, chopped
4 ounces white baking chocolate, chopped

1 Preheat oven to 350°F. Line a 13x9x2-inch baking pan with foil, extending the foil over the edges of the pan; set aside. Place cookie dough in a large bowl; let stand for 15 minutes. Knead in the ginger, cinnamon, and cloves. Press the dough evenly into the bottom of the prepared pan. Bake for 20 minutes.

2 Meanwhile, for filling, in a medium bowl stir together the eggs, walnuts, brown sugar, molasses, and cranberries. Pour over baked crust, spreading evenly.

3 Bake for 18 to 20 minutes or until filling is set. Cool in pan on a wire rack. In a small saucepan heat and stir white baking chocolate over low heat until melted and smooth. Drizzle over uncut bars. Let stand until set. Use foil to lift uncut bars out of pan. Transfer to a cutting board. Cut into narrow bars.

to store: Place bars in a single layer in an airtight container; cover. Store in the refrigerator up to 5 days or freeze up to 3 months.

nutrition facts per bar: 150 cal., 7 g total fat (2 g sat. fat), 18 mg chol., 78 mg sodium, 20 g carb., 0 g fiber, 2 g pro.

Don't confuse sweetened condensed milk with evaporated milk—they aren't interchangeable in recipes.

peppermint cream bars

prep: 30 minutes bake: 27 minutes at 350°F
makes: 36 bars

1   17.5-ounce package
      sugar cookie mix
2   tablespoons all-
      purpose flour
½   cup butter
4   egg yolks
1   14-ounce can
      sweetened
      condensed milk
½   teaspoon peppermint
      extract
½   cup crushed
      peppermint candies
1   recipe White
      Chocolate Ganache

1 Preheat oven to 350°F. Line a 13×9×2-inch baking pan with foil, extending the foil over edges of pan. Lightly grease foil; set pan aside.

2 For crust, in a large bowl stir together cookie mix and flour. Using a pastry blender, cut in butter until mixture resembles fine crumbs. Press mixture evenly onto the bottom of the prepared baking pan. Bake for 12 to 15 minutes or until edges are lightly browned.

3 For filling, in a medium bowl combine egg yolks, sweetened condensed milk, and peppermint extract. Stir in crushed candies. Carefully pour filling over hot crust.

4 Bake for 15 to 20 minutes or until filling is set. Cool in pan on a wire rack.

5 Pour White Chocolate Ganache over uncut bars, spreading evenly. Cover and chill about 1 hour or until firm. Using the edges of the foil, lift uncut bars out of pan. Cut into bars.

nutrition facts per bar: 171 cal., 7 g total fat (4 g sat. fat), 33 mg chol., 75 mg sodium, 24 g carb., 0 g fiber, 2 g pro.

white chocolate ganache: In a medium saucepan bring ¼ cup whipping cream just to boiling over medium-high heat. Remove from heat. Add 6 ounces chopped white baking chocolate with cocoa butter (do not stir). Let stand for 5 minutes. Stir until smooth. Cool about 5 minutes.

201

Serve with a scoop of banana or coconut ice cream, and you'll be doling out seconds!

caramel-nut chocolate chip bars

prep: 15 minutes **bake:** 35 minutes at 350°F
makes: 36 bars

1 18-ounce roll refrigerated chocolate chip cookie dough
2 cups quick-cooking rolled oats
1½ cups chopped honey-roasted peanuts or cashews
1 14-ounce can sweetened condensed milk
¼ cup caramel-flavor ice cream topping
½ cup flaked coconut
Caramel-flavor ice cream topping (optional)

1 Preheat oven to 350°F. Line a 13×9×2-inch baking pan with foil, extending the foil over edges of pan. Grease foil; set pan aside.

2 For crust, in a large bowl stir together cookie dough, oats, and ½ cup of the nuts until combined. Press filling evenly onto the bottom of the prepared baking pan. Bake for 15 minutes.

3 Meanwhile, in a small bowl stir together sweetened condensed milk and caramel topping. Drizzle filling over partially baked crust. Sprinkle with the remaining 1 cup nuts and the coconut.

4 Bake for 20 to 25 minutes or until top is golden. Cool in pan on a wire rack. Using the edges of the foil, lift uncut bars out of pan. Cut into bars. If desired, serve with additional caramel topping.

to store: Place bars in a single layer in an airtight container; cover. Store in the refrigerator up to 3 days.

nutrition facts per bar: 157 cal., 7 g total fat (2 g sat. fat), 7 mg chol., 74 mg sodium, 21 g carb., 1 g fiber, 3 g pro.

Fig and apricot add Moroccan flair to these bars.

apricot-fig meringue bars

prep: 30 minutes bake: 15 minutes at 350°F + 18 minutes at 325°F
makes: 24 bars

Nonstick cooking
     spray
1   17.5-ounce package
     oatmeal cookie mix
⅓   cup butter
1   egg, lightly beaten
2   cups dried
     Calimyrna (light)
     figs (12 ounces),
     stemmed
¾   cup apricot preserves
3   egg whites
½   teaspoon cream of
     tartar
⅔   cup granulated sugar

1 Preheat oven to 350°F. Line a 13×9×2-inch baking pan with foil, extending the foil over edges of pan. Coat foil with cooking spray; set pan aside.

2 For crust, place cookie mix in a large bowl. Using a pastry blender, cut in butter until resembles coarse crumbs. Stir in the lightly beaten egg until mixture starts to cling. Press mixture evenly onto the bottom of the prepared baking pan. Bake for 15 to 18 minutes or until set and lightly browned. Cool in pan on a wire rack for 5 minutes. Reduce oven temperature to 325°F.

3 Meanwhile, in a food processor combine figs and preserves. Cover and process until a thick paste forms. Carefully spread fig filling over crust.

4 For meringue, in a large mixing bowl beat egg whites and cream of tartar with an electric mixer on medium speed until soft peaks form (tips curl). Gradually add sugar, about 1 tablespoon at a time, beating on high speed until stiff peaks form (tips stand straight). Spread meringue over fig fillling, swirling to create peaks.

5 Bake for 18 to 22 minutes or until meringue is set and lightly browned. Cool in pan on a wire rack. Using the edges of the foil, lift uncut bars out of pan. Cut into bars.

to store: Place bars in a single layer in an airtight container; cover. Store in the refrigerator up to 3 days.

nutrition facts per bar: 208 cal., 7 g total fat (3 g sat. fat), 15 mg chol., 135 mg sodium, 36 g carb., 1 g fiber, 3 g pro.

This treat is perfect for any autumn gathering.

pumpkin cheesecake bars with chocolate topping

prep: 35 minutes bake: 40 minutes at 350°F chill: 2 hours
makes: 48 bars

1   17.5-ounce package
    oatmeal cookie mix
¾   cup butter
2   8-ounce packages
    cream cheese,
    softened
1¾ cups granulated
    sugar
3   eggs
1   15-ounce can
    pumpkin
1   teaspoon vanilla
½   teaspoon pumpkin
    pie spice
¼   teaspoon salt
1   cup semisweet
    chocolate pieces
48 pecan halves

1 Preheat oven to 350°F. Line a 15×10×1-inch baking pan with foil, extending the foil over edges of pan. Lightly grease foil; set pan aside. For crust, place cookie mix in a large bowl. Using a pastry blender, cut in ½ cup of the butter until mixture resembles coarse crumbs. Press evenly onto the bottom of the prepared baking pan. Bake about 10 minutes or until set.

2 For filling, in a large mixing bowl beat cream cheese and sugar with an electric mixer on medium speed until combined. Add eggs, one at a time, beating on low speed after each addition just until combined. Stir in pumpkin, vanilla, pumpkin pie spice, and salt. Pour filling over hot crust, spreading evenly.

3 Bake for 30 to 35 minutes or until filling is slightly puffed around edges and just set in center. Cool in pan on a wire rack.

4 In a small microwave-safe bowl microwave chocolate and the remaining ¼ cup butter on 100 percent power (high) for 30 to 60 seconds or until softened; stir until smooth. Spread chocolate mixture over uncut bars. Top with pecan halves. Cover and chill for 2 to 24 hours. Using the edges of the foil, lift uncut bars out of pan. Cut into bars.

to store: Place bars in a single layer in an airtight container; cover. Store in the refrigerator up to 3 days.

nutrition facts per bar: 173 cal., 11 g total fat (5 g sat. fat), 31 mg chol., 117 mg sodium, 18 g carb., 1 g fiber, 2 g pro.

Baking the crust layer before spreading the filling creates a solid base for the nutty bars.

gooey mixed-nut bars

prep: 25 minutes **bake:** 45 minutes at 350°F
makes: 32 bars

Nonstick cooking
    spray
1   package 2-layer-size
    yellow cake mix
½ cup butter
4   eggs, lightly beaten
1   cup packed brown
    sugar
½ cup light-color corn
    syrup
⅓ cup butter, melted
1   teaspoon vanilla
½ teaspoon ground
    cinnamon
2   cups mixed nuts,
    coarsely chopped

1 Preheat oven to 350°F. Line a 13×9×2-inch baking pan with foil, extending the foil over edges of pan. Coat foil with cooking spray; set baking pan aside.

2 For crust, place cake mix in a large bowl. Using a pastry blender, cut in the ½ cup butter until mixture resembles coarse crumbs. Press evenly onto the bottom of the prepared baking pan. Bake for 15 to 20 minutes or until lightly browned and set.

3 Meanwhile, in a medium bowl combine eggs, brown sugar, corn syrup, melted ⅓ cup butter, vanilla, and cinnamon. Stir in mixed nuts. Pour nut layer over hot crust.

4 Bake about 30 minutes or until bubbly around the edges. Cool in pan on a wire rack. Using the edges of the foil, lift uncut bars out of pan. Cut into bars.

to store: Layer bars between sheets of waxed paper in an airtight container; cover. Store in the refrigerator up to 1 week or freeze up to 3 months.

nutrition facts per bar: 207 cal., 11 g total fat (4 g sat. fat), 39 mg chol., 155 mg sodium, 26 g carb., 1 g fiber, 3 g pro.

Just five ingredients and you're ready for your next potluck.

dark chocolate revel bars

prep: 25 minutes **bake:** 25 minutes at 350°F
makes: 36 bars

2   16.5-ounce packages refrigerated chocolate chip cookie dough
2   cups rolled oats
1   cup red and green candy-coated milk chocolate pieces
1   14-ounce can sweetened condensed milk
1½ cups dark chocolate pieces

1 Preheat oven to 350°F. Line a 13×9×2-inch baking pan with foil, extending the foil over the edges of the pan; set aside. In a large bowl stir together the cookie dough, oats, and candy-coated chocolate pieces. Press two-thirds of the dough into the bottom of the prepared baking pan; set aside.

2 In a medium saucepan combine the condensed milk and dark chocolate pieces. Heat over low heat until chocolate melts, stirring occasionally. Pour over dough in pan, spreading evenly. Dot remaining dough mixture on chocolate mixture.

3 Bake for 25 to 30 minutes or until top is lightly browned. Cool in pan on a wire rack. Use foil to lift uncut bars out of pan. Transfer to a cutting board. Cut into bars.

nutrition facts per bar: 252 cal., 10 g total fat (5 g sat. fat), 11 mg chol., 74 mg sodium, 36 g carb., 2 g fiber, 4 g pro.

Cream cheese and four sweet spices dress up a basic mix.

spiced brownies with cream cheese swirl

prep: 20 minutes **bake:** 25 minutes at 350°F
makes: 32 bars

1 3-ounce package
   cream cheese,
   softened
¼ cup granulated sugar
1 egg yolk
1 tablespoon all-
   purpose flour
1 18.3-ounce package
   fudge brownie mix
½ teaspoon ground
   cinnamon
½ teaspoon ground
   ginger
¼ teaspoon ground
   nutmeg
⅛ teaspoon ground
   cloves

1 Preheat oven to 350°F. Line a 13×9×2-inch baking pan with foil, extending the foil over edges of pan. Lightly grease foil; set pan aside.

2 In a small mixing bowl beat cream cheese and sugar with an electric mixer on medium to high speed until smooth. Beat in egg yolk and flour; set aside.

3 In a large bowl combine brownie mix, cinnamon, ginger, nutmeg, and cloves. Prepare brownie mix according to package directions, substituting melted butter for the oil. Pour batter into the prepared baking pan, spreading evenly. Spoon cream cheese mixture into small mounds on top of batter. Using a narrow metal spatula or a table knife, swirl gently to marble.

4 Bake for 25 to 30 minutes or until center is set (cream cheese swirl will be lightly browned). Cool in pan on a wire rack. Cover and chill until ready to serve. Using the edges of the foil, lift uncut brownies out of pan. Cut into bars.

to store: Place brownies in a single layer in an airtight container; cover. Store in the refrigerator up to 4 days or freeze up to 3 months.

nutrition facts per bar: 128 cal., 7 g total fat (4 g sat. fat), 33 mg chol., 88 mg sodium, 15 g carb., 0 g fiber, 1 g pro.

These PB&C bars feature the flavors of a favorite candy.

honey-roasted peanut butter bars with chocolate ganache

prep: 40 minutes **bake:** 12 minutes at 350°F **cool:** 15 minutes **chill:** 1 hour
makes: 48 bars

1	package 2-layer-size devil's food cake mix
⅓	cup butter, melted
1	egg
¾	cup butter, softened
¾	cup honey-roasted peanut butter
2	teaspoons vanilla
3	cups powdered sugar
2	tablespoons whipping cream or milk
¾	cup honey-roasted peanuts, chopped
½	cup whipping cream
1	11.5-ounce package (2 cups) milk chocolate pieces

1 Preheat oven to 350°F. Line a 15×10×1-inch baking pan with foil, extending the foil over edges of pan. Lightly grease foil; set pan aside.

2 For crust, in a large mixing bowl beat cake mix, the ⅓ cup melted butter, and egg with an electric mixer on low speed for 1 to 2 minutes or until combined. Press mixture evenly onto the bottom of the prepared pan. Bake for 12 minutes. Cool in pan on a wire rack.

3 In another large mixing bowl beat the ¾ cup butter, the peanut butter, and vanilla on medium speed for 30 seconds. Gradually add powdered sugar, beating until combined. Beat in the 2 tablespoons whipping cream. Stir in peanuts. Pour mixture over baked crust, spreading evenly. Chill while preparing the ganache.

4 For ganache, in a small saucepan bring the ½ cup whipping cream just to boiling over medium-high heat. Remove from heat. Add chocolate (do not stir). Let stand for 5 minutes. Stir until smooth. Cool for 15 minutes. Gently pour ganache over bars, spreading evenly. Cover and chill for 1 to 2 hours or until set. Using the edges of the foil, lift uncut bars out of pan. Cut into bars.

to store: Place bars in a single layer in an airtight container; cover. Store in the refrigerator up to 3 days or freeze up to 3 months. Before serving, let bars stand at room temperature for 15 minutes. Or thaw bars if frozen.

nutrition facts per bar: 189 cal., 11 g total fat (5 g sat. fat), 21 mg chol., 143 mg sodium, 22 g carb., 1 g fiber, 2 g pro.

Two off-the-shelf mixes give you a head start with this delectable concoction.

cookie and coffee brownies

prep: 20 minutes bake: 40 minutes at 350°F
makes: 24 bars

1   16-ounce roll
    refrigerated sugar
    cookie dough
1   19.5-ounce package
    milk chocolate
    brownie mix
2   eggs
½   cup vegetable oil
⅓   cup coffee liqueur or
    cooled strong coffee
1   cup semisweet
    or bittersweet
    chocolate pieces
    (6 ounces)

1 Preheat oven to 350°F. Press cookie dough evenly onto the bottom of an ungreased 13×9×2-inch baking pan.

2 In a large bowl beat brownie mix, eggs, oil, and liqueur with a wooden spoon just until combined. Pour batter over cookie dough, spreading evenly. Sprinkle with chocolate pieces.

3 Bake about 40 minutes or until edges are set. Cool in pan on a wire rack. Cut into bars.

nutrition facts per bar: 279 cal., 15 g total fat (3 g sat. fat), 23 mg chol., 159 mg sodium, 36 g carb., 1 g fiber, 3 g pro.

express treats

Extra cake mix batter creates a streusel-like topping.

chewy chocolate-caramel bars

prep: 25 minutes **bake:** 25 minutes at 350°F
makes: 48 bars

1 package 2-layer-size German chocolate cake mix
¾ cup butter, melted
1 5-ounce can evaporated milk
1 14-ounce package vanilla caramels, unwrapped
1 cup chopped walnuts
1 cup semisweet chocolate pieces (6 ounces)

1 Preheat oven to 350°F. Grease a 13×9×2-inch baking pan; set aside.

2 In a large mixing bowl beat cake mix, melted butter, and ⅓ cup of the evaporated milk with an electric mixer on medium speed until smooth. Spread half the batter in the prepared baking pan.

3 In a large heavy saucepan heat and stir caramels and the remaining evaporated milk over medium-low heat until melted and smooth. Pour caramel mixture over dough in pan. Sprinkle with nuts and chocolate pieces. Crumble the remaining batter over layers in pan.

4 Bake for 25 minutes. Cool in pan on a wire rack. Cut into bars.

nutrition facts per bar: 140 cal., 8 g total fat (4 g sat. fat), 9 mg chol., 115 mg sodium, 17 g carb., 1 g fiber, 1 g pro.

Hint: When bananas get overripe, stash them in the freezer so you always have a banana on call for baking. Just thaw before mashing it.

banana-chocolate chip bars

prep: 20 minutes **bake:** 25 minutes at 350°F
makes: 36 bars

1 16.5-ounce package refrigerated peanut butter cookie dough
1 cup rolled oats
½ cup mashed banana
½ cup miniature semisweet chocolate pieces
½ cup chopped peanuts
1 16-ounce can chocolate or vanilla frosting

1 Preheat oven to 350°F. Lightly grease a 13×9×2-inch baking pan; set aside. In a large bowl stir together cookie dough, oats, mashed banana, chocolate pieces, and peanuts until combined. Spread dough evenly in the prepared baking pan.

2 Bake about 25 minutes or until golden. Cool in pan on a wire rack.

3 Frost with chocolate or vanilla frosting. Or use one-half can chocolate frosting and one-half can vanilla frosting then swirl frostings gently to marble. Cut into bars.

to store: Cover frosted bars in pan and store at room temperature overnight. Or place unfrosted bars in a single layer in an airtight container; cover. Freeze up to 3 months. Thaw bars before frosting as directed in Step 3.

nutrition facts per bar: 158 cal., 8 g total fat (2 g sat. fat), 4 mg chol., 75 mg sodium, 21 g carb., 1 g fiber, 3 g pro.

Transform cookie dough into a quick-and-easy biscotti.

chocolate chip cookie sticks

prep: 15 minutes **bake:** 15 minutes at 375°F + 8 minutes at 300°F
makes: 25 cookies

1   16.5-ounce package
      refrigerated
      chocolate chip
      cookie dough
½   cup all-purpose flour
1   egg
½   teaspoon ground
      cinnamon
¼   cup semisweet
      chocolate pieces
½   teaspoon shortening

1 Preheat oven to 375°F. Lightly grease a cookie sheet; set aside. In a large bowl stir together the cookie dough, flour, egg, and cinnamon. If necessary, work the dough with your hands to mix well. Divide dough in half. Shape each half into a 5×4-inch rectangle on the prepared cookie sheet, spacing about 3 inches apart.

2 Bake about 15 minutes or until lightly browned. Cool on cookie sheet on a wire rack.

3 Preheat oven to 300°F. Cut rectangles crosswise into ½-inch slices. Turn slices, cut sides up, on cookie sheet. Bake for 8 minutes. Cool on cookie sheet on a wire rack.

4 Transfer cookies to a sheet of waxed paper. In a small microwave-safe bowl combine semisweet chocolate and shortening. Microwave, uncovered, on 100 percent power (high) for 30 seconds; stir. Continue to microwave at 10-second intervals until smooth, stirring after each interval. Drizzle over cookies. Let stand until set.

nutrition facts per cookie: 130 cal., 6 g total fat (2 g sat. fat), 15 mg chol., 53 mg sodium, 18 g carb., 1 g fiber, 2 g pro.

This favorite candy bar gets star treatment in these elegant bites, perfect for a holiday cookie tray.

snickering tartlets

prep: 30 minutes **bake:** 5 minutes at 450°F + 15 minutes at 325°F **Chill:** 2 hours
makes: 24 cookies

1   15-ounce package rolled refrigerated unbaked piecrust (2 crusts)*

2   2.07-ounce chocolate-coated caramel-topped nougat bars with peanuts such as Snickers

½   of an 8-ounce package cream cheese, softened

2   tablespoons sour cream

2   tablespoons creamy peanut butter

2   teaspoons granulated sugar

1   egg

½   cup milk chocolate pieces

2   tablespoons whipping cream

1 Preheat oven to 450°F. On a lightly floured surface, unroll piecrusts. Roll each crust into a 12-inch circle. Using a 3-inch round cutter, cut 24 circles from crusts, rerolling scraps as necessary. Press each dough circle into bottom and up sides of 24 ungreased 1¾-inch muffin cups, pleating as necessary and extending slightly above sides of cups. Bake for 5 to 7 minutes or until very light golden brown; cool. Reduce oven temperature to 325°F.

2 Chop candy bars. Reserve 24 pieces for garnish. Place remaining candy bar pieces in bottoms of crust-lined cups.

3 In a small bowl beat cream cheese, sour cream, peanut butter, and sugar with an electric mixer on medium speed until smooth. Beat in egg until well combined. Spoon about 1 teaspoon cream cheese mixture over candy bar pieces in each tart.

4 Bake for 15 to 20 minutes or until centers are set. Cool in pan on a wire rack.

5 In a small saucepan combine chocolate pieces and whipping cream. Cook and stir over low heat until melted. Cool slightly. Spoon chocolate on top of each tartlet; garnish with reserved candy bar pieces. Chill for 2 hours before serving.

*tip: For an option, omit the piecrusts. Place 30 baked miniature phyllo dough shells (two 1.9-ounce packages) on a cookie sheet. Add candy pieces and cream cheese mixture and bake as above. Top with chocolate mixture and garnish with remaining candy. Store in refrigerator up to 24 hours or freeze up to 3 months. Makes 30 tartlets.

nutrition facts per cookie: 169 cal., 11 g total fat (5 g sat. fat), 17 mg chol., 119 mg sodium, 17 g carb., 1 g fiber, 2 g pro.

express treats

*Call on these gems for
St. Patrick's Day parties.*

mint-chocolate cookies

prep: 20 minutes **bake:** 8 minutes at 350°F per batch
makes: 36 cookies

1   17.5-ounce package
      sugar cookie mix
½   cup butter, softened
1   egg
½   teaspoon mint extract
4   ounces layered
      chocolate-mint
      candies (1 package),
      coarsely chopped,
      or 1 cup crème de
      menthe baking
      pieces
36 green candy coating
      disks or wafers*

1 Preheat oven to 350°F. Line cookie sheets with parchment paper; set aside.

2 In a large bowl stir together cookie mix, butter, egg, and mint extract until a soft dough forms. Stir in chopped chocolate-mint candies. Drop dough by rounded teaspoons 2 inches apart onto the prepared cookie sheets.

3 Bake for 8 to 10 minutes or until set. Place a coating disk on each cookie. Cool cookies on cookie sheet for 1 minute. Transfer to a wire rack; cool.

*tip: Look for green candy coating disks or wafers, such as Walton brand, in the cake decorating section of hobby and crafts stores.

nutrition facts per cookie: 112 cal., 6 g total fat (4 g sat. fat), 12 mg chol., 64 mg sodium, 15 g carb., 0 g fiber, 1 g pro.

Here's an easy and cute cookie for young children to help make.

peanut butter snappers

prep: 25 minutes   bake: 10 minutes at 375°F per batch
makes: 22 cookies

1⅓ cups pecan halves
1   16.5-ounce package
    refrigerated peanut
    butter cookie dough
½   cup caramel baking
    bits
1   cup semisweet
    chocolate pieces

1 Preheat oven to 375°F. Line two large cookie sheets with parchment paper. Arrange 22 to 24 clusters of 4 to 5 pecans about 2 inches apart on prepared cookie sheets; set aside.

2 In a medium bowl stir together the cookie dough and baking bits. Shape dough into 1-inch balls. Place a ball on each cluster of pecans, pressing lightly into nuts.

3 Bake for 10 to 12 minutes or until edges are golden. Immediately sprinkle each cookie with a slightly rounded teaspoon of chocolate pieces. Let stand for 2 minutes, then spread chocolate on cookies. Transfer cookies warm parchment paper to a wire rack; cool.

nutrition facts per cookie: 195 cal., 13 g total fat (3 g sat. fat), 6 mg chol., 98 mg sodium, 21 g carb., 1 g fiber, 3 g pro.

easy black-and-white star stacks

prep: 1 hour bake: 6 to 10 minutes at 375°F per batch
makes: 20 cookies

2   16.5 to 18-ounce rolls refrigerated sugar cookie dough
¾   cup all-purpose flour
¼   cup unsweetened cocoa powder
1   16-ounce can vanilla frosting
    Small silver or white pearl candies
1   16-ounce can chocolate frosting

1 Preheat oven to 375°F. In a large bowl combine one roll of cookie dough and ½ cup of the flour; knead until well mixed. On a lightly floured surface roll dough to about ¼-inch thickness. Using a set of graduated-size (3-inch, 2¼-inch, and 1 inch) star-shape cookie cutters, cut out dough to make 10 to 15 large cookies, 10 to 15 medium cookies, and 10 to 15 small cookies, rerolling scraps as necessary. Place similar-size cookies 2 inches apart on an ungreased cookie sheet. Bake large cookies for 10 to 12 minutes, medium cookies for 8 to 10 minutes, and small cookies for 6 to 8 minutes or until edges are firm and bottoms are light brown. Cool on cookie sheet for 1 minute. Transfer to a wire rack; cool completely.

2 In the same large bowl combine the remaining roll of cookie dough, the remaining ¼ cup flour, and the cocoa powder; knead until well mixed. Roll, cut, bake, and cool cookies as directed in Step 1.

3 Transfer vanilla frosting to a microwave-safe bowl. Microwave on 100 percent power (high) about 30 seconds or until the consistency of thick cream, stirring every 10 seconds. Dip the tops of the small plain and medium sized cookies into vanilla frosting. Place a pearl candy on each star point. Let stand on a wire rack set over waxed paper until set. (If frosting becomes firm, reheat in the microwave.) Repeat with chocolate frosting and chocolate cookies.

4 To assemble, place the large cookies on a work surface. Top each large cookie with an alternating color of medium cookie, securing in place with a small amount of frosting. Top each medium cookie with an alternating color of small cookie, securing with frosting. Let stand until set.

nutrition facts per cookie: 406 cal., 17 g total fat (4 g sat. fat), 13 mg chol., 295 mg sodium, 60 g carb., 1 g fiber, 2 g pro.

Creamy white chocolate fills the center of each cookie.

swirled peppermint thumbprints

prep: 30 minutes **bake:** 10 minutes at 350°F per batch **chill:** 1 hour
makes: 34 cookies

2   16- to 16.5-ounce packages refrigerated sugar cookie dough
1   cup all-purpose flour
10 ounces white baking chocolate with cocoa butter, chopped
½   cup whipping cream
¼   teaspoon peppermint extract
    Red food coloring
1   recipe White Chocolate Drizzle (optional)

1 Preheat oven to 350°F. In a large bowl combine cookie dough and flour; knead until smooth. Shape dough into 1½-inch balls. Place balls 2 inches apart on an ungreased cookie sheet. Using your thumb, make an indentation in the center of each ball.

2 Bake for 10 to 12 minutes or until edges are very lightly browned. Cool on cookie sheet for 1 minute. Transfer cookies to a wire rack; cool.

3 For filling, in a medium microwave-safe bowl combine white chocolate and whipping cream. Microwave, uncovered, on 100 percent power (high) for 1 to 2 minutes or until white chocolate is melted, stirring twice. Stir in peppermint extract. Divide mixture in half. Tint one portion with food coloring. Cover and chill both portions for 1 to 2 hours or until spreading consistency.

4 Spoon about 1 teaspoon of the white chocolate and about 1 teaspoon of the pink chocolate into the center of each cookie. Gently swirl a knife through filling to marble. Let stand until set. If desired, drizzle cookies with White Chocolate Drizzle.

nutrition facts per cookie: 190 cal., 9 g total fat (4 g sat. fat), 8 mg chol., 85 mg sodium, 25 g carb., 0 g fiber, 2 g pro.

white chocolate drizzle: In a small microwave-safe bowl combine 2 to 3 ounces white baking chocolate with cocoa butter and 2 teaspoons shortening. Microwave on 100 percent power (high) about 1 minute or until melted and smooth, stirring every 30 seconds. Stir in 1 to 2 teaspoons peppermint extract.

Creamy mascarpone gives these quick bites star quality.

coffee sandwich cookies with mascarpone cinnamon filling

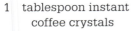

prep: 15 minutes **bake:** 10 minutes at 350°F per batch
makes: 20 cookies

1 tablespoon instant coffee crystals
1 tablespoon milk
1 16.5-ounce package refrigerated sugar cookie dough
¼ cup all-purpose flour
1 8-ounce carton mascarpone
¼ cup powdered sugar
⅛ teaspoon ground cinnamon

1 Preheat oven to 350°F. In a large bowl dissolve coffee crystals in milk. Add cookie dough and flour; mix with a wooden spoon until combined. Drop dough by rounded teaspoons 2 inches apart on an ungreased cookie sheet. Bake for 10 to 13 minutes or until edges are browned. Cool for 1 minute on cookie sheet. Transfer to a wire rack; cool.

2 For filling, in a medium bowl stir together the mascarpone, powdered sugar, and cinnamon. Spread filling on bottoms of half the cookies. Top with remaining cookies, bottom sides down.

to store: Layer filled cookies between sheets of waxed paper in an airtight container; cover. Store in the refrigerator up to 3 days or freeze up to 2 months. Serve cookies at to room temperature.

nutrition facts per bar: 164 cal., 10 g total fat (4 g sat. fat), 21 mg chol., 106 mg sodium, 17 g carb., 0 g fiber, 4 g pro.

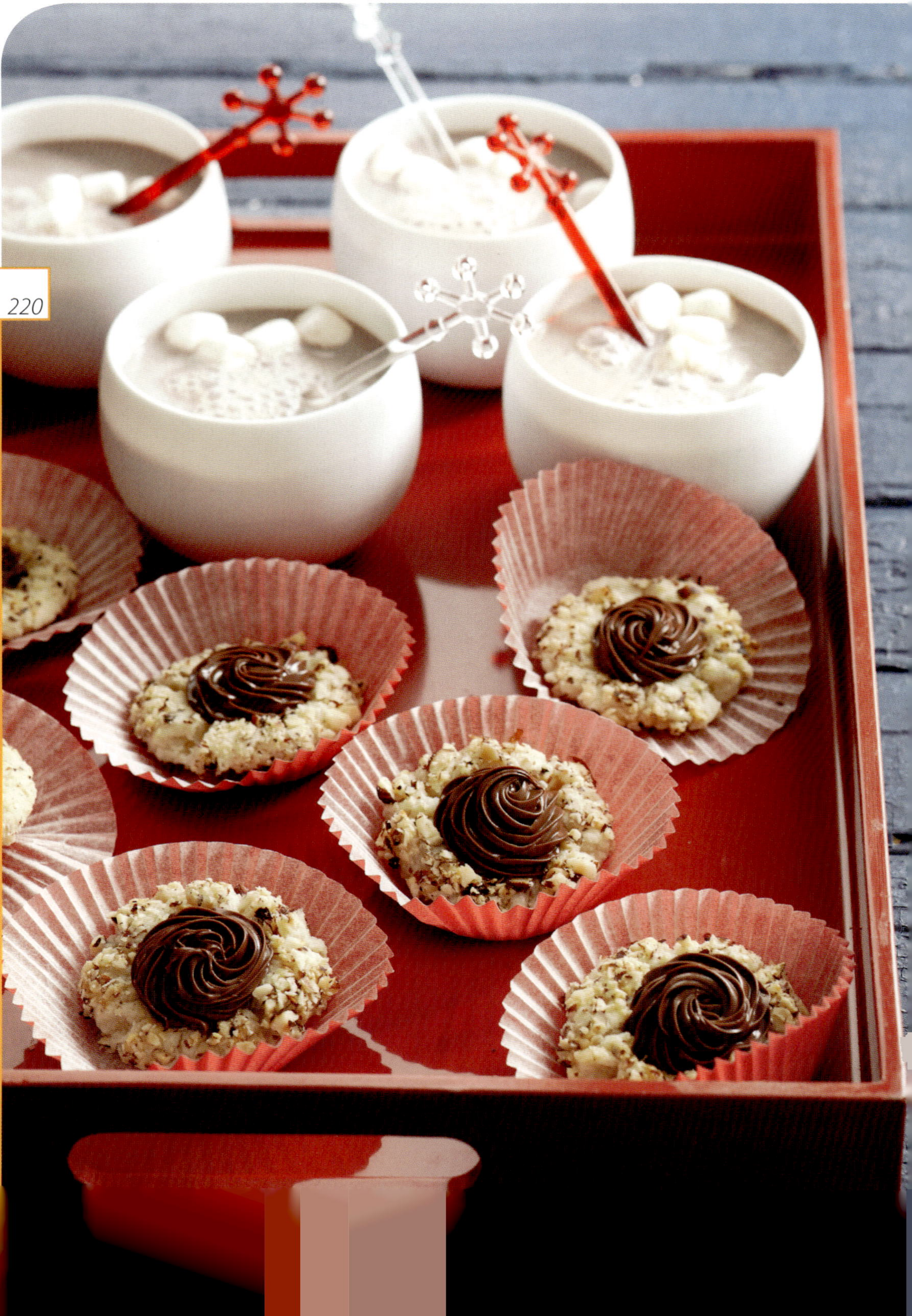

Warm up after a day of outdoor winter sports with hot cocoa and these nutty sweets.

hazelnut kisses

prep: 20 minutes bake: 10 minutes at 375°F per batch
makes: 24 cookies

1   16.5-ounce package refrigerated sugar cookie dough
½   cup all-purpose flour
1   egg
1   tablespoon water
½   cup finely chopped hazelnuts (filberts)
½   cup purchased chocolate-hazelnut spread

1 Preheat oven to 375°F. Line cookie sheets with parchment paper; set aside. In a large bowl stir together the cookie dough and flour. Shape dough into 1¼-inch balls. In a small bowl whisk together egg and the water. Place nuts in a shallow dish. Roll balls in egg mixture, then in nuts to coat. Place balls 2 inches apart on the prepared cookie sheets. Press your thumb into the center of each ball.

2 Bake for 10 minutes or until golden. If cookie centers puff during baking, indent warm cookies with the back of a measuring teaspoon. Transfer to a wire rack; cool. Pipe or spoon cookies with chocolate-hazelnut spread.

to store: Layer unfilled cookies between sheets of waxed paper in an airtight container; cover. Store at room temperature up to 3 days or freeze up to 3 months. If frozen, thaw cookies. Fill cookies as directed in Step 2.

nutrition facts per bar: 139 cal., 7 g total fat (1 g sat. fat), 14 mg chol., 90 mg sodium, 17 g carb., 0 g fiber, 2 g pro.

8

Spectacular cookie recipes are cherished by bakers around the globe, from Germany to Italy. This international assortment of sumptuous cookies features unique shapes, flavors, and techniques.

worldly

favo

mint tuile bowls, page 241

rites

Norwegian sandbakkelse, traditionally baked in mini fluted tins, will remind you of shortbread cookies.

hazelnut sandbakkelse

prep: 45 minutes **bake:** 9 minutes at 350°F per batch
makes: 72 cookies

3½ cups all-purpose flour
½ cup finely ground blanched hazelnuts (filberts)* or almonds
1½ cups butter, softened
¾ cup granulated sugar
¼ cup packed brown sugar
¼ teaspoon salt
1 egg
  Purchased chocolate-hazelnut spread (optional)

1 Line seventy-two 1¾-inch muffins cups with paper bake cups; set aside. In a large bowl combine flour and ground nuts.

2 In a large mixing bowl beat butter with an electric mixer on medium to high speed for 30 seconds. Add granulated sugar, brown sugar, and salt. Beat until combined, scraping sides of bowl occasionally. Beat in egg until combined. Beat in as much of the flour mixture as you can with the mixer. Using a wooden spoon, stir in any remaining flour mixture until dough no longer sticks to fingers when handled. If necessary, cover and chill about 1 hour or until dough is easy to handle.

3 Preheat oven to 350°F. Press 1-inch balls of dough into the center of the paper bake cups. Using your thumb, make an indentation in the center of each ball.

4 Bake for 9 to 11 minutes or until edges are firm and very lightly browned. Remove from oven. Let cool in pan for 3 minutes. Transfer paper bake cups to a wire rack; cool.

5 If desired, spoon chocolate-hazelnut spread into a decorating bag fitted with a star tip. Pipe chocolate-hazelnut spread into each cookie indent.

*tip: If you can't find blanched hazelnuts, toast ½ cup hazelnuts in a 350°F oven about 10 minutes or until skins begin to crack. Remove from oven; cool slightly. Rub hazelnuts vigorously in a clean towel to remove as much of the skin as you can.

nutrition facts per cookie: 74 cal., 5 g total fat (3 g sat. fat), 13 mg chol., 37 mg sodium, 8 g carb., 0 g fiber, 1 g pro.

You'll need a rosette iron, found in specialty shops around the holidays, to shape the batter for frying.

swedish cardamom rosettes

start to finish: 40 minutes
makes: 60 cookies

1	tablespoon powdered sugar
1½	teaspoons ground cardamom
2	eggs, lightly beaten
1	cup all-purpose flour
1	cup milk
1	tablespoon granulated sugar
1	teaspoon vanilla
¼	teaspoon salt
	Vegetable oil for deep-fat frying

1 In a small bowl stir together powdered sugar and ½ teaspoon of the cardamom; set aside. In a medium mixing bowl combine eggs, flour, milk, granulated sugar, the remaining 1 teaspoon cardamom, the vanilla, and salt. Beat with an electric mixer on medium speed until smooth. Transfer batter to a shallow bowl or platter.

2 Heat a rosette iron in deep hot oil (365°F). Dip hot iron into batter for 2 to 3 seconds. (Batter should come only three-fourths the way up the sides of the iron.) Dip iron into hot oil for 30 to 45 seconds or until cookie is golden. Lift out iron and tip slightly to drain. With a fork, push rosette off iron onto a wire rack set over paper towels. Repeat with remaining batter, reheating rosette iron in oil each time before dipping into the batter. Sift powdered sugar mixture over cooled rosettes.

to store: Layer cookies between waxed paper in an airtight container; cover. Store at room temperature for 1 day or freeze up to 3 months.

nutrition facts per cookie: 93 cal., 9 g total fat (1 g sat. fat), 7 mg chol., 14 mg sodium, 2 g carb., 0 g fiber, 1 g pro

sweet citrus krumkaker

prep: 40 minutes **stand:** 30 minutes
makes: 30 cookies

3 eggs
½ cup granulated sugar
½ cup butter, melted
      and cooled slightly
½ cup all-purpose flour
1 teaspoon vanilla
½ teaspoon finely
      shredded lemon
      peel and/or orange
      peel (optional)
3 ounces vanilla-flavor
      candy coating
¼ cup crushed lemon
      drop candies
1 recipe Lemon Cream

1 In a mixing bowl beat eggs with an electric mixer on medium speed for 1 minute. Gradually add sugar; beat about 3 minutes or until sugar is almost dissolved, scraping sides of bowl occasionally. Gradually beat in cooled butter. Stir in flour, vanilla, and, if desired, lemon peel just until mixture is smooth.

2 Heat a nonelectric krumkake iron on the range top over medium-low heat. Lightly grease the krumkake grid. If using a 6-inch iron, spoon about 1 tablespoon of the batter onto the krumkake grid. Close iron gently but firmly. Cook over medium-low heat about 30 seconds. (Or cook batter in an electric krumkake iron according to manufacturer's directions.) Carefully open iron. Using a narrow spatula, loosen cookie from grid. Invert cookie onto a wire rack. Immediately roll the cookie around a metal cone. Let cookie cool around cone until it holds a cone shape. Repeat, heating the krumkake iron and cooking the remaining batter 1 tablespoon at a time.

3 In a small microwave-safe bowl microwave the candy coating, uncovered, on 100 percent power (high) for 30 to 60 seconds or until melted and smooth, stirring twice. Carefully dip the rim of a cooled cookie into melted coating, letting excess drip back into bowl. Immediately dip rim into crushed lemon drops to coat. Place krumkake on a cookie sheet lined with waxed paper. Repeat with remaining cookies, candy coating, and crushed lemon drops. Let stand 30 minutes or until set.

4 Pipe Lemon Cream into the cones. Serve immediately.

lemon cream: In a medium mixing bowl beat two 8-ounce packages cream cheese, softened, and one 10-ounce jar lemon curd with an electric mixer on medium speed until smooth.

to store: Store undipped and unfilled cookies in an airtight container at room temperature up to 3 days. Coat and fill before serving.

nutrition facts per cookie: 159 cal., 10 g total fat (6 g sat. fat), 53 mg chol., 85 mg sodium, 16 g carb., 1 g fiber, 2 g pro.

Nothing beats the rich aromatics that come from the seeds of dried vanilla beans. Look for Tahitian or Madagascar beans for the sweetest flavor.

swedish vanilla butter cookies

prep: 40 minutes **chill:** 2 hours **bake:** 6 minutes at 375°F per batch
makes: 60 cookies

1   vanilla bean or
       1 teaspoon vanilla
1   cup butter, softened
½   cup granulated sugar
⅛   teaspoon salt
2   cups all-purpose flour
4   ounces white
       chocolate with
       cocoa butter,
       chopped
2   teaspoons shortening

1 Cut vanilla bean in half lengthwise; using the tip of a knife, scrape the seeds from the bean halves into a small bowl; set aside.

2 In a medium mixing bowl beat butter with an electric mixer on medium to high speed for 30 seconds. Add sugar, half the vanilla bean seeds, and the salt. Beat until combined, scraping sides of bowl occasionally. Beat in as much of the flour as you can with the mixer. Using a wooden spoon, stir in any remaining flour.

3 Divide dough in half. Shape each half into an 8-inch log. Wrap each log in plastic wrap or waxed paper. Chill about 2 hours or until dough is firm enough to slice.

4 Preheat oven to 375°F. If necessary, reshape logs to make them round. Using a serrated knife, cut logs into ¼-inch slices. Place slices 2 inches apart on an ungreased cookie sheet.

5 Bake for 6 to 8 minutes or just until cookies begin to brown on edges. Cool on cookie sheet for 1 minute. Transfer to a wire rack; cool.

6 For white chocolate drizzle, in a small saucepan stir white chocolate and shortening over low heat until melted and smooth. Stir in the remaining vanilla bean seeds. Arrange cookies side by side on parchment paper or cookie sheets lined with waxed paper. Spoon drizzle over cookies. Let stand until set. If necessary, chill about 10 minutes or until drizzle is set.

nutrition facts per cookie: 61 cal., 4 g total fat (2 g sat. fat), 8 mg chol., 29 mg sodium, 6 g carb., 0 g fiber, 1 g pro.

Use kitchen shears to easily and quickly cut chilled dough into petite cookies.

danish peppernuts

prep: 1 hour   **stand:** 15 minutes   **chill:** 2 hours   **bake:** 7 minutes at 375°F per batch
makes: 48 cookies

1 cup granulated sugar
1 cup molasses
¼ cup butter
2 eggs, lightly beaten
2 tablespoons finely chopped crystallized ginger
½ teaspoon baking powder
½ teaspoon baking soda
½ teaspoon ground cardamom
½ teaspoon vanilla
¼ teaspoon salt
¼ teaspoon crushed anise seeds
⅛ teaspoon ground black pepper
4 cups all-purpose flour
Coarse sugar

1 In a large saucepan combine granulated sugar, molasses, and butter. Bring to boiling, stirring until sugar is dissolved. Remove from heat. Let stand at room temperature for 15 minutes.

2 Stir in eggs, ginger, baking powder, baking soda, cardamom, vanilla, salt, anise seeds, and pepper. Stir in the flour until combined. Cover and chill about 2 hours or until dough is firm enough to handle.

3 Preheat oven to 375°F. Grease a large cookie sheet; set aside. On a surface sprinkled with coarse sugar, roll about 2 tablespoons of the dough into a ¼-inch-thick rope. Cut each rope into ⅜-inch-long pieces. Place pieces ½ inch apart on prepared cookie sheet.

4 Bake for 7 to 8 minutes or until cookies are lightly browned on bottoms. Immediately remove cookies from cookie sheet. Cool on paper towels.

nutrition facts per cookie: 89 cal., 1 g total fat (1 g sat. fat), 10 mg chol., 45 mg sodium, 18 g carb., 0 g fiber, 1 g pro

Cooking the sugar mixture to 238°F is critical to re-creating Italy's candylike cookie.

lacy florentines

prep: 40 minutes **bake:** 8 minutes at 350°F per batch
makes: 36 cookies

¾   cup granulated sugar
½   cup butter
⅓   cup whipping cream
2   tablespoons honey
1   cup quick-cooking
     rolled oats
1   cup finely chopped
     blanched almonds
½   cup finely chopped
     crystallized ginger
2   tablespoons all-
     purpose flour
¼   teaspoon finely
     shredded lemon
     peel
4   ounces bittersweet
     chocolate, melted

1 Preheat oven to 350°F. Line two large cookie sheets with foil. Grease foil; set cookie sheets aside. In a medium-sized heavy saucepan combine sugar, butter, cream, and honey. Stir over low heat about 5 minutes or until butter is melted and sugar is dissolved.

2 Increase heat and bring mixture to boiling. To prevent sugar from crystallizing, brush down sides of saucepan with a damp pastry brush. Clip a candy thermometer to side of saucepan. Cook until thermometer registers 238°F (soft-ball stage). Remove from heat. Quickly stir in oats, almonds, ginger, flour, and lemon peel.

3 Drop dough by tablespoons 3 inches apart onto prepared cookie sheets. Dip tines of a fork into cold water and press top of each cookie to flatten.

4 Bake on separate racks for 8 to 10 minutes or until light golden brown and set, switching cookie sheets halfway through baking. Cool completely on cookie sheets. Gently lift cookies from foil. Drizzle with melted chocolate. Let stand until chocolate is set.

nutrition facts per cookie: 110 cal., 7 g total fat (3 g sat. fat), 10 mg chol., 25 mg sodium, 12 g carb., 1 g fiber, 1 g pro.

Plan to prepare and serve this Italian treat on the same day.

chocolate pizzelle

start to finish: 1 hour
makes: 64 cookies

1½ cups hazelnuts
(filberts), toasted
(see tip, page 70)
2¼ cups all-purpose flour
3 tablespoons
unsweetened cocoa
powder
1 tablespoon baking
powder
3 eggs
1 cup granulated sugar
⅓ cup butter, melted
and cooled
2 teaspoons vanilla
1 recipe Chocolate
Glaze

1 Finely chop 1 cup of the hazelnuts; set aside. Place the remaining ½ cup hazelnuts in a food processor or blender. Cover and process until very finely ground but still dry (not oily); set aside. In a medium bowl stir together the ground hazelnuts, flour, cocoa powder, and baking powder; set aside.

2 In a large mixing bowl beat eggs with an electric mixer on high speed about 4 minutes or until thick and lemon color. Gradually add sugar, beating on medium speed. Beat in the butter and vanilla until combined. Add flour mixture, beating on low speed until combined.

3 Heat an electric pizzelle iron according to manufacturer's directions. (Or heat a nonelectric pizzelle iron on range top over medium heat until a drop of water sizzles on the grid. Reduce heat to medium-low.)

4 For each pizzelle, place a slightly rounded tablespoon of batter on pizzelle grid, slightly off-center toward the back. Close lid. Bake according to manufacturer's directions. (For a nonelectric iron, bake about 2 minutes or until golden brown, turning once.) Transfer pizzelle to a paper towel to cool. Repeat with remaining batter.

5 Dip the edges of each pizzella into Chocolate Glaze and then into the reserved chopped hazelnuts to coat edges. Place pizzelle on wire racks until glaze is set.

nutrition facts per cookie: 120 cal., 5 g total fat (1 g sat. fat), 22 mg chol., 54 mg sodium, 17 g carb., 1 g fiber, 2 g pro.

chocolate glaze: In a medium bowl stir together 3 cups powdered sugar, ⅓ cup unsweetened cocoa powder, and 1 teaspoon vanilla. Stir in enough milk (4 to 6 tablespoons) to make a glaze of dipping consistency.

Egg whites, ground nuts, and powdered sugar add to the unique quality of these treats from the Tuscany region of Italy.

tuscan-style cookies

prep: 30 minutes   **chill:** overnight   **bake:** 10 minutes at 350°F per batch
makes: 36 cookies

232

1½   cups slivered almonds
1   cup pistachio nuts
2½   cups powdered sugar
¼   cup all-purpose flour
1   tablespoon finely shredded orange peel
2   teaspoons finely shredded lemon peel
¼   teaspoon baking powder
¼   teaspoon salt
2   egg whites
½   teaspoon almond extract
½   teaspoon vanilla
    Powdered sugar

1 In a food processor combine almonds, pistachios, and ½ cup of the powdered sugar. Cover and process until nuts are very finely ground but still dry (not oily). Add 1½ cups of the powdered sugar, the flour, orange peel, lemon peel, baking powder, and ¼ teaspoon salt. Cover and process with on/off pulses until combined; set aside.

2 In a large mixing bowl beat egg whites, almond extract, and vanilla with an electric mixer on medium speed until soft peaks form (tips curl). Gradually add the remaining ½ cup powdered sugar, beating until medium-stiff peaks form (tips stand almost straight). Gently fold nut mixture into beaten egg whites until combined.

3 Line a shallow baking pan with plastic wrap. Using damp hands or a rubber spatula, shape dough into a 12×6-inch rectangle in the baking pan. Cover with plastic wrap and chill overnight.

4 Preheat oven to 350°F. Line a cookie sheet with parchment paper or foil; set aside. Using a long sharp knife, cut dough into 2-inch squares. Cut each square in half diagonally to form two triangles. Place 1 inch apart on the prepared cookie sheet.

5 Bake for 10 to 12 minutes or until bottoms are lightly browned. Transfer cookies to a wire rack. While warm, sprinkle lightly with additional powdered sugar; cool.

nutrition facts per cookie: 84 cal., 4 g total fat (0 g sat fat), 0 mg chol., 22 mg sodium, 11 g carb., 1 g fiber, 2 g pro.

A pocket of nut and orange—delizioso!

walnut crescents (pressnitz)

prep: 40 minutes **chill:** 1 hour **bake:** 18 minutes at 375°F per batch
makes: 20 cookies

½ cup butter, softened
½ cup ricotta cheese
¼ teaspoon salt
1½ cups all-purpose flour
½ cup chopped walnuts, toasted (see tip, page 13)
⅓ cup granulated sugar
2 tablespoons orange marmalade
½ teaspoon finely shredded orange peel
¼ teaspoon ground cinnamon
1 egg
1 tablespoon water

1 In a large mixing bowl beat butter, ricotta cheese, and salt with an electric mixer on medium to high speed about 30 seconds or until smooth. Using a wooden spoon, stir in flour. Shape dough into a ball. Wrap in plastic wrap. Chill for 1 hour.

2 Preheat oven to 375°F. Lightly grease a cookie sheet. On a lightly floured surface, roll dough to ½-inch thickness. Fold in half; roll to a 15×12-inch rectangle, about ⅛ inch thick. Cut into 3-inch squares.

3 For filling, in a small bowl combine walnuts, sugar, orange marmalade, orange peel, and cinnamon. Place a slightly rounded teaspoon of filling on each dough square. Fold one corner of each dough square over the filling; roll to the opposite corner and press to seal. If necessary, brush underside of each dough point with water before pressing to seal. Shape into slight crescents. Place crescents on prepared cookie sheets. In a small bowl beat together the egg and water. Brush egg mixture over crescents.

4 Bake for 18 to 20 minutes or until golden brown. Transfer to a wire rack; cool.

to store: Layer cookies between sheets of waxed paper in an airtight container; cover. Store at room temperature up to 3 days or freeze up to 1 month.

nutrition facts per cookie: 126 cal., 8 g total fat (4 g sat. fat), 25 mg chol., 80 mg sodium, 12 g carb., 0 g fiber, 2 g pro.

Similar to Mexican wedding cakes (which are actually butter cookies), this version has roots in Spain.

walnut polvorones

prep: 40 minutes **chill:** 1 hour **bake:** 15 minutes at 325°F per batch
makes: 16 cookies

1½ cups finely chopped
walnuts, toasted
(see tip, page 13)
1 cup butter, softened
1 cup powdered sugar
1 tablespoon milk
1½ teaspoons ground
cinnamon
1 teaspoon vanilla
1½ cups all-purpose flour
Granulated sugar

1 Place ¾ cup of the walnuts in a food processor. Cover and process until very finely ground but still dry (not oily); set aside. In a large mixing bowl beat butter with an electric mixer on medium to high speed for 30 seconds. Add ½ cup of the powdered sugar. Beat until combined, scraping sides of bowl occasionally. Beat in milk, 1 teaspoon of the cinnamon, and the vanilla until combined. Beat in as much of the flour as you can with the mixer. Using a wooden spoon, stir in any remaining flour, the ground walnuts, and the remaining finely chopped walnuts. Cover and chill about 1 hour or until dough is easy to handle.

2 Preheat oven to 325°F. Shape dough into 2-inch balls. Place balls 2½ inches apart on an ungreased cookie sheet. Dip the bottom of a drinking glass with a distinctive design into granulated sugar; use glass bottom to flatten balls slightly.

3 Bake about 15 minutes or until bottoms are lightly browned. Cool on cookie sheet for 2 minutes. Transfer to a wire rack; cool.

4 Before serving, in a small bowl combine the remaining ½ cup powdered sugar and the remaining ½ teaspoon cinnamon. Sprinkle cookies with powdered sugar-cinnamon mixture.

to store: Layer plain cookies between sheets of waxed paper in an airtight container; cover. Store at room temperature up to 3 days or freeze up to 3 months. Before serving, sprinkle with powdered sugar-cinnamon mixture.

nutrition facts per cookie: 249 cal., 19 g total fat (8 g sat. fat), 31 mg chol., 83 mg sodium, 19 g carb., 1 g fiber, 3 g pro.

See pages 107–113 for more biscotti recipes with Italian roots.

lemon-nut biscotti sticks

prep: 40 minutes **bake:** 30 minutes at 350°F + 10 minutes at 300°F per batch
makes: 68 cookies

2¾ cups all-purpose flour
1½ cups granulated sugar
2 tablespoons cornmeal
1½ teaspoons baking powder
1 teaspoon salt
½ teaspoon anise seeds
3 eggs
1 egg yolk
⅓ cup butter, melted
2 teaspoons finely shredded lemon peel
½ cup whole almonds
½ cup pine nuts

1 Preheat oven to 350°F. Line two cookie sheets with parchment paper; set aside. In a large bowl stir together flour, sugar, cornmeal, baking powder, salt, and anise seeds. Make a well in the center of flour mixture. In a small bowl beat eggs and egg yolk with a fork until combined. Add eggs, melted butter, and lemon peel all at once to flour mixture; stir until combined. Stir in almonds and pine nuts. Dough will be sticky.

2 Turn dough out onto a lightly floured surface. Divide dough into four portions. Shape each portion into a 14-inch roll. Place two of the rolls about 3 inches apart on each prepared cookie sheet.

3 Bake on separate racks about 30 minutes or until lightly browned, rotating cookie sheets once halfway through baking. Cool completely on cookie sheets.

4 Preheat oven to 300°F. Transfer rolls to a cutting board. Using a serrated knife, cut rolls diagonally into ½-inch slices. Place slices on cookie sheets. Bake for 10 to 15 minutes or until crisp. Cool on wire racks.

nutrition facts per cookie: 61 cal., 2 g total fat (1 g sat. fat), 13 mg chol., 56 mg sodium, 9 g carb., 0 g fiber, 1 g pro.

orange-nut biscotti sticks: Prepare as directed, except substitute 1 tablespoon finely shredded orange peel for the lemon peel and stir in ¼ cup chopped purchased candied orange peel with the nuts.

nutrition facts per cookie: 64 cal., 2 g total fat (1 g sat. fat), 13 mg chol., 56 mg sodium, 9 g carb., 0 g fiber, 1 g pro.

The crown of pine nuts adds a crunchy finish to these buttery cookies.

italian cornmeal-apricot cookies

prep: 30 minutes **bake:** 10 minutes at 350°F per batch
makes: 42 cookies

1¾ cups all-purpose flour
¾   cup yellow cornmeal
½   teaspoon salt
1   cup butter, softened
¾   cup granulated sugar
2   eggs
1½ teaspoons vanilla
1   teaspoon finely
    shredded lemon
    peel
¾   cup snipped dried
    apricots
½   cup pine nuts

1 Preheat oven to 350°F. Line a cookie sheet with parchment paper; set aside. In a medium bowl stir together flour, cornmeal, and salt; set aside.

2 In a large mixing bowl beat butter with an electric mixer on medium to high speed for 30 seconds. Add sugar. Beat mixture about 2 minutes or until light and fluffy, scraping sides of bowl occasionally. Add eggs, one at a time, beating on low speed after each addition. Beat in vanilla and lemon peel. Beat in flour mixture on low speed until combined. Stir in dried apricots. Let dough stand for 5 minutes.

3 Place pine nuts in a shallow dish. Shape dough into 1¼-inch balls. Lightly press one side of each ball into pine nuts. Place balls, nut sides up, 2 inches apart on the prepared cookie sheet. Using your fingers, flatten each ball slightly.

4 Bake about 10 minutes or until edges are set. Cool on cookie sheet for 3 minutes. Transfer cookies to a wire rack; cool.

nutrition facts per cookie: 99 cal., 6 g total fat (3 g sat. fat), 20 mg chol., 70 mg sodium, 11 g carb., 0 g fiber, 1 g pro.

This crisp meringue cookie replicates the texture and almond flavor of a classic Italian import.

italian amaretti cookies

prep: 30 minutes bake: 13 minutes at 325°F per batch
makes: 48 cookies

1 cup whole blanched
    or unblanched
    almonds
½ cup powdered sugar
2 egg whites
1 tablespoon amaretto
    or ½ teaspoon
    almond extract
⅛ teaspoon cream of
    tartar
½ cup granulated sugar
    Whole blanched
    or unblanched
    almonds (optional)
    Coarse or regular
    granulated sugar
    (optional)

1 Preheat oven to 325°F. Line a large cookie sheet with parchment paper or foil. Lightly grease foil, if using. Set aside. In a food processor combine the 1 cup almonds and the powdered sugar. Cover and process until finely ground. Set aside.

2 In a large mixing bowl combine egg whites, amaretto, and cream of tartar. Beat with an electric mixer on high speed until soft peaks form (tips curl). Gradually beat in the ½ cup granulated sugar, about 1 tablespoon at a time, until stiff peaks form (tips stand straight). Fold half the almond mixture into the egg white mixture. Fold in the remaining almond mixture.

3 Spoon batter in 1-inch mounds 2 inches apart on the prepared cookie sheets. If desired, place a whole almond on top of each cookie and sprinkle lightly with coarse sugar.

4 Bake for 13 to 15 minutes or until tops are set and lightly browned. Cool on cookie sheets on a wire rack. Peel cookies from parchment paper or foil.

nutrition facts per cookie: 32 cal., 2 g total fat (1 g sat. fat), 0 mg chol., 3 mg sodium, 4 g carb., 0 g fiber, 1 g pro.

pineapple-filled macarons

prep: 35 minutes **stand:** 30 minutes **bake:** 10 minutes at 325°F per batch
makes: 24 sandwich cookies

½   cup coarsely chopped macadamia nuts (about 3 ounces)
½   cup slivered almonds (about 3 ounces)
2   cups powdered sugar
3   egg whites
½   teaspoon vanilla
    Salt
¼   cup shredded coconut, finely chopped
1   recipe Creamy Pineapple Filling

creamy pineapple filling: Drain ½ cup crushed pineapple in a sieve, reserving drained liquid. In a large bowl beat ¼ cup butter, softened, with an electric mixer on medium speed until smooth. Add drained pineapple and ½ teaspoon vanilla. Beat until combined. Gradually beat in 3 cups powdered sugar and enough reserved pineapple juice (1 to 2 tablespoons) to make a filling of spreading consistency.

1 Line two large cookie sheets with parchment paper; set aside. In a food processor combine macadamia nuts and almonds. Add 1 cup of the powdered sugar. Cover and process until nuts are very finely ground; set aside.

2 In a large mixing bowl combine egg whites, vanilla, and salt. Beat with an electric mixer on medium speed until soft peaks form (tips curl). Gradually add the remaining 1 cup powdered sugar, about 1 tablespoon at a time, beating on high speed just until stiff peaks form (tips stand straight). Sprinkle one-fourth of the nut mixture over the egg mixture; gently fold in with a large spatula. Continue sprinkling and folding in nut mixture, one-fourth at a time, until the two mixtures are combined.

3 Spoon macaron batter into a large decorating bag fitted with a large round tip (about ½-inch). Pipe batter in 1½-inch flat circles on the prepared cookie sheets. Sprinkle half the macaroons with coconut. Let stand for 30 minutes.

4 Preheat oven to 325°F. Bake for 10 to 15 minutes or just until set. Cool completely on cookie sheets on a wire rack. Peel cookies off parchment paper.

5 Spread about 1 tablespoon of the Creamy Pineapple Filling on flat sides (bottoms) of the cookies without coconut. Top each with a coconut-topped cookie, flat side down.

to store: Layer unfilled cookies between sheets of waxed paper in an airtight container; cover. Store at room temperature up to 3 days or freeze up to 3 months. To serve, thaw cookies, if frozen. Fill as directed in Step 5.

nutrition facts per sandwich cookie: 188 cal., 7 g total fat (2 g sat. fat), 6 mg chol., 45 mg sodium, 33 g carb., 1 g fiber, 1 g pro.

Lining the baking sheets with parchment paper is critical, for the cookies to easily removed after cooling.

cocoa-hazelnut macarons

prep: 35 minutes **stand:** 30 minutes **bake:** 9 minutes at 325°F per batch
makes: 20 sandwich cookies

1¼   cups powdered sugar
1   cup finely ground hazelnuts (filberts)
2   tablespoons unsweetened cocoa powder
3   egg whites
½   teaspoon vanilla
    Dash salt
¼   cup granulated sugar
¾   cup purchased chocolate-hazelnut spread

1 Line two large cookie sheets with parchment paper; set aside. In a medium bowl stir together powdered sugar, hazelnuts, and cocoa powder; set aside.

2 In a large mixing bowl combine egg whites, vanilla, and salt. Beat with an electric mixer on medium speed until frothy. Gradually add granulated sugar, about 1 tablespoon at a time, beating on high speed just until soft peaks form (tips curl). Stir in nut mixture.

3 Spoon batter into a large decorating bag fitted with a large (about ½-inch) round tip.* Pipe 1½-inch circles 1 inch apart onto the prepared cookie sheets. Let stand for 30 minutes before baking.

4 Meanwhile, preheat oven to 325°F. Bake for 9 to 10 minutes or until set. Cool on cookie sheets on wire racks. Carefully peel cookies off parchment paper.

5 Spread chocolate-hazelnut spread on bottoms of half the cookies. Top with remaining cookies, bottom sides down.

*tip: If you don't have a decorating bag, spoon batter into a large resealable plastic bag, snip a ½ inch from one corner of the bag.

to store: Layer unfilled cookies between sheets of waxed paper in an airtight container; cover. Store in the refrigerator up to 3 days or freeze up to 3 months. To serve, thaw cookies if frozen. Fill as directed in Step 5.

nutrition facts per sandwich cookie: 133 cal., 7 g total fat (0 g sat. fat), 0 mg chol., 25 mg sodium, 17 g carb., 1 g fiber, 2 g pro.

chocolate-glazed madeleines

prep: 25 minutes **bake:** 10 minutes at 375°F per batch **chill:** 30 minutes
makes: 24 cookies

½ cup granulated sugar
2 egg yolks
½ cup butter, melted and cooled
½ teaspoon finely shredded orange peel
1 tablespoon orange-flavor liqueur or orange juice
1 teaspoon vanilla
½ cup all-purpose flour
½ teaspoon baking powder
⅛ teaspoon baking soda
⅛ teaspoon salt
2 egg whites, lightly beaten
1 recipe Chocolate Glaze
Finely chopped pistachios (optional)

1 Preheat oven to 375°F. Grease and flour twenty-four 3-inch madeleine molds; set aside.

2 In a medium mixing bowl beat sugar and egg yolks with an electric mixer on medium to high speed about 30 seconds or until combined. Add the melted butter, orange peel, orange liqueur, and vanilla. Beat on low speed until combined.

3 In a small bowl combine the flour, baking powder, baking soda, and salt. Sprinkle about one-fourth of the flour mixture over the egg-yolk mixture; stir in gently. Repeat, sprinkling and stirring in one-fourth of the flour mixture at a time. Gently stir in the egg whites.

4 Spoon the batter into the prepared molds, filling each mold about one-half full.

5 Bake for 10 to 12 minutes or until edges are golden brown and tops spring back when lightly touched. Cool in molds for 1 minute. Using the point of a knife, loosen each madeleine from the mold. Invert mold onto a wire rack. Remove mold; cool.

6 Dip half of each cookie in warm Chocolate Glaze, letting excess drip off. Place on a waxed paper-lined pan. If desired, sprinkle pistachios onto Chocolate Glaze. Chill madeleines about 30 minutes or until Chocolate Glaze is set.

chocolate glaze: In a medium saucepan heat ½ cup whipping cream, ½ teaspoon vanilla, and, if desired, 1 tablespoon orange-flavor liqueur over medium-high heat just until boiling. Remove from heat. Add 6 ounces bittersweet or semisweet chocolate, chopped. Do not stir. Let stand for 5 minutes; stir until smooth.

to store: Layer unglazed cookies between sheets of waxed paper in an airtight container; cover. Store at room temperature up to 3 days or freeze up to 3 months. Layer glazed cookies between sheets of waxed paper in an airtight container; cover. Store in the refrigerator up to 2 days. Bring to room temperature before serving.

nutrition facts per cookie: 126 cal., 9 g total fat (6 g sat. fat), 52 mg chol., 62 mg sodium, 10 g carb., 1 g fiber, 2 g pro.

These thin crisp cookies, originally from France, double as edible cups. Pictured on page 223.

mint tuile bowls

prep: 30 minutes **bake:** 5 minutes at 375°F per batch **cool:** 30 minutes
makes: 32 cookies

4 egg whites
6 tablespoons butter, melted
2 tablespoons white creme de menthe or anise-, almond-, or hazelnut-flavor liqueur
½ teaspoon vanilla
1 cup granulated sugar
1 cup all-purpose flour
1 recipe Crème de Menthe Whipped Cream or small scoops mint ice cream
   Fresh raspberries (optional)

crème de menthe whipped cream: In a large chilled mixing bowl beat 1 cup whipping cream, 2 tablespoons granulated sugar, 2 tablespoons white crème de menthe, and ½ teaspoon vanilla with an electric mixer on medium speed until stiff peaks form.

1 In a medium bowl let egg whites stand at room temperature for 30 minutes. Meanwhile, line a large cookie sheet with foil; lightly grease foil. Place desired bowl molds* on a work surface. In a small bowl combine melted butter, crème de menthe, and vanilla; set aside.

2 Preheat oven to 375°F. In a large mixing bowl beat egg whites with an electric mixer on medium speed until soft peaks form (tips curl). Gradually add sugar, beating on high speed until stiff peaks form (tips stand straight). Fold in about half the flour. Gently stir in butter mixture. Fold in the remaining flour until thoroughly combined.

3 For each cookie, drop a level tablespoon of batter onto the prepared cookie sheet (bake only three or four cookies at a time). Using the back of a spoon, spread batter into 3-inch circles.

4 Bake for 5 to 7 minutes or until cookies are golden brown around edges. Using a wide spatula, immediately remove the cookies and drape, in a single layer, over bowl molds. Cool cookies on molds about 30 minutes or until they hold their shape; then carefully remove. Cool completely on a wire rack.

5 Just before serving, pipe or spoon Crème de Menthe Whipped Cream into tuile bowls. If desired, garnish each with a raspberry.

*tip: A variety of kitchen objects will work as molds to shape these bowl-shape cookies. Use overturned shot glasses, ramekins, 1¾-inch muffin cups, or individual egg cups cut from an egg carton.

to store: Layer unfilled tuile bowls between sheets of waxed paper in an airtight container; cover. Store at room temperature up to 3 days or freeze up to 3 months. To serve, thaw tuile bowls, if frozen. Fill tuile bowls as directed in Step 5.

nutrition facts per cookie: 97 cal., 5 g total fat (3 g sat. fat), 16 mg chol., 25 mg sodium, 11 g carb., 0 g fiber, 1 g pro.

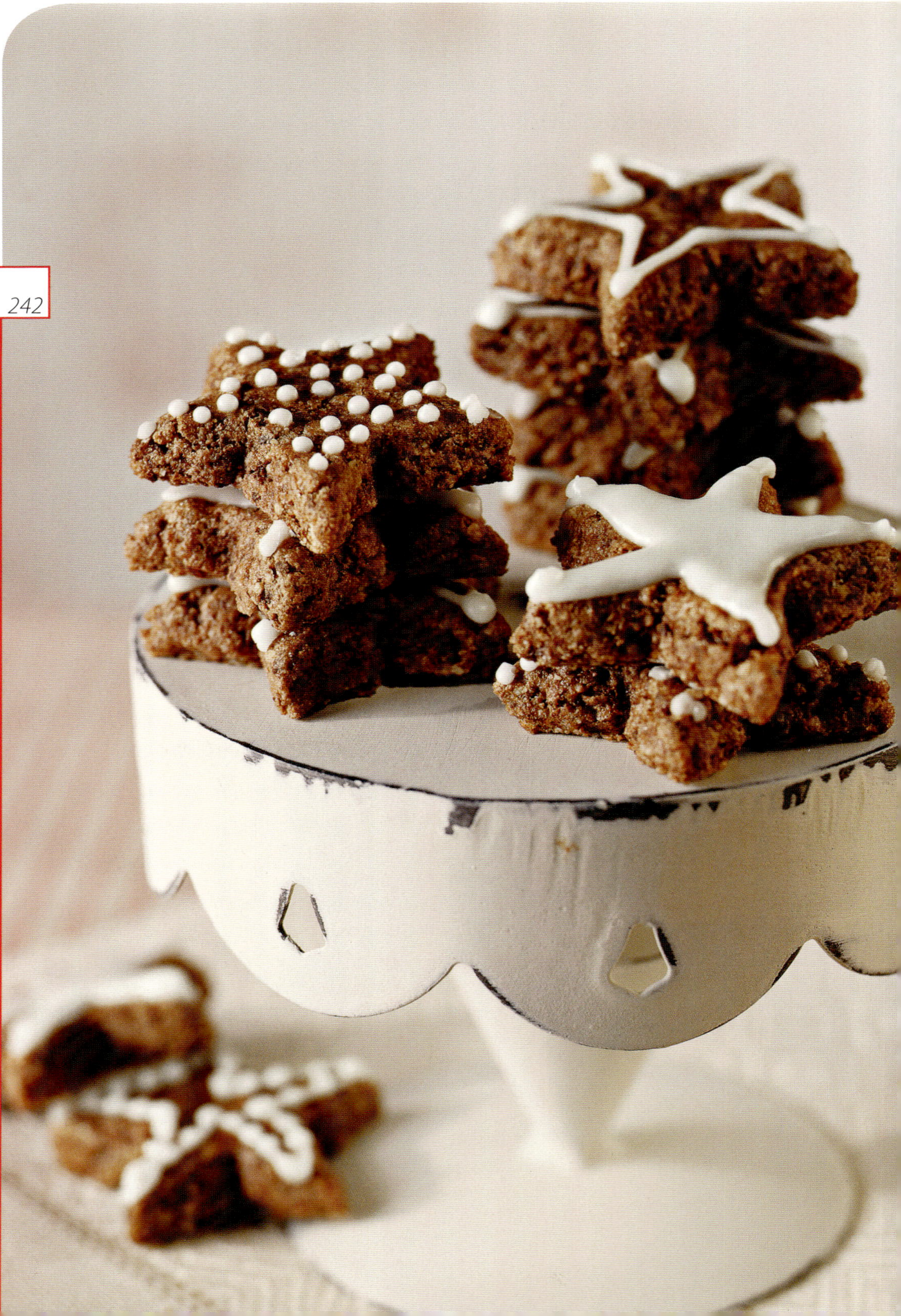

swiss basler brunsli

prep: 30 minutes **chill:** 1 hour **bake:** 12 minutes at 350°F per batch
makes: 30 cookies

5   ounces almonds (about
       1 cup)
¾   cup granulated sugar
¾   teaspoon ground
       cinnamon
¼   teaspoon ground cloves
3   ounces bittersweet
       chocolate, coarsely
       chopped
1   egg white
1   to 2 tablespoons kirsch
       Powdered sugar
1   recipe Powdered Sugar
       Icing (see recipe,
       page 18)

1 In a food processor* combine almonds, granulated sugar, cinnamon, and cloves. Cover and process until finely ground. Add chocolate and process with several on/off turns until finely ground. Add egg white and 1 tablespoon of the kirsch; process to form a stiff dough. If necessary, add additional kirsch, 1 teaspoon at a time, until dough holds together. Wrap dough in plastic wrap and chill about 1 hour or until easy to handle.

2 Preheat oven to 350°F. Line a cookie sheet with parchment paper; set aside. Place dough on a surface lightly coated with powdered sugar. Using a rolling pin coated with powdered sugar, roll dough to ⅜-inch thickness. Using a 1½-inch star- or heart-shape cookie cutter, cut out dough. Place cutouts 1 inch apart on the prepared cookie sheet.

3 Bake about 12 minutes or until edges are firm and surface is dry (center will be soft). Do not overbake. Let stand for 2 minutes on cookie sheet. Transfer to a wire rack; cool. Decorate as desired with Powdered Sugar Icing.

*tip: To prepare dough using a blender, place almonds, ½ cup of the granulated sugar, the cinnamon, and cloves in the blender. Cover and blend until finely ground; do not overblend. Transfer to a large mixing bowl; set aside. Finely chop the chocolate and transfer to blender; add remaining ¼ cup sugar. Cover and blend until very finely chopped. Add to mixture in bowl. Stir in the egg white and 1 tablespoon of the kirsch until well mixed. If necessary, stir in additional kirsch until dough holds together. Continue as above.

to store: Layer uniced cookies between sheets of waxed paper in an airtight container; cover. Store at room temperature up to 3 days or freeze unfrosted cookies up to 3 months. Thaw cookies, if frozen. Decorate with Powdered Sugar Icing.

nutrition facts per cookie: 87 cal.,3 g total fat (1 g sat. fat), 0 mg chol., 2 mg sodium, 14 g carb., 1 g fiber, 1 g pro.

This quick version of the Swiss treat bypasses the traditional wooden molds.

leckerle

prep: 30 minutes **bake:** 10 minutes at 350°F per batch
makes: 60 cookies

2½   cups all-purpose flour
1   cup granulated sugar
1   cup unblanched almonds, finely chopped
¼   cup candied orange peel, finely chopped
¼   cup candied lemon peel, finely chopped
1   teaspoon baking powder
1   teaspoon ground cinnamon
½   teaspoon ground nutmeg
¼   teaspoon ground cloves
¾   cup honey
2   tablespoons kirsch or brandy
1   egg, lightly beaten
1   recipe Citrus Glaze

1 Preheat oven to 350°F. Grease a cookie sheet; set aside. In a large mixing bowl stir together flour, sugar, almonds, candied peels, baking powder, cinnamon, nutmeg, and cloves. Make a well in the center of the flour mixture. Add honey, kirsch, and the egg. Stir and knead the dough until it forms a ball. Divide dough in half.

2 On a lightly floured surface, roll one dough portion at a time to ¼-inch thickness. Cut dough into 2½×1-inch strips. Place strips 1 inch apart on the prepared cookie sheet.

3 Bake about 10 minutes or until golden brown. Transfer cookies to a wire rack. While still warm, brush cookies with Citrus Glaze; cool.

nutrition facts per cookie: 67 cal., 1 g total fat (0 g sat. fat), 3 mg chol., 10 mg sodium, 14 g carb., 0 g fiber, 1 g pro.

citrus glaze: In a small bowl stir together ½ cup powdered sugar, 1 teaspoon melted butter, ¼ teaspoon finely shredded lemon peel, and 1 teaspoon lemon juice. Stir in additional water, 1 teaspoon at a time, until glaze is of brushing consistency.

Make sure you get marzipan and not almond paste for this recipe. Almond paste has a higher proportion of almonds to sugar than marzipan and a slightly grainier texture.

german biberli

prep: 45 minutes **chill:** 2 hours **bake:** 8 minutes at 350°F per batch
makes: 30 cookies

½ cup packed brown sugar
⅓ cup honey
2 cups all-purpose flour
1½ teaspoons ground cinnamon
½ teaspoon baking powder
½ teaspoon ground nutmeg
1 egg
¼ cup butter, softened
½ cup mixed candied fruits and peels, finely chopped
½ cup chopped, slivered almonds
1 7- to 8-ounce package marzipan
Powdered sugar
1 recipe Lemon Glaze
Chopped almonds (optional)
Maraschino cherries (optional)

1 In a small saucepan heat and stir brown sugar and honey over low heat until sugar is dissolved. Remove from heat; cool slightly. In a medium bowl stir together flour, cinnamon, baking powder, and nutmeg; set aside. In a large mixing bowl combine honey mixture, egg, and butter. Beat with an electric mixer on low to medium speed until combined. Stir in candied fruits and peels and the ½ cup almonds. Stir in flour mixture. Cover and chill dough for 2 hours or until easy to handle.

2 In a small bowl knead marzipan with your hands until softened. Shape marzipan into a ball; flatten slightly. Sprinkle with powdered sugar. Roll ball between two sheets of waxed paper into an 8-inch square; set aside.

3 Preheat oven to 350°F. Lightly grease a cookie sheet; set aside. On a lightly floured surface, roll dough into a 16×8-inch rectangle. Place marzipan square on half of rectangle; lift unlayered dough portion and fold it over marzipan. Using a rolling pin, roll layered dough to ½ inch thickness (about a 9-inch square). Using a sharp knife, cut square into diamonds about 3 inches long and 1½-inches wide. Place diamonds 1 inch apart on prepared cookie sheet.

4 Bake about 8 minutes or until golden. Let stand for 2 minutes on cookie sheet. Transfer to a wire rack. While still warm, brush cookies with Lemon Glaze. If desired, sprinkle with chopped almonds and top with a maraschino cherry. Let stand until set.

nutrition facts per cookie: 115 cal., 4 g total fat (1 g sat. fat), 11 mg chol., 30 mg sodium, 19 g carb., 1 g fiber, 2 g pro.

lemon glaze: In a small bowl stir together ½ cup powdered sugar, 1 teaspoon melted butter, ¼ teaspoon finely shredded lemon peel, and 1 teaspoon lemon juice. Stir in additional water, 1 teaspoon at a time, until glaze is of brushing consistency.

Add this classic cookie from Germany to your holiday baking.

lebkuchen

prep: 35 minutes   **chill:** 3 hours   **bake:** 8 minutes at 350°F per batch
makes: 48 cookies

1   egg
¾   cup packed brown
      sugar
½   cup full-flavor
      molasses
⅓   cup honey
3   cups all-purpose flour
1   teaspoon ground
      cinnamon
½   teaspoon baking soda
½   teaspoon ground
      cloves
½   teaspoon ground
      ginger
¼   teaspoon ground
      cardamom
½   cup chopped almonds
½   cup finely chopped
      diced mixed
      candied fruits and
      peels
1   recipe Lemon Glaze
      Candied fruit pieces

1 In a medium mixing bowl beat egg with an electric mixer on high speed for 1 minute. Add brown sugar; beat on medium speed until light and fluffy. Beat in molasses and honey.

2 In a large bowl stir together flour, cinnamon, baking soda, cloves, ginger, and cardamom. Add beaten egg mixture. Using a wooden spoon, stir until combined (dough will be stiff.) Stir in almonds and the ½ cup candied fruits and peels. Divide dough in half. Cover and chill about 3 hours or until dough is easy to handle.

3 Preheat oven to 350°F. Lightly grease a cookie sheet; set aside. On a lightly floured surface, roll one dough portion at a time into a 12×8-inch rectangle. Cut into 2-inch squares. Place on prepared cookie sheet.

4 Bake for 8 to 10 minutes or until lightly browned around edges. Cool on cookie sheet for 1 minute. Transfer cookies to a wire rack. Brush warm cookies with Lemon Glaze. Garnish with candied fruit pieces. Allow glaze to thoroughly dry and cookies to cool. Place cookies in a single layer in an airtight container; cover. Store cookies at room temperature overnight to soften.

to store: Store cookies in the covered container at room temperature up to 7 days or freeze up to 3 months.

nutrition facts per cookie: 82 cal., 1 g total fat (0 g sat. fat), 5 mg chol., 19 mg sodium, 17 g carb., 0 g fiber, 1 g pro.

lemon glaze: In a small bowl stir together 1½ cups powdered sugar; 1 tablespoon butter, melted; and 1 tablespoon lemon juice. Add enough water (3 to 4 teaspoons) to make glaze drizzling consistency.

The filling in these dainty cookies borrows raspberry jam from Austria's famous linzertorte.

linzer jam sandwiches

prep: 40 minutes   **chill:** 1 hour   **bake:** 7 minutes at 375°F per batch
makes: 20 sandwich cookies

⅓   cup butter, softened
⅓   cup shortening
¾   cup granulated sugar
1½ teaspoons baking
     powder
¼   teaspoon salt
¼   teaspoon ground
     cinnamon
⅛   teaspoon ground
     cloves
1   egg
1   tablespoon milk
½   teaspoon vanilla
½   teaspoon finely
     shredded lemon
     peel
2   cups all-purpose flour
     Powdered sugar
⅓   to ½ cup raspberry,
     strawberry, or
     cherry preserves or
     jam

1 In a large mixing bowl beat butter and shortening with an electric mixer on medium to high speed for 30 seconds. Add granulated sugar, baking powder, salt, cinnamon, and cloves. Beat until combined, scraping sides of bowl occasionally. Beat in egg, milk, vanilla, and lemon peel until combined. Beat in as much of the flour as you can with the mixer. Using a wooden spoon, stir in any remaining flour. Divide dough in half. Cover and chill dough about 1 hour or until easy to handle.

2 Preheat oven to 375°F. On a lightly floured surface, roll half the dough at a time to ⅛- to ¼-inch thickness. Using 2½-inch cookie cutters, cut dough into shapes. Place cutouts 1 inch apart on an ungreased cookie sheet. Using ¾-inch cookie cutters, cut shapes from centers half of the cookies. Reroll scraps as necessary.

3 Bake for 7 to 10 minutes or until edges are lightly browned. Transfer cookies to a wire rack; cool.

4 Sift powdered sugar onto the cookies with cutout centers. Spread a scant teaspoon of preserves on the bottoms of the cookies without cutouts. Press the bottoms of the sugared cookies against the preserves. Serve within 2 hours.

to store: Layer unfilled cookies between sheets of waxed paper in an airtight container; cover. Store at room temperature up to 3 days or freeze up to 3 months. Thaw cookies, if frozen. Assemble as directed in Step 4.

nutrition facts per sandwich cookie: 154 cal., 7 g total fat (3 g sat. fat), 17 mg chol., 89 mg sodium, 22 g carb., 0 g fiber, 2 g pro.

Delicious anytime of year, Rugalach is traditionally served during Hanukkah.

chocolate rugalach

prep: 30 minutes **chill:** 1 hour **bake:** 20 minutes at 350°F per batch
makes: 48 cookies

1 cup butter, softened
1 8-ounce carton sour cream
1 egg yolk
2 cups all-purpose flour
¾ cup granulated sugar
¾ cup miniature semisweet chocolate pieces
1 teaspoon ground cinnamon
Powdered sugar (optional)

1 In large mixing bowl beat butter with an electric mixer on medium to high speed for 30 seconds. Add sour cream and egg yolk. Beat until combined. Using a wooden spoon, stir in flour until combined. (Dough will be sticky.) Divide dough into four portions. Cover and chill for 1 hour or until dough is easy to handle.

2 For filling, in a small bowl combine sugar, chocolate pieces, and cinnamon; set aside.

3 Preheat oven to 350°F. Line a cookie sheet with parchment paper; set aside. On a lightly floured surface, roll one portion of the dough into a 10-inch circle. Spread one-fourth of the filling on dough . Cut dough into 12 wedges. Roll up each wedge, starting at wide end. Repeat with remaining dough and filling. Place cookies, tip sides down, about 2 inches apart on prepared cookie sheet.

4 Bake for 20 minutes or until golden brown. Transfer cookies to wire racks; cool. If desired, sprinkle with powdered sugar.

nutrition facts per cookie: 89 cal., 6 g total fat (4 g sat. fat), 17 mg chol., 30 mg sodium, 9 g carb., 0 g fiber, 1 g pro.

apricot rugalach: Prepare as directed except omit miniature chocolate pieces and cinnamon. For filling, in a small saucepan combine 1 cup finely snipped dried apricots or finely snipped dried cherries, ¼ cup granulated sugar, and ¼ cup warm water. Bring to boiling; reduce heat. Simmer, uncovered, about 5 minutes or until thickened, stirring occasionally. Remove from heat; cool. Stir in ½ cup finely chopped toasted walnuts (see tip, page 13). Continue as directed in Step 3.

nutrition facts per cookie: 94 cal., 6 g total fat (3 g sat. fat), 16 mg chol., 38 mg sodium, 10 g carb., 0 g fiber, 1 g pro.

Windmill-shape cookies represent the landscape throughout the Netherlands.

speculaas

prep: 45 minutes chill: 1 hour bake: 8 minutes at 350°F per batch
makes: 48 cookies

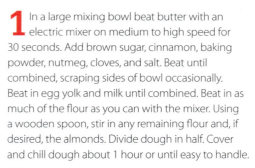

½ cup butter, softened
¾ cup packed brown sugar
¾ teaspoon ground cinnamon
½ teaspoon baking powder
¼ teaspoon ground nutmeg
¼ teaspoon ground cloves
⅛ teaspoon salt
1 egg yolk
1 tablespoon milk
1⅓ cups all-purpose flour
3 tablespoons finely chopped blanched almonds (optional)
1 recipe Powdered Sugar Icing (see recipe, page 18) (optional)

1 In a large mixing bowl beat butter with an electric mixer on medium to high speed for 30 seconds. Add brown sugar, cinnamon, baking powder, nutmeg, cloves, and salt. Beat until combined, scraping sides of bowl occasionally. Beat in egg yolk and milk until combined. Beat in as much of the flour as you can with the mixer. Using a wooden spoon, stir in any remaining flour and, if desired, the almonds. Divide dough in half. Cover and chill dough about 1 hour or until easy to handle.

2 Preheat oven to 350°F. Lightly grease a cookie sheet; set aside. Lightly oil a cookie mold. Press a small amount of dough into the prepared cookie mold. Unmold dough onto the prepared cookie sheet. If cookie does not unmold easily, tap the mold on the counter to release the dough. (Or, on a lightly floured surface, roll one half of the dough at a time to ⅛-inch thickness. Use desired cookie cutters to cut out dough.) Place cookies 1 inch apart on the prepared cookie sheet.

3 Bake for 8 to 10 minutes or until edges are golden. Let stand for 1 minute on cookie sheet. Transfer to a wire rack; cool. If desired, prepare Powdered Sugar Icing as directed except reduce milk to 2 to 3 teaspoons to make icing piping consistency. Pipe frosting on cookies.

to store: Layer cookies between sheets of waxed paper in an airtight container; cover. Store at room temperature up to 3 days or freeze undecorated cookies up to 3 months. Thaw cookies. If desired, decorate with Powdered Sugar Icing.

nutrition facts per cookie: 40 cal., 2 g total fat (1 g sat. fat), 10 mg chol., 30 mg sodium, 5 g carb., 0 g fiber, 0 g pro.

Stick with tradition by serving with hot brewed English tea.

english lemon-curd sandwich cookies

prep: 30 minutes **chill:** 1 hour **bake:** 12 minutes at 350°F per batch
makes: 48 sandwich cookies

1 recipe Lemon Curd or
  2 cups purchased
  lemon curd
2½ cups all-purpose flour
½ teaspoon baking soda
½ teaspoon salt
1 cup butter, softened
¾ cup granulated sugar
1 egg
1 teaspoon vanilla
1 cup finely ground
  pecans

1 In a medium bowl stir together flour, baking soda, and salt; set aside. In a large mixing bowl beat butter with an electric mixer on medium to high speed for 30 seconds. Add sugar. Beat until combined, scraping sides of bowl occasionally. Beat in egg and vanilla until combined. Beat in pecans and as much of the flour mixture as you can with the mixer. Using a wooden spoon, stir in any remaining flour mixture. Divide dough in half. Cover and chill about 1 hour or until dough is easy to handle.

2 Preheat oven to 350°F. On a lightly floured surface, one portion of the dough at a time to ⅛-inch thickness. Using a floured 2-inch round scalloped-edge round cookie cutter, cut out dough. Place cutouts 1 inch apart on an ungreased cookie sheet. Using a ½-inch round cookie cutter, cut and remove a circle from the center of half the cookies.

3 Bake for 12 to 15 minutes or until lightly browned. Transfer cookies to a wire rack; cool.

4 Spread 1½ teaspoons of the Lemon Curd on bottoms of the cookies without cutout centers. Top with cookies with cutout centers, bottom sides down.

lemon curd: In a medium saucepan stir together 1 cup granulated sugar and 2 tablespoons cornstarch. Stir in 1 tablespoon finely shredded lemon peel, 6 tablespoons lemon juice, and 6 tablespoons water. Cook and stir over medium heat until thickened and bubbly. Stir half the lemon mixture into 6 lightly beaten egg yolks. Return egg mixture to the saucepan. Cook, stirring constantly, over medium heat until mixture comes to a gentle boil. Cook and stir for 2 minutes more. Remove from heat. Add ½ cup butter, cut into pieces, stirring until melted. Cover surface of the curd with plastic wrap. Chill at least 1 hour. Store, covered, in refrigerator up to 1 week or freeze up to 2 months. Thaw in refrigerator before serving. Makes about 2 cups.

to store: Place sandwich cookies in a single layer in an airtight container; cover. Store in the refrigerator up to 3 days. Freeze unfilled cookies up to 3 months. To serve, thaw cookies and fill as directed.

nutrition facts per sandwich cookie: 126 cal., 8 g total fat (4 g sat. fat), 42 mg chol., 91 mg sodium, 13 g carb., 0 g fiber, 1 g pro.

Although brandy is the traditional liquor in this English recipe, you can substitute rum or orange liqueur.

brandy snaps

prep: 40 minutes **bake:** 9 minutes at 350°F per batch
makes: 30 cookies

½   cup granulated sugar
½   cup butter
⅓   cup golden syrup* or
        dark-color corn syrup
¾   cup all-purpose flour
½   teaspoon ground ginger
1   tablespoon brandy
1   recipe Sweetened
        Whipped Cream
        (optional)

1 Preheat oven to 350°F. Line a cookie sheet with foil. Lightly grease the foil; set aside.

2 In a medium saucepan heat and stir sugar, butter, and syrup over low heat until butter is melted. Remove from heat. In a small bowl stir together flour and ginger; add to butter mixture, mixing well. Stir in brandy.

3 Drop batter by rounded teaspoons 3 to 4 inches apart onto the prepared cookie sheet. (Bake only two or three cookies at a time.)

4 Bake for 9 to 10 minutes or until bubbly and golden brown. Let stand for 1 to 2 minutes on cookie sheet. Quickly invert cookies onto another cookie sheet, and wrap each cookie around the greased handle of a wooden spoon or a metal cone. When cookie is set, transfer to a wire rack; cool. If desired, fill cooled cookies with Sweetened Whipped Cream.

*tip: Golden syrup, popular in England, is available in specialty stores and large supermarkets.

to store: Place unfilled cookies in a single layer in an airtight container; cover. Store at room temperature up to 3 days or freeze up to 3 months. Thaw cookies; if desired, fill with Sweetened Whipped Cream.

nutrition facts per snap: 62 cal., 3 g total fat (2 g sat. fat), 8 mg chol., 34 mg sodium, 8 g carb., 0 g fiber, 0 g pro.

sweetened whipped cream: In a medium size chilled mixing bowl combine 1 cup whipping cream, 2 tablespoons granulated or powdered sugar, and ½ teaspoon vanilla. Beat with an electric mixer on medium speed until soft peaks form (tips curl).

new zealand yo-yos

prep: 30 minutes **bake:** 8 minutes at 375°F per batch
makes: 24 sandwich cookies

½   cup butter
½   cup granulated sugar
1   egg
1   teaspoon vanilla
1¾ cups all-purpose flour
¾   cup finely chopped
    red and/or green
    candied cherries
    Granulated sugar
    (optional)
1   recipe Cherry
    Frosting

1 Preheat oven to 375°F. In a large mixing bowl beat butter with an electric mixer on medium to high speed for 30 seconds. Add the ½ cup sugar. Beat until combined, scraping sides of bowl occasionally. Beat in egg and vanilla until combined. Beat in as much flour as you can with the mixer. Using a wooden spoon, stir in any remaining flour and the candied cherries.

2 Shape dough into 1-inch balls. Place balls 2 inches apart on an ungreased cookie sheet. Flatten each ball by criss-crossing with the tines of a fork. If desired, sprinkle with sugar.

3 Bake about 8 minutes or until edges are golden. Transfer cookies to wire racks; cool.

4 Spread Cherry Frosting on the flat sides of half of the cookies. Top with remaining cookies, bottom sides down.

to store: Layer sandwich cookies between sheets of waxed paper in an airtight container; cover. Store in the refrigerator up to 2 days. (Or layer unfilled cookies between sheets of waxed paper in an airtight container; cover. Freeze up to 3 months. To serve, thaw cookies and fill with Cherry Frosting as directed.)

nutrition facts per sandwich cookie: 163 cal., 5 g total fat (3 g sat. fat), 22 mg chol., 49 mg sodium, 28 g carb., 0 g fiber, 1 g pro.

cherry frosting: In a medium mixing bowl beat one 3-ounce package cream cheese, softened, until fluffy. Gradually add 1 cup powdered sugar, beating well. Add ¼ teaspoon vanilla. Beat in an additional 1 cup powdered sugar to make frosting spreading consistency. Stir in ¼ cup finely chopped red or green candied cherries. Makes about ¾ cup.

melomacarona (greek honey-dipped cookies)

prep: 1 hour 15 minutes **bake:** 9 minutes at 375°F per batch **stand:** 30 minutes
makes: 60 cookies

1¾ cups mild-flavor olive oil
1¼ cups granulated sugar
1 tablespoon finely shredded orange peel
½ cup orange juice
2 tablespoons cognac or orange juice
2 teaspoons ground cinnamon
1½ teaspoons baking soda
¾ teaspoon freshly grated nutmeg or ½ teaspoon ground nutmeg
¼ teaspoon salt
¼ teaspoon ground cloves
7 cups all-purpose flour
½ cup granulated sugar
½ teaspoon ground cinnamon
1 egg white, lightly beaten
¼ cup sliced almonds
1 recipe Spiced Honey Glaze

1 Preheat oven to 375°F. In an extra-large bowl whisk together oil, the 1¼ cups sugar, orange peel, orange juice, cognac, 2 teaspoons cinnamon, the baking soda, nutmeg, salt, and cloves until well combined. Stir in flour with a wooden spoon. Dough will be stiff.

2 Turn dough out onto a lightly floured surface and knead for 5 minutes. Dough will be crumbly as you knead it. Shape dough into a ball.

3 In a small bowl combine the ½ cup sugar and the ½ teaspoon cinnamon. Using a slightly rounded tablespoon of dough for each cookie, shape dough into 2½×1½-inch ovals, ¼ to ½ inch thick. Dip dough ovals in cinnamon-sugar mixture, turning to coat both sides. Place ovals 1 inch apart on an ungreased cookie sheet. Brush tops of ovals very lightly with beaten egg white. Place 2 to 3 almond slices on each cookie, pressing lightly onto cookies.

4 Bake for 9 to 11 minutes or just until edges are firm when lightly touched and tops are lightly browned. Cool cookies on cookie sheet for 1 minute. Transfer cookies to wire racks; cool.

5 Place wire racks over sheets of waxed paper. Dip cooled cookies into Spiced Honey Glaze, turning to coat both sides. Remove from galze with two forks, allowing excess glaze to drip off. Set cookies on prepared racks. Let stand 30 minutes before serving.

nutrition facts per cookie: 147 cal., 7 g total fat (1 g sat. fat), 0 mg chol., 43 mg sodium, 22 g carb., 1 g fiber, 2 g pro.

spiced honey glaze: In a small saucepan combine ⅓ cup granulated sugar, ⅓ cup water, ⅓ cup honey, 1 teaspoon finely shredded lemon peel, 1 tablespoon lemon juice, one 3-inch cinnamon stick, and 1 whole clove. Bring to boiling, stirring constantly to dissolve sugar. Reduce heat; simmer, uncovered, for 10 minutes. Cool completely before dipping cookies.

Each wedge is a mini taste of the Greek dessert, baklava.

greek honey-nut wedges

prep: 30 minutes **chill:** 1 hour **bake:** 15 minutes at 350°F per batch
makes: 24 cookies

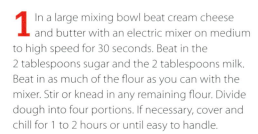

1	8-ounce package cream cheese, softened
½	cup butter, softened
2	tablespoons granulated sugar
2	tablespoons milk
2	cups all-purpose flour
⅔	cup granulated sugar
1½	teaspoons ground cinnamon
⅓	cup honey
2	tablespoons lemon juice
2	cups finely chopped walnuts
1	tablespoon granulated sugar
⅛	teaspoon ground cinnamon
	Milk

1 In a large mixing bowl beat cream cheese and butter with an electric mixer on medium to high speed for 30 seconds. Beat in the 2 tablespoons sugar and the 2 tablespoons milk. Beat in as much of the flour as you can with the mixer. Stir or knead in any remaining flour. Divide dough into four portions. If necessary, cover and chill for 1 to 2 hours or until easy to handle.

2 Meanwhile, for filling, in a small bowl stir together the ⅔ cup sugar, the 1½ teaspoons cinnamon, the honey, and lemon juice. Stir in walnuts; set aside. In another small bowl stir together the 1 tablespoon sugar and the ⅛ teaspoon cinnamon; set aside.

3 Preheat oven to 350°F. On a lightly floured surface, roll one portion of dough into an 8-inch circle. Carefully transfer circle to an ungreased cookie sheet. Spread half the filling to within ½ inch of edges. Roll another portion of dough into an 8-inch circle. Place over the nut-topped circle. Seal edges with a fork. Brush with milk; sprinkle with sugar-cinnamon mixture. Repeat with remaining dough and filling.

4 Bake for 15 to 20 minutes or until edges start to brown. Let stand for 10 minutes on cookie sheet. Cut each round into 12 wedges. Transfer to a wire rack; cool.

nutrition facts per cookie: 212 cal., 14 g total fat (5 g sat. fat), 21 mg chol., 66 mg sodium, 21 g carb., 1 g fiber, 3 g pro.

Almonds, a favorite ingredient in Mediterranean sweets, lend a characteristic flavor to these melt-in-your mouth cookies.

greek almond shortbread rounds

prep: 45 minutes **chill:** 1 hour **bake:** 12 minutes at 325°F per batch
makes: 84 cookies

1½ cups butter, softened
1 cup powdered sugar
2 egg yolks
2 tablespoons brandy
   or orange juice
2 teaspoons vanilla
3½ cups cake flour
1 cup blanched
   almonds, lightly
   toasted (see tip,
   page 13) and finely
   ground
Powdered sugar
2 tablespoons orange
   juice (optional)
Powdered sugar

1 In a large mixing bowl beat butter with an electric mixer on medium to high speed for 30 seconds. Add the 1 cup powdered sugar. Beat until fluffy and light in color, scraping sides of bowl occasionally. Beat in egg yolks, brandy, and vanilla until combined. Using a wooden spoon, stir in flour and almonds. Cover and chill about 1 hour or until dough is easy to handle.

2 Preheat oven to 325°F. Shape dough into 1-inch balls. Place balls 2 inches apart on an ungreased cookie sheet. Using the bottom of a glass that has been dipped in additional powdered sugar, flatten each ball to ¼-inch thickness.

3 Bake for 12 to 14 minutes or until set. Transfer cookies to a wire rack. If desired, lightly brush warm cookies with orange juice. Sprinkle cookies with additional powdered sugar. Cool completely on wire rack.

nutrition facts per cookie: 69 cal., 4 g total fat (2 g sat. fat), 13 mg chol., 30 mg sodium, 7 g carb., 0 g fiber, 1 g pro.

This Lebanese butter cookie gets it name from the Arabic word for "swoon."

middle eastern ghraybeh

prep: 30 minutes **bake:** 12 minutes at 325°F per batch
makes: 24 cookies

1 cup butter
2 cups all-purpose flour
1 cup sifted powdered sugar
2 tablespoons milk
1 tablespoon orange-flower water or rose water, or 1 teaspoon vanilla
12 blanched almonds, halved lengthwise, and toasted, if desired (see tip, page 13)

1 Preheat oven to 325°F. To clarify butter, in a small saucepan melt butter over low heat without stirring. Skim off solids that float to the surface; discard. Pour the clear layer into a measuring cup; discard the milky bottom layer. You should have about ¾ cup clarified butter.

2 In a medium mixing bowl stir together clarified butter, the flour, powdered sugar, milk, and orange-flower water.

3 Divide dough in half. Divide each half into 12 portions. Roll each portion into a ½-inch-thick rope about 5 inches long. Place ropes on an ungreased cookie sheet. Form ropes into S and/or O shapes. Place an almond half on top of each cookie.

4 Bake about 12 minutes or until bottoms are lightly browned. Transfer to a wire rack; cool.

nutrition facts per cookie: 125 cal., 8 g total fat (5 g sat. fat), 21 mg chol., 78 mg sodium, 12 g carb., 0 g fiber, 1 g pro.

cochinitos de jengibre

prep: 30 minutes **chill:** 3 hours **bake:** 7 minutes at 375°F per batch
makes: 18 cookies

⅔   cup butter, softened
¾   cup packed brown
    sugar
2   teaspoons ground
    ginger
1   teaspoon baking soda
1   teaspoon ground
    cinnamon
1   teaspoon finely
    shredded orange
    peel
½   teaspoon salt
¼   teaspoon ground
    cloves
1   egg
½   cup molasses
3   cups all-purpose flour
    Canned vanilla
    frosting (optional)
    White nonpareils or
    small decorative
    candies (optional)

1 In a large bowl beat butter with an electric mixer on medium to high speed for 30 seconds. Add brown sugar, ginger, baking soda, cinnamon, orange peel, salt, and cloves. Beat until combined, scraping sides of bowl occasionally. Beat in egg and molasses until combined. Beat in as much of the flour as you can with the mixer. Using a wooden spoon, stir in any remaining flour. Divide dough in half. Cover and chill about 3 hours or until dough is easy to handle.

2 Preheat oven to 375°F. Lightly grease a cookie sheet or line the sheet with parchment paper; set aside. On a lightly floured surface, roll one portion of the dough at a time to ¼-inch thickness. Using a lightly floured 4- to 5-inch pig-shape cookie cutter, cut out dough. Place cutouts 2 inches apart on prepared cookie sheet.*

3 Bake for 7 to 8 minutes or until edges are lightly browned. Cool on cookie sheet for 1 minute. Transfer to a wire rack; cool.

4 To decorate, if desired, spoon canned vanilla frosting into a decorating bag fitted with a small round tip. (Or fill a heavy resealable plastic bag with frosting; snip a small hole from one corner of the bag.) To outline each cookie, pipe a border around the edge. For the pig's eye, pipe a small dot of frosting, then add a white nonpareil or small decorative candy.

*tip: To easily transfer cutouts from the floured surface to the cookie sheet, use a thin, wide, and flexible metal spatula.

to store: Layer undecorated cookies between sheets of waxed paper in an airtight container; cover. Store at room temperature up to 3 days or freeze up to 3 months. To serve, thaw cookies, if frozen. If desired, decorate cookies as directed in Step 4.

nutrition facts per cookie: 205 cal., 7 g total fat (4 g sat. fat), 30 mg chol., 193 mg sodium, 33 g carb., 1 g fiber, 3 g pro.

Variations of this filled cookie are common throughout South America.

alfajores

prep: 30 minutes **chill:** 2 hours **bake:** 8 minutes at 350°F per batch
makes: 36 sanwiches cookies

1½ cups butter, softened
1 cup powdered sugar
1 cup granulated sugar
¼ teaspoon salt
1 egg
1 teaspoon finely
   shredded orange or
   lemon peel
1 teaspoon vanilla
⅓ cup finely ground
   blanched almonds
3 cups all-purpose flour
   Powdered sugar
1 13.4-ounce can dulce
   de leche
6 ounces semisweet
   chocolate pieces,
   melted

1 In a large mixing bowl beat butter with an electric mixer on medium to high speed for 30 seconds. Add the 1 cup powdered sugar, the granulated sugar, and salt. Beat until combined, scraping sides of bowl occasionally. Add egg, orange peel, and vanilla; beat until combined. Beat in the ground almonds. Beat in as much of the flour as you can with the mixer. Using a wooden spoon, stir in any remaining flour. Divide dough into three portions. Cover and chill about 2 hours or until dough is easy to handle.

2 Preheat oven to 350°F. Lightly grease a cookie sheet; set aside. On a surface dusted with powdered sugar, roll one portion of dough at a time to ⅛-to ¼-inch thickness. Using a fluted round and/or square 2- to 2½-inch cookie cutter, cut out dough, making an equal number of each shape. Place cutouts 1 inch apart on the prepared cookie sheet.

3 Bake for 8 to 10 minutes or until tops are very lightly browned. Carefully transfer to a wire rack; cool.

4 Fill sandwich cookies within 2 hours of serving. For each cookie, spread 1 rounded teaspoon of dulce de leche on the bottom of a cookie. Spoon about 1 teaspoon melted chocolate over dulce de leche; use the back of a spoon to gently spread chocolate. Top with another cookie, bottom side down. Sift with additional powdered sugar.

nutrition facts per sandwich cookie: 233 cal., 12 g total fat (7 g sat. fat), 33 mg chol., 99 mg sodium, 29 g carb., 1 g fiber, 3 g pro.

This Latin American sweet will remind you of macaroons.

lime-piloncillo cocada

prep: 30 minutes **bake:** 15 minutes at 325°F per batch
makes: 60 cookies

4 egg whites
1 teaspoon vanilla
¼ teaspoon cream of
    tartar
⅛ teaspoon salt
1⅓ cups grated piloncillo
    (Mexican dark
    brown sugar) (about
    5 ounces) or packed
    brown sugar
1 14-ounce package
    flaked coconut
½ cup chopped roasted
    and salted pistachio
    nuts or chopped
    toasted almonds
    (see tip, page 13)
2 tablespoons finely
    shredded lime peel

1 Preheat oven to 325°F. Line cookie sheets with parchment paper; set aside. In an extra-large mixing bowl combine egg whites, vanilla, cream of tartar, and salt. Beat with an electric mixer on high speed until soft peaks form (tips curl). Gradually add grated piloncillo, about 1 tablespoon at a time, beating until stiff peaks form (tips stand straight).

2 In a medium bowl stir together coconut, nuts, and lime peel. Fold coconut mixture into egg white mixture, half at a time. Drop dough by teaspoons 1 inch apart onto prepared cookie sheets.

3 Bake for about 15 minutes or until golden brown. Transfer to wire racks; cool.

to store: Layer cookies between sheets of waxed paper in an airtight container; cover. Store in the refrigerator up to 3 days or freeze up to 1 month.

nutrition facts per cookie: 57 cal., 3 g total fat (2 g sat. fat), 0 mg chol., 32 mg sodium, 8 g carb., 1 g fiber, 1 g pro.

four-layer caramel crunch
nougat brownies, page 279

irresistible

brow

9

When it comes to bar cookies, brownies are, hands down, the universal favorite. Many brownie recipes are made with chocolate, but several "blondie" versions are offered here. Alongside a cup of hot coffee or cold milk, you'll surely enjoy these top-rated recipes.

nies

Look for the truffle-filled chocolate squares in the candy aisle at supermarkets.

milk chocolate truffle brownies

prep: 25 minutes **bake:** 25 minutes at 325°F
makes: 20 brownies

Nonstick cooking
   spray
½ cup butter
½ cup milk chocolate
   pieces
3 ounces unsweetened
   chocolate, chopped
1 cup granulated sugar
1½ teaspoons vanilla
3 eggs
⅔ cup all-purpose flour
½ teaspoon baking
   powder
½ teaspoon salt
1 4.63-ounce package
   (10 squares) truffle-
   filled chocolate
   squares

1 Preheat oven to 325°F. Line a 9×9×2-inch baking pan with foil, extending the foil over edges of pan. Coat foil with cooking spray; set pan aside.

2 In a medium saucepan heat and stir butter, milk chocolate pieces, and unsweetened chocolate over low heat until melted and smooth; cool slightly. Stir in sugar and vanilla until combined. Add eggs, one at a time, beating with a wooden spoon after each addition. In a small bowl stir together flour, baking powder, and salt. Add flour mixture to chocolate mixture; stir just until combined. Pour batter into the prepared baking pan, spreading evenly.

3 Bake for 25 minutes. Break milk chocolate squares into irregular-shape pieces. Sprinkle over warm brownies. Cool in pan on a wire rack. Using the edges of the foil, lift uncut brownies out of pan. Cut into bars.

nutrition facts per brownie: 192 cal., 12 g total fat (7 g sat. fat), 44 mg chol., 131 mg sodium, 22 g carb., 1 g fiber, 3 g pro.

orange-kissed chocolate brownies

prep: 40 minutes **bake:** 25 minutes at 350°F **cool:** 1 hour **chill:** 75 minutes
makes: 32 brownies

4 eggs
2 cups granulated sugar
1¼ cups all-purpose flour
1 cup unsweetened Dutch-process cocoa powder
1 cup butter, melted
¼ cup butter, softened
1 teaspoon finely shredded orange peel
3½ cups powdered sugar
2 to 3 tablespoons orange juice
4 ounces semisweet chocolate, chopped
½ cup butter
2 tablespoons light-color corn syrup

1 Preheat oven to 350°F. Line a 13×9×2-inch baking pan with foil, extending the foil over edges of pan. Lightly grease foil; set pan aside. In a large mixing bowl beat eggs and sugar with an electric mixer on medium speed for 3 to 5 minutes or until pale yellow and thickened. In a small bowl stir together flour and cocoa powder. Add flour mixture to egg mixture, beating just until smooth. Using a wooden spoon, stir in the 1 cup melted butter until combined. Spread batter evenly in the prepared pan.

2 Bake for 25 to 30 minutes or until a wooden toothpick inserted near the center comes out clean. Cool in pan on a wire rack.

3 For frosting, in a medium mixing bowl beat the ¼ cup softened butter and orange peel on medium speed until smooth. Add 1 cup of the powdered sugar and 1 tablespoon of the orange juice, beating until combined. Beat in the remaining 2½ cups powdered sugar and enough of the remaining 1 to 2 tablespoons orange juice to reach spreading consistency. Spread frosting over brownies. Cover and chill for 30 minutes.

4 Meanwhile, in a medium saucepan melt chocolate and the ½ cup butter over low heat. Remove from heat; stir in corn syrup. Cool for 15 minutes.

5 Gradually pour melted chocolate mixture over frosted brownies. Tilt pan gently to spread chocolate over entire surface. Chill about 30 minutes or until chocolate is set. Using the edges of the foil, lift uncut brownies out of pan. Cut into bars.

to store: Place brownies in a single layer in an airtight container; cover. Store in the refrigerator up to 5 days or freeze up to 3 months. Before serving, let refrigerated brownies stand at room temperature for 15 minutes. Or thaw brownies, if frozen.

nutrition facts per brownie: 244 cal., 12 g total fat (7 g sat. fat), 53 mg chol., 82 mg sodium, 34 g carb., 1 g fiber, 2 g pro.

fudgy brownies

prep: 15 minutes **bake**: 35 minutes at 350°F
makes: 64 brownies

9   ounces unsweetened chocolate, coarsely chopped
1   cup butter
⅓   cup water
4   teaspoons instant coffee crystals
1½ cups granulated sugar
1½ cups packed brown sugar
5   eggs
1½ teaspoons vanilla
2   cups all-purpose flour
¾   cup ground almonds
½   teaspoon ground cinnamon
¼   teaspoon salt
1   recipe Bittersweet Ganache (optional)

1 Preheat oven to 350°F. Line a 13×9×2-inch baking pan with foil, extending foil over edges of pan. Grease foil; set pan aside.

2 In a large microwave-safe mixing bowl combine the chocolate, butter, the water, and the coffee crystals. Microwave, uncovered, on 100 percent power (high) for 2 to 4 minutes or until butter is melted, stirring once or twice. Remove bowl from microwave oven. Stir until chocolate is melted.

3 Beat in granulated sugar and brown sugar with an electric mixer on low to medium speed until combined. Add eggs and vanilla; beat on medium speed for 2 minutes. Add flour, almonds, cinnamon, and salt. Beat on low speed until combined. Spread batter evenly in the prepared pan.

4 Bake about 35 minutes or until top appears set and dry. Cool in pan on a wire rack. Using foil edges, lift brownies out of pan. Cut into bars. If desired, evenly pour Bittersweet Ganache over brownies.

tip: To add an extra drizzle of chocolate, in a small microwave-safe bowl combine 2 ounces chopped white baking chocolate, 2 ounces chopped milk chocolate, and 2 teaspoons shortening. Microwave on 100 percent power (high) about 2 minutes or until melted and smooth, stirring every 30 seconds. Drizzle melted chocolate over brownies.

nutrition facts per brownie: 302 cal., 17 g total fat (9 g sat. fat), 66 mg chol., 127 mg sodium, 37 g carb., 2 g fiber, 4 g pro.

bittersweet ganache: In a saucepan bring 1 cup whipping cream just to boiling over medium-high heat. Remove from heat. Add 12 ounces bittersweet chocolate, chopped (do not stir). Let stand 5 minutes. Stir until smooth. Cool for 15 minutes.

Nutty caramel is sandwiched between chocolate layers.

caramel-hazelnut brownies

prep: 35 minutes **bake:** 45 minutes at 350°F
makes: 36 brownies

Nonstick cooking spray
2⅔ cups granulated sugar
1½ cups butter, melted
4 eggs, lightly beaten
2 teaspoons vanilla
3 cups all-purpose flour
1½ cups unsweetened
cocoa powder
2 teaspoons baking
powder
1 teaspoon salt
1 14-ounce package
vanilla caramels,
unwrapped
2 tablespoons milk
1 cup hazelnuts (filberts),
toasted* and chopped
2 tablespoons hazelnut
liqueur
2 cups dark or
bittersweet chocolate
pieces

1 Preheat oven to 350°F. Line a 13×9×2-inch baking pan with foil, extending the foil over edges of pan. Generously coat foil with cooking spray; set pan aside.

2 In an extra-large mixing bowl beat sugar and melted butter with an electric mixer on low speed until combined. Beat in eggs and vanilla. In a medium bowl stir together flour, cocoa powder, baking powder, and salt. Add flour mixture, ½ cup at a time, beating well after each addition (batter will be thick). Spread batter evenly in the prepared baking pan.

3 In a large microwave-safe bowl microwave caramels and milk on 100 percent power (high) for 1¼ to 2 minutes or until caramels are melted, stirring every 30 seconds. Immediately stir in ½ cup of the hazelnuts and the liqueur. Drizzle caramel mixture over batter.

4 Bake for 45 minutes. Immediately sprinkle with chocolate pieces; let stand on a wire rack for 2 minutes to soften chocolate. Spread chocolate over top of brownies. Sprinkle with the remaining ½ cup hazelnuts.

5 Cool in pan on wire rack. If necessary, chill about 15 minutes or until chocolate is set. Using the edges of the foil, lift uncut brownies out of pan. Cut into bars.

*tip: To toast hazelnuts, preheat oven to 350°F. Spread nuts in a single layer in a shallow baking pan. Bake about 10 minutes or until slightly golden, stirring once. Place warm nuts on a clean kitchen towel. Rub the nuts with the towel to remove the loose skins.

to store: Place bars in a single layer in an airtight container; cover. Store in the refrigerator up to 3 days.

nutrition facts per brownie: 280 cal., 16 g total fat (8 g sat. fat), 44 mg chol., 168 mg sodium, 38 g carb., 1 g fiber, 4 g pro.

You may need a fork to enjoy these gooey sweets.

dulce de leche fluff brownies

prep: 30 minutes **bake:** 20 minutes at 350°F
makes: 32 brownies

6   ounces unsweetened chocolate, coarsely chopped
1   cup butter
2   cups granulated sugar
4   eggs
2   teaspoons vanilla
1⅓ cups all-purpose flour
½   teaspoon baking soda
1   cup miniature semisweet chocolate pieces
1   13.4-ounce can dulce de leche
1   7-ounce jar marshmallow creme
½   cup chopped pecans, toasted (see tip, page 13)

1 In a medium saucepan heat and stir unsweetened chocolate and butter over low heat until melted and smooth. Remove from heat; cool slightly. Meanwhile, preheat oven to 350°F. Line a 13×9×2-inch baking pan with foil, extending the foil over edges of pan. Grease foil; set pan aside.

2 Stir sugar into chocolate mixture. Add eggs, one at a time, beating with a wooden spoon after each addition just until combined. Stir in vanilla. In a small bowl stir together flour and baking soda. Add flour mixture to chocolate mixture; stir just until combined. Stir in semisweet chocolate pieces. Pour batter into the prepared baking pan, spreading evenly.

3 Bake for 20 to 25 minutes or until edges are set and center is almost set. Meanwhile, transfer dulce de leche to a small microwave-safe bowl. Microwave on 100 percent power (high) about 1 minute or until softened, stirring once.

4 Remove brownies from oven and set pan on a wire rack. Immediately spoon marshmallow creme in mounds on hot brownies. Drop spoonfuls of dulce de leche between mounds of marshmallow creme. Let stand for a few minutes to soften. Using a table knife or narrow metal spatula, gently swirl marshmallow creme and dulce de leche together to marble. Sprinkle with pecans. Cool in pan on rack.

5 Using the edges of the foil, lift uncut brownies out of pan. Cut into squares, wiping knife as needed between cuts. Serve brownies the same day they are prepared.

nutrition facts per brownie: 264 cal., 13 g total fat (8 g sat. fat), 45 mg chol., 91 mg sodium, 35 g carb., 1 g fiber, 4 g pro.

A soda fountain favorite is baked into this dream dessert.

chocolate malted-milk brownies

prep: 45 minutes **bake:** 30 minutes at 325°
makes: 24 brownies

¾ cup butter
4 ounces unsweetened chocolate, chopped
4 eggs
2 cups granulated sugar
1 teaspoon vanilla
1½ cups all-purpose flour
⅓ cup chocolate malted-milk powder
½ teaspoon salt
1 cup coarsely chopped chocolate malted-milk balls
1 recipe Chocolate Malted-Milk Filling
12 chocolate malted-milk balls, halved

1 Preheat oven to 325°F. Line a 15×10×1-inch baking pan with foil, extending the foil over edges of pan. Grease foil; set pan aside.

2 In a saucepan melt butter and chocolate over low heat. Whisk in eggs, sugar, and vanilla.

3 In a small bowl combine flour, malted-milk powder, and salt. Add flour mixture to chocolate mixture; stir just until combined. Stir in the 1 cup chopped malted-milk balls. Spread batter in prepared pan.

4 Bake about 30 minutes or until set. Cool in pan on a wire rack. Using edges of the foil, lift brownies out of pan. Using a 2-inch round cutter, cut brownies into rounds.

5 Pipe or spread Chocolate Malted-Milk Filling on each brownie round. Place half a chocolate malted-milk ball on the chocolate filling on each brownie round.

nutrition facts per brownie: 460 cal., 24 g total fat (14 g sat. fat), 102 mg chol., 220 mg sodium, 59 g carb., 2 g fiber, 6 g pro.

chocolate malted-milk filling: In a medium microwave-safe bowl combine 1 cup milk chocolate pieces and ½ cup whipping cream. Microwave, uncovered, on 100 percent power (high) for 1 minute. Whisk until chocolate is melted and mixture is smooth. Stir in 1 tablespoon chocolate malted-milk powder. Cover and chill for 30 minutes, stirring every 10 minutes. Beat with an electric mixer on medium-high speed until filling is fluffy, being careful not to overbeat. (Or instead of chilling chocolate filling, place the bowl in a larger bowl filled with ice cubes. Beat filling with an electric mixer on medium-high speed until fluffy, being careful not to overbeat.)

marbled chocolate-pumpkin brownies

prep: 30 minutes bake: 1 hour at 325°F
makes: 36 brownies

1 3-ounce package cream cheese, softened
1 tablespoon butter, softened
2¾ cups granulated sugar
5 eggs
1 cup canned pumpkin
3 teaspoons vanilla
½ teaspoon ground cinnamon
¼ teaspoon ground ginger
1 tablespoon all-purpose flour
6 ounces unsweetened chocolate, chopped
¾ cup butter, cut up
¼ cup milk
1¼ cups all-purpose flour
¾ teaspoon baking powder
½ teaspoon salt
¾ cup coarsely chopped toasted walnuts (see tip, page 13) (optional)

1 Preheat oven to 325°F. Line a 13×9×2-inch baking pan with foil, extending the foil over edges of pan. Grease foil; set pan aside.

2 In a medium mixing bowl beat cream cheese and the 1 tablespoon softened butter with an electric mixer on medium to high speed for 30 seconds. Add ½ cup of the sugar. Beat until combined, scraping sides of bowl occasionally. Beat in one of the eggs, the pumpkin, 1 teaspoon of the vanilla, the cinnamon, and the ginger until combined. Stir in the 1 tablespoon flour; set aside. Wash beaters.

3 In a large saucepan heat and stir chocolate and the ¾ cup butter over low heat until melted. Remove from heat. Gradually add the remaining 2¼ cups sugar, beating with an electric mixer on low speed just until combined. Add the remaining 4 eggs, one at a time, beating well after each addition. Beat in milk and the remaining 2 teaspoons vanilla. In a small bowl stir together the 1¼ cups flour, baking powder, and salt. Add flour mixture to chocolate mixture; beat just until combined.

4 Spread chocolate batter in the prepared baking pan. Spoon cream cheese mixture into small mounds of chocolate batter. Using a narrow metal spatula or a table knife, swirl gently to marble. If desired, sprinkle with walnuts.

5 Bake about 1 hour or just until center is set when pan is gently shaken. Cool in pan on a wire rack. Using the edges of the foil, lift uncut brownies out of pan. Cut into bars.

to store: Layer brownies between sheets of waxed paper in an airtight container; cover. Store in the refrigerator up to 3 days.

nutrition facts per brownie: 159 cal., 8 g total fat (5 g sat. fat), 43 mg chol., 92 mg sodium, 21 g carb., 1 g fiber, 2 g pro.

270

Pecans plus lots of chocolate are the signature ingredients in any "turtle" recipe.

incredible turtle brownies

prep: 30 minutes   **bake:** 35 minutes at 325°F   **stand:** 10 minutes
makes: 25 brownies

6	ounces bittersweet chocolate, coarsely chopped
½	cup butter
1	cup pecan halves, toasted (see tip, page 13)
1	cup granulated sugar
2	eggs
1	teaspoon vanilla
¾	cup all-purpose flour
2	teaspoons unsweetened Dutch-process cocoa powder
½	teaspoon baking powder
¼	teaspoon salt
⅓	cup semisweet chocolate pieces
1	recipe Caramel Sauce

1 Preheat oven to 325°F. Lightly grease a 9×9×2-inch baking pan; set aside. In a small saucepan heat and stir bittersweet chocolate and butter over low heat until melted; cool slightly.

2 Reserve 25 of the pecan halves for garnish. Finely chop the remaining pecan halves; set aside.

3 In a large mixing bowl beat sugar, eggs, and vanilla with an electric mixer on medium to high speed about 4 minutes or until pale and thickened. Beat in melted chocolate mixture. In a medium bowl stir together flour, cocoa powder, baking powder, and salt. Gently fold in flour mixture and the finely chopped pecans until combined. Pour batter into the prepared pan, spreading evenly.

4 Bake for 35 to 45 minutes or until a wooden toothpick inserted in the center comes out clean. Sprinkle with chocolate pieces. Cover loosely with foil and let stand for 10 minutes. Spread melted chocolate evenly over uncut brownies. Cool in pan. Cut into squares. Spoon caramel sauce on each square then top with a pecan half.

nutrition facts per brownie: 202 cal., 13 g total fat (6 g sat. fat), 35 mg chol., 81 mg sodium, 20 g carb., 1 g fiber, 2 g pro.

caramel sauce: In a small heavy saucepan combine ¼ cup butter, ⅓ cup packed dark brown sugar, ¼ cup whipping cream, and 1 tablespoon light-color corn syrup. Bring to boiling over medium-high heat, stirring occasionally; reduce heat. Boil gently, uncovered, for 3 minutes. Remove from heat. Stir in ½ teaspoon vanilla; cool slightly.

Some brownie lovers prefer fudgy recipes; this version will appeal to those who prefer cake-like brownies.

red velvet-buttermilk brownies

prep: 40 minutes **bake:** 25 minutes at 350°F
makes: 36 brownies

2 cups all-purpose flour
2 cups granulated
   sugar
1 teaspoon baking soda
¼ teaspoon salt
1 cup butter
1 cup water
⅓ cup unsweetened
   cocoa powder
2 eggs
½ cup buttermilk or
   sour milk*
1½ teaspoons vanilla
1 1-ounce bottle red
   food coloring
   (2 tablespoons)
1 recipe Buttercream
   Frosting

1 Preheat oven to 350°F. Grease a 15×10×1-inch baking pan; set aside. In a large mixing bowl stir together the flour, sugar, baking soda, and salt; set aside.

2 In a medium saucepan combine butter, the water, and cocoa powder. Bring just to boiling, stirring constantly. Remove from heat. Add the cocoa mixture to flour mixture; beat with an electric mixer on medium to high speed until thoroughly combined. Add eggs, buttermilk, vanilla, and red food coloring. Beat for 1 minute (batter will be thin). Pour batter into the prepared pan.

3 Bake about 25 minutes or until a wooden toothpick inserted in center comes out clean. Cool in pan on a wire rack. Frost with Buttercream Frosting

*tip: For ½ cup sour milk, place 1½ teaspoons lemon juice or vinegar in a glass measuring cup. Add enough milk to equal ½ cup total liquid; stir. Let stand for 5 minutes before using.

to store: Place frosted brownies in a single layer in an airtight container; cover. Store in the refrigerator up to 3 days or freeze up to 3 months.

nutrition facts per brownie: 232 cal., 14 g total fat (8 g sat. fat), 45 mg chol., 181 mg sodium, 27 g carb., 1 g fiber, 2 g pro.

buttercream frosting: In a medium saucepan whisk together 1½ cups granulated sugar, 1½ cups milk, ⅓ cup all-purpose flour, and a dash of salt. Cook and stir over medium heat until bubbly. Reduce heat; cook and stir for 1 minute more. Remove from heat. Stir in 2 teaspoons vanilla. Cover and cool completely. Transfer to a large mixing bowl. Gradually beat in 1½ cups butter, softened, beating with an electric mixer on medium speed until smooth, scraping sides of bowl occasionally. (Frosting might look curdled until all of the butter is incorporated.)

The recipe name comes from the hazelnut-infused chocolate from Switzerland.

gianduja cheesecake brownies

prep: 25 minutes **bake:** 50 minutes at 325°F
makes: 32 brownies

8   eggs
2⅓ cups granulated
       sugar
1   13-ounce jar
       purchased
       chocolate-hazelnut
       spread or 1 recipe
       Chocolate-Hazelnut
       Spread
1¼ cups butter, melted
       and cooled
2   cups all-purpose flour
½   cup unsweetened
       Dutch-process
       cocoa powder
2   8-ounce packages
       reduced-fat cream
       cheese (Neufchâtel),
       softened
       Powdered sugar
       (optional)

1 Preheat oven to 325°F. Grease and lightly flour a 13x9x2-inch baking pan; set aside.

2 In a large mixing bowl beat 4 of the eggs, 2 cups of the granulated sugar, ½ cup of the chocolate-hazelnut spread, and the melted butter with an electric mixer on low to medium speed until combined. In a medium bowl stir together flour and cocoa powder. Add flour mixture to egg mixture; stir just until combined. Spread batter in the prepared baking pan.

3 Wash beaters. In another large mixing bowl beat cream cheese and the remaining ⅓ cup granulated sugar on medium speed until light and fluffy. Beat in the remaining 4 eggs and the remaining chocolate-hazelnut spread until combined. Carefully spread over batter in pan.

4 Bake for 50 to 55 minutes or until cream cheese layer is firm and set. Cool in pan on a wire rack. Cover and chill before cutting into bars. If desired, sprinkle brownies with powdered sugar.

nutrition facts per brownie: 268 cal., 15 g total fat (8 g sat. fat), 76 mg chol., 134 mg sodium, 29 g carb., 1 g fiber, 5 g pro.

chocolate-hazelnut spread: Place 6 ounces milk chocolate, finely chopped, in a medium bowl; set aside. In a small heavy saucepan combine ¼ cup milk, 2 tablespoons powdered sugar, 1 tablespoon honey, and ⅛ teaspoon salt. Bring just to boiling. Pour hot milk mixture over chopped chocolate. Let stand for 5 minutes. Stir until smooth. Cool slightly. In a food processor combine ¾ cup hazelnuts (filberts), toasted, and 1 tablespoon unsweetened cocoa powder. Cover and process until nuts start to form a paste. Add 1 tablespoon vegetable oil; cover and process until a paste forms. Add chocolate mixture; cover and process until nearly smooth. Transfer spread to an airtight container; cover. Store in the refrigerator up to 1 week. Let stand at room temperature for 30 minutes before using.

A dream dessert for chocolate and coffee lovers.

triple-chocolate and espresso brownies

prep: 30 minutes **bake:** 30 minutes at 350°F
makes: 20 brownies

½ cup butter
4 ounces bittersweet chocolate, coarsely chopped
3 ounces unsweetened chocolate, coarsely chopped
1 cup granulated sugar
2 eggs
1 tablespoon instant espresso coffee powder
1 teaspoon vanilla
⅔ cup all-purpose flour
¼ teaspoon baking soda
⅛ teaspoon salt
1 cup miniature semisweet chocolate pieces
1 recipe Chocolate Cream Cheese Frosting
Chocolate-covered coffee beans, chopped (optional)

1 In a medium saucepan heat and stir butter, bittersweet chocolate, and unsweetened chocolate over low heat until melted; cool. Preheat oven to 350°F. Line an 8×8×2-inch baking pan with foil, extending the foil over edges of pan. Grease foil; set pan aside.

2 Stir sugar into chocolate mixture. Add eggs, one at a time, beating with a wooden spoon after each addition just until combined. Stir in espresso powder and vanilla. In a small bowl stir together flour, baking soda, and salt. Add flour mixture to chocolate mixture; stir just until combined. Stir in semisweet chocolate pieces. Spread batter evenly in the prepared baking pan.

3 Bake for 30 minutes. Cool in pan on a wire rack. Spread with Chocolate Cream Cheese Frosting. Using the edges of the foil, lift uncut brownies out of pan. Cut into bars. If desired, sprinkle with chocolate-covered coffee beans.

nutrition facts per brownie: 258 cal., 16 g total fat (9 g sat. fat), 38 mg chol., 85 mg sodium, 30 g carb., 2 g fiber, 3 g pro.

chocolate cream cheese frosting: In a small saucepan heat and stir ½ cup semisweet chocolate pieces over low heat until melted and smooth. Remove from heat; cool. In a medium bowl stir together one 3-ounce package cream cheese, softened, and ¼ cup powdered sugar. Stir in melted chocolate until smooth.

goat cheese brownies with honey swirl

prep: 30 minutes bake: 45 minutes at 325°F
makes: 32 brownies

8   ounces semisweet
     or bittersweet
     chocolate, chopped
3   tablespoons butter
6   ounces goat cheese
     (chèvre), softened
2   tablespoons butter,
     softened
¼   cup granulated sugar
¼   cup all-purpose flour
2   tablespoons honey
3   eggs
1¼ cups granulated sugar
⅓   cup water
1   teaspoon vanilla
1   cup all-purpose flour
¾   teaspoon baking
     powder
½   teaspoon salt
1   cup chopped almonds,
     toasted (see tip,
     page 13)
1   recipe Honey and
     Cream Cheese
     Frosting (optional)

1 Preheat oven to 325°F. Line a 13x9x2-inch baking pan with foil, extending the foil over edges of pan. Grease foil; set pan aside. In a medium-size heavy saucepan melt the chocolate and the 3 tablespoons butter over low heat. Remove from heat; cool.

2 For filling, in a medium mixing bowl beat goat cheese and the 2 tablespoons butter with an electric mixer on medium speed for 30 seconds. Add the ¼ cup sugar; beat until fluffy. Add ¼ cup flour, the honey, and one of the eggs; beat well. Set aside. Wash and dry beaters thoroughly.

3 For batter, in a large mixing bowl beat the 2 remaining eggs with an electric mixer on medium speed until foamy. Add the 1¼ cups sugar, the water, and vanilla; beat well. Beat in the cooled chocolate. Stir in the 1 cup flour, baking powder, and salt. Stir in nuts. Spread half the batter in the prepared pan.

4 Evenly spread goat cheese filling over chocolate layer. Spoon the remaining chocolate batter in small mounds over cheese layer. Drag a thin metal spatula or table knife through chocolate mounds to marble.

5 Bake about 45 minutes or until center is set. Cool in pan on a wire rack.

6 If desired, frost brownies with Honey and Cream Cheese Frosting. Using the edges of the foil, lift uncut brownies out of pan. Cut into bars.

nutrition facts per brownie: 151 cal., 7 g total fat (4 g sat. fat), 29 mg chol., 93 mg sodium, 20 g carb., 1 g fiber, 3 g pro.

honey and cream cheese frosting: In a large mixing bowl combine 4 ounces cream cheese, softened, and ¼ cup butter, softened. Beat with an electric mixer on medium speed until smooth. Gradually add 2 cups powdered sugar and 2 tablespoons honey, beating until combined. Add an additional 1 cup powdered sugar and 1 tablespoon milk, beating until smooth.

For primo brownies, buy the best white chocolate you can find. The extra cost is worth it!

white chocolate brownies

prep: 15 minutes **cool:** 10 minutes **bake:** 25 minutes at 350°F
makes: 16 brownies

6   ounces white baking chocolate with cocoa butter, chopped
6   tablespoons butter
2   eggs
¼   cup granulated sugar
1   cup all-purpose flour
½   teaspoon vanilla
½   cup chopped macadamia nuts
2   ounces white baking chocolate with cocoa butter, chopped

1 Preheat oven to 350°F. Line an 8×8×2-inch baking pan with foil, extending foil over the edges of the pan. Grease foil; set aside.

2 In a small heavy saucepan combine the 6 ounces white chocolate and the butter. Heat and stir over low heat until melted. Cool for 10 minutes. Add eggs and sugar. Beat with a wooden spoon until combined. Add flour and vanilla; stir just until smooth. Stir in macadamia nuts. Spread batter evenly in the prepared pan.

3 Bake about 25 minutes or until top is lightly browned. Immediately sprinkle with the 2 ounces white chocolate. Let stand until chocolate is melted; spread over uncut brownies. Cool in pan on a wire rack. Using edges of foil, lift uncut brownies out of pan. Cut into squares.

nutrition facts per brownie: 195 cal., 13 g total fat (6 g sat. fat), 41 mg chol., 50 mg sodium, 18 g carb., 1 g fiber, 3 g pro.

chocolate-covered cherry squares

prep: 25 minutes stand: 30 minutes bake: 25 minutes at 350°
makes: 36 brownies

¾ cup snipped dried sweet cherries
¼ cup amaretto or cranberry juice
4 ounces unsweetened chocolate, coarsely chopped
½ cup butter
1½ cups granulated sugar
3 eggs
1 teaspoon vanilla
1 cup all-purpose flour
1 tablespoon unsweetened cocoa powder
¼ teaspoon baking soda
⅓ cup miniature semisweet chocolate pieces
½ cup butter, softened
2 tablespoons maraschino cherry juice
2 cups powdered sugar
1 recipe Chocolate Ganache
36 maraschino cherries with stems (about 1½ cups), well drained and patted dry (optional)

1 In a small bowl combine dried cherries and amaretto. Let stand for 30 minutes. Drain cherries, discarding liquid. Meanwhile, preheat oven to 350°F. Line a 9×9×2-inch baking pan with foil, extending the foil over edges of pan. Grease foil; set pan aside.

2 In a medium saucepan melt unsweetened chocolate and the ½ cup butter over low heat. Stir in granulated sugar. Add eggs, one at a time, beating with a wooden spoon after each addition just until combined. Stir in vanilla. In a small bowl stir together flour, cocoa powder, and baking soda. Add flour mixture to chocolate mixture; stir just until combined. Stir in miniature chocolate pieces and soaked cherries.

3 Pour batter into the prepared baking pan, spreading evenly. Bake for 25 to 28 minutes or until edges are set. Cool in pan on a wire rack.

4 For frosting, in a medium mixing bowl beat the ½ cup softened butter with an electric mixer on medium speed for 30 seconds. Beat in cherry juice. Gradually beat in powdered sugar until combined. Spread frosting over brownie layer. Carefully spread Chocolate Ganache over frosting. If desired, arrange maraschino cherries on ganache. Chill until set. Using the edges of the foil, lift uncut brownies out of pan. Cut into squares.

to store: Cover and refrigerate brownies in the refrigerator up to 3 days. If desired, top with maraschino cherries before serving.

nutrition facts per brownie: 196 cal., 10 g total fat (6 g sat. fat), 34 mg chol., 63 mg sodium, 26 g carb., 1 g fiber, 2 g pro.

chocolate ganache: In a small saucepan bring ½ cup whipping cream just to boiling over medium-high heat. Remove from heat. Add 4 ounces bittersweet or semisweet chocolate, chopped (do not stir). Let stand for 5 minutes. Stir until smooth. Let stand at room temperature, stirring occasionally, about 4 to 5 minutes or until slightly thickened.

Appease the toffee lovers in your family with this decadent delight.

almond brittle brownies

prep: 30 minutes **bake:** 10 minutes + 27 minutes at 350°F
makes: 36 brownies

1	recipe Almond Brittle
½	cup butter, softened
2½	cups granulated sugar
2½	cups all-purpose flour
¾	cup butter
4	ounces unsweetened chocolate, coarsely chopped
2	teaspoons vanilla
4	eggs

1 Prepare Almond Brittle. Place cooled Almond Brittle in a heavy plastic bag. Using a rolling pin or meat mallet, coarsely crush brittle; set aside.

2 Preheat oven to 350°F. Grease and flour a 13×9×2-inch baking pan; set aside.

3 For crust, in a medium mixing bowl beat the ½ cup softened butter and ½ cup of the sugar with an electric mixer on medium to high speed until smooth. Stir in 1 cup of the flour. Press evenly onto the bottom of prepared pan. Bake about 10 minutes or until edges are lightly browned.

4 Meanwhile, in a medium saucepan heat and stir the ¾ cup butter and the chocolate over low heat until melted. Remove from heat. Stir in the remaining 2 cups sugar and the vanilla. Add eggs, one at a time, beating with a wooden spoon after each addition just until combined. Stir in the remaining 1½ cups flour. Pour batter over hot crust, spreading evenly.

5 Bake for 15 minutes. Sprinkle with crushed almond brittle; press lightly into chocolate layer. Bake for 12 to 15 minutes more or until top is set. Cool in pan on a wire rack. Cut into bars.

nutrition facts per brownie: 164 cal., 10 g total fat (5 g sat. fat), 41 mg chol., 56 mg sodium, 20 g carb., 1 g fiber, 2 g pro.

almond brittle: Line a baking sheet with foil. Butter foil; set baking sheet aside. In a medium skillet combine ⅓ cup slivered almonds, ¼ cup granulated sugar, and 1 tablespoon butter. Cook over medium-high heat until sugar starts to melt, shaking skillet occasionally. Do not stir. When sugar starts to melt, reduce heat to low and cook until sugar is golden, stirring as needed with a wooden spoon. Pour onto the prepared baking sheet; cool.

Crispy rice cereal adds a nice crunch to the caramel layer.
Pictured on page 260.

four-layer caramel crunch nougat brownies

prep: 50 minutes **bake:** 15 minutes at 350°F **chill:** 2 hours
makes: 64 brownies

3	ounces unsweetened chocolate, coarsely chopped
½	cup butter
2¼	cups granulated sugar
2	eggs
1	teaspoon vanilla
⅔	cup all-purpose flour
¼	teaspoon baking soda
1½	14-ounce packages vanilla caramels (68 caramels total), unwrapped
⅔	cup evaporated milk
1	tablespoon water
1½	cups crisp rice cereal
⅓	cup butter
1	7-ounce jar marshmallow creme
¼	cup creamy peanut butter
1	12-ounce package (2 cups) semisweet chocolate pieces
⅓	cup whipping cream
3	tablespoons butter

1 In a saucepan melt unsweetened chocolate and the ½ cup butter over low heat; cool slightly. Preheat oven to 350°F. Line a 13×9×2-inch baking pan with foil, extending foil over edges of pan. Grease foil; set pan aside.

2 For brownie layer, stir 1 cup of the sugar into chocolate mixture. Add eggs, one at a time, beating with a wooden spoon after each addition just until combined. Stir in vanilla. Stir in flour and baking soda just until combined. Spread batter evenly in the prepared pan. Bake for 15 to 17 minutes or until edges start to pull away from sides of pan. Cool in pan on a wire rack.

3 For caramel layer, in a large microwave-safe bowl combine caramels, 2 tablespoons of the evaporated milk, and the water. Microwave on 100 percent power (high) for 2½ to 3 minutes or until caramels are melted, stirring every 30 seconds. Stir in rice cereal. Spread caramel mixture over brownie layer, spreading to edges. Place pan in freezer while preparing nougat layer.

4 For nougat layer, in a medium saucepan combine the remaining 1¼ cups sugar, the remaining evaporated milk, and the ⅓ cup butter. Bring to boiling over medium-high heat, stirring constantly; reduce heat to medium. Boil at a moderate, steady rate without stirring for 10 minutes. Place marshmallow creme and peanut butter in a large heat-proof bowl. Gradually whisk hot mixture into marshmallow mixture until combined. Pour over caramel layer, spreading to edges. Return to freezer.

5 For chocolate layer, in a small saucepan heat and stir semisweet chocolate pieces, whipping cream, and the 3 tablespoons butter over low heat until melted. Pour chocolate mixture over nougat layer, spreading to edges. Cover loosely; chill for 2 hours. Using the edges of the foil, lift uncut brownies out of pan. Cut into bars.

nutrition facts per brownie: 156 cal., 8 g total fat (5 g sat. fat), 16 mg chol., 68 mg sodium, 22 g carb., 1 g fiber, 2 g pro.

280

Kids love these bars with all their favorite campfire flavors.

inside-out s'mores brownies

prep: 20 minutes **bake:** 25 minutes at 350°F
makes: 15 brownies

½   cup butter
2   ounces unsweetened chocolate, chopped
1   cup granulated sugar
2   eggs
1   teaspoon vanilla
¾   cup all-purpose flour
9   graham cracker squares
1   cup tiny marshmallows

1 In a medium saucepan heat and stir butter and chocolate over low heat until melted; cool. Meanwhile, preheat oven to 350°F. Line an 11×7×1½-inch baking pan with parchment paper or lightly grease pan; set aside.

2 Stir sugar into cooled chocolate mixture. Add eggs, one at a time, beating with a wooden spoon just until combined. Stir in vanilla. Stir in flour just until combined.

3 Spread half the batter in the prepared baking pan. Top with graham crackers, cutting as necessary to fit. Sprinkle with marshmallows, without letting them touch the sides of the pan. Carefully spread the remaining batter over layers, covering completely.

4 Bake about 25 minutes or until set. Cool in pan on a wire rack. Cut into bars.

nutrition facts per brownie: 189 cal., 9 g total fat (5 g sat. fat), 44 mg chol., 84 mg sodium, 26 g carb., 1 g fiber, 2 g pro.

Smoked almonds set this bar apart from all others.

salted almond brownies

prep: 25 minutes **bake:** 25 minutes at 350°F
makes: 16 brownies

- 4   ounces unsweetened chocolate, coarsely chopped
- ½   cup butter
- 1½ cups granulated sugar
- 3   eggs
- 1   teaspoon vanilla
- 1   cup all-purpose flour
- 1   tablespoon unsweetened cocoa powder
- ¼   teaspoon baking soda
- 1   cup milk chocolate pieces (6 ounces)
- 1½ cups chopped smoked almonds
- ¼   teaspoon sea salt

1 In a medium saucepan heat and stir unsweetened chocolate and butter over low heat until melted and smooth; cool slightly. Meanwhile, preheat oven to 350°F. Line a 9×9×2-inch baking pan with foil, extending foil over edges of pan. Grease foil; set pan aside.

2 Stir sugar into chocolate mixture. Add eggs, one at a time, beating with a wooden spoon after each addition just until combined. Stir in vanilla. In a small bowl stir together flour, cocoa powder, and baking soda. Add flour mixture to chocolate mixture; stir just until combined. Stir in ¾ cup of the milk chocolate pieces. Pour batter into the prepared baking pan, spreading evenly. Sprinkle with the remaining ¼ cup milk chocolate pieces, the almonds, and salt.

3 Bake for 25 minutes. Cool in pan on a wire rack. Using the edges of the foil, lift uncut brownies out of pan. Cut into bars.

nutrition facts per brownie: 347 cal., 21 g total fat (10 g sat. fat), 53 mg chol., 195 mg sodium, 38 g carb., 3 g fiber, 6 g

For a wow dessert, tuck each wedge into a bowl of ice cream.

pistachio brownie wedges

prep: 25 minutes **bake:** 25 minutes at 325°F
makes: 16 brownies

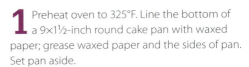

½   cup butter
3   ounces unsweetened
      chocolate
2   eggs
¾   cup granulated sugar
1   teaspoon vanilla
¾   cup all-purpose flour
¾   cup coarsely chopped
      pecans, toasted
      (see tip, page 13)
1   ounce semisweet
      or bittersweet
      chocolate squares
1   teaspoon shortening
1   ounce white baking
      chocolate with
      cocoa butter
½   cup finely chopped
      pistachio nuts or
      pecans

1 Preheat oven to 325°F. Line the bottom of a 9×1½-inch round cake pan with waxed paper; grease waxed paper and the sides of pan. Set pan aside.

2 In a small saucepan heat and stir butter and unsweetened chocolate over low heat until melted and smooth. Remove from heat; cool.

3 In a large mixing bowl beat eggs about 1 minute or until frothy. Add sugar and vanilla; beat for 2 minutes or until thickened. Beat in melted chocolate mixture. Stir in flour. Spread evenly into the prepared pan. Sprinkle with the ¾ cup toasted pecans; press lightly into batter.

4 Bake for 25 minutes. Cool in pan on a wire rack. Remove brownie from pan. Remove waxed paper. Cut brownie into quarters. Cut each quarter into four wedges.

5 In a small saucepan heat and stir semisweet chocolate and ½ teaspoon of the shortening until smooth. In another small saucepan over low heat stir the white chocolate and the remaining ½ teaspoon shortening over low heat until smooth.

6 Carefully dip outer edges of eight brownie wedges into melted semisweet chocolate, then into pistachios. Dip outer edges of remaining brownie wedges in melted white chocolate, then in pistachios. Place on waxed paper; let stand until set.

nutrition facts per brownie: 224 cal., 16 g total fat (7 g sat. fat), 39 mg chol., 79 mg sodium, 20 g carb., 2 g fiber, 4 g pro.

A double chocolate layer caps the tender buttery crust, providing two cookie tastes in each bite.

shortbread brownies

prep: 25 minutes **bake:** 45 minutes at 350°F
makes: brownies

2½ cups all-purpose flour
⅓ cup packed brown sugar
¾ cup butter
1¼ cups miniature semisweet chocolate pieces
2 cups granulated sugar
¾ cup unsweetened cocoa powder
2¼ teaspoons baking powder
1 teaspoon salt
5 eggs
½ cup butter, melted
1 tablespoon vanilla

1 Preheat oven to 350°F. Line a 13×9×2-inch baking pan with foil, extending the foil over edges of pan; set aside. For crust, in a medium bowl stir together 1½ cups of the flour and the brown sugar. Cut in the ¾ cup butter until mixture resembles coarse crumbs. Stir in ½ cup of the chocolate pieces. Press dough evenly into the prepared pan. Bake for 10 minutes.

2 Meanwhile, in a large bowl stir together granulated sugar, the remaining 1 cup flour, the cocoa powder, baking powder, and salt. Add eggs, the melted butter, and vanilla; beat by hand until smooth. Stir in the remaining ¾ cup chocolate pieces. Carefully spoon over crust in pan, spreading evenly.

3 Bake for 35 minutes. Cool in pan on a wire rack. Using edges of foil, lift brownies out of pan. Cut into bars.

nutrition facts per brownie: 193 cal., 10 g total fat (6 g sat. fat), 43 mg chol., 162 mg sodium, 26 g carb., 1 g fiber, 2 g pro.

Ground chipotle adds a kick to each bite.

chocolate-chipotle brownies

prep: 30 minutes **bake:** 35 minutes at 325°F
makes: 32 brownies

8	ounces semisweet chocolate, coarsely chopped
1	cup butter
2½	cups granulated sugar
1	tablespoon instant espresso coffee powder
1	to 2 teaspoons ground chipotle chile pepper
1½	teaspoons ground cinnamon
6	eggs
2	teaspoons vanilla
2	cups all-purpose flour
¼	cup unsweetened Dutch-process cocoa powder
	Unsweetened Dutch-process cocoa powder

1 In a small saucepan melt chocolate and butter over low heat; cool slightly.

2 Preheat oven to 325°F. Line a 13×9×2-inch baking pan with foil, extending the foil over edges of pan. Grease foil; set pan aside.

3 In a large mixing bowl stir together sugar, espresso powder, ground chipotle pepper, and cinnamon. Add chocolate mixture. Beat with an electric mixer on medium speed for 1 minute, scraping sides of bowl occasionally. Add eggs, one at a time, beating on low speed after each addition just until combined. Beat in vanilla. In a small bowl stir together flour and the ¼ cup cocoa powder. Add flour mixture to chocolate mixture; beat just until combined. Beat on medium speed for 1 minute. Pour batter into the prepared baking pan, spreading evenly.

4 Bake for 35 to 40 minutes or until edges start to pull away from sides of pan. Cool in pan on a wire rack. Using the edges of the foil, lift uncut brownies out of pan. Sprinkle with additional cocoa powder. Cut into bars.

nutrition facts per brownie: 194 cal., 9 g total fat (5 g sat. fat), 55 mg chol., 55 mg sodium, 26 g carb., 1 g fiber, 3 g pro.

Cherry and chocolate define any "black forest" dessert.

black forest brownies

prep: 30 minutes bake: 35 minutes at 350°F
makes: 24 brownies

2   10-ounce jars maraschino cherries with stems
1   cup semisweet chocolate pieces
½   cup butter
3   eggs, lightly beaten
1¼ cups granulated sugar
1¼ cups all-purpose flour
1   teaspoon vanilla
¾   teaspoon salt
½   teaspoon baking powder
1   cup white baking pieces
½   cup slivered almonds, toasted (see tip, page 13)
1   3-ounce package cream cheese, softened
⅔   cup powdered sugar

1 Preheat oven to 350°F. Grease a 13×9×2-inch baking pan; set aside. Drain one jar of cherries; remove stems and coarsely chop cherries. Drain on paper towels. Reserve the remaining jar of whole cherries for garnish.

2 In a large microwave-safe bowl microwave semisweet chocolate and butter on 100 percent power (high) for 1 minute; stir. Microwave for 10 to 20 seconds more or until melted. Stir in eggs, granulated sugar, flour, vanilla, salt, and baking powder until combined. Fold in the chopped cherries, white baking pieces, and almonds. Pour batter into the prepared baking pan.

3 Bake for 35 minutes. Cool in pan on a wire rack. Cut into bars.

4 For cream cheese topping, in a medium mixing bowl beat cream cheese and powdered sugar with an electric mixer on medium speed until smooth. Pipe or spoon a small amount of cream cheese topping onto each brownie. Drain the reserved cherries. Top each brownie with a cherry.

to store: Place brownies in a single layer in an airtight container; cover. Store in the refrigerator up to 3 days.

nutrition facts per brownie: 240 cal., 11 g total fat (5 g sat. fat), 40 mg chol., 128 mg sodium, 33 g carb., 1 g fiber, 3 g pro.

Check the brownies at 25 minutes of baking to prevent them from overbaking.

caramel-swirl brownies

prep: 25 minutes **bake:** 25 minutes at 350°F
makes: 16 brownies

1	3-ounce package cream cheese, cut up
12	vanilla caramels, unwrapped
1	tablespoon granulated sugar
1	tablespoon milk
1	egg yolk
¾	cup butter
3	ounces unsweetened chocolate, chopped
1½	cups granulated sugar
3	eggs, lightly beaten
1½	teaspoons vanilla
1	cup all-purpose flour

1 Preheat oven to 350°F. Line a 9×9×2-inch baking pan with foil, extending the foil over the edges of the pan. Grease foil; set pan aside.

2 For caramel, in a small saucepan combine cream cheese, caramels, the 1 tablespoon sugar, and the milk. Cook and stir over medium-low heat just until caramels melt. In a small bowl lightly beat egg yolk; gradually stir into the caramel mixture. Remove from heat; set aside.

3 In a medium saucepan heat and stir butter and chocolate over medium-low heat until melted and smooth. Remove from heat. Stir in the 1½ cups sugar, the eggs, and vanilla. Stir in flour just until combined. Spread batter evenly in the prepared pan. Top evenly with spoonfuls of the caramel. Using a thin metal spatula, swirl caramel into batter.

4 Bake for 25 to 30 minutes or until top springs back when lightly touched and edges start to pull away from sides of the pan. Cool in pan on a wire rack. Using the edges of the foil, lift the uncut brownies out of the pan. Cut into bars.

to store: Place bars in a single layer in an airtight container; cover. Store in the refrigerator up to 3 days or freeze up to 3 months.

nutrition facts per brownie: 274 cal., 15 g total fat (9 g sat. fat), 75 mg chol., 129 mg sodium, 33 g carb.,1 g fiber, 4 g pro.

Cardamom and ginger spice these gems.

white chocolate spiced brownies

prep: 25 minutes **bake:** 30 minutes at 350°F
makes: 32 brownies

1   cup butter, softened
1¾   cups packed brown
        sugar
3   eggs
1   tablespoon rum
        (optional)
1   teaspoon vanilla
2½   cups all-purpose flour
1½   teaspoons baking
        powder
1   teaspoon ground
        cardamom
1   teaspoon ground
        cinnamon
½   teaspoon ground
        ginger
¼   teaspoon salt
6   ounces white baking
        chocolate with
        cocoa butter,
        chopped
1   tablespoon
        finely chopped
        crystallized ginger
     Powdered sugar
        (optional)

1 Preheat oven to 350°F. Line a 13×9×2-inch baking pan with foil, extending the foil over edges of pan. Grease foil; set pan aside.

2 In a large mixing bowl beat butter with an electric mixer on medium to high speed for 30 seconds. Add brown sugar. Beat until combined, scraping sides of bowl occasionally. Beat in eggs, rum (if using), and vanilla until combined. In a medium bowl stir together flour, baking powder, 1 teaspoon cardamom, 1 teaspoon cinnamon, ground ginger, and salt. Beat in as much of the flour mixture as you can with the mixer. Using a wooden spoon, stir in any remaining flour mixture, the white chocolate, and crystallized ginger. Spread batter evenly in the prepared pan.

3 Bake for 30 minutes. Cool in pan on a wire rack. Using the edges of the foil, lift uncut brownies out of pan. If desired, sprinkle lightly with powdered sugar. Cut into bars.

nutrition facts per brownie: 171 cal., 8 g total fat (5 g sat. fat), 36 mg chol., 92 mg sodium, 23 g carb., 0 g fiber, 2 g pro.

Give an enthusiastic young kitchen helper the job of unwrapping the caramels.

fudge ripple pecan brownies

prep: 30 minutes **bake:** 30 minutes at 350°F **stand:** 2 hours
makes: 16 brownies

½   cup butter
3   ounces unsweetened chocolate, coarsely chopped
1   cup granulated sugar
2   eggs
1   teaspoon vanilla
⅔   cup all-purpose flour
¼   teaspoon baking soda
1   cup chopped pecans, toasted (see tip, page 13)
¾   cup semisweet chocolate pieces
20 vanilla caramels, unwrapped
1   tablespoon milk

1 In a medium saucepan heat and stir butter and unsweetened chocolate over low heat until melted; cool.

2 Preheat oven to 350°F. Line an 8×8×2-inch baking pan with foil, extending the foil over edges of pan. Grease foil; set pan aside.

3 Stir sugar into chocolate mixture in saucepan. Add eggs, one at a time, beating with a wooden spoon after each addition just until combined. Stir in vanilla. Stir in flour and baking soda just until combined. Stir in ½ cup of the pecans and ½ cup of the semisweet chocolate pieces. Spread batter evenly in the prepared baking pan.

4 Bake for 30 minutes. Cool in pan on a wire rack.

5 Meanwhile, in a small saucepan heat and stir caramels and milk over medium-low heat until melted and smooth. Spread caramel mixture over brownies. Sprinkle with the remaining ½ cup pecans.

6 In another small saucepan heat and stir the remaining ¼ cup semisweet chocolate pieces over low heat until melted. Drizzle melted chocolate over brownies. Let stand for 2 hours. Before serving. Using the edges of the foil, lift uncut brownies out of pan. Cut into bars.

to store: Cover pan of brownies and store in the refrigerator up to 3 days. Before serving, let brownies stand at room temperature for 1 hour.

nutrition facts per brownie: 291 cal., 18 g total fat (9 g sat. fat), 42 mg chol., 102 mg sodium, 33 g carb., 2 g fiber, 4 g pro.

Perfect for when you want just a bite of cheescake!

cream cheese brownies

prep: 40 minutes **bake:** 45 minutes at 350°F
makes: 32 brownies

8	ounces semisweet chocolate, coarsely chopped
3	tablespoons butter
4	eggs
1¼	cups granulated sugar
⅓	cup water
2	teaspoons vanilla
1	cup all-purpose flour
1	teaspoon baking powder
¼	teaspoon salt
¾	cup chopped macadamia nuts, pecans, or walnuts; toasted (see tip, page 13)
1	8-ounce package cream cheese, softened
⅔	cup granulated sugar
2	tablespoons all-purpose flour
1	tablespoon lemon juice
1	recipe Chocolate Glaze (optional)

1 In a large heavy saucepan melt chocolate and butter over low heat; cool. Preheat oven to 350°F. Line a 13×9×2-inch baking pan with foil, extending the foil over edges of pan. Grease foil; set pan aside.

2 In a large mixing bowl beat 2 of the eggs with an electric mixer on medium speed until foamy. Add 1¼ cups sugar, the water, and 1 teaspoon of the vanilla. Beat on medium speed about 6 minutes or until mixture is slightly thickened and lemon color. Beat in chocolate mixture. Stir in the 1 cup flour, baking powder, and salt; stir in nuts. Pour half the batter into the prepared baking pan, spreading evenly.

3 In a medium mixing bowl beat the remaining 2 eggs, the remaining 1 teaspoon vanilla, the cream cheese, the ⅔ cup sugar, the 2 tablespoons flour, and lemon juice on medium speed until smooth. Carefully spread cream cheese mixture over batter in pan. Spoon the remaining batter on cream cheese layer. Using a narrow metal spatula, swirl gently to marble.

4 Bake for 45 minutes. Cool in pan on a wire rack. If desired, spread with Chocolate Glaze. Chill 1 hour or until set. Using the edges of the foil, lift uncut brownies out of pan. Cut into bars.

to store: Place brownies in a single layer in an airtight container; cover. Store in the refrigerator up to 3 days.

nutrition facts per brownie: 164 cal., 9 g total fat (4 g sat. fat), 34 mg chol., 67 mg sodium, 20 g carb., 1 g fiber, 2 g pro.

chocolate glaze: In a small saucepan heat and stir ⅓ cup whipping cream and 6 ounces semisweet chocolate, finely chopped, over low heat until smooth. Cool slightly.

irresistible brownies

This popular recipe is frequently named Texas Sheet Cake.

chocolate-buttermilk brownies

prep: 30 minutes **bake:** 25 minutes at 350°F **cool:** 1 hour
makes: 24 brownies

2	cups all-purpose flour
2	cups granulated sugar
1	teaspoon baking soda
¼	teaspoon salt
1	cup butter
1	cup water
⅓	cup unsweetened cocoa powder
2	eggs
½	cup buttermilk or sour milk (see tip, page 12)
1½	teaspoons vanilla
1	recipe Chocolate-Buttermilk Frosting

1 Preheat oven to 350°F. Grease a 15×10×1-inch or a 13×9×2-inch baking pan; set aside. In a medium mixing bowl stir together flour, sugar, baking soda, and salt; set aside.

2 In a medium saucepan combine butter, the water, and cocoa powder. Bring mixture just to boiling, stirring constantly. Remove from heat. Add the cocoa mixture to flour mixture. Beat with an electric mixer on medium to high speed until thoroughly combined. Add eggs, buttermilk, and vanilla. Beat for 1 minute (batter will be thin). Pour batter into the prepared pan.

3 Bake about 25 minutes for the 15×10×1-inch pan, 35 minutes for the 13×9×2-inch pan, or until a wooden toothpick inserted in the center comes out clean.

4 Pour warm Chocolate-Buttermilk Frosting over brownies, spreading evenly. Cool in pan on wire rack for 1 hour. Cut into bars.

nutrition facts per brownie: 245 cal., 10 g total fat (6 g sat. fat), 43 mg chol., 158 mg sodium, 37 g carb., 1 g fiber, 2 g pro.

chocolate-buttermilk frosting: In a medium saucepan combine ¼ cup butter, 3 tablespoons unsweetened cocoa powder, and 3 tablespoons buttermilk or sour milk (see tip, page 12). Bring to boiling. Remove from heat. Add 2¼ cup powdered sugar and ½ teaspoon vanilla. Beat until smooth. If desired, stir in ¾ cup coarsely chopped pecans, toasted (optional).

These brownies may be a bit fussy to make, but they're fancy enough to take to a party.

crème de menthe brownies

prep: 35 minutes bake: 30 minutes at 350°F chill: 1 hour
makes: 48 brownies

1. In a medium saucepan melt ¾ cup of the dark chocolate pieces, the unsweetened chocolate, and butter over low heat; cool. Preheat oven to 350°F. Line a 13×9×2-inch baking pan with foil, extending the foil over edges of pan. Grease foil; set pan aside.

2. Stir sugar into chocolate mixture. Add eggs, one at a time, beating with a wooden spoon after each addition just until combined. Stir in vanilla. In a small bowl stir together flour, baking soda, and salt. Add flour mixture to chocolate mixture, stirring just until combined. Stir in the remaining dark chocolate pieces. Spread batter evenly in the prepared baking pan.

3. Bake for 30 minutes. Cool in pan on a wire rack. Spread Crème de Menthe Filling over brownies. Chill while preparing Dark Chocolate Ganache.

4. Spread ganache evenly over filling. Cover and chill about 1 hour or until ganache is set. Using the edges of the foil, lift uncut brownies out of pan. Cut into bars.

1	12-ounce package (2 cups) dark chocolate pieces
3	ounces unsweetened chocolate, chopped
½	cup butter
1	cup granulated sugar
2	eggs
1	teaspoon vanilla
⅔	cup all-purpose flour
¼	teaspoon baking soda
⅛	teaspoon salt
1	recipe Crème de Menthe Filling
1	recipe Dark Chocolate Ganache

to store: Place brownies in a single layer in an airtight container; cover. Store in the refrigerator up to 3 days or freeze up to 3 months.

nutrition facts per brownie: 186 cal., 11 g total fat (6 g sat. fat), 25 mg chol., 53 mg sodium, 22 g carb., 1 g fiber, 2 g pro.

crème de menthe filling: In a large mixing bowl beat one 3-ounce package cream cheese, softened, and ½ cup butter, softened, with an electric mixer on medium speed for 30 seconds. Gradually beat in 1 cup powdered sugar. Beat in 2 tablespoons crème de menthe (or 2 tablespoons milk, ½ teaspoon mint extract, and several drops of green food coloring). Gradually beat in an additional 2 cups powdered sugar. Beat in 1 tablespoon of additional milk, if necessary, to make the filling slightly thicker than a frosting.

dark chocolate ganache: In a medium saucepan bring ½ cup whipping cream just to boiling over medium-high heat. Remove from heat. Add one 12-ounce package dark chocolate pieces (do not stir). Let stand for 5 minutes. Stir until smooth. Cool for 15 minutes.

bourbon-brownie petits fours

prep: 35 minutes bake: 30 minutes at 350°F
makes: 64 brownies

½   cup butter
3   ounces unsweetened chocolate, coarsely chopped
¼   cup bourbon or milk
3   tablespoons instant coffee granules
1   cup granulated sugar
2   eggs
1   teaspoon vanilla
¾   cup all-purpose flour
¼   teaspoon baking soda
1   recipe Milk Chocolate Glaze and Frosting

1 In a medium saucepan heat and stir butter and unsweetened chocolate over low heat until melted and smooth. Remove from heat; cool.

2 Preheat oven to 350°F. Line an 8×8×2-inch baking pan with foil, extending the foil over the edges of the pan. Grease foil; set pan aside. In a small bowl stir together bourbon and coffee granules; set aside.

3 Stir the sugar into the cooled chocolate mixture in saucepan. Add the eggs, one at a time, beating with a wooden spoon just until combined. Stir in vanilla and bourbon mixture.

4 In a small bowl stir together the flour and baking soda. Add flour mixture to chocolate mixture, stirring just until combined. Spread batter evenly in the prepared pan.

5 Bake for 30 minutes. Cool in pan on a wire rack. Using the edges of the foil, lift the uncut brownies out of the pan. Cut off brownie edges; save for another use.

6 For petits fours, cut brownies into 1- to 1½-inch squares. Coat petits fours with Milk Chocolate Glaze.

7 For Milk Chocolate Frosting, beat the reserved cooled Milk Chocolate Glaze with an electric mixer about 30 seconds or until fluffy. Spoon frosting into a decorating bag fitted with a large star tip. Pipe a large rosette in the center of each petit four.

milk chocolate glaze and frosting: In a medium saucepan bring 1 cup whipping cream just to boiling over medium-high heat. Remove from heat. Add one 12-ounce package milk chocolate pieces (do not stir). Let stand for 5 minutes. Stir until smooth. Pour half the chocolate mixture into a large bowl; cover loosely and chill for 1 to 2 hours to reserve for Milk Chocolate Frosting. When ready to glaze petits fours, heat and stir remaining Milk Chocolate Glaze in pan over medium-low heat until it is drizzling consistency.

to store: Place petits fours in a single layer in an airtight container; cover. Store in the refrigerator up to 3 days or freeze up to 3 months. To serve, thaw, if frozen, or let refrigerated petits fours stand at room temperature for 15 minutes before serving.

nutrition facts per brownie: 157 cal., 10 g total fat (6 g sat. fat), 43 mg chol., 90 mg sodium, 18 g carb., 1 g fiber, 2 g pro.

Be ready to get requests for this recipe when you show up with a pan of these bars.

chewy butterscotch-pecan brownies

prep: 30 minutes **bake:** 20 minutes at 350°F
makes: 24 brownies

⅓ cup butter
1⅓ cups flaked or shredded coconut
¾ cup chopped pecans
1⅔ cups packed brown sugar
½ cup butter, softened
½ teaspoon baking soda
¼ teaspoon salt
3 eggs
½ teaspoon vanilla
1½ cups all-purpose flour
½ cup chopped pecans
½ cup tiny marshmallows
Caramel-flavor ice cream topping (optional)
Pecan halves (optional)

1 Preheat oven to 350°F. Grease a 13×9×2-inch baking pan; set aside. In a small saucepan heat the ⅓ cup butter over medium heat until melted. Stir in coconut, ¾ cup pecans, and ⅔ cup of the brown sugar. Press mixture evenly onto the bottom of the prepared baking pan; set aside.

2 In a large mixing bowl beat the ½ cup butter with an electric mixer on medium to high speed for 30 seconds. Add the remaining 1 cup brown sugar, the baking soda, and salt. Beat until combined, scraping sides of bowl occasionally. Add eggs and vanilla; beat until combined. Beat in flour until combined. Stir in the ½ cup pecans and marshmallows. Carefully spread over coconut layer.

3 Bake about 20 minutes or until top is evenly browned (center may jiggle slightly when gently shaken). Cool in pan on a wire rack. Cut into bars. If desired, drizzle with caramel topping and top with pecan halves.

nutrition facts per brownie: 211 cal., 13 g total fat (6 g sat. fat), 43 mg chol., 113 mg sodium, 23 g carb., 1 g fiber, 2 g pro.

Use creamy or chunky in this recipe—whichever you prefer.

peanut butter brownies

prep: 30 minutes **bake:** 30 minutes at 350°F
makes: 24 brownies

4　ounces bittersweet
　　chocolate, coarsely
　　chopped
¼　cup butter
¼　cup peanut butter
1　cup packed brown
　　sugar
2　eggs
1　teaspoon vanilla
⅔　cup all-purpose flour
¼　teaspoon baking soda
⅛　teaspoon salt
1　cup chopped
　　chocolate-covered
　　peanut butter cups
1　recipe Nutty Frosting
　　Chocolate-covered
　　peanut butter cups,
　　halved or quartered
　　(optional)

1 In a medium saucepan combine bittersweet chocolate, butter, and peanut butter. Cook and stir over low heat until melted; cool slightly. Preheat oven to 350°F. Line an 8×8×2-inch baking pan with foil, extending the foil over edges of pan. Grease foil; set pan aside.

2 Stir brown sugar into chocolate mixture. Add eggs, one at a time, beating with a wooden spoon after each addition just until combined. Stir in vanilla. In a small bowl stir together flour, baking soda, and salt. Add flour mixture to chocolate mixture; stir just until combined. Stir in the 1 cup chopped peanut butter cups. Pour batter into the prepared baking pan, spreading evenly.

3 Bake about 30 minutes or until set. Cool in pan on a wire rack. Cut into bars. Spoon Nutty Frosting onto bars. If desired, top with halved or quartered peanut butter cups.

nutrition facts per brownie: 252 cal., 14 g total fat (6 g sat. fat), 33 mg chol., 134 mg sodium, 30 g carb., 1 g fiber, 4 g pro.

nutty frosting: In a medium mixing bowl combine ½ cup peanut butter; ½ cup butter, softened; 1 tablespoon milk; and 1 teaspoon vanilla. Beat with an electric mixer on medium speed until combined. Gradually beat in 2 cups powdered sugar.

For the ultimate presentation, spoon whipped cream over each brownie and serve with fresh raspberries.

raspberry and white chocolate brownies

prep: 30 minutes **bake:** 30 minutes at 350°F
makes: 20 brownies

½ cup butter
2 ounces white baking chocolate with cocoa butter, chopped
2 eggs
⅔ cup granulated sugar
1 teaspoon vanilla
1 cup all-purpose flour
½ cup chopped almonds, toasted (see tip, page 13)
½ teaspoon baking powder
   Dash salt
1 cup fresh raspberries
2 ounces white baking chocolate with cocoa butter, melted

1 Preheat oven to 350°F. Line an 8×8×2-inch baking pan with foil, extending the foil over edges of pan. Grease foil; set pan aside.

2 In a medium saucepan heat and stir butter and 2 ounces chopped white chocolate over low heat until melted and smooth. Remove from heat. Add eggs, sugar, and vanilla. Beat lightly with a wooden spoon just until combined. Stir in flour, almonds, baking powder, and salt. Spread batter evenly in the prepared baking pan. Sprinkle with raspberries.

3 Bake for 30 to 35 minutes or until golden. Cool in pan on a wire rack.

4 Using the edges of the foil, lift uncut brownies out of pan. Cut into bars or with a 2-inch round cutter. Drizzle brownies with the 2 ounces melted white chocolate.

nutrition facts per brownie: 146 cal., 8 g total fat (4 g sat. fat), 34 mg chol., 62 mg sodium, 16 g carb., 1 g fiber, 2 g pro.

white chocolate, coconut, and pecan brownies: Prepare as directed except omit almonds and raspberries. After adding flour mixture, stir in ⅓ cup white baking pieces, ⅓ cup flaked coconut, and ⅓ cup chopped pecans, toasted (see tip, page 13).

nutrition facts per brownie: 165 cal., 10 g total fat (6 g sat. fat), 33 mg chol., 81 mg sodium, 18 g carb., 0 g fiber, 2 g pro.

10

unbeatable

bar

With flavors adopted from drop cookies, cakes, pies, even ice cream bars are super solutions when time is short. In less than an hour, you can prep and bake dozens of servings, often calling on one of the kitchen's most-favored pans: the 13×9.

S

frosted apple slab pie, page 340

Substitute raisins for the figs, if you prefer.

white chocolate blondies with macadamia nuts and figs

prep: 20 minutes **bake:** 25 minutes at 350°F
makes: 36 bars

2   cups packed brown sugar
⅔   cup butter
2   eggs
2   teaspoons vanilla
2   cups all-purpose flour
1   teaspoon baking powder
¼   teaspoon baking soda
½   cup chopped macadamia nuts
½   cup snipped dried figs
3   ounces white baking chocolate with cocoa butter, cut into chunks
2   ounces white baking chocolate with cocoa butter, melted (optional)

1 Preheat oven to 350°F. Grease a 13×9×2-inch baking pan; set aside.

2 In a medium saucepan heat and stir brown sugar and butter over medium heat until butter is melted and mixture is smooth. Cool slightly. Add eggs, one at a time, beating with a wooden spoon until combined. Stir in vanilla. Stir in flour, baking powder, and baking soda until combined. Stir in macadamia nuts, figs, and white chocolate chunks. Spread batter evenly in the prepared baking pan.

3 Bake for 25 to 30 minutes or until a wooden toothpick inserted near the center comes out clean. If desired, drizzle melted white chocolate over uncut bars. Cut into bars while warm. Leave cut bars in pan; cool on a wire rack.

nutrition facts per bar: 139 cal., 6 g total fat (3 g sat. fat), 19 mg chol., 62 mg sodium, 21 g carb., 1 g fiber, 2 g pro.

Package these for holiday giftgiving.

cranberry-candied ginger blondies with toasted macadamias

prep: 30 minutes   **cool:** 15 minutes   **bake:** 28 minutes at 350°F
makes: 32 bars

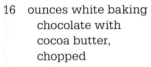

16 ounces white baking chocolate with cocoa butter, chopped
½ cup butter, cut up
3 eggs, lightly beaten
½ cup granulated sugar
1¾ cups all-purpose flour
1 teaspoon vanilla
1 cup macadamia nuts, coarsely chopped
½ cup dried cranberries, snipped
¼ cup finely chopped crystallized ginger
1 tablespoon shortening
Snipped dried cranberries (optional)

1 Preheat oven to 350°F. Line a 13×9×2-inch baking pan with foil, extending the foil over edges of pan. Lightly grease foil; set pan aside.

2 In a medium saucepan heat and stir 12 ounces of the white chocolate over low heat until melted. Remove from heat. Stir in butter until melted. Cool for 15 minutes.

3 Whisk eggs and sugar into white chocolate mixture until smooth. Stir in flour and vanilla just until combined. Fold in nuts, ½ cup dried cranberries, and 2 tablespoons of the ginger. Spread batter evenly in the prepared baking pan.

4 Bake for 28 to 30 minutes or until top is lightly browned and edges start to pull away from sides of pan. Cool in pan on a wire rack.

5 In a small saucepan heat and stir the remaining 4 ounces white chocolate and the shortening over low heat until melted. Drizzle over uncut bars. Sprinkle with the remaining 2 tablespoons ginger and, if desired, additional dried cranberries. Using the edges of the foil, lift uncut bars out of pan. Cut into bars.

nutrition facts per bar: 191 cal., 11 g total fat (6 g sat. fat), 30 mg chol., 48 mg sodium, 19 g carb., 1 g fiber, 3 g pro.

Here's a clever way to use the last bits of broken pretzels.

peanut-pretzel bars

prep: 30 minutes   **bake:** 20 minutes at 350°F
makes: 48 bars

½   cup butter, softened
½   cup peanut butter
2   cups packed brown sugar
1   teaspoon baking soda
2   eggs
2   teaspoons vanilla
2½ cups all-purpose flour
3   cups quick-cooking rolled oats
1½ cups peanut butter-flavor pieces
1   14-ounce can sweetened condensed milk
1   cup chopped peanuts
1   cup broken pretzel twists (2½ ounces)

1 Preheat oven to 350°F. In a large mixing bowl beat butter and peanut butter with an electric mixer on medium to high speed for 30 seconds. Add brown sugar and baking soda. Beat until combined, scraping sides of bowl occasionally. Beat in eggs and 1 teaspoon of the vanilla until combined. Beat in as much of the flour as you can with the mixer. Using a wooden spoon, stir in any remaining flour and the oats.

2 For filling, in a medium saucepan heat and stir peanut butter pieces and sweetened condensed milk over low heat until mixture is melted and smooth. Remove from heat. Stir in peanuts, pretzels, and the remaining 1 teaspoon vanilla.

3 Press two-thirds of the oat mixture onto the bottom of an ungreased 15×10×1-inch baking pan. Spread filling over oat mixture. Drop the remaining oat mixture in spoonfuls on filling.

4 Bake for 20 to 25 minutes or until top is golden. Cool in pan on a wire rack. Cut into bars to serve.

nutrition facts per bar: 203 cal., 8 g total fat (4 g sat. fat), 16 mg chol., 109 mg sodium, 28 g carb., 2 g fiber, 5 g pro.

Melted chocolate pieces are the no-fuss frosting on these toffee-and-nut goodies.

milk chocolate-toffee bars

prep: 25 minutes **bake:** 25 minutes at 350°F
makes: 36 bars

2	cups all-purpose flour
1	cup packed brown sugar
½	teaspoon ground cinnamon
1	cup butter, softened
1	teaspoon vanilla
¾	cup chopped pecans
1	cup milk chocolate pieces
½	cup toffee pieces

1 Preheat oven to 350°F. Line a 13×9×2-inch baking pan with foil, extending foil over the edges of the pan. Grease foil; set pan aside.

2 In a large mixing bowl stir together flour, brown sugar, and cinnamon. Add butter and vanilla. Beat with an electric mixer on low speed until mixture resembles coarse crumbs. Stir in pecans and ½ cup of the milk chocolate pieces. Press mixture evenly into the bottom of the prepared pan.

3 Bake for 25 to 30 minutes or until golden brown. Sprinkle bars with the remaining ½ cup milk chocolate pieces; let stand on a wire rack for 5 minutes to soften. Using a table knife, swirl the chocolate pieces and spread a thin layer of chocolate over the bars. Immediately sprinkle with the toffee pieces. Cool completely in pan on a wire rack. Using the foil edges, lift uncut bars out of pan. Cut into bars.

nutrition facts per bar: 151 cal., 9 g total fat (5 g sat. fat), 17 mg chol., 55 mg sodium, 16 g carb., 1 g fiber, 1 g pro.

A chocolate crust is the foundation for blondie filling and coconut topping—it's like eating three cookies in one!

chocolate shortbread blondies with macaroon topping

prep: 25 minutes **bake:** 40 minutes at 350°F
makes: 32 bars

3½   cups all-purpose flour
⅔   cup granulated sugar
½   cup unsweetened cocoa powder
1⅔   cups butter
½   cup miniature semisweet chocolate pieces
1   recipe Macaroon Topping
2   cups packed brown sugar
2   eggs
2   teaspoons vanilla
1   teaspoon baking powder
¼   teaspoon baking soda
1   cup chopped salted cashews or peanuts
    Milk chocolate, melted (optional)

1 Preheat oven to 350°F. Line a 13×9×2-inch baking pan with foil, extending the foil over edges of pan. Grease foil; set pan aside. For crust, in a medium bowl stir together 1½ cups of the flour, the granulated sugar, and cocoa powder. Using a pastry blender, cut in 1 cup of the butter until mixture resembles coarse crumbs. Stir in chocolate pieces. Press crust evenly onto the bottom of the prepared baking pan. Bake about 8 minutes or until set. Prepare Macaroon Topping; set aside.

2 Meanwhile, in a medium saucepan heat and stir brown sugar and the remaining ⅔ cup butter over medium heat until melted and smooth; cool slightly. Add eggs, one at a time, beating with a wooden spoon after each addition just until combined. Stir in vanilla. Stir in the remaining 2 cups flour, baking powder, and baking soda. Stir in cashews.

3 Pour batter evenly over crust. Spoon Macaroon Topping into small mounds on batter; carefully spread to edges of pan. Bake for 32 to 34 minutes or until topping is lightly browned. Cool in pan on a wire rack.

4 If desired, drizzle with melted milk chocolate. Using the edges of the foil, lift uncut bars out of pan. Cut into bars.

nutrition facts per bar: 291 cal., 15 g total fat (9 g sat. fat), 37 mg chol., 160 mg sodium, 38 g carb., 1 g fiber, 4 g pro.

macaroon topping: In a medium bowl stir together ⅓ cup granulated sugar and ¼ cup all-purpose flour. Stir in 1¼ cups sweetened flaked coconut; 3 egg whites, lightly beaten; and ½ teaspoon vanilla.

These double-chocolate and peppermint brownies make a fun holiday treat.

peppermint blondies

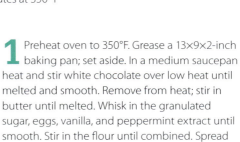

prep: 30 minutes **bake:** 28 minutes at 350 °F
makes: 32 bars

12   ounces white chocolate with cocoa butter, chopped
½   cup butter
½   cup granulated sugar
3   eggs, lightly beaten
2   teaspoons vanilla
1   teaspoon peppermint extract
1½   cups all-purpose flour
1   cup miniature semisweet chocolate pieces
1   recipe White Chocolate-Peppermint Frosting
     Coarsely crushed striped round peppermint candies (optional)

1 Preheat oven to 350°F. Grease a 13×9×2-inch baking pan; set aside. In a medium saucepan heat and stir white chocolate over low heat until melted and smooth. Remove from heat; stir in butter until melted. Whisk in the granulated sugar, eggs, vanilla, and peppermint extract until smooth. Stir in the flour until combined. Spread the batter evenly in the prepared pan.

2 Bake for 28 to 30 minutes or until top is lightly browned and sides begin to pull away from pan. Immediately sprinkle semisweet chocolate pieces evenly over bars. Cool in pan on a wire rack.

3 Spread White Chocolate-Peppermint Frosting evenly over cooled bars. If desired, sprinkle with crushed peppermint candies.

to store: Place bars in a single layer in an airtight container; cover. Store in the refrigerator up to 3 days or freeze up to 2 months.

nutrition facts per bar: 273 cal., 14 g total fat (9 g sat. fat), 39 mg chol., 94 mg sodium, 34 g carb., 0 g fiber, 3 g pro.

white chocolate-peppermint frosting: In a small saucepan heat and stir 6 ounces white baking chocolate with cocoa butter, chopped, over low heat until melted and smooth. Set aside to cool. In a large mixing bowl beat 1¾ cups powdered sugar and ½ cup butter, softened, with an electric mixer on low speed until combined. Beat in ⅓ cup sour cream, ½ teaspoon vanilla, ½ teaspoon peppermint extract, and ¼ teaspoon salt until combined. Beat in an additional 1¾ cups powdered sugar. Beat in the melted white chocolate until combined.

For extra crunch, sprinkle chopped roasted peanuts on the frosting before it sets.

chocolate-peanut butter bars

prep: 25 minutes **bake:** 20 minutes at 350°F
makes: 36 bars

¾ cup butter, softened
1 cup packed brown
   sugar
1 egg
2 teaspoons vanilla
½ teaspoon salt
2 cups all-purpose flour
1 12-ounce package
   semisweet
   chocolate pieces
3 tablespoons butter
¼ cup peanut butter
¼ cup hot strong coffee
1 cup powdered sugar

1 Preheat oven to 350°F. Line a 15×10×1-inch baking pan with parchment paper or foil or lightly grease pan; set aside.

2 In a large mixing bowl beat the ¾ cup butter with an electric mixer on medium to high speed for 30 seconds. Add brown sugar. Beat until combined, scraping sides of bowl occasionally. Beat in egg, vanilla, and salt until combined. Beat in as much of the flour as you can with the mixer. Using a wooden spoon, stir in any remaining flour.

3 Transfer dough to the prepared baking pan, spreading evenly. Bake for 20 to 22 minutes or until edges are golden. Cool in pan on a wire rack.

4 For frosting, in a small saucepan heat and stir chocolate pieces and the 3 tablespoons butter over low heat until melted and smooth. Transfer to a medium bowl. Stir in peanut butter and coffee until combined. Stir in powdered sugar until smooth. Spread uncut bars with frosting. Let stand until frosting is set. Cut into bars.

to store: Place bars in a single layer in an airtight container; cover. Store at room temperature up to 2 days.

nutrition facts per bar: 164 cal., 9 g total fat (5 g sat. fat), 19 mg chol., 78 mg sodium, 18 g carb., 2 g fiber, 1 g pro.

Pat dry the fresh or frozen cranberries before sprinkling over the batter.

white chocolate and nutmeg bars

prep: 25 minutes **bake:** 40 minutes at 350°F
makes: 24 bars

Nonstick cooking
    spray
2   cups all-purpose flour
2   teaspoons freshly
    grated nutmeg or
    1 teaspoon ground
    nutmeg
1   teaspoon baking
    powder
¼   teaspoon baking soda
2   cups packed brown
    sugar
⅔   cup butter
2   eggs
2   teaspoons vanilla
¾   cup dried cranberries
1½ cups fresh or frozen
    cranberries, thawed
¾   cup coarsely chopped
    white chocolate
    (3 ounces)

1 Preheat oven to 350°F. Line a 13×9×2-inch baking pan with foil, extending foil over pan edges. Lightly coat foil with cooking spray; set aside. In a small bowl combine flour, nutmeg, baking powder, and baking soda; set aside.

2 In a medium saucepan combine brown sugar and butter. Cook and stir over medium heat until melted and smooth. Cool slightly. Stir in eggs, one at a time, beating well after each addition. Stir in vanilla. Add flour mixture; stir just until combined. Stir in dried cranberries. Spread batter in prepared pan. Sprinkle with fresh cranberries.

3 Bake about 40 minutes or until a wooden toothpick inserted near the center comes out clean. Remove pan from oven. Sprinkle top of bars with white chocolate. Cool in pan on a wire rack. Using the foil, lift the uncut bars out of the pan. Cut into bars.

nutrition facts per bar: 196 cal., 7 g total fat (4 g sat. fat), 29 mg chol., 93 mg sodium, 32 g carb., 1 g fiber, 2 g pro.

If you can't find the raspberry-chocolate candies, semisweet chocolate pieces work just as well.

raspberry-dark chocolate chip bars

prep: 25 minutes **bake:** 30 minutes at 350°F
makes: 36 bars

1	cup granulated sugar
1	cup packed brown sugar
⅔	cup butter
2	eggs
1	tablespoon vanilla
2¼	cups all-purpose flour
1½	teaspoons baking powder
¼	teaspoon salt
1½	cups white baking pieces
1	8-ounce package raspberry-filled dark chocolate pieces
1	teaspoon shortening

1 Preheat oven to 350°F. Line a 13×9×2-inch baking pan with foil, extending the foil over edges of pan. Lightly grease foil; set pan aside.

2 In a large saucepan combine granulated sugar, brown sugar, and butter. Cook over medium-low heat until butter is melted, stirring frequently. Add eggs, one at a time, beating with a wooden spoon after each addition. Stir in vanilla. Stir in flour, baking powder, and salt. Stir in 1 cup of the white baking pieces. Pour batter into the prepared baking pan, spreading evenly.

3 Bake for 20 minutes. Remove from oven. Sprinkle with raspberry-filled chocolate pieces. Bake for 10 minutes more. Cool in pan on a wire rack.

4 In a small saucepan heat and stir the remaining ½ cup white baking pieces and shortening over low heat until melted and smooth. Drizzle over uncut bars. Let stand until set. Using the edges of the foil, lift uncut bars out of pan. Cut into bars.

nutrition facts per bar: 184 cal., 8 g total fat (5 g sat. fat), 19 mg chol., 82 mg sodium, 28 g carb., 0 g fiber, 1 g pro.

Butterscotch- and vanilla-flavor bars, sans chocolate, are often called "blondies."

browned-butter blondies

prep: 20 minutes bake: 35 minutes at 325°F
makes: 32 bars

1 cup butter, cut up
2 cups all-purpose flour
1 teaspoon baking powder
1 teaspoon salt
¼ teaspoon baking soda
1½ cups packed brown sugar
½ cup granulated sugar
2 eggs
2 teaspoons vanilla
1 cup coarsely chopped pecans, toasted (see tip, page 13) (optional)
⅔ cup almond toffee bits

1 Preheat oven to 325°F. Line a 13×9×2-inch baking pan with foil, extending the foil over the edges of the pan. Grease the foil; set pan aside. In a small saucepan melt the butter over medium heat until foamy. When foaming subsides, swirl pan constantly over medium heat until butter is golden brown and fragrant. Immediately remove from heat; set aside. In a small bowl stir together the flour, baking powder, salt, and baking soda. Set aside.

2 In a large mixing bowl combine the browned butter, brown sugar, granulated sugar, eggs, and vanilla. Beat with an electric mixer on medium speed until thick and smooth. With mixer on low speed, add flour mixture, one third at a time, beating just until combined after each addition. Batter will be very thick. If desired, stir in pecans. Using a rubber spatula and moist hands, spread and pat the batter evenly into the prepared pan. Sprinkle evenly with almond toffee bits.

3 Bake about 35 minutes or until a wooden toothpick inserted near the center comes out clean. Cool in pan on a wire rack. Use the foil to lift the uncut bars out of the pan. Place on cutting board. Cut into bars.

tip: If desired, drizzle bars with caramel-flavor ice cream topping and sprinkle with additional chopped toasted pecans and almond toffee bits before serving.

nutrition facts per bar: 186 cal., 10 g total fat (5 g sat. fat), 29 mg chol., 176 mg sodium, 23 g carb., 1 g fiber, 2 g pro.

A low oven temperature ensures the bars bake through without overbrowning.

lemony glazed shortbread bars

prep: 40 minutes bake: 40 minutes at 300°F
makes: 32 bars

3   cups all-purpose flour
⅓   cup cornstarch
1¼ cups powdered sugar
¼   cup finely shredded
     lemon peel (5 to
     6 lemons)
1½ cups butter, softened
1   tablespoon lemon
     juice
½   teaspoon salt
½   teaspoon vanilla
1   recipe Lemony Glaze
     Finely shredded
     lemon peel
     (optional)

1 Preheat oven to 300°F. Line a 13×9×2-inch baking pan with foil, extending the foil over edges of pan. Lightly grease foil; set pan aside.

2 In a medium bowl stir together flour and cornstarch; set aside. In a small bowl combine powdered sugar and lemon peel. Pressing against side of bowl with a wooden spoon, work the ¼ cup lemon peel into powdered sugar until sugar is yellow color and fragrant;* set aside.

3 In a large mixing bowl beat butter, lemon juice, salt, and vanilla with an electric mixer on medium speed until combined. Gradually beat in lemon peel-sugar mixture. Stir in flour mixture.

4 Using lightly floured fingers, press dough evenly into the prepared baking pan. Bake about 40 minutes or until lightly browned and edges start to brown. Remove from oven.

5 Immediately spoon Lemony Glaze over top, spreading gently to edges. If desired, sprinkle with lemon peel. Cool in pan on a wire rack. Using the edges of the foil, lift uncut bars out of pan. Cut into bars.

*tip: Rubbing the lemon peel with the sugar releases the lemon oils.

nutrition facts per bar: 181 cal., 9 g total fat (5 g sat. fat), 23 mg chol., 98 mg sodium, 25 g carb., 0 g fiber, 1 g pro.

lemony glaze: In a medium bowl combine 2½ cups powdered sugar, 2 teaspoons finely shredded lemon peel, 3 tablespoons lemon juice, 1 tablespoon light-color corn syrup, and ½ teaspoon vanilla. Stir until smooth.

Warm preserves make these bars glisten.

almond-apricot blondies

prep: 30 minutes bake: 35 minutes at 350°F
makes: 32 bars

1   cup dried apricots,
      coarsely snipped
¼   cup amaretto or apricot
      nectar
2   cups packed brown
      sugar
⅔   cup butter
2   eggs
2   teaspoons vanilla
2   cups all-purpose flour
1   teaspoon baking powder
¼   teaspoon baking soda
¼   teaspoon salt
2   cups sliced almonds,
      toasted (see tip,
      page 13)
1   cup apricot preserves

1 In a small saucepan combine dried apricots and amaretto. Bring just to boiling; cool. Preheat oven to 350°F. Line a 13×9×2-inch baking pan with foil, extending the foil over edges of pan. Lightly grease foil; set pan aside.

2 In a medium saucepan heat and stir brown sugar and butter over medium heat until melted and smooth; cool slightly. Add eggs, one at a time, beating with a wooden spoon after each addition just until combined. Stir in vanilla. Stir in flour, baking powder, baking soda, and salt until combined. Stir in the undrained apricots. Fold in 1½ cups of the almonds. Spread batter evenly in the prepared pan.

3 Bake about 35 minutes or until a wooden toothpick inserted near the center comes out clean. Cool slightly in pan on a wire rack.

4 Meanwhile, in a small saucepan bring apricot preserves to boiling over medium-high heat. Reduce heat to medium-low; simmer, uncovered, about 10 minutes or until slightly thickened. Cool for 5 minutes.

5 Gently spread preserves over warm uncut bars. Sprinkle with the remaining ½ cup almonds. Using the edges of the foil, lift uncut bars out of pan. Cut into bars.

to store: Place bars in a single layer in an airtight container; cover. Store in the refrigerator up to 3 days or freeze up to 2 months.

nutrition facts per bar: 198 cal., 7 g total fat (3 g sat. fat), 22 mg chol., 89 mg sodium, 31 g carb., 1 g fiber, 3 g pro.

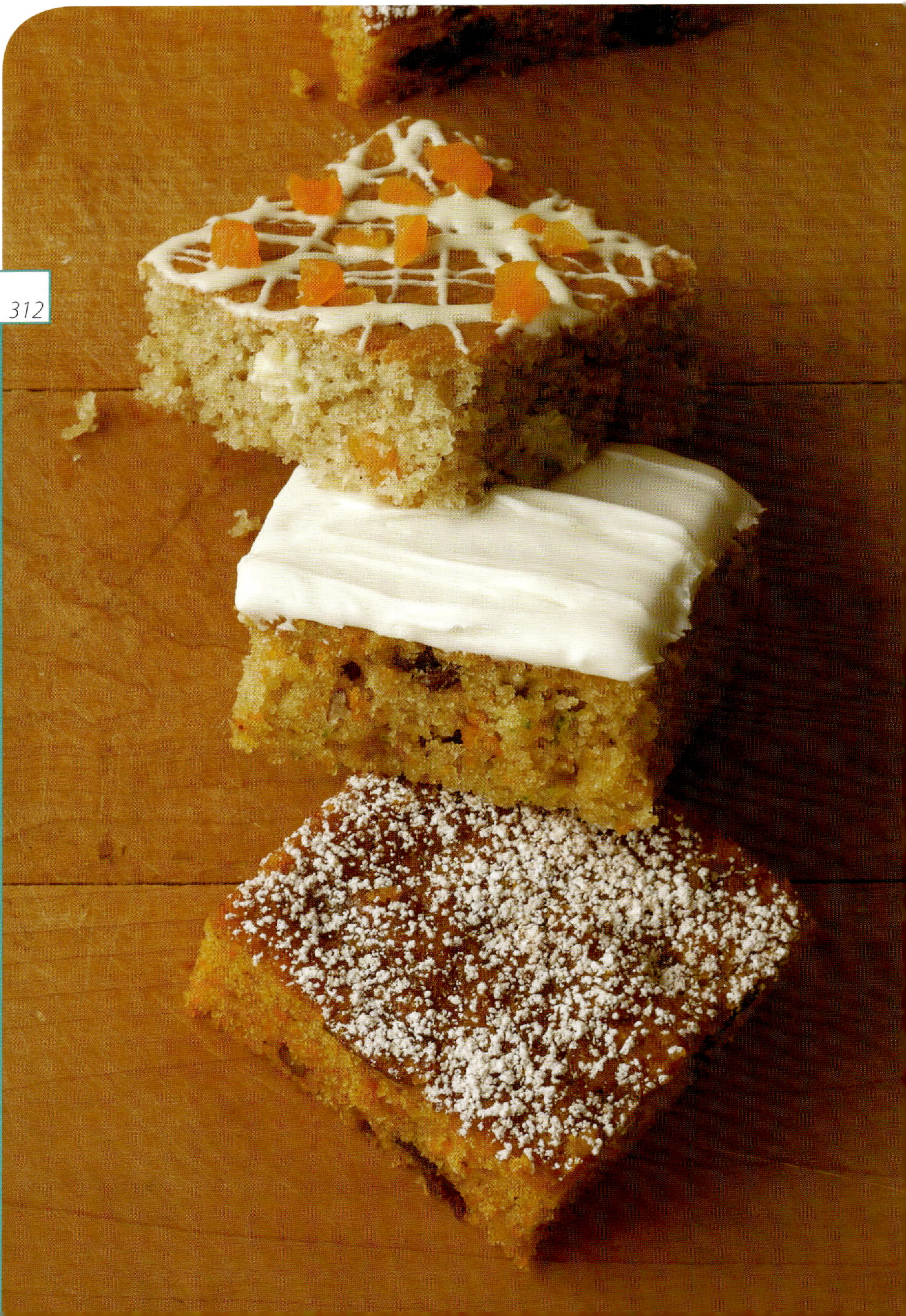

Shredded carrot adds moistness and sweetness to all three variations of these bars, pictured at left.

carrot cake bars

prep: 25 minutes bake: 25 minutes at 350°F
makes: 36 bars

2 cups all-purpose flour
2 cups granulated sugar
2 teaspoons baking powder
1 teaspoon ground cinnamon
½ teaspoon salt
½ teaspoon baking soda
3 cups finely shredded carrots (6 medium)
1 cup vegetable oil
4 eggs, lightly beaten
1 cup chopped pecans
1 recipe Cream Cheese Frosting (see recipe, page 19)

1 Preheat oven to 350°F. In a large bowl stir together flour, sugar, baking powder, cinnamon, salt, and baking soda. Add carrots, oil, and eggs; stir until combined. Stir in pecans. Spread batter evenly in an ungreased 15×10×1-inch baking pan.

2 Bake about 25 minutes or until a wooden toothpick inserted near the center comes out clean. Cool in pan on a wire rack for 2 hours. Spread with Cream Cheese Frosting. Cut into bars.

to store: Cover bars and store in the refrigerator up to 3 days.

nutrition facts per bar: 224 cal., 10 g total fat (2 g sat. fat), 29 mg chol., 100 mg sodium, 31 g carb., 1 g fiber, 2 g pro.

confetti carrot-cake bars: Prepare as directed, except use 1 cup finely shredded zucchini, 1 cup finely shredded carrots, and 1 cup finely shredded yellow summer squash instead of the 3 cups carrots. Sprinkle cooled bars with powdered sugar.
nutrition facts per bar: 222 cal., 10 g total fat (2 g sat. fat), 29 mg chol., 96 mg sodium, 31 g carb., 1 g fiber, 2 g pro.,

cashew-apricot-parsnip bars: Prepare as directed, except substitute finely shredded parsnips for the carrots; substitute ½ cup each chopped cashews and snipped dried apricots for the pecans; add 4 ounces white baking bar, chopped; and substitute ground allspice for the cinnamon. Omit Cream Cheese Frosting. After baking and cooling, place 4 ounces white baking bar, chopped, in a small saucepan; cook and stir over low heat until melted. Drizzle over uncut bars. Sprinkle with ¼ finely chopped dried apricots. Let stand until set.
nutrition facts per bar: 192 cal., 10 g total fat (2 g sat. fat), 25 mg chol., 86 mg sodium, 25 g carb., 1 g fiber, 2 g pro.

Ya man ... the rum frosting adds a Jamaican note to these treats.

banana bars with butter-rum frosting

prep: 20 minutes **bake:** 25 minutes at 350°F
makes: 48 bars

½	cup butter, softened
1⅓	cups granulated sugar
1½	teaspoons baking powder
½	teaspoon baking soda
¼	teaspoon salt
1	egg
1	cup mashed bananas (3 medium)
½	cup sour cream
1	teaspoon vanilla
2	cups all-purpose flour
¾	cup chopped almonds, toasted (see tip, page 13)
1	recipe Butter-Rum Frosting
	Dried banana slices (optional)

1 Preheat oven to 350°F. Grease a 15×10×1-inch baking pan; set aside. In a large mixing bowl beat butter with an electric mixer on medium to high speed for 30 seconds. Add sugar, baking powder, baking soda, and salt. Beat until combined, scraping sides of bowl occasionally. Beat in egg, mashed bananas, sour cream, and vanilla until combined. Beat in as much of the flour as you can with the mixer. Using a wooden spoon, stir in any remaining flour and the almonds. Pour batter into the prepared baking pan, spreading evenly.

2 Bake about 25 minutes or until a wooden toothpick inserted near the center comes out clean. Cool in pan on a wire rack.

3 Spread with Butter-Rum Frosting. Cut into bars. If desired, top with dried banana slices before serving.

nutrition facts per bar: 111 cal., 4 g total fat (2 g sat. fat), 12 mg chol., 60 mg sodium, 18 g carb., 0 g fiber, 1 g pro.

butter-rum frosting: In a medium mixing bowl beat 3 tablespoons butter, softened, with an electric mixer on medium speed for 30 seconds. Gradually beat in 1½ cups powdered sugar. Beat in 1 tablespoon rum and 1 teaspoon vanilla. Beat in an additional 1½ cups powdered sugar and enough milk to make frosting spreading consistency.

These crowd-pleasing bars get an updated twist with Browned Butter Frosting, but you can stick with tradition and use Cream Cheese Frosting instead (see recipe, page 19).

pumpkin bars

prep: 25 minutes **bake:** 25 minutes at 350°F
makes: 36 bars

- 2 cups all-purpose flour
- 1½ cups granulated sugar
- 2 teaspoons baking powder
- 2 teaspoons ground cinnamon
- 1 teaspoon baking soda
- ½ teaspoon salt
- ¼ teaspoon ground cloves
- 4 eggs, lightly beaten
- 1 15-ounce can pumpkin
- 1 cup vegetable oil
- 1 recipe Browned Butter Frosting

1 Preheat oven to 350°F. In a large bowl stir together flour, sugar, baking powder, cinnamon, baking soda, salt, and cloves. Add eggs, pumpkin, and oil; stir until combined. Spread batter evenly in an ungreased 15×10×1-inch baking pan.

2 Bake for 25 to 30 minutes or until a wooden toothpick inserted near the center comes out clean. Cool in pan on a wire rack for 2 hours.

3 Spread with Browned Butter Frosting. Cut into bars.

to store: To store, place bars in a single layer in an airtight container; cover. Store in the refrigerator up to 3 days.

nutrition facts per bar: 178 cal., 8 g total fat (2 g sat. fat), 28 mg chol., 109 mg sodium, 25 g carb., 1 g fiber, 2 g pro.

browned butter frosting: In a small saucepan melt ⅓ cup butter over low heat. Continue heating until butter turns a light golden brown. Remove from heat. In a large mixing bowl combine 3 cups powdered sugar, 2 tablespoons milk, and 1 teaspoon vanilla. Add browned butter. Beat with an electric mixer on medium speed until spreading consistency, adding additional milk if necessary.

While classic baklava is made with walnuts, peanuts give these bars kid appeal.

peanut baklava

prep: 45 minutes bake: 35 minutes at 325°F
makes: 32 bars

3 cups peanuts, finely chopped
1½ cups granulated sugar
1 teaspoon ground cinnamon
¾ cup butter, melted
20 sheets (14×9-inch rectangles) frozen phyllo dough, thawed
¾ cup water
3 tablespoons honey
2 inches stick cinnamon

1 Preheat oven to 325°F. In a medium bowl stir together peanuts, ½ cup of the sugar, and the ground cinnamon; set aside.

2 Brush the bottom of a 13×9×2-inch baking pan with some of the melted butter. Unroll phyllo dough. Place one sheet of phyllo in the prepared baking pan. (While you work, keep the remaining phyllo covered with plastic wrap to prevent it from drying out). Brush phyllo sheet generously with some of the melted butter. Layer four more phyllo sheets in the pan, brushing each sheet with melted butter. Sprinkle with about 1 cup of the nut mixture. Repeat layering phyllo sheets and sprinkling with nut mixture twice, brushing each sheet with melted butter.

3 Layer the remaining five phyllo sheets on the filling, brushing each sheet with melted butter. Drizzle with any remaining melted butter. Using a sharp knife, cut layers into 32 to 48 pieces.

4 Bake for 35 to 45 minutes or until top is golden brown. Cool slightly in pan on a wire rack.

5 Meanwhile, in a medium saucepan stir together the remaining 1 cup sugar, the water, honey, and stick cinnamon. Bring to boiling; reduce heat. Simmer, uncovered, for 20 minutes. Remove and discard stick cinnamon. Pour honey mixture evenly over slightly cooled baklava; cool completely.

nutrition facts per bar: 182 cal., 12 g total fat (4 g sat. fat), 11 mg chol., 73 mg sodium, 18 g carb., 1 g fiber, 4 g pro.

Anyone who loves pecan pie will go nuts for this updated recipe.

maple-nut pie bars

prep: 25 minutes **bake:** 40 minutes at 350°F
makes: 24 bars

Nonstick cooking spray
1¼ cups all-purpose flour
½ cup powdered sugar
¼ teaspoon salt
½ cup butter
2 eggs, lightly beaten
1 cup chopped mixed nuts
½ cup packed brown sugar
½ cup pure maple syrup
2 tablespoons butter, melted
½ teaspoon maple flavoring
½ cup white baking pieces (optional)
1 teaspoon shortening (optional)
24 pecan halves (optional)

1 Preheat oven to 350°F. Line an 11×7×1½-inch baking pan with foil, extending the foil over edges of pan. Lightly coat foil with cooking spray; set pan aside.

2 For crust, in a medium bowl stir together flour, powdered sugar, and salt. Using a pastry blender, cut in the ½ cup butter until mixture resembles coarse crumbs. Evenly press crumb mixture onto the bottom of the prepared baking pan. Bake about 20 minutes or until lightly browned.

3 Meanwhile, for filling, in another medium bowl combine eggs, mixed nuts, brown sugar, maple syrup, 2 tablespoons melted butter, and maple flavoring. Evenly spread filling over hot crust.

4 Bake about 20 minutes more or until filling is set. Cool in pan on a wire rack. Using the edges of the foil, lift uncut bars out of pan. Cut into bars.

5 If desired for topping, in a large glass measuring cup combine white baking pieces and shortening. Microwave on 100 percent power (high) about 1 minute or until melted, stirring after 30 seconds. Dollop melted white chocolate on bars and top with pecan halves.

to store: Place bars in a single layer in an airtight container; cover. Store in the refrigerator up to 2 days.

nutrition facts per bar: 153 cal., 9 g total fat (4 g sat. fat), 30 mg chol., 91 mg sodium, 18 g carb., 1 g fiber, 2 g pro.

pecan pie bars: Prepare as directed except substitute chopped pecans for the mixed nuts and light-color corn syrup for the maple syrup. Omit the maple flavoring and add 1 teaspoon vanilla to the filling.

nutrition facts per bar: 152 cal., 9 g total fat (4 g sat. fat), 28 mg chol., 78 mg sodium, 18 g carb., 1 g fiber, 2 g pro.

These nutty, chunky, super-rich bars eat like candy.

chocolate-drizzled caramel-hazelnut bars

prep: 45 minutes bake: 38 minutes at 350°F cool: 20 minutes
makes: 36 bars

3½ cups hazelnuts
    (filberts)
    Nonstick cooking
    spray
2   cups all-purpose flour
⅔   cup powdered sugar
¾   cup cold butter, cut
    up
½   cup packed brown
    sugar
½   cup honey
⅔   cup butter
3   tablespoons
    whipping cream
¾   cup semisweet
    chocolate pieces
2   teaspoons shortening

1 Preheat oven to 350°F. Place hazelnuts in a 15×10×1-inch baking pan. Bake about 10 minutes or until toasted, stirring once. Place the warm nuts on a clean kitchen towel. Rub the nuts with the towel to remove the loose skins; discard skins. Set nuts aside.

2 Line a 13×9×2-inch baking pan with heavy foil, extending foil over the edges of the pan. Lightly coat foil with cooking spray; set pan aside.

3 In a food processor combine flour, powdered sugar, and the ¾ cup cold butter. Cover and pulse until mixture forms coarse crumbs. Press flour mixture firmly and evenly onto the bottom and ¾ inch up the sides of the prepared pan. Bake for 18 to 20 minutes or until edges begin to brown. Transfer pan to a wire rack; cool for 20 minutes.

4 In a medium saucepan combine brown sugar, honey, the ⅔ cup butter, and the whipping cream. Cook and stir over medium heat until mixture boils. Stir in toasted hazelnuts. Spoon nut mixture into the partially-baked crust, spreading evenly.

5 Bake for 20 to 25 minutes or until filling is golden and bubbly. Transfer pan to a wire rack; cool completely. Use foil to lift uncut bars out of pan. Place on a cutting board. Using a sharp knife, trim edges. Cut into bars.

6 In a small saucepan combine chocolate pieces and shortening. Cook and stir over low heat until melted and smooth. Drizzle over bars; let stand until chocolate is set.

nutrition facts per bar: 227 cal., 17 g total fat (6 g sat. fat), 21 mg chol., 66 mg sodium, 19 g carb., 2 g fiber, 3 g pro.

Use coarse sea salt rather than table salt in the topping.

salted chewy cashew-caramel bars

prep: 40 minutes   bake: 20 minutes at 350°F
makes: 60 bars

1   cup butter, softened
1   cup granulated sugar
1   cup packed brown
      sugar
2   eggs
1½ cups all-purpose flour
1   cup finely crushed
      pretzels
1   teaspoon baking soda
½   teaspoon salt
3   cups rolled oats
1   14-ounce can
      sweetened
      condensed milk
1   11-ounce package
      caramel baking bits
2   teaspoons vanilla
1   cup milk chocolate
      pieces
1   cup chopped salted
      cashews
¼   teaspoon sea salt

1 Preheat oven to 350°F. Line a 15×10×1-inch baking pan with foil, extending the foil over edges of pan; set aside.

2 In a large mixing bowl beat butter with an electric mixer on medium to high speed for 30 seconds. Add granulated sugar and brown sugar. Beat until light and fluffy, scraping sides of bowl occasionally. Beat in eggs until combined. In a medium bowl stir together flour, pretzels, baking soda, and ½ teaspoon salt. Gradually add flour mixture to butter mixture, beating until combined. Stir in oats. Remove 1 cup of the oat mixture for topping. For crust, press the remaining evenly onto the bottom of the prepared baking pan.

3 For filling, in a medium saucepan heat and stir sweetened condensed milk and caramel bits over medium-low heat until caramel is melted and mixture is smooth. Remove from heat. Stir in vanilla. Pour caramel mixture over crust layer in pan. Sprinkle with chocolate pieces, cashews, and sea salt. Drop topping in spoonfuls on filling.

4 Bake for 20 to 25 minutes or until lightly browned. Cool in pan on a wire rack. Using the edges of the foil, lift uncut bars out of pan. Cut into bars.

nutrition facts per bar: 176 cal., 7 g total fat (3 g sat. fat), 18 mg chol., 144 mg sodium, 26 g carb., 1 g fiber, 3 g pro.

A coffee glaze melts into the bars after baking.

cappuccino-caramel-oat bars

prep: 30 minutes **bake:** 20 minutes at 350°F
makes: 48 bars

3 cups rolled oats
2⅓ cups all-purpose flour
1 cup chopped pecans
1 teaspoon baking soda
¼ teaspoon salt
1 cup butter, softened
2 cups packed brown sugar
2 eggs
1 tablespoon instant coffee crystals or espresso coffee powder
2 teaspoons vanilla
¾ cup caramel-flavor ice cream topping
½ cup chopped pecans
1 recipe Coffee Glaze (optional)

1 Preheat oven to 350°F. Lightly grease a 15×10×1-inch baking pan; set aside.

2 In a large bowl stir together oats, flour, the 1 cup pecans, baking soda, and salt; set aside. In a large mixing bowl beat butter with an electric mixer on medium speed for 30 seconds. Add brown sugar. Beat until combined, scraping sides of bowl occasionally. Beat in eggs, the 1 tablespoon coffee crystals, and vanilla until combined. Beat in as much of the oat mixture as you can with the mixer. Stir in any remaining oat mixture. Remove 2 cups for topping.

3 Using floured hands, press the remaining oat mixture evenly onto the bottom of the prepared baking pan. Carefully spread with caramel topping to within ¼ inch of the edges. Spoon reserved oat mixture into small mounds on caramel topping; sprinkle with the ½ cup pecans.

4 Bake for 20 to 25 minutes or until edges are set (do not overbake). Cool in pan on a wire rack. If desired, drizzle with Coffee Glaze; let stand for 15 minutes to set glaze. Cut into bars.

to store: Place bars in a single layer in an airtight container; cover. Store at room temperature up to 3 days or freeze up to 1 month.

nutrition facts per bar: 158 cal., 7 g total fat (3 g sat. fat), 18 mg chol., 96 mg sodium, 23 g carb., 1 g fiber, 2 g pro.

coffee glaze: In a small bowl combine 2 tablespoons very hot milk and 1 teaspoon instant coffee crystals; stir until dissolved. Stir in 1 cup sifted powdered sugar until smooth.

Two large pans of bars will serve a crowd.

date-walnut honey bars

prep: 30 minutes **bake:** 25 minutes at 350°F **chill:** 30 minutes
makes: 36 bars

1	recipe Oatmeal Crust
¾	cup honey
¾	cup apple jelly
¼	cup butter
¼	cup all-purpose flour
¼	cup packed brown sugar
½	teaspoon baking powder
½	teaspoon salt
4	eggs, lightly beaten
1	teaspoon vanilla
2½	cups coarsely chopped walnuts
2	cups snipped pitted whole dates

1 Preheat oven to 350°F. Prepare Oatmeal Crust; cool. In a medium saucepan combine honey, apple jelly, and butter. Melt over low heat about 5 minutes, stirring frequently. Remove from heat.

2 In a large mixing bowl stir together flour, brown sugar, baking powder, and salt. Add eggs and vanilla. Beat with an electric mixer on medium speed until smooth. Stir in honey mixture.

3 Pour half the batter over each baked crust, spreading evenly. Top with walnuts and dates. Bake for 25 minutes. Cool in pans on wire racks. Cover and chill for 30 minutes. Cut into bars.

nutrition facts per bar: 243 cal., 12 g total fat (5 g sat. fat), 38 mg chol., 139 mg sodium, 32 g carb., 2 g fiber, 3 g pro.

oatmeal crust: In a blender or food processor combine ¾ cup regular rolled oats, ¾ cup granulated sugar, and ½ teaspoon salt. Cover and blend or process until oats are finely chopped. Transfer to a large bowl. Stir in 2 cups all-purpose flour. Using a pastry blender, cut in 1 cup butter until the mixture resembles coarse crumbs. Sprinkle 1 tablespoon water over mixture. Continue to blend until mixture forms loose crumbs. Press evenly onto bottoms of two greased 13×9×2-inch baking pans. Bake each pan on the center rack of the 350°F oven for 12 minutes. Cool on wire racks.

Tote this dessert in a cooler for summer potlucks.

chocolaty caramel-nut s'more bars

prep: 30 minutes **bake:** 27 minutes at 325°F
makes: 24 bars

2   cups finely crushed chocolate wafers (38 cookies)
½   cup butter, melted
1   11-ounce package caramel baking bits*
¼   cup whipping cream*
2   cups tiny marshmallows
1½ cups mixed nuts, cashews, or cocktail peanuts, coarsely chopped
1   cup semisweet chocolate pieces

1 Preheat oven to 325°F. Line a 13×9×2-inch baking pan with foil, extending the foil over the edges of the pan. Lightly grease foil; set pan aside.

2 In a large bowl stir together the crushed cookies and butter. Press crumb mixture firmly and evenly into the bottom of the prepared pan. Bake for 15 minutes. Cool crust in pan on a wire rack for 5 minutes.

3 Meanwhile, in a small heavy saucepan heat and stir caramel bits and whipping cream until caramel is melted and smooth. Pour caramel mixture evenly over crust.

4 In a medium bowl combine marshmallows, nuts, and chocolate pieces; sprinkle over caramel mixture and press in lightly.

5 Bake about 12 minutes or until marshmallows just begin to brown. Cool in pan on a wire rack. Using the foil edges, lift uncut bars out of pan. Cut into bars.

*tip: If you cannot locate caramel baking bits, substitute a 14-ounce package of vanilla caramels, unwrapped, and increase the whipping cream to ⅓ cup.

to store: Layer bars between sheets of waxed paper in an airtight container; cover. Store in the refrigerator up to 3 days or freeze up to 3 months.

nutrition facts per bar: 237 cal., 15 g total fat (7 g sat. fat), 14 mg chol., 163 mg sodium, 27 g carb., 1 g fiber, 3 g pro.

The ultimate quick dessert for anyone who craves cashews!

caramel-cashew bars

prep: 15 minutes bake: 23 minutes at 325°F
makes: 24 bars

3   cups finely crushed
      shortbread cookies
¼   cup granulated sugar
½   cup butter, melted
36 vanilla caramels,
      unwrapped
½   cup whipping cream
2   cups coarsely
      chopped cashews or
      dry-roasted peanuts
2   cups tiny
      marshmallows

1 Preheat oven to 325°F. Line a 13×9×2-inch baking pan with foil, extending the foil over edges of pan. Lightly grease foil; set pan aside.

2 For crust, in a large bowl stir together crushed cookies and sugar. Stir in melted butter until combined. Press mixture evenly onto the bottom of the prepared baking pan. Bake about 15 minutes or until golden and dry around edges.

3 Meanwhile, in a medium size heavy saucepan heat and stir caramels and whipping cream over medium-low heat until caramels are melted and mixture is smooth. Stir in nuts. Sprinkle marshmallows evenly over baked crust. Carefully spread caramel mixture over marshmallows.

4 Bake for 8 to 10 minutes or until caramel layer is set and bubbly around edges. Cool in pan on a wire rack. Using the edges of the foil, lift uncut bars out of pan. Cut into bars.

nutrition facts per bar: 317 cal., 18 g total fat (8 g sat. fat), 22 mg chol., 245 mg sodium, 34 g carb., 1 g fiber, 4 g pro.

Please PB&J fans by spreading different jams on each side of the baking pan.

peanut butter jammin' bars

prep: 20 minutes **bake:** 25 minutes at 375°F
makes: 32 bars

¾   cup butter, softened
½   cup creamy peanut butter
1½   cups packed brown sugar
1   teaspoon vanilla
½   teaspoon baking soda
½   teaspoon salt
2¼   cups quick-cooking rolled oats
2   cups all-purpose flour
1   12-ounce jar seedless blackberry, raspberry, or strawberry jam
1   cup chocolate-covered peanuts, coarsely chopped

1 Preheat oven to 375°F. Line a 13×9×2-inch baking pan with foil, extending the foil over edges of the pan. Lightly grease foil; set pan aside.

2 For crust, in a large mixing bowl beat butter and peanut butter with an electric mixer on medium to high speed for 30 seconds. Add brown sugar, vanilla, baking soda, and salt. Beat until combined, scraping sides of bowl occasionally. Beat in oats. Beat in as much of the flour as you can with the mixer. Using a wooden spoon, stir in any remaining flour (mixture will be crumbly). Remove 2 cups of the oat mixture for topping. Press remaining evenly onto the bottom of the prepared pan; set aside.

3 In a small bowl stir jam until smooth. Carefully spread jam over crust to within 1 inch of the edges. Sprinkle with the reserved oat mixture and chocolate-covered peanuts.

4 Bake for 25 to 30 minutes or until jam is bubbly and topping is golden. Cool in pan on a wire rack. Using the edges of the foil, lift uncut bars out of pan. Cut into bars.

nutrition facts per bar: 213 cal., 9 g total fat (4 g sat. fat), 12 mg chol., 121 mg sodium, 32 g carb., 2 g fiber, 3 g pro.

If necessary, break the graham crackers to fit into the pan.

oat 'n' toffee grahams

prep: 15 minutes **bake:** 21 minutes at 350°F
makes: 32 bars

24   graham crackers
      (12 rectangles)
1½   cups rolled oats
¾   cup granulated sugar
¾   cup packed brown
      sugar
3   tablespoons all-
      purpose flour
⅔   cup butter, melted
1   egg, lightly beaten
1   teaspoon vanilla
1   12-ounce package
      (2 cups) semisweet
      chocolate pieces
½   cup smoke-flavor
      whole almonds,
      coarsely chopped

1 Preheat oven to 350°F. Line a 15×10×1-inch baking pan with foil, extending the foil over edges of pan. Arrange graham crackers in a single layer in the prepared baking pan.

2 In a large bowl stir together oats, granulated sugar, brown sugar, and flour. Stir in melted butter, egg, and vanilla until combined. Spoon oat mixture onto graham cracker layer, carefully spreading to cover crackers completely.

3 Bake for 20 to 25 minutes or until top is lightly browned and bubbly. Sprinkle with chocolate pieces. Bake for 1 minute more. Spread melted chocolate evenly over top. Sprinkle with almonds. Cool in pan on a wire rack. Using the edges of the foil, lift uncut bars out of pan. Cut or break into bars.

nutrition facts per bar: 193 cal., 9 g total fat (5 g sat. fat), 17 mg chol., 77 mg sodium, 26 g carb., 2 g fiber, 3 g pro.

Use light cream cheese if you want to trim a few calories.

pumpkin-chocolate cheesecake bars

prep: 25 minutes **bake:** 55 minutes at 325°F **chill:** 3 hours
makes: 24 bars

1¼ cups finely crushed graham crackers
¼ cup granulated sugar
⅓ cup butter, melted
2 8-ounce packages cream cheese, softened
1¾ cups granulated sugar
3 eggs
1 cup canned pumpkin
½ teaspoon pumpkin pie spice
½ teaspoon vanilla
¼ teaspoon salt
6 ounces semisweet chocolate, coarsely chopped, or 1 cup semisweet chocolate pieces
2 tablespoons butter
1¼ cups sour cream
¼ cup granulated sugar
    Freshly grated nutmeg and/or milk chocolate or semisweet chocolate curls

1 Preheat oven to 325°F. Lightly grease a 13×9×2-inch baking pan; set aside. In a medium bowl stir together crushed graham crackers and the ¼ cup sugar. Stir in ⅓ cup melted butter. Press mixture evenly onto the bottom of the prepared baking pan; set aside.

2 In a large mixing bowl beat cream cheese and 1¾ cups sugar with an electric mixer on medium speed until smooth. Add eggs, one at a time, beating on low speed after each addition just until combined. Beat in pumpkin, pumpkin pie spice, vanilla, and salt on low speed just until combined. Transfer 1¼ cups of the mixture to a medium bowl.

3 In a small heavy saucepan heat and stir 6 ounces chocolate and 2 tablespoons butter over low heat until melted. Stir chocolate mixture into the 1¼ cups pumpkin mixture. Pour over crust, spreading evenly. Bake for 15 minutes.

4 Carefully pour the remaining pumpkin mixture over baked chocolate layer, spreading evenly. Bake for 40 to 45 minutes or until filling is puffed and center is set. Cool in pan on a wire rack for 30 minutes.

5 In a small bowl combine sour cream and the ¼ cup sugar. Gently spread sour cream mixture over uncut bars. Cool completely. Cover and chill for at least 3 hours. Cut into bars.* Before serving, sprinkle with nutmeg and/or chocolate curls.

*tip: To make triangle-shapes, cut the bars crosswise into four strips. Then cut each strip into five triangles (you'll have two half-triangles at the ends of each strip).

to store: Place bars in a single layer in an airtight container; cover. Store in the refrigerator up to 3 days.

nutrition facts per bar: 256 cal., 15 g total fat (9 g sat. fat), 62 mg chol., 151 mg sodium, 28 g carb., 1 g fiber, 3 g pro.

Orange peel and orange juice can be used instead of tangerine.

tangy tangerine cheesecake bars

prep: 20 minutes **bake:** 38 minutes 350°F **cool:** 1 hour **chill:** 2 hours
makes: 16 bars

¼ cup butter, softened
¼ cup packed brown
    sugar
⅔ cup all-purpose flour
12 ounces cream cheese,
    softened
⅓ cup granulated sugar
1 egg
¼ cup whipping cream
2 teaspoons finely
    shredded tangerine
    peel
3 tablespoons tangerine
    juice
½ teaspoon vanilla
1 recipe Candied
    Tangerine Peel
    (optional)

1 Preheat oven to 350°F. Line an 8×8×2-inch baking pan with foil, extending the foil over the edges of the pan; set aside.

2 In a small mixing bowl beat butter and brown sugar with an electric mixer on medium to high speed until light and fluffy. Add flour, beating until combined (mixture will be crumbly). Press mixture evenly onto the bottom of the prepared baking pan. Bake for 8 minutes.

3 Meanwhile, for filling, in a medium mixing bowl beat cream cheese and granulated sugar with an electric mixer on medium speed until smooth. Beat in egg, whipping cream, tangerine peel, tangerine juice, and vanilla until combined. Pour filling over crust.

4 Bake about 30 minutes or just until filling is set. Cool in pan on a wire rack for 1 hour. Cover and chill for at least 2 hours. Cut into squares or triangles. If desired, top with Candied Tangerine Peel.

to store: Place bars in a single layer in an airtight container; cover. Store in the refrigerator up to 3 days or freeze up to 3 months.

nutrition facts per bar: 166 cal., 12 g total fat (7 g sat. fat), 48 mg chol., 101 mg sodium, 13 g carb., 0 g fiber, 2 g pro.

candied tangerine peel: Using a paring knife, cut peels from 3 tangerines into lengthwise quarters, cutting just to the surface of the fruit. Pry back the quartered peel and pull away to remove. Reserve fruit for another use. Using a spoon, scrape away the white pith inside the peel. Cut peel into thin strips. In a 2-quart saucepan combine 1⅓ cups sugar and ⅓ cup water. Cover and bring to boiling. Uncover and add tangerine peel strips. Return to boiling, stirring to dissolve sugar. Reduce heat to medium-low. (Mixture should boil at a moderate, steady rate over entire surface.) Cook, uncovered, about 15 minutes or until peel is almost translucent, stirring occasionally. Using a slotted spoon, remove peel from syrup, allowing syrup to drain. Transfer peel to a wire rack set over waxed paper. Set cooked peel aside until cool enough to handle but still warm and slightly sticky. Roll peel in additional sugar to coat. Dry on the rack for 1 to 2 hours more. To store: candied peel, place in an airtight container; cover. Store in a cool, dry place up to 1 week or freeze up to 6 months.

swirls-of-peppermint cheesecake bars

prep: 25 minutes **bake:** 25 minutes at 350°F **chill:** 4 hours **cool:** 1 hour
makes: 32 bars

Nonstick cooking
spray
2 cups finely crushed
chocolate wafer
cookies (about
38 cookies)
2 tablespoons
granulated sugar
⅓ cup butter, melted
2 8-ounce packages
cream cheese,
softened
1 cup granulated sugar
1 teaspoon vanilla
½ teaspoon peppermint
extract
¼ cup milk
4 eggs, lightly beaten
Several drops red
food coloring
¼ cup crushed
peppermint candies

1 Preheat oven to 350°F. Coat a 13×9×2-inch baking pan with cooking spray; set aside.

2 For crust, in a medium bowl combine crushed cookies and the 2 tablespoons sugar; stir in melted butter. Press mixture evenly onto the bottom of the prepared baking pan.

3 In a large mixing bowl beat cream cheese, the 1 cup sugar, vanilla, and peppermint extract with an electric mixer on medium speed until smooth. Beat in milk until combined. Stir in eggs until combined.

4 Pour cream cheese mixture over crust, spreading evenly. Randomly drop red food coloring in random spots over cream cheese mixture. Using a thin metal spatula, swirl slightly to marble.*

5 Bake about 25 minutes or until edges are puffed and center is set. Cool in pan on a wire rack for 1 hour. Cover and chill for 4 to 24 hours. Cut into bars, wiping knife between cuts. Sprinkle with crushed candies before serving.

***tip:** To keep layers and colors separate, swirl the food coloring gently into the batter.

to store: Place bars in a single layer in an airtight container; cover. Store in the refrigerator up to 3 days or freeze up to 3 months.

nutrition facts per bar: 139 cal., 8 g total fat (4 g sat. fat), 44 mg chol., 119 mg sodium, 14 g carb., 0 g fiber, 2 g pro.

Thoroughly chill before cutting into bars.

coconut-blueberry cheesecake bars

prep: 30 minutes **bake:** 26 minutes at 350°F **chill:** 3 hours
makes: 32 bars

½ cup butter
¾ cup finely crushed graham crackers
½ cup all-purpose flour
½ cup flaked coconut
½ cup ground pecans
¼ cup granulated sugar
12 ounces cream cheese, softened
⅔ cup granulated sugar
4 eggs
1 tablespoon brandy or milk
1 teaspoon vanilla
2 cups fresh blueberries

1 Preheat oven to 350°F. Lightly grease a 13×9×2-inch baking pan; set aside.

2 For crust, in a small saucepan heat butter over medium heat until the color of light brown sugar. Remove from heat. In a medium bowl stir together crushed graham crackers, flour, coconut, pecans, and ¼ cup sugar. Stir in browned butter until combined. Press mixture evenly onto the bottom of the prepared baking pan. Bake for 8 to 10 minutes or until lightly browned.

3 Meanwhile, in a large mixing bowl beat cream cheese and ⅔ cup sugar with an electric mixer on medium speed until smooth. Beat in eggs, brandy, and vanilla until combined. Pour mixture over hot crust, spreading evenly. Sprinkle with blueberries.

4 Bake for 18 to 20 minutes or until center appears set. Cool in pan on a wire rack. Cover and chill at least 3 hours. Cut into bars.

to store: Place bars in a single layer in an airtight container; cover. Store in the refrigerator up to 2 days.

nutrition facts per bar: 136 cal., 9 g total fat (5 g sat. fat), 46 mg chol., 78 mg sodium, 11 g carb., 1 g fiber, 2 g pro.

unbeatable bars

Divvy the fresh raspberries over the cream cheese so each square has a fruit topping.

chocolate-raspberry cheesecake bars

prep: 30 minutes **bake:** 25 minutes at 350°F **chill:** 1 hour
makes: 16 bars

1 cup crushed chocolate wafer cookies
3 tablespoons butter, melted
½ of an 8-ounce package cream cheese, softened
⅓ cup sour cream
¼ cup granulated sugar
1 egg
1 tablespoon raspberry liqueur (optional)
1 teaspoon cornstarch
½ teaspoon finely shredded lemon peel
1 cup fresh raspberries
 Seedless raspberry jam or currant jelly, melted (optional)

1 Preheat oven to 350°F. Line an 8×8×2-inch baking pan with foil, extending the foil over edges of pan. Lightly grease foil; set pan aside. For crust, in a small bowl stir together cookie crumbs and melted butter. Press mixture evenly onto the bottom of the prepared baking pan; set aside.

2 In a medium mixing bowl beat cream cheese with an electric mixer on medium to high speed until smooth. Add sour cream and sugar. Beat until combined, scraping sides of bowl occasionally. Beat in egg just until combined. Add liqueur (if desired), cornstarch, and lemon peel; beat on low speed just until combined. Pour cream cheese mixture over crust, spreading evenly. Arrange raspberries in 16 mounds on cream cheese mixture.

3 Bake for 25 to 30 minutes or until center is set. Cool in pan on a wire rack. Cover and chill for at least 1 hour. If desired, drizzle melted jam over raspberries before serving. Cut into bars.

to store: Place bars in a single layer in an airtight container; cover. Store in the refrigerator up to 3 days or freeze up to 1 month.

nutrition facts per bar: 106 cal., 7 g total fat (4 g sat. fat), 27 mg chol., 101 mg sodium, 10 g carb., 1 g fiber, 2 g pro.

Here's a handy idea for hot summer days. These bars won't melt in the midday sun.

oatmeal jam bars

prep: 15 minutes **bake:** 35 minutes at 350°F
makes: 36 bars

1⅓ cups all-purpose flour
¼ teaspoon baking soda
¼ teaspoon salt
¾ cup quick-cooking rolled oats
⅓ cup packed brown sugar
1 teaspoon finely shredded lemon peel
2 3-ounce packages cream cheese, softened
¼ cup butter, softened
¾ cup seedless blackberry, red raspberry, or black raspberry jam
1 teaspoon lemon juice

1 Preheat oven to 350°F. Grease a 9×9×2-inch baking pan; set aside. In a medium bowl stir together flour, baking soda, and salt. Stir in oats, brown sugar, and lemon peel; set aside.

2 In a large mixing bowl combine cream cheese and butter. Beat with an electric mixer on medium to high speed for 30 seconds. Add flour mixture; beat on low speed until mixture is crumbly. Remove 1 cup of the crumb mixture for topping; set aside.

3 Press the remaining crumb mixture onto the bottom of the prepared baking pan. Bake for 20 minutes.

4 Meanwhile, in a small bowl combine jam and lemon juice. Carefully spread jam mixture over hot crust. Sprinkle with the reserved 1 cup crumb mixture. Bake about 15 minutes or until top is golden. Cool in pan on a wire rack. Cut into bars.

to store: Layer bars between sheets of waxed paper in an airtight container; cover. Store in the refrigerator up to 3 days or freeze up to 1 month.

nutrition facts per bar: 173 cal., 7 g total fat (5 g sat. fat), 20 mg chol., 121 mg sodium, 25 g carb., 0 g fiber, 2 g pro.

unbeatable bars

These bars have a chocolate cookie crust.

macaroon chocolate bars

prep: 30 minutes **bake:** 33 minutes at 350°F
makes: 48 bars

2 cups crushed
   chocolate sandwich
   cookies with white
   filling
½ cup granulated sugar
⅓ cup unsweetened
   cocoa powder
½ cup butter, melted
1 teaspoon vanilla
⅔ cup all-purpose flour
⅓ cup granulated sugar
¼ teaspoon salt
2¾ cups flaked coconut
3 egg whites, lightly
   beaten
½ teaspoon vanilla
½ cup semisweet
   chocolate pieces
1 teaspoon shortening

1 Preheat oven to 350°F. Line a 13×9×2-inch baking pan with foil, extending the foil over edges of pan. Lightly grease foil; set pan aside.

2 For crust, in a large bowl stir together crushed cookies, the ½ cup sugar, and the cocoa powder. Drizzle with melted butter and the 1 teaspoon vanilla; toss gently to coat. Press evenly onto the bottom of the prepared baking pan. Bake for 8 minutes.

3 Meanwhile, for filling, in a large bowl stir together flour, the ⅓ cup sugar, and the salt. Stir in coconut. Add egg whites and the ½ teaspoon vanilla, stirring until combined. Spoon filling over hot crust. Using moistened hands, carefully press filling to edges of pan.

4 Bake for 25 to 28 minutes or until filling is set and lightly browned. Cool in pan on a wire rack.

5 In a small saucepan heat and stir chocolate pieces and shortening over low heat until melted and smooth. Drizzle melted chocolate over uncut bars. Chill until chocolate is set. Using the edges of the foil, lift uncut bars out of pan. Cut into bars.

tip: If you like, arrange the bars on a serving plate, then drizzle the melted chocolate over both the bars and the plate.

to store: Place bars in a single layer in an airtight container; cover. Store at room temperature up to 3 days or freeze up to 3 months.

nutrition facts per bar: 85 cal., 5 g total fat (3 g sat. fat), 5 mg chol., 51 mg sodium, 10 g carb., 1 g fiber, 1 g pro.

A lengthy ingredient list, yes. But the flavor combo is irresistible.

creamy raspberry bars

prep: 25 minutes   **bake:** 45 minutes at 350°F   **chill:** 2 hours
makes: 24 bars

1   cup unsalted butter, softened
2   cups all-purpose flour
¼   cup packed brown sugar
½   teaspoon kosher salt
    Unsalted butter, softened
¾   cup seedless raspberry jam or preserves
2   cups fresh raspberries
4   ounces cream cheese, softened
4   ounces soft goat cheese (chèvre) or cream cheese, softened
½   cup granulated sugar
1   tablespoon all-purpose flour
1   egg
1   egg yolk
2   tablespoons finely shredded lemon peel
2   tablespoons lemon juice
½   teaspoon vanilla

1 Preheat oven to 350°F. Line a 13×9×2-inch baking pan with foil, extending the foil over edges of pan. Set aside.

2 For crust, in a medium mixing bowl beat 1 cup butter with an electric mixer on medium to high speed for 30 seconds. Beat in the 2 cups flour, brown sugar, and salt until combined. Press mixture evenly onto the bottom of the prepared baking pan. Bake about 20 minutes or until set and lightly browned. Cool on a wire rack for 5 minutes.

3 Lightly brush exposed foil on sides of pan with additional softened butter to keep filling from sticking. Carefully spread jam evenly over crust. Sprinkle with raspberries.

4 For filling, in a large mixing bowl beat cream cheese and goat cheese on medium speed for 30 seconds. Beat in granulated sugar and the 1 tablespoon flour. Beat in egg, yolk, lemon peel and juice, and vanilla until smooth; pour over raspberries.

5 Bake for 25 to 30 minutes or until set. Cool in pan on wire rack. Cover and chill for 2 hours (top may crack slightly). Using the edges of the foil, lift uncut bars out of pan. Cut into bars.

to store: Place bars in a single layer in an airtight container; cover. Store in the refrigerator up to 2 days.

nutrition facts per bar: 209 cal., 12 g total fat (7 g sat. fat), 48 mg chol., 88 mg sodium, 23 g carb., 1 g fiber, 3 g pro.

Cream of coconut—an ingredient in piña coladas—can usually be found in the aisle with rum and other spirits.

coconut cream pie bars

prep: 30 minutes **bake:** 40 minutes at 350°F **cool:** 1hour **chill:** 3 hours
makes: 32 bars

2 cups all-purpose flour
¾ cup flaked coconut
½ cup powdered sugar
1 teaspoon finely shredded lime peel
1 cup butter, softened
1 cup granulated sugar
¼ cup cornstarch
¼ teaspoon salt
3 cups whole milk
⅔ cup cream of coconut (such as Coco López brand)*
5 egg yolks, lightly beaten
1¼ teaspoons coconut extract
1 teaspoon vanilla
Whipped cream (optional)
Fresh coconut curls or coconut shards, toasted (optional)

1 Preheat oven to 350°F. Line a 13×9×2-inch baking pan with foil, extending the foil over edges of pan. Set aside.

2 For crust, in a large bowl stir together flour, the ¾ cup flaked coconut, powdered sugar, and lime peel. Add butter, stirring to combine. (Mixture will be crumbly; keep stirring until it comes together.) Press evenly onto the bottom of the prepared baking pan. Bake about 20 minutes or until crust is lightly browned. Cool on a wire rack.

3 For filling, in a large saucepan stir together granulated sugar, cornstarch, and salt. Gradually stir in milk and cream of coconut. Cook and stir over medium-high heat until thickened and bubbly; reduce heat. Cook and stir for 2 minutes more. Remove from heat. Gradually stir about 1 cup of the hot filling into egg yolks. Return egg yolk mixture to saucepan. Bring to a gentle boil, stirring constantly; reduce heat. Cook and stir for 2 minutes more. Remove from heat. Stir in coconut extract and vanilla. Pour warm filling over crust.

4 Bake about 20 minutes or until filling is set. Cool on a wire rack for 1 hour. Cover and chill for 3 to 6 hours before serving. Using the edges of the foil, lift uncut bars out of pan. Cut into bars. If desired, top with whipped cream and coconut curls.

nutrition facts per bar: 197 cal., 12 g total fat (8 g sat. fat), 57 mg chol., 92 mg sodium, 21 g carb., 1 g fiber, 2 g pro.

It's like pumpkin pie, gingerbread, and pecan pie in each bite.

toffee-pumpkin pie bars

prep: 30 minutes **bake:** 40 minutes at 375°F
makes: 32 bars

2   cups crushed gingersnaps (about 35 cookies)
¼   cup granulated sugar
¼   cup all-purpose flour
½   cup butter, melted
1   15-ounce can pumpkin
¾   cup packed brown sugar
1   teaspoon ground cinnamon
¾   teaspoon ground ginger
½   teaspoon salt
¼   teaspoon ground cloves
4   eggs, lightly beaten
1½   cups half-and-half or light cream
½   cup toffee pieces
½   cup chopped pecans, toasted (see tip, page 13)
     Caramel-flavor ice cream topping (optional)

1 Preheat oven to 375°F. Grease a 13×9×2-inch baking pan; set pan aside.

2 For crust, in a medium bowl combine crushed gingersnaps, the granulated sugar, and flour. Add butter and stir until well combined. Press the crumb mixture evenly onto the bottom of prepared pan; set aside.

3 For filling, in a large bowl combine pumpkin, brown sugar, cinnamon, ginger, salt, and cloves. Add eggs, beating lightly with a fork until combined. Gradually add half-and-half; stir just until combined. Pour filling into crust-lined pan.

4 Bake for 40 to 45 minutes or until a knife inserted near the center comes out clean. Sprinkle top with toffee pieces and pecans. Cool in pan on a wire rack. Cut into bars. Cover and chill within 2 hours. If desired, drizzle with caramel topping just before serving.

to store: Place bars in a single layer in an airtight container; cover. Store in the refrigerator up to 2 days. Do not freeze.

nutrition facts per bar: 145 cal., 8 g total fat (4 g sat. fat), 41 mg chol., 139 mg sodium, 17 g carb., 1 g fiber, 2 g pro.

pomegranate-raspberry bars

prep: 20 minutes **bake:** 44 minutes at 350°F
makes: 32 bars

Nonstick cooking
  spray
1½ cups all-purpose flour
⅓ cup powdered sugar
¾ cup butter, softened
6 cups frozen
  raspberries
⅔ cup pomegranate
  juice
¼ cup lemon juice
¾ cup granulated sugar
⅓ cup cornstarch
¼ teaspoon salt
4 eggs, lightly beaten
Pomegranate seeds
  (optional)

1 Preheat oven to 350°F. Line a 13×9×2-inch baking pan with foil, extending the foil over edges of pan. Coat foil with cooking spray; set pan aside.

2 For crust, in a large mixing bowl stir together flour and powdered sugar; add butter. Beat with an electric mixer on low speed just until mixture starts to cling (mixture may seem crumbly at first but will come together with continued beating). Press mixture evenly onto the bottom of the prepared baking pan. Bake for 14 minutes.

3 Meanwhile, in a medium saucepan combine frozen raspberries and pomegranate juice. Cook over medium-high heat about 5 minutes or until most of the berries are softened. Pour mixture through a fine-mesh sieve, pressing berries with a spoon to release their juices. Measure 2 cups juice, adding more pomegranate juice if necessary. Stir in lemon juice.

4 In a medium bowl stir together granulated sugar, cornstarch, and salt. Stir in eggs until combined. Stir in juice mixture. Pour mixture evenly over hot crust.

5 Bake about 30 minutes or until edges begin to brown and center appears set. Cool in pan on a wire rack. If desired, cover and chill until serving time. Using the edges of the foil, lift uncut bars out of pan. Cut into bars. If desired, sprinkle with pomegranate seeds before serving.

to store: Layer bars between sheets of waxed paper in an airtight container; cover. Store in the refrigerator up to 1 week.

nutrition facts per bar: 113 cal., 5 g total fat (3 g sat. fat), 35 mg chol., 66 mg sodium, 16 g carb., 1 g fiber, 2 g pro.

From cocktail glass to baking pan, lime and mint prove their undeniable appeal.

pecan-crusted mojito bars

prep: 25 minutes **bake:** 40 minutes at 350°F
makes: 36 bars

1¾	cups all-purpose flour
1	cup chopped pecans
¾	cup granulated sugar
1	cup butter, cut into slices
4	eggs, lightly beaten
1½	cups granulated sugar
2	tablespoons finely shredded lime peel
½	cup lime juice
¼	cup all-purpose flour
2	tablespoons milk
1	tablespoon snipped fresh mint
½	teaspoon baking powder
¼	teaspoon salt
	Powdered sugar
	Finely shredded lime peel (optional)
	Small fresh mint leaves (optional)

1 Preheat oven to 350°F. Line a 13×9×2-inch baking pan with foil, extending the foil over edges of pan; set aside.

2 For crust, in a food processor combine 1¾ cups flour, the pecans, and the ¾ cup granulated sugar. Add butter. Cover and process with several on/off pulses until mixture resembles coarse crumbs. Press mixture evenly onto the bottom of the prepared baking pan. Bake for 20 to 22 minutes or until lightly browned.

3 Meanwhile, for filling, in a medium bowl combine eggs, the 1½ cups granulated sugar, the 2 tablespoons lime peel, lime juice, the ¼ cup flour, milk, snipped mint, baking powder, and salt. Pour filling over hot crust.

4 Bake for 20 to 25 minutes or just until filling is set and edges begin to brown. Cool in pan on a wire rack. Using the edges of the foil, lift uncut bars out of pan. Cut into bars. Sprinkle with powdered sugar. If desired, garnish with lime peel and mint leaves.

to store: Layer bars between sheets of waxed paper in an airtight container; cover. Store in the refrigerator up to 1 week.

nutrition facts per bar: 150 cal., 8 g total fat (4 g sat. fat), 37 mg chol., 64 mg sodium, 19 g carb., 1 g fiber, 1 g pro.

Our Test Kitchen has baked lemon bars for decades—and this is absolutely our most requested version.

lemon bars deluxe

prep: 20 minutes **bake:** 45 minutes at 350°F
makes: 24 bars

2   cups all-purpose flour
½   cup powdered sugar
1   cup butter, softened
4   eggs, lightly beaten
1½ cups granulated
    sugar
1   tablespoon finely
    shredded lemon
    peel
⅓   cup lemon juice
¼   cup all-purpose flour
    Powdered sugar
    Crushed lemon drops
    (optional)

1 Preheat oven to 350°F. For crust, in a large mixing bowl stir together 2 cups flour and ½ cup powdered sugar; add butter. Beat with an electric mixer on low to medium speed just until mixture begins to cling. Press evenly onto the bottom of an ungreased 13×9×2-inch baking pan. Bake about 25 minutes or until lightly browned.

2 Meanwhile, in a medium bowl combine eggs, granulated sugar, and lemon juice. Whisk in ¼ cup flour and the lemon peel. Pour evenly over crust.

3 Bake about 20 minutes or until edges begin to brown and center is set. Cool in pan on a wire rack. Cut into bars. Sprinkle with powdered sugar and, if desired, crushed lemon drops.

to store: Place bars in a single layer in an airtight container; cover. Store in the refrigerator up to 2 days.

nutrition facts per bar: 184 cal., 9 g total fat (5 g sat. fat), 55 mg chol., 66 mg sodium, 25 g carb., 0 g fiber, 3 g pro.

Enjoy this as German families do—for breakfast!

cherry kuchen bars

prep: 25 minutes **bake:** 42 minutes at 350°F
makes: 32 bars

½ cup butter, softened
½ cup shortening
1¾ cups granulated
    sugar
1½ teaspoons baking
    powder
½ teaspoon salt
3 eggs
1 teaspoon vanilla
3 cups all-purpose flour
1 21-ounce can cherry
    pie filling
1 recipe Powdered
    Sugar Icing

1 Preheat oven to 350°F. For crust, in a large mixing bowl beat butter and shortening with an electric mixer on medium to high speed for 30 seconds. Add sugar, baking powder, and salt. Beat until combined, scraping sides of bowl occasionally. Beat in eggs and vanilla until combined. Beat in as much of the flour as you can with the mixer. Using a wooden spoon, stir in any remaining flour. Remove 1½ cups of the dough for topping. Press the remaining dough evenly onto the bottom of an ungreased 15x10x1-inch baking pan.

2 Bake for 12 minutes. Spread pie filling over hot crust. Spoon the reserved dough into small mounds on top of pie filling. Bake about 30 minutes more or until topping is lightly browned.

3 Cool in pan on a wire rack for 10 minutes. Drizzle with Powdered Sugar Icing. Cool completely.

to store: Place bars in a single layer in an airtight container; cover. Store in the refrigerator up to 2 days.

nutrition facts per bar: 189 cal., 6 g total fat (3 g sat. fat), 27 mg chol., 84 mg sodium, 31 g carb., 0 g fiber, 2 g pro.

powdered sugar icing:
In a small bowl stir together 1½ cups powdered sugar, ¼ teaspoon almond extract or vanilla, and enough milk (3 to 4 teaspoons) to make icing drizzling consistency.

Cornflakes soak up the fruit syrup in the filling, making the squares easy to eat out of hand at picnics. Pictured on page 299.

frosted apple slab pie

prep: 40 minutes **bake:** 45 minutes at 350°F
makes: 32 bars

3   cups all-purpose flour
2   tablespoons granulated
       sugar
½   teaspoon salt
½   cup shortening
½   cup butter, cut up
2   egg yolks, lightly
       beaten
⅓   cup milk
1   to 2 tablespoons cold
       water
6   cups thinly sliced,
       peeled cooking
       apples (6 medium)
1   cup granulated sugar
1   cup crushed cornflakes
½   teaspoon ground
       cinnamon
½   teaspoon freshly
       grated nutmeg or
       ¼ teaspoon ground
       nutmeg
1   egg white, lightly
       beaten
1   recipe Powdered Sugar
       Icing
       Freshly grated nutmeg
       or ground nutmeg
       (optional)

powdered sugar icing: In a medium bowl combine 1½ cups powdered sugar, ¼ teaspoon vanilla, and enough milk (1 to 2 tablespoons) to make icing a drizzling consistency.

1 For pastry, in a large bowl stir together flour, the 2 tablespoons sugar, and salt. Using a pastry blender, cut in shortening and butter until pieces are pea size. In a small bowl combine egg yolks, milk, and 1 tablespoon of the water. Gradually stir yolk mixture into flour mixture just until all of the flour mixture is moistened. If necessary, stir in enough of the remaining 1 tablespoon water, 1 teaspoon at a time, to moisten. Gather slightly more than half of the flour mixture into a ball, kneading gently until it holds together. Repeat with the remaining flour mixture. Cover and chill until needed.

2 In an extra-large bowl combine apples, 1 cup sugar, the cornflakes, cinnamon, and the ½ teaspoon nutmeg.

3 Preheat oven to 350°F. Press the larger pastry ball onto the bottom and up the sides of a 15×10×1-inch baking pan. Spoon apple filling into pastry-lined pan.

4 Roll the smaller pastry ball between two sheets of waxed paper into a 15×10-inch rectangle. Carefully peel off top sheet of waxed paper. Invert pastry over filling; carefully peel off waxed paper. Using moist fingers, press edges of the two pastry rectangles together. Cut a few slits in the top; brush lightly with egg white.

5 Bake for 45 to 50 minutes or until pastry is golden, apples are tender, and filling is bubbly. Cool in pan on a wire rack.

6 Drizzle with Powdered Sugar Icing. If desired, sprinkle with additional nutmeg. Let stand until icing is set. Cut into bars.

nutrition facts per bar: 171 cal., 6 g total fat (3 g sat. fat), 21 mg chol., 81 mg sodium, 27 g carb., 1 g fiber, 2 g pro.

Puff pastry and berries—who can resist?

berry slab pie bars

prep: 30 minutes **bake:** 25 minutes at 400°F
makes: 16 bars

½	17.3-ounce package (1 sheet) frozen puff pastry sheets, thawed
¼	cup granulated sugar
1	tablespoon cornstarch
1	tablespoon finely chopped crystallized ginger
1	12-ounce package frozen mixed berries, thawed and drained
1	egg, lightly beaten
2	tablespoons water
	Coarse sugar (optional)

1 Preheat oven to 400°F. Line a large baking sheet with parchment paper or foil. Unfold pastry on a lightly floured surface. Roll pastry into a 15×12-inch rectangle. Transfer to the prepared baking sheet; set aside.

2 For filling, in a medium bowl stir together ¼ cup granulated sugar, cornstarch, and crystallized ginger. Halve any large berries. Add berries to sugar mixture; toss gently to coat.

3 Spoon filling crosswise onto half the pastry rectangle, spreading to within 1 inch of the edges. In a small bowl combine egg and the water. Brush some of the egg mixture on pastry edges.

4 Fold the pastry over filling. Using a fork, firmly press edges of pastry together to seal. Brush top pastry with egg mixture and, if desired, sprinkle with coarse sugar. Cut two or three slits in top pastry.

5 Bake for 25 to 30 minutes or until pastry is golden. Cool on a wire rack. Cut into bars.

to store: Place bars in a single layer in an airtight container; cover. Store in the refrigerator up to 1 day.

nutrition facts per bar: 116 cal., 6 g total fat (2 g sat. fat), 13 mg chol., 43 mg sodium, 14 g carb., 1 g fiber, 2 g pro.

Even better served warm with homemade vanilla ice cream!

cherry crumble pie bars

prep: 25 minutes **bake:** 55 minutes at 350°F
makes: 32 bars

2	cups all-purpose flour
1¼	cups ground almonds
¾	cup packed brown sugar
1	cup butter, cut up
¾	cup granulated sugar
1	tablespoon cornstarch
½	teaspoon finely shredded lemon peel
4	cups frozen unsweetened pitted tart red cherries, thawed and drained
½	teaspoon almond extract

1 Preheat oven to 350°F. Line a 13×9×2-inch baking pan with foil, extending the foil over edges of pan; set aside.

2 For crust, in a large bowl stir together flour, almonds, and brown sugar. Using a pastry blender, cut in butter until mixture resembles fine crumbs. Remove 1½ cups of the crumb mixture for topping. Press the remaining mixture evenly onto the bottom of the prepared baking pan. Bake for 15 minutes.

3 For filling, in another large bowl combine granulated sugar, cornstarch, and lemon peel. Add cherries and almond extract; toss gently. Spread filling over hot crust (mixture will be wet). Sprinkle with reserved crumb mixture.

4 Bake about 40 minutes more or until topping is golden and filling is bubbly. Cool in pan on a wire rack. Using the edges of the foil, lift uncut bars out of pan. Cut into bars.

to store: Layer bars between sheets of waxed paper in an airtight container; cover. Store in the refrigerator up to 2 days or freeze up to 3 months.

nutrition facts per bar: 148 cal., 7 g total fat (4 g sat. fat), 15 mg chol., 43 mg sodium, 19 g carb., 1 g fiber, 2 g pro.

Your kitchen will smell amazing while these bake. You'll be anxious to dig into a warm bar!

apple-cinnamon streusel bars

prep: 30 minutes **bake:** 35 minutes at 350°F
makes: 32 bars

2	cups all-purpose flour
1½	cups rolled oats
¾	cup granulated sugar
2	teaspoons ground cinnamon
1	teaspoon ground ginger
1	cup butter, cut up
1	8-ounce package cream cheese, softened
½	cup finely snipped dried apples
½	cup chopped walnuts, toasted (see tip, page 13)
½	cup sweetened condensed milk
¼	cup pure maple syrup
1	teaspoon ground cinnamon
1	cup powdered sugar
3	to 4 teaspoons milk

1 Preheat oven to 350°F. For crust, in a large bowl stir together flour, oats, granulated sugar, the 2 teaspoons cinnamon, and ginger. Using a pastry blender, cut in butter until mixture resembles coarse crumbs. Remove 1 cup of the crumb mixture for topping. Press the remaining mixture evenly onto the bottom of an ungreased 13×9×2-inch baking pan.

2 For filling, in a medium mixing bowl beat cream cheese, dried apples, walnuts, sweetened condensed milk, maple syrup, and the 1 teaspoon cinnamon with an electric mixer on medium speed until combined. Spread filling over crust. Sprinkle with reserved topping.

3 Bake for 35 to 40 minutes or until topping is lightly browned. Cool in pan on a wire rack.

4 For icing, in a small bowl stir together powdered sugar and enough of the milk to make icing drizzling consistency. Drizzle icing over uncut bars. Cut into bars.

to store: Place bars in a single layer in an airtight container; cover. Store in the refrigerator up to 3 days.

nutrition facts per bar: 203 cal., 10 g total fat (6 g sat. fat), 25 mg chol., 72 mg sodium, 25 g carb., 1 g fiber, 3 g pro.

raspberry french silk pie bars

prep: 25 minutes **bake:** 10 minutes at 375°F **chill:** 2 hours
makes: 32 bars

1 recipe Raspberry Ganache
2 cups finely crushed chocolate wafers
¼ cup all-purpose flour
2 tablespoons granulated sugar
½ cup butter, melted
1 cup whipping cream
3 ounces semisweet chocolate, chopped
3 ounces bittersweet chocolate, chopped
⅓ cup granulated sugar
⅓ cup butter
2 egg yolks, lightly beaten
3 tablespoons crème de cacao or whipping cream
½ cup raspberry preserves or seedless raspberry jam
   Fresh raspberries (optional)

1 Prepare Raspberry Ganache; let stand. Preheat oven to 375°F. Line a 13×9×2-inch baking pan with foil, extending the foil over edges of pan. For crust, combine crushed wafers, flour, and the 2 tablespoons sugar. Add butter; stir until well combined. Press crumbs evenly onto the bottom and slightly up the sides of the pan. Bake about 10 minutes or until set. Cool in pan on a wire rack.

2 Meanwhile, for filling, in a medium-size heavy saucepan combine whipping cream, semisweet chocolate, bittersweet chocolate, the ⅓ cup sugar, and the ⅓ cup butter. Cook and stir over low heat about 10 minutes or until melted and smooth. Remove from heat. Gradually stir half the hot mixture into egg yolks. Return egg yolk mixture to saucepan. Cook and stir over medium-low heat about 5 minutes or until slightly thickened and bubbly. Remove from heat (mixture may appear curdled). Stir in crème de cacao.

3 Place saucepan in a bowl of ice water. Cool about 20 minutes or until filling stiffens and becomes difficult to stir, stirring occasionally. Transfer filling to a medium mixing bowl.

4 Carefully spread preserves over crust. Beat filling with an electric mixer on medium speed for 2 to 3 minutes or until light and fluffy. Spread filling over preserves. Cover; chill for 1 to 2 hours or until firm.

5 Spread Raspberry Ganache over layers in pan. Cover; chill for 1 to 2 hours or until firm. Using the edges of the foil, lift uncut bars out of pan. Cut into bars. If desired, garnish with fresh raspberries.

raspberry ganache: In a large glass measuring cup combine 1 cup chopped semisweet chocolate or chocolate pieces, ⅓ cup whipping cream, and 1 tablespoon seedless raspberry jam. Microwave on 100 percent power (high) about 1 minute or until melted, stirring every 30 seconds. Let stand about 1 hour or until slightly thickened.

to store: Place bars in a single layer in an airtight container; cover. Chill up to 3 days.

nutrition facts per bar: 201 cal., 13 g total fat (8 g sat. fat), 39 mg chol., 104 mg sodium, 21 g carb., 1 g fiber, 2 g pro.

Layer rich and creamy caramel mixture over a sugar cookie crust then top it all with chocolate.

twixy shortbread bars

prep: 35 minutes **chill:** 1 hour 30 minutes **bake:** 20 minutes at 350°F
makes: 48 bars

1½ cups butter, softened
½ cup granulated sugar
2¼ teaspoons vanilla
3 cups all-purpose flour
1 13.4-ounce can dulce de leche
¾ cup whipping cream
6 tablespoons butter
3 tablespoons light-color corn syrup
12 ounces semisweet chocolate, chopped

1 For crust, in a large mixing bowl beat 1½ cups butter with an electric mixer on medium to high speed for 30 seconds. Add sugar and 1½ teaspoons of the vanilla. Beat until combined, scraping sides of bowl occasionally. Beat in as much of the flour as you can with the mixer. Using a wooden spoon, stir in any remaining flour. Cover and chill for 30 to 60 minutes or until dough is easy to handle.

2 Preheat oven to 350°F. Line a 13×9×2-inch baking pan with foil, extending the foil over edges of pan. Press dough evenly onto the bottom of the prepared baking pan. Bake for 20 to 25 minutes or until top is lightly browned. Cool in pan on a wire rack.

3 Spread dulce de leche evenly over crust. In a medium saucepan bring whipping cream, the 6 tablespoons butter, and the corn syrup just to boiling over medium heat. Remove from heat. Add chocolate and the remaining ¾ teaspoon vanilla (do not stir). Let stand for 5 minutes. Stir until smooth. Cool for 10 minutes. Gradually pour chocolate mixture over dulce de leche layer, spreading evenly. Cover and chill for 1 to 2 hours or until chocolate is set.

4 Using the edges of the foil, lift uncut bars out of pan. Cut into bars.

nutrition facts per bar: 171 cal., 11 g total fat (7 g sat. fat), 26 mg chol., 64 mg sodium, 17 g carb., 1 g fiber, 2 g pro.

Our food editors rave about this recipe.

peanut butter-chocolate revel bars

prep: 30 minutes bake: 30 minutes at 350°F
makes: 24 bars

1	cup butter, softened
1½	cups packed brown sugar
1	teaspoon baking soda
½	teaspoon salt
2	eggs
2	cups creamy peanut butter
4	teaspoons vanilla
3	cups all-purpose flour
1	14-ounce can sweetened condensed milk
1½	cups semisweet chocolate pieces
2	tablespoons creamy peanut butter
2	teaspoons vanilla
½	cup chopped salted peanuts (optional)

1 Preheat oven to 350°F. Line a 13×9×2-inch baking pan with foil, extending the foil over edges of pan. Grease foil; set pan aside.

2 In an extra-large mixing bowl beat butter with an electric mixer on medium to high speed for 30 seconds. Add brown sugar, baking soda, and salt. Beat until combined, scraping sides of bowl occasionally. Beat in eggs, 2 cups peanut butter, and 2 teaspoons of the vanilla until combined. Beat in as much of the flour as you can with the mixer. Using a wooden spoon, stir in any remaining flour. Set aside.

3 For filling, in a medium saucepan combine sweetened condensed milk, chocolate pieces, and the 2 tablespoons peanut butter. Cook over low heat until chocolate is melted, stirring occasionally. Remove from heat. Stir in the remaining 2 teaspoons vanilla.

4 Remove 2 cups of the dough for topping. Press the remaining dough evenly onto the bottom of the prepared baking pan. Spread filling over dough in pan. Drop the remaining dough in spoonfuls on filling. If desired, sprinkle with peanuts.

5 Bake for 30 to 35 minutes or until topping is lightly browned. Cool in pan on a wire rack. Using the edges of the foil, lift uncut bars out of pan. Cut into bars.

nutrition facts per bar: 218 cal., 9 g total fat (5 g sat. fat), 26 mg chol., 84 mg sodium, 32 g carb., 2 g fiber, 3 g pro.

We accepted the challenge and put everyone's favorite ingredients into one outstanding bar.

bit o' everything bars

prep: 30 minutes **bake:** 25 minutes at 325°F
makes: 36 bars

3   cups crushed pretzels
⅓   cup granulated sugar
1   cup butter, melted
½   cup butter
½   cup whipping cream
¼   cup packed brown sugar
1   11-ounce package caramel baking bits or one 14-ounce package vanilla caramels, unwrapped
2   cups cocktail peanuts
1   cup dark or semisweet chocolate pieces (6 ounces)
1   cup milk chocolate and peanut butter swirled pieces (6 ounces)
1   cup almond toffee bits

1 Preheat oven to 325°F. Line a 13×9×2-inch baking pan with foil, extending the foil over edges of pan. Grease foil; set pan aside. For crust, in a medium bowl stir together crushed pretzels and granulated sugar. Stir in melted butter until combined. Press mixture evenly onto the bottom of the prepared baking pan.

2 In a medium saucepan combine the ½ cup butter, whipping cream, and brown sugar. Cook and stir over medium-low heat until butter is melted and brown sugar is dissolved. Stir in caramel bits. Cook and stir until caramels are melted and mixture is smooth. Stir in peanuts.

3 Quickly pour caramel mixture over crust, spreading evenly. Sprinkle with dark chocolate pieces, milk chocolate pieces, and toffee bits.

4 Bake about 25 minutes or until edges are bubbly and lightly browned. Cool in pan on a wire rack. Using the edges of the foil, lift uncut bars out of pan. Cut into bars.

nutrition facts per bar: 286 cal., 19 g total fat (10 g sat. fat), 29 mg chol., 238 mg sodium, 27 g carb., 1 g fiber, 3 g pro.

Quick-cooking oats form a chewy, moist crust and topping.

caramel chocolitas

prep: 35 minutes **bake:** 20 minutes at 350°F
makes: 48 bars

2 cups all-purpose flour
1¾ cups quick-cooking rolled oats
1½ cups packed brown sugar
1 teaspoon baking soda
¼ teaspoon salt
1 cup butter, melted
1 14-ounce package vanilla caramels, unwrapped
⅓ cup milk
1 12-ounce package (2 cups) semisweet chocolate pieces
1 cup milk chocolate pieces (6 ounces)
1 cup chopped pecans

1 Preheat oven to 350°F. Line a 13×9×2-inch baking pan with foil, extending the foil over edges of pan. Grease foil; set pan aside.

2 For crust, in a large bowl stir together flour, oats, brown sugar, baking soda, and salt. Stir in melted butter until crumbly. Remove half the crumb mixture for topping. Press remaining mixture evenly onto the bottom of the prepared baking pan.

3 In a small microwave-safe bowl microwave caramels and milk on 50 percent power (medium) for 4 to 6 minutes or until caramels are melted, stirring twice.

4 Sprinkle semisweet chocolate pieces, milk chocolate pieces, and pecans over crust. Drizzle with caramel mixture. Sprinkle with reserved topping.

5 Bake for 20 to 25 minutes or until lightly browned. Cool in pan on a wire rack. Using the edges of the foil, lift uncut bars out of pan. Cut into bars.

to store: Place bars in a single layer in an airtight container; cover. Store in the refrigerator up to 3 days.

nutrition facts per bar: 194 cal., 10 g total fat (5 g sat. fat), 11 mg chol., 93 mg sodium, 25 g carb., 1 g fiber, 2 g pro.

candy-crunch peanut butter
bars, page 363

no-fuss

no-b

Even when you don't want to turn on the oven, you can share cookie joy. These recipes don't exclude "preheat" in the directions. Some require a saucepan and a stovetop— but each recipe comes together fast with little fuss.

ake

Select plain butter crackers layer for this quick dessert.

coconut-date cracker bars with browned butter glaze

prep: 30 minutes **chill:** 2 hours
makes: 24 bars

36   rich rectangular
     crackers
¾   cup packed brown
     sugar
½   cup whipping cream
⅓   cup butter
2   egg yolks
½   teaspoon salt
1   cup flaked coconut
1   cup snipped pitted
     whole dates
¾   cup chopped pecans
     or walnuts
1   tablespoon dark rum
1   teaspoon vanilla
¼   cup butter
1   cup powdered sugar
1   tablespoon milk
⅛   teaspoon salt
     Milk (optional)
⅓   cup chopped pecans
     or walnuts

1 Line an 8×8×2-inch pan with foil, extending the foil over edges of pan. Lightly grease foil. Arrange half the crackers in a single layer in the prepared pan, cutting to fit if necessary.

2 For filling, in a medium saucepan combine brown sugar, whipping cream, ⅓ cup butter, egg yolks, and ½ teaspoon salt. Cook and stir over medium heat until butter is melted. Stir in coconut, dates, and the ¾ cup nuts. Cook and stir about 8 minutes or until filling is glossy and turns a rich shade of brown. Remove from heat. Stir in rum and vanilla.

3 Pour filling over cracker layer in pan, carefully spreading to cover crackers completely. Arrange the remaining crackers over filling, pressing lightly.

4 For glaze, in a small saucepan melt the ¼ cup butter over medium heat. Cook until butter is light brown. Transfer to a small bowl. Stir in powdered sugar, 1 tablespoon milk, and the ⅛ teaspoon salt until smooth. If necessary, stir in additional milk to reach spreading consistency. Carefully spread glaze over cracker layer. Sprinkle with ⅓ cup pecans. Cover and chill about 2 hours or until set.

5 Using the edges of the foil, lift uncut bars out of pan. Using a serrated knife, cut into bars.

to store: Place bars in a single layer in an airtight container; cover. Store in the refrigerator up to 3 days or freeze up to 1 month.

nutrition facts per bar: 205 cal., 12 g total fat (5 g sat. fat), 34 mg chol., 161 mg sodium, 23 g carb., 2 g fiber, 1 g pro.

One saucepan and a bowl makes cleanup a snap.

caramel apple bars

prep: 25 minutes **stand:** 1 hour
makes: 16 bars

1   cup creamy peanut
     butter
¾   cup caramel-flavor ice
     cream topping
3   tablespoons packed
     brown sugar
3   cups apple-
     cinnamon-flavor
     round toasted oat
     cereal
1   cup coarsely snipped
     dried apples
½   cup salted peanuts,
     coarsely chopped

1 Line an 8×8×2-inch pan with foil, extending
the foil over edges of pan. Lightly grease
foil; set pan aside. In a large saucepan combine
¾ cup of the peanut butter, ½ cup of the caramel
topping, and the brown sugar. Cook and stir over
medium heat just until mixture starts to boil.
Remove from heat. Add cereal and dried apples,
stirring gently to coat. Press mixture into the
prepared pan.

2 In a small bowl stir together the remaining
¼ cup peanut butter and the remaining
¼ cup caramel topping. Spread mixture over
cereal layer. Sprinkle with peanuts; press gently. Let
stand about 1 hour or until set. Using the edges of
the foil, lift uncut bars out of pan. Cut into bars.

nutrition facts per bar: 233 cal., 11 g total fat (2 g sat. fat),
0 mg chol., 174 mg sodium, 28 g carb., 2 g fiber, 6 g pro.

These crunchy bars are an ideal lunchbox treat; just wrap each bar individually in plastic wrap.

butterscotch-peanut treats

prep: 20 minutes **chill:** 2 hours
makes: 48 bars

nonstick cooking
   spray
1½ cups sifted powdered
   sugar
1 cup creamy peanut
   butter
6 tablespoons butter,
   melted
1 9-ounce package
   chocolate wafers,
   crushed
1 11-ounce package
   (about 2 cups)
   butterscotch-flavor
   pieces
¼ cup whipping cream
¾ cup chopped peanuts

1 Line a 13×9×2-inch pan with foil, extending the foil over edges of pan. Lightly coat foil with cooking spray; set pan aside. For crust, in a large bowl stir together powdered sugar, peanut butter, and butter. Stir in the crushed chocolate wafers. Press mixture into the bottom of an ungreased 13×9×2-inch baking pan.

2 In a medium-size heavy saucepan combine butterscotch pieces and cream. Stir over low heat just until pieces are melted.

3 Carefully spread butterscotch mixture over crust. Sprinkle with the peanuts.

4 Cover and chill for 2 to 24 hours. Using the edges of the foil, lift uncut bars out of pan. Cut into bars or use 2-inch cookie cutters to cut shapes. Store in refrigerator.

to store: Layer bars between sheets of waxed paper in an airtight container; cover. Store in the refrigerator up to 1 week.

nutrition facts per cookie: 130 cal., 8 g total fat (4 g sat. fat), 6 mg chol., 96 mg sodium, 13 g carb., 0 g fiber, 2 g pro.

Perennial favorite Rice Krispies Treats get updated with dried fruit, white chocolate, and spice.

white chocolate-cranberry crispy treats

prep: 30 minutes **stand:** 1 hour
makes: 48 bars

¼ cup butter
5 cups tiny marshmallows
⅛ to ¼ teaspoon ground nutmeg or ground cinnamon
6 cups crisp rice cereal
1 cup white baking pieces (6 ounces)
¾ cup dried cranberries
½ cup finely chopped pecans or walnuts, toasted (see tip, page 13)
1 recipe Marshmallow Topping (optional)
  Chopped pecans or walnuts, toasted (see tip, page 13) (optional)

1 Lightly grease a 13×9×2-inch pan; set aside. In a 4- to 5-quart Dutch oven heat butter over low heat until melted. Add marshmallows, stirring until melted. Stir in nutmeg. Add cereal, white baking pieces, dried cranberries, and the ½ cup pecans, stirring until combined.

2 Using the back of a greased spoon, press cereal mixture into of the prepared pan. If desired, drizzle with Marshmallow Topping and sprinkle with additional pecans. Let stand for 1 hour before serving. Cut into bars.

to store: Layer bars between sheets of waxed paper in an airtight container; cover. Store at room temperature up to 3 days.

nutrition facts per bar: 80 cal., 3 g total fat (2 g sat. fat), 3 mg chol., 57 mg sodium, 12 g carb., 0 g fiber, 1 g pro.

marshmallow topping:
In a medium saucepan melt 1 tablespoon butter over low heat. Add 1½ cups tiny marshmallows, stirring until melted.

356

Crush a favorite chocolate sandwich cookies for the crust.

chocolate cheesecake bars

prep: 20 minutes **stand:** 15 minutes **chill:** 4 hours
makes: 24 bars

1¾ cups crushed chocolate sandwich cookies with white filling
¼ cup butter, melted
1 ounce semisweet chocolate, melted
8 ounces semisweet chocolate, chopped
¾ cup whipping cream
1 3-ounce package cream cheese, softened
1 tablespoon chocolate liqueur (optional)
½ cup miniature semisweet chocolate pieces
Sweetened whipped cream (optional)
Chopped semisweet chocolate (optional)

1 Line a 9×9×2-inch pan with foil, extending the foil over edges of pan. Lightly grease foil; set pan aside. For crust, in a large bowl combine crushed cookies, melted butter, and melted chocolate. Press mixture onto the bottom of the prepared pan. Chill while preparing the filling.

2 For filling, in a small microwave-safe bowl microwave the 8 ounces chopped chocolate and whipping cream on 100 percent power (high) about 2 minutes or until melted and smooth, stirring once.

3 In a medium mixing bowl beat cream cheese and, if desired, liqueur with an electric mixer on medium to high speed until smooth. Gradually add melted chocolate mixture, beating until combined. Spread filling over crust. Let stand for 15 minutes. Sprinkle with the ½ cup miniature chocolate pieces. Cover and chill for 4 hours or until set. Cut into bars. If desired, top with sweetened whipped cream and additional chopped chocolate.

nutrition facts per: 215 cal., 16 g total fat (9 g sat. fat), 33 mg chol., 80 mg sodium, 18 g carb., 1 g fiber, 2 g pro.

Energize out on the hiking trail with this treat, but skip the chocolate drizzle for less mess.

trail mix granola bars

prep: 25 minutes **chill:** 15 minutes **stand:** 15 minutes
makes: 16 bars

½ cup packed dark
    brown sugar
¼ cup honey
2 tablespoons butter
2 tablespoons creamy
    peanut butter
2 cups peanut butter-
    flavor granola, large
    clusters broken up
½ cup dry-roasted
    sunflower kernels
½ cup chocolate-
    covered or salted
    soy nuts
¼ cup honey-roasted
    almonds, coarsely
    chopped
¼ cup peanut butter-
    flavor pieces
½ cup dark chocolate
    pieces, melted

1 Grease a 9×9×2-inch pan; set aside. In a small saucepan combine brown sugar, honey, butter, and peanut butter. Bring to boiling over medium heat; reduce heat. Simmer, uncovered, for 2 minutes. Remove from heat.

2 In a large bowl combine granola, sunflower kernels, soy nuts, almonds, and peanut butter pieces. Add brown sugar mixture to granola mixture; toss gently to combine.

3 Immediately press granola mixture onto the prepared pan. Chill about 15 minutes or until firm.

4 Cut into bars. Drizzle with melted chocolate. Let stand about 15 minutes or until chocolate is set.

nutrition facts per bar: 229 cal., 12 g total fat (5 g sat. fat), 4 mg chol., 80 mg sodium, 29 g carb., 3 g fiber, 5 g pro.

No one will guess these have with a pudding layer!

butterscotch bites

prep: 30 minutes **chill:** 2 hours
makes: 40 bars

1½ cups powdered sugar
1 cup creamy peanut
   butter
6 tablespoons butter,
   melted
1 9-ounce package
   chocolate wafer
   cookies, crushed
⅓ cup milk
3 tablespoons
   butterscotch or
   cheesecake instant
   pudding and pie
   filling mix
¾ cup butter, softened
½ teaspoon vanilla
3½ cups powdered sugar
½ cup butterscotch-
   flavor pieces
1 teaspoon shortening

1 Line a 13×9×2-inch pan with foil, extending the foil over edges of pan; set aside. For crust, in a large bowl stir together the 1½ cups powdered sugar, the peanut butter, and 6 tablespoons melted butter. Stir in crushed cookies. Press mixture evenly onto the bottom of the prepared pan. Chill while preparing the pudding layer.

2 For pudding layer, in a small bowl combine milk and pudding mix; set aside. In a large mixing bowl beat ¾ cup butter with an electric mixer on medium to high speed for 30 seconds. Beat in pudding mixture and vanilla until smooth. Gradually add the 3½ cups powdered sugar, beating until smooth. Spread pudding layer over crust.

3 In a small microwave-safe bowl microwave butterscotch pieces and shortening on 100 percent power (high) about 1 minute or until melted, stirring every 30 seconds. Pour butterscotch mixture into a heavy resealable plastic bag; snip a small hole from one corner of the bag. Drizzle in crisscross patterns over pudding layer.

4 Cover and chill for at least 2 hours. Using edges of the foil, lift uncut bars out of pan. Cut into bars or triangles.

nutrition facts per bar: 194 cal., 10 g total fat (5 g sat. fat), 14 mg chol., 135 mg sodium, 25 g carb., 1 g fiber, 2 g pro.

If you have only large marshmallows, snip each one into four pieces before measuring the six cups.

nutty marshmallow cheer bars

prep: 30 minutes **stand:** 30 minutes
makes: 32 bars

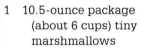

1	10.5-ounce package (about 6 cups) tiny marshmallows
¼	cup butter, cut up
2	teaspoons vanilla
8	cups round toasted oat cereal with nuts and honey
1	cup lightly salted cashews, coarsely chopped
½	cup coarsely crushed peanut brittle or almond toffee bits
1	cup chocolate-covered peanuts, whole or coarsely chopped
1	cup caramel baking bits
1	tablespoon water
3	ounces semisweet or bittersweet chocolate, chopped
¼	teaspoon shortening

1 Grease a 13×9×2-inch pan; set aside. In a large microwave-safe bowl microwave marshmallows and butter on 100 percent power (high) for 1½ to 2 minutes or until mixture is puffed and melted, stirring once. Stir in vanilla. Add cereal, cashews, and peanut brittle, stirring until mixed. Gently stir in chocolate-covered peanuts. Press mixture onto the bottom of the prepared pan.

2 In a small microwave-safe bowl microwave caramel bits and the water on high for 1 to 1½ minutes or until melted, stirring once. Drizzle over cereal mixture.

3 In another small microwave-safe bowl microwave chocolate and shortening on high for 1 to 1½ minutes or until melted and smooth, stirring every 30 seconds. Drizzle over cereal mixture. Let stand about 30 minutes or until set. Cut into bars.

to store: Layer bars between sheets of waxed paper in an airtight container; cover. Store at room temperature up to 2 days.

nutrition facts per bar: 172 cal., 7 g total fat (3 g sat. fat), 5 mg chol., 107 mg sodium, 25 g carb., 1 g fiber, 2 g pro.

Combine pantry staples for these quick and delightfully salty-sweet treats. Mix and match what you have on hand to make this goody your verson.

make-it-mine chewy popcorn drops

start to finish: 30 minutes
makes: 50 drops

6   cups popped popcorn
3   cups pretzels
2   cups mixed nuts
1   cup dried fruit
1   20-ounce package
     candy coating
     (almond bark),
     coarsely chopped
⅔   cup nut butter

1 In an extra-large bowl combine popcorn, pretzels, mixed nuts, and dried fruit.

2 For coating in a medium-sized heavy saucepan heat and stir candy coating over low heat just until melted and smooth, being careful not to overheat. Remove from heat. Stir in nut butter just until combined (do not overstir).

3 Pour melted coating over popcorn mixture. Stir gently to coat. Immediately drop by rounded tablespoons (or use a medium cookie scoop) onto a tray lined with waxed paper,

pressing mixture into the sides of the bowl as you scoop (this will help hold the mixture together). Let stand until set.

to store: Place drops between sheets of waxed paper in an airtight container; cover. Store in the refrigerator up to 2 days.

popcorn *(pick one)*
Plain popcorn
Cheese popcorn
Kettle popcorn

pretzels *(pick one)*
Pretzel sticks
Tiny pretzel twists, broken
Pretzel squares, broken

mixed nuts *(pick one)*
Roasted cashews, coarsely
  chopped
Roasted peanuts, coarsely
  chopped
Toasted almonds, chopped

dried fruit *(pick one)*
Golden raisins
Snipped apricots
Cranberries
Cherries

candy coating *(pick one)*
Vanilla
Chocolate

nut butter *(pick one)*
Peanut butter
Chocolate-hazelnut spread

Introduce young chefs to microwave cooking with this super-simple snack.

chocolate, coconut, and almond bars

prep: 20 minutes **stand:** 1 hour
makes: 32 bars

1   10-ounce package
    large marshmallows
3   tablespoons butter,
    softened
½   teaspoon coconut
    flavoring
2   cups sweetened
    flaked coconut
2   cups crispy flake and
    crunchy oat cluster
    cereal with honey
    and almonds
1⅓ cups honey-flavor
    sliced almonds
1   cup miniature
    semisweet
    chocolate pieces

1 Line a 9×9×2-inch pan with foil, extending the foil over edges of pan. Lightly grease foil; set pan aside.

2 In a large microwave-safe bowl microwave marshmallows and butter on 100 percent power (high) for 1 to 2 minutes or until butter is melted. Stir in coconut flavoring. Add coconut, cereal, and almonds, stirring gently to mix evenly. Cool slightly. Gently fold in chocolate pieces.

3 Press cereal mixture lightly into the prepared pan. Let stand about 1 hour or until set. Using edges of the foil, lift uncut bars out of pan. Cut into bars.

nutrition facts per bar: 147 cal., 8 g total fat (4 g sat. fat), 3 mg chol., 55 mg sodium, 18 g carb., 1 g fiber, 2 g pro.

*If you're a fan of burnt peanuts, you'll
love these peanut-buttery bars.*

candy-crunch
peanut butter
bars

prep: 30 minutes chill: 1 hour
makes: 48 bars

30   peanut butter
       sandwich cookies
       with peanut butter
       filling
¼   teaspoon salt
½   cup butter, melted
2   cups powdered sugar
1⅓ cups creamy peanut
       butter
½   cup butter, softened
2   tablespoons
       whipping cream
½   cup finely crushed
       burnt peanuts or
       other candy-coated
       peanuts
1   cup semisweet
       chocolate pieces
       (6 ounces)
½   cup creamy peanut
       butter
       Coarsely crushed
       burnt peanuts or
       other candy-coated
       peanuts (optional)

1 Line a 13×9×2-inch pan with foil, extending
the foil over edges of pan; set aside. For
crust, in a food processor combine peanut
butter cookies and salt. Cover and process until
fine crumbs form. Add melted butter. Cover
and process with several on/off pulses just until
combined. Press mixture evenly into prepared pan.

2 In a large mixing bowl beat powdered sugar,
the 1⅓ cups peanut butter, softened butter, and
whipping cream with an electric mixer on low to
medium speed until smooth. Stir in ½ cup crushed
peanuts. Carefully spread mixture over crust.

3 In a small heavy saucepan heat and stir
chocolate pieces and the ½ cup peanut
butter over low heat until melted. Spread mixture
over layers in pan. If desired, sprinkle with
additional peanuts.

4 Cover and chill about 1 hour or until set.
Using edges of the foil, lift uncut bars out of
pan. Cut into bars.

to store: Layer bars between sheets of waxed
paper in an airtight container; cover. Store in the
refrigerator up to 1 week.

nutrition facts per bar: 182 cal., 12 g total fat (5 g sat. fat),
11 mg chol., 127 mg sodium, 17 g carb., 1 g fiber, 4 g pro.

Also try banana instant pudding in the filling.

chocolate-glazed pudding bars

prep: 30 minutes **chill:** 1 hour
makes: 64 bars

1 cup granulated sugar
1 cup light-color corn syrup
2 cups peanut butter
3 cups crisp rice cereal
3 cups cornflakes
¾ cup butter
4 cups powdered sugar
2 4-serving-size packages vanilla instant pudding and pie filling mix
¼ cup milk
1 12-ounce package (2 cups) semisweet chocolate pieces
½ cup butter

1 Line a 15×10×1-inch pan with foil, extending the foil over edges of pan; set aside.

2 For crust layer in a large saucepan combine granulated sugar and corn syrup; heat and stir just until bubbly around the edges. Cook and stir for 1 minute more. Remove from heat. Stir in peanut butter until melted. Using a wooden spoon, stir in rice cereal and cornflakes until coated. Press crust into the prepared baking pan.

3 For fillin in a medium saucepan heat the ¾ cup butter over low heat until melted. Stir in powdered sugar, pudding mix, and milk. Spread filling layer over cereal mixture.

4 For frosting, in a small saucepan heat and stir chocolate pieces and the ½ cup butter over low heat until melted. Spread frosting over filling. Cover loosely and chill about 1 hour or until set. Using edges of the foil, lift uncut bars out of pan. Cut into bars.

to store: Layer bars between sheets of waxed paper in an airtight container; cover. Store in the refrigerator up to 2 days.

nutrition facts per cookie: 175 cal., 9 g total fat (4 g sat. fat), 10 mg chol., 133 mg sodium, 23 g carb., 1 g fiber, 2 g pro.

Pretzels are a salty companion to the sweet filling.

butterscotch-pretzel bars

prep: 25 minutes **chill:** 2 hours
makes: 36 bars

Nonstick cooking
   spray
1½ cups powdered sugar
1   cup creamy peanut
   butter
6   tablespoons butter,
   melted
2   cups crushed pretzels
1   11-ounce package
   (about 2 cups)
   butterscotch-flavor
   pieces
¼   cup whipping cream
½   cup coarsely crushed
   pretzels
½   cup chopped peanuts

1 Line a 13×9×2-inch pan with foil, extending the foil over edges of pan. Lightly coat foil with cooking spray; set pan aside. For crust, in a large bowl combine powdered sugar, peanut butter, and melted butter. Stir in 2 cups crushed pretzels. Press mixture evenly onto the bottom of the prepared pan.

2 In a medium-size heavy saucepan heat and stir butterscotch pieces and whipping cream over low heat just until butterscotch pieces are melted.

3 Spread butterscotch mixture over crust. Sprinkle with ½ cup crushed pretzels and peanuts; press gently. Cover and chill for at least 2 hours. Using edges of the foil, lift uncut bars out of pan. Cut into bars.

to store: Layer bars between sheets of waxed paper in an airtight container; cover. Store in the refrigerator up to 1 week.

nutrition facts per bar: 166 cal., 10 g total fat (5 g sat. fat),

For holiday gifts, wrap each cluster in cellophane or paper.

salted chocolate-caramel clusters

prep: 20 minutes stand: 1 hour
makes: 24 clusters

1   8-ounce package
    pecan halves,
    toasted (see tip,
    page 13)
1   14-ounce package
    vanilla caramels,
    unwrapped
1   tablespoon milk
1   12-ounce package
    dark chocolate
    pieces
2   ounces white
    chocolate with
    cocoa butter,
    chopped (⅓ cup)
    (optional)
1   teaspoon shortening
    (optional)
    Coarse sea salt
    or Fleur de Sel
    (optional)

1 Line two baking sheets or trays with foil or parchment paper; grease the foil or parchment. For each bar, arrange 5 pecan halves in a single-layer cluster.

2 In a small heavy saucepan combine caramels and milk. Heat and stir over medium-low heat until caramel are melted and mixture is smooth. Spoon some of the caramel mixture over each cluster of pecans. Let stand about 30 minutes or until firm.

3 In a medium-size heavy saucepan heat and stir the dark chocolate pieces over low heat until chocolate is melted and smooth. Remove ¼ cup of the melted chocolate; set aside. Spoon the remaining melted chocolate over clusters, gently spreading to the edges. Let clusters stand about 30 minutes or until firm. (If necessary, place trays in refrigerator for 5 to 10 minutes until firm.)

4 Meanwhile, if desired, in a small microwave-safe bowl combine white chocolate and shortening. Microwave, uncovered, on 100 percent power (high) about 1 minute or until chocolate is melted and smooth, stirring every 30 seconds. Spread some of the white chocolate over the top of each cluster. Pour reserved melted chocolate into a small resealable plastic bag. Snip off a very small piece from one corner. Drizzle chocolate over the top of each cluster. If desired, sprinkle each cluster with coarse sea salt.

to store: Layer clusters between sheets of waxed paper in an airtight container; cover. Store in the refrigerator up to 1 week.

nutrition facts per cluster: 255 cal., 16 g total fat (6 g sat. fat), 1 mg chol., 53 mg sodium, 26 g carb., 2 g fiber, 3 g pro.

Crush gingersnaps by placing in a resealable plastic bag and then pound with the flat side of a meat mallet.

gingersnap logs

prep: 45 minutes   chill: 1 hour   stand: 30 minutes
makes: 36 logs

1¼	cups crushed gingersnaps
½	cup powdered sugar
⅓	cup sweetened condensed milk
1	tablespoon molasses or 1½ teaspoons rum or coffee liqueur
1½	teaspoons vanilla
1	teaspoon ground cinnamon
3	ounces white baking chocolate with cocoa butter, chopped
1	cup canned vanilla frosting
	Red decorative sugar

1 In a food processor combine 1 cup of the gingersnap crumbs, the powdered sugar, sweetened condensed milk, molasses, vanilla, and cinnamon. Cover and process until well combined. Transfer to a bowl; stir in the remaining ¼ cup gingersnap crumbs. Cover and chill for 1 hour or until easy to handle.

2 Line an extra-large cookie sheet with waxed paper; set aside. Shape rounded teaspoonfuls of crumb mixture into 1x½-inch logs. Place on prepared baking sheet.

3 In a small saucepan heat and stir white chocolate over low heat until melted. Add frosting; heat and stir until smooth. Using a fork, dip logs, one at a time, into white chocolate mixture, allowing excess to drip off. Return to cookie sheet. Sprinkle logs with red decorative sugar. Let stand about 30 minutes or until set.

to store: Layer logs between sheets of waxed paper in an airtight container; cover. Store at room temperature up to 3 days or freeze up to 3 months.

nutrition facts per log: 81 cal., 3 g total fat (1 g sat. fat), 1 mg chol., 46 mg sodium, 13 g carb., 0 g fiber, 1 g pro.

For ease of transporting and serving, place each morsel in a paper bake cup and arrange in a single layer in a baking pan.

dark chocolate chews

prep: 20 minutes **stand:** 1 hour
makes: 42 chews

2   cups granulated sugar
½   cup butter
½   cup half-and-half or light cream
¾   cup dark chocolate pieces
¼   cup unsweetened cocoa powder
1   teaspoon vanilla
¼   teaspoon mint extract
2   cups quick-cooking rolled oats
1   cup sweetened flaked coconut
½   cup sliced or coarsely chopped almonds, toasted (see tip, page 13)

1 Line an extra-large cookie sheet with waxed paper or set paper bake cups on a cookie sheet; set cookie sheet aside. In a large saucepan bring sugar, butter, and half-and-half to boiling, stirring to dissolve sugar. Remove from heat. Stir in chocolate pieces, cocoa powder, vanilla, and mint extract. Stir until chocolate is melted and mixture is smooth. Stir in oats, coconut, and almonds.

2 Drop mixture by rounded teaspoons onto prepared cookie sheet or into paper bake cups. Let stand about 1 hour or until set.

to store: Layer cookies between sheets of waxed paper in an airtight container; cover. Store in the refrigerator up to 1 week or freeze up to 1 month.

nutrition facts per chew: 110 cal., 5 g total fat (3 g sat. fat), 7 mg chol., 27 mg sodium, 16 g carb., 1 g fiber, 1 g pro.

Indulge in a cookie and candy all in one serving.

white chocolate-almond butter balls

prep: 30 minutes chill: 50 minutes
makes: 36 butter balls

1 cup almond butter
¼ cup butter, softened
1 cup powdered sugar
2 tablespoons
     unsweetened cocoa
     powder
2 cups crisp rice cereal
8 ounces white baking
     chocolate with
     cocoa butter,
     chopped
4 ounces vanilla-flavor
     candy coating
2 teaspoons shortening
2 ounces white baking
     chocolate with
     cocoa butter,
     chopped

1 Line a large cookie sheet with parchment paper; set aside. In a large mixing bowl beat almond butter and butter with an electric mixer on medium to high speed for 30 seconds. Gradually add powdered sugar and cocoa powder, beating until combined. Stir in rice cereal.

2 Using buttered hands, shape mixture into 1-inch balls. Place balls on the prepared cookie sheet. Chill for 30 minutes.

3 In a small heavy saucepan heat and stir 8 ounces white chocolate, the candy coating, and shortening over low heat until melted and smooth.

4 Line another large cookie sheet or tray with waxed paper. Using a fork, dip chilled balls, one at a time, into melted white chocolate mixture, allowing excess to drip back into pan.* Place on the prepared cookie sheet or tray. Chill about 20 minutes or until firm.

5 Place 2 ounces chopped white chocolate in a small microwave-safe bowl. Microwave on 50 percent power (medium) for 1½ to 2 minutes or until chocolate is melted and smooth, stirring twice. Drizzle melted white chocolate over cookies.

*tip: If the coating mixture in the pan becomes too shallow for dipping, transfer the mixture to a 1-cup glass measuring cup or a custard cup to dip the last few cookies.

to store: Place butter balls in a single layer in an airtight container; cover. Store in the refrigerator up to 2 weeks.

nutrition facts per butter ball: 137 cal., 9 g total fat (4 g sat. fat), 5 mg chol., 41 mg sodium, 13 g carb., 1 g fiber, 2 g pro.

They look and taste like chocolate truffles with crunchy cereal centers.

crunchy peanut butter balls

prep: 30 minutes   **chill:** 1 hour 50 minutes
makes: 50 bars

1   cup crunchy peanut butter
¼   cup butter, softened
1   cup powdered sugar
2   tablespoons unsweetened cocoa powder
2   cups crispy rice cereal
2   cups dry-roasted peanuts, chopped
8   ounces semisweet chocolate, chopped
8   ounces chocolate-flavor candy coating
1   tablespoon shortening

1 In a large mixing bowl beat peanut butter and butter with an electric mixer on medium to high speed for 30 seconds. Beat in powdered sugar and unsweetened cocoa powder on low speed until combined. Using a wooden spoon, stir in rice cereal and 1 cup of the chopped peanuts. Cover and chill for 1 hour or until easy to handle.

2 Line a large cookie sheet with parchment paper; set aside. With buttered hands, shape mixture into 1-inch balls. Place balls on prepared cookie sheet; chill for 30 minutes.

3 In a small heavy saucepan heat and stir semisweet chocolate, chocolate candy coating, and shortening over low heat until melted and smooth. Cool about 5 minutes or until slightly thickened.

4 Line a second large cookie sheet with waxed paper. Using a fork, dip chilled balls, one at a time, into chocolate mixture, allowing excess to drip off. Place on the prepared cookie sheet. Immediately sprinkle each ball with about ½ teaspoon of the remaining chopped peanuts. Chill balls about 20 minutes or until chocolate is set.

to store: Place peanut butter balls in a single layer in an airtight container; cover. Store in the refrigerator up to 2 weeks.

nutrition facts per peanut butter ball: 136 cal., 10 g total fat (4 g sat. fat), 2 mg chol., 39 mg sodium, 12 g carb., 1 g fiber, 3 g pro.

Count on these treats to be a hit with adults and children.

caramel-popcorn drops

start to finish: 30 minutes
makes: 48 drops

6 cups popped popcorn
3 cups square pretzels or tiny pretzel twists
2 cups mixed nuts, coarsely chopped
1 cup golden raisins
1 20-ounce package vanilla-flavor candy coating, coarsely chopped
⅔ cup caramel-flavor ice cream topping

1 Line an extra-large cookie sheet or tray with waxed paper; set aside. In an extra-large bowl combine popcorn, pretzels, mixed nuts, and raisins.

2 In a medium-size heavy saucepan heat and stir candy coating over low heat until melted and smooth. Remove from heat. Stir in caramel topping.

3 Pour melted coating mixture over popcorn mixture. Stir gently to coat, slightly crushing pretzels. Drop mixture by rounded tablespoons onto prepared cookie sheet. Let stand until set.

to store: Place drops between sheets of waxed paper in an airtight container; cover. Store in the refrigerator up to 2 days.

nutrition facts per drop: 138 cal., 7 g total fat (4 g sat. fat), 0 mg chol., 53 mg sodium, 18 g carb., 1 g fiber, 2 g pro.

12

Dozens of popular cookie brands appear on supermarket shelves. But why buy cookies when you can re-create some of America's most-loved cookies at home? Use our insider recipes—and you'll enjoy the satisfaction of tasting these impersonators fresh from your oven.

double take

S

fig cookies, page 379

Thin wafers encased in minty chocolate will remind you of store-bought patties.

chocolate-glazed peppermint cookies

prep: 45 minutes   chill: 1 hour   bake: 6 minutes at 375°F per batch
makes: 68 cookies

1   cup butter, softened
1   cup granulated sugar
½   cup unsweetened cocoa powder
1½ teaspoons baking powder
½   teaspoon salt
1   egg
1   teaspoon vanilla
2½ cups all-purpose flour
1   recipe Chocolate-Peppermint Coating
½   cup crushed peppermint candies (optional)

chocolate-peppermint coating: In a medium saucepan combine two 12-ounce packages (about 4 cups) semisweet chocolate pieces, ¼ cup shortening, and ½ teaspoon peppermint extract. Cook and stir over low heat until chocolate melts.

1 In a large mixing bowl beat butter with an electric mixer on medium to high speed for 30 seconds. Add sugar, cocoa powder, baking powder, and salt. Beat until combined, scraping sides of bowl occasionally. Beat in egg and vanilla until combined. Beat in as much of the flour as you can with the mixer. Using a wooden spoon, stir in any remaining flour.

2 Divide dough in half. Shape each half into a 10-inch log. Wrap each log in plastic wrap or waxed paper. Chill about 1 hour or until dough is firm enough to slice.

3 Preheat oven to 375°F. Cut logs into ¼-inch slices. Place slices 1 inch apart on an ungreased cookie sheet.

4 Bake for 6 to 8 minutes or until edges are firm. Transfer cookies to a wire rack; cool.

5 Dip each cookie into Chocolate-Peppermint Coating, turning to coat all sides of cookie. Using a thin metal spatula, scrape off excess coating so cookie is covered with a thin layer. (Reheat coating as necessary.) Place cookies on cookie sheets lined with waxed paper. If desired, sprinkle with crushed candies while coating is wet. Chill until coating is set.

to store: Layer cookies between sheets of waxed paper in an airtight container; cover. Store in the refrigerator up to 3 days or freeze up to 3 months.

nutrition facts per cookie: 110 cal., 7 g total fat (4 g sat. fat), 10 mg chol., 51 mg sodium, 13 g carb., 1 g fiber, 1 g pro.

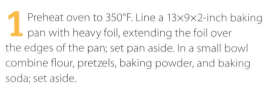

Salted nut rolls (even deep-fried versions!) are popular eats at Midwestern state fairs.

salted peanut bars

prep: 25 minutes bake: 12 minutes at 350°F per batch
makes: 48 bars

1 cup all-purpose flour
½ cup crushed pretzels
½ teaspoon baking powder
¼ teaspoon baking soda
½ cup butter, softened
⅔ cup packed brown sugar
2 egg yolks
2 teaspoons vanilla
1 7-ounce jar marshmallow creme
½ cup creamy peanut butter
¼ cup powdered sugar
1 cup salted cocktail peanuts
1 14-ounce package vanilla caramels, unwrapped
3 tablespoons milk

1 Preheat oven to 350°F. Line a 13×9×2-inch baking pan with heavy foil, extending the foil over the edges of the pan; set pan aside. In a small bowl combine flour, pretzels, baking powder, and baking soda; set aside.

2 In a large mixing bowl beat butter with an electric mixer on medium to high speed for 30 seconds. Add brown sugar, egg yolks, and vanilla. Beat until combined, scraping sides of bowl occasionally. Beat in as much of the flour mixture as you can with the mixer. Using a wooden spoon, stir in any remaining flour mixture. Press mixture into the prepared pan.

3 Bake for 12 to 14 minutes or until lightly browned. Meanwhile, in a medium microwave-safe bowl combine marshmallow creme and peanut butter. Microwave on 100 percent power (high) for 1 minute or until softened and slightly melted, stirring after 30 seconds. Stir in powdered sugar. Spread mixture over crust. Sprinkle with peanuts.

4 In a large heavy saucepan combine caramels and milk. Cook and stir over medium-low heat until melted and smooth. Pour caramel mixture evenly over peanut layer. Cool in pan on a wire rack. Using the foil, lift the uncut bars out of the pan. Cut into bars.

to store: Place bars in a single layer in an airtight container; cover. Store in the refrigerator up to 1 week.

nutrition facts per bar: 127 cal., 6 g total fat (3 g sat. fat), 14 mg chol., 81 mg sodium, 16 g carb., 0 g fiber, 2 g pro.

Some things never go out of fashion—that includes serving ice-cold milk with these popular marshmallow sandwiches.

homemade oatmeal cream pies

prep: 40 minutes **bake:** 8 minutes at 350°F per batch
makes: 13 sandwiches

¾   cup all-purpose flour
½   teaspoon baking soda
½   teaspoon salt
¼   teaspoon baking
       powder
½   cup butter, softened
½   cup peanut butter
½   cup granulated sugar
½   cup packed brown
       sugar
1   egg
1   teaspoon vanilla
1   cup quick-cooking
       rolled oats
2   teaspoons hot water
¼   teaspoon salt
1   7-ounce jar
       marshmallow creme
½   cup shortening
⅓   cup powdered sugar

1 Preheat oven to 350°F. Grease a cookie sheet; set aside. In a small bowl stir together flour, baking soda, salt, and baking powder; set aside.

2 In a large mixing bowl beat butter and peanut butter with an electric mixer on medium to high speed until combined. Add granulated sugar and brown sugar. Beat until fluffy, scraping sides of bowl occasionally. Beat in egg and vanilla until combined. Using a wooden spoon, stir in flour mixture and oats just until combined. Drop dough by rounded teaspoons 2 inches apart onto the prepared cookie sheet.

3 Bake for 8 to 10 minutes or until edges are lightly browned and centers are set. Cool on cookie sheet for 1 minute. Transfer to a wire rack; cool.

4 For marshmallow filling, in a medium mixing bowl combine the hot water and salt, stirring until salt is dissolved. Add marshmallow creme, shortening, and powdered sugar. Beat with an electric mixer on medium speed until combined.

5 Spread marshmallow filling on bottoms of half the cookies. Top with the remaining cookies, bottom sides down.

to store: Layer unfilled cookies between sheets of waxed paper in an airtight container; cover. Store at room temperature up to 3 days. Continue as directed in Step 4.

nutrition facts per sandwich cookie: 367 cal., 20 g total fat (8 g sat. fat), 35 mg chol., 305 mg sodium, 43 g carb., 1 g fiber, 5 g pro.

Peanut butter and pecans make this a standout cookie, just like those found in cafes around the country.

bake shop chocolate chip cookies

prep: 30 minutes **bake:** 15 minutes at 325°F per batch
makes: 24 cookies

2¼ cups all-purpose flour
  1 teaspoon baking soda
  1 teaspoon salt
  1 cup unsalted butter, softened
  ⅔ cup creamy peanut butter
  1 cup granulated sugar
  1 cup packed brown sugar
  2 eggs
  2 teaspoons vanilla
  1 12-ounce package semisweet chocolate pieces or one 11.5-ounce package bittersweet chocolate pieces (2 cups)
1¼ cups coarsely chopped pecans

1 Preheat oven to 325°F. In a medium bowl stir together flour, baking soda, and salt; set aside.

2 In a large mixing bowl combine butter, peanut butter, granulated sugar, brown sugar, and eggs. Beat with an electric mixer on medium speed until light in color, about 3 minutes. Beat in vanilla. Beat in flour mixture on low speed. Stir in chocolate and nuts. Using a ¼-cup measure, drop dough about 2 inches apart onto an ungreased baking sheet.

3 Bake for 15 to 17 minutes or until golden brown on edges and lightly browned on top. Cool on cookie sheet for 3 minutes. Transfer cookies to a wire rack; cool.

nutrition facts per cookie: 323 cal., 20 g total fat (8 g sat. fat), 39 mg chol., 186 mg sodium, 35 g carb., 2 g fiber, 5 g pro.

double takes

Irish Cream Butter Frosting (see recipe, page 19) is a primo option to this classic.

chocolate sandwich cookies

prep: 35 minutes **chill:** 1 hour **bake:** 7 minutes at 375°F per batch
makes: 24 sandwich cookies

3 cups all-purpose flour
1 cup unsweetened cocoa powder
1½ teaspoons baking powder
½ teaspoon salt
2 cups granulated sugar
1 cup shortening
2 eggs
¼ cup milk
½ recipe Butter Frosting or Chocolate Butter Frosting (see recipes, page 19)

1 In a large bowl stir together flour, cocoa powder, baking powder, and salt; set aside.

2 In a large mixing bowl beat sugar and shortening with an electric mixer on medium to high speed until combined. Beat in eggs and milk until combined. Beat in as much of the flour mixture as you can with the mixer. Using a wooden spoon, stir in any remaining flour mixture. Divide dough in half. Cover and chill for 1 to 2 hours or until dough is easy to handle.

3 Preheat oven to 375°F. On a lightly floured surface, roll half the dough at a time until ¼-inch thickness. Using 2- to 2½-inch round scalloped-edge cookie cutters, cut out dough. Place cutouts 1 inch apart on an ungreased cookie sheet.

4 Bake about 7 minutes or until firm. Transfer to a wire rack; cool. Spread bottoms of half the cookies with Butter Frosting. Top with remaining cookies, bottom sides down.

tip: To make frosted cookies instead of sandwich cookies, make a whole recipe of Butter Frosting or Chocolate Butter Frosting. Spread the frosting on tops of all the cookies. Makes 48.

to store: Layer filled cookies between sheets of waxed paper in an airtight container; cover. (Place frosted cookies in a single layer in an airtight container.) Store at room temperature up to 3 days or freeze up to 3 months.

nutrition facts per cookie: 157 cal., 6 g total fat (2 g sat. fat), 12 mg chol., 57 mg sodium, 25 g carb., 1 g fiber, 2 g pro.

The original version of these cookies was invented near Newton, Massachusetts, in the late 1800s. Pictured on page 373.

fig cookies

prep: 45 minutes **chill:** 3 hours **bake:** 10 minutes at 375°F per batch
makes: 36 cookies

½   cup butter, softened
¼   cup granulated sugar
¼   cup packed brown sugar
¼   teaspoon baking soda
1   egg
1   teaspoon vanilla
1¾ cups all-purpose flour
1   recipe Fig Filling
1   recipe Lemon Glaze or powdered sugar

1 In a medium bowl beat butter with an electric mixer on medium to high speed for 30 seconds. Add granulated sugar, brown sugar, and baking soda. Beat until combined, scraping sides of bowl occasionally. Beat in egg and vanilla until combined. Beat in as much of the flour as you can with the mixer. Using a wooden spoon, stir in any remaining flour. Divide dough in half. Cover and chill dough about 3 hours or until dough is easy to handle.

2 Preheat oven to 375°F. On a floured pastry cloth, roll one portion of dough at a time into a 10×8- inch rectangle. Cut rectangle into two 10×4- inch strips. Spread one-fourth of the Fig Filling lengthwise down the middle of each strip. Using the pastry cloth, lift up one long side of each dough strip and fold it over the filling. Lift up opposite side and fold it to enclose filling; seal edges. Place filled strips, seam sides down, on an ungreased cookie sheet. Repeat with remaining dough and Fig Filling.

3 Bake for 10 to 12 minutes or until lightly browned. Immediately slice each strip crosswise into 1-inch pieces. Transfer to a wire rack; cool. Drizzle cookies with Lemon Glaze or dust with powdered sugar.

nutrition facts per cookie: 102 cal., 3 g total fat (2 g sat. fat), 13 mg chol., 38 mg sodium, 17 g carb., 1 g fiber, 1 g pro.

fig filling: Remove stems from 1 cup dried figs; chop figs. In a small saucepan combine the chopped figs; ⅔ cup raisins, finely chopped; ½ cup orange juice; ⅓ cup diced candied fruits and peels, finely chopped; 2 tablespoons granulated sugar; 1 teaspoon finely shredded lemon peel; and ¼ teaspoon ground cinnamon. Bring just to boiling; reduce heat. Cover and simmer for 5 to 8 minutes or until fruit is soft and filling is thick, stirring occasionally. Stir in ⅓ cup blanched almonds, finely chopped. Cool to room temperature.

lemon glaze: In a medium bowl stir together 2 cups powdered sugar, 2 tablespoons milk, 2 teaspoons lemon juice, and ¼ teaspoon salt until smooth.

380

During hectic holiday seasons, prepare the dough and chill it for several days before baking.

sandies

prep: 35 minutes **chill:** 30 minutes **bake:** 20 minutes at 325°F per batch
makes: 30 cookies

1	cup butter, softened
½	cup powdered sugar
1	tablespoon water
1	teaspoon vanilla
2¼	cups all-purpose flour
1	cup chopped pecans
1	cup powdered sugar

1 Preheat oven to over to 325°F. In a large mixing bowl beat butter with an electric mixer on medium to high speed for 30 seconds. Add the ½ cup powdered sugar. Beat in water and vanilla until combined, scraping sides of bowl occasionally. Beat in as much of the flour as you can with the mixer. Stir in any remaining flour and the pecans. Wrap dough and chill for 30 to 60 minutes or until firm enough to shape.

2 Shape dough into 1-inch balls. Bake about 20 minutes or until bottoms are lightly browned. Cool cookies on a wire rack.

3 Gently shake cooled cookies in a bag containing the 1 cup powdered sugar.

nutrition facts per sandies or chocolate-covered cookie variation: 109 cal., 7 g total fat (3 g sat. fat), 14 mg chol., 52 mg sodium, 11 g carb., 1 g fiber, 1 g pro.

chocolate-covered sandies: Bake and cool cookies as directed through Step 3. In a large shallow bowl stir together ¾ cup powdered sugar and ¼ cup unsweetened cocoa powder. Add cooled cookies, in batches, to powdered sugar mixture, turning to coat.

These cherry-topped cookies look exactly like those found in a gift tin of assorted cookies, yet these have a richer buttery taste.

butter dream cookies

prep: 30 minutes **bake:** 12 minutes at 350°F per batch
makes: 48 cookies

24 maraschino cherries
   (about half of a
   10-ounce jar)
¾ cup butter, softened
¼ cup shortening
½ cup granulated sugar
1 teaspoon almond
   extract
½ teaspoon salt
2¼ cups all-purpose flour

1 Drain maraschino cherries. Pat cherries dry with paper towels. Cut each cherry in half. Set halved cherries aside.

2 Preheat oven to 350°F. In a large mixing bowl beat butter and shortening with an electric mixer on medium to high speed for 30 seconds. Add sugar; beat until combined, scraping sides of bowl occasionally. Beat in almond extract and salt until combined. Beat in as much of the flour as you can with the mixer. Using a wooden spoon, stir in any remaining flour. Continue stirring until dough comes together, or use your hands to knead dough, if necessary.

3 Shape dough into 1-inch balls. Place balls about 1 inch apart on ungreased cookie sheets. Press your thumb into the center of each ball. Place a cherry half, cut side down, in the indentation of each cookie.

4 Bake for 12 to 14 minutes or until bottoms are lightly browned. Cool on cookie sheet 2 minutes. Transfer cookies to wire racks; cool.

nutrition facts per cookie: 69 cal., 4 g total fat (2 g sat. fat), 8 mg chol., 46 mg sodium, 8 g carb., 0 g fiber, 1 g pro.

double takes

Why purchase the original when you can bake the jumbo version at home—and then sample a warm-from-the-oven cookie?

giant gingersnaps

prep: 25 minutes **chill:** 30 minutes **bake:** 16 minutes at 350°F per batch
makes: 15 cookies

2 cups all-purpose flour
2 teaspoons ground ginger
2 teaspoons ground cinnamon
1 teaspoon baking soda
¼ teaspoon salt
¼ teaspoon ground nutmeg
¼ teaspoon ground cloves
½ cup butter, softened
¼ cup shortening
¾ cup granulated sugar
½ cup packed brown sugar
⅓ cup light molasses
1 egg
⅓ cup granulated sugar

1 In a medium bowl combine flour, ginger, cinnamon, baking soda, salt, nutmeg, and cloves; set aside. In a large mixing bowl beat butter and shortening with an electric mixer on medium to high speed for 30 seconds. Beat in the ¾ cup granulated sugar and the brown sugar until fluffy. Beat in molasses and egg until combined. Beat in as much of the flour mixture as you can with the mixer. Using a wooden spoon, stir in any remaining flour mixture. Cover and chill dough about 30 minutes or until easy to handle.

2 Preheat oven to 350°F. Lightly grease a cookie sheet. Place the ⅓ cup granulated sugar in a shallow bowl. Using ¼ cup of dough per cookie, shape dough into balls. Coat balls with the sugar. Place balls 4 inches apart on prepared cookie sheet.

3 Bake for 16 to 17 minutes or until golden brown. Cool on cookie sheets for 5 minutes. Transfer cookies to wire racks; cool.

nutrition facts per cookie: 260 cal., 10.5 g total fat (5 g sat. fat), 31 mg chol., 195 mg sodium, 40 g carb., 0 g fiber, 2 g pro.

The peanut butter-honey filling is also a tasty frosting on sugar cookies.

peanut butter cookie sandwiches

prep: 40 minutes chill: 1 hour bake: 8 minutes at 375°F per batch
makes: 48 sandwich cookies

¾ cup creamy peanut
    butter
½ cup butter, softened
½ cup granulated sugar
½ cup packed brown
    sugar
½ teaspoon baking
    powder
½ teaspoon baking soda
1 egg
1 teaspoon vanilla
1½ cups all-purpose flour
1 recipe Peanut Butter-
    Honey Filling
    Chopped honey-
    roasted peanuts
    (optional)

1 In a large mixing bowl beat the ¾ cup peanut butter and butter with an electric mixer on medium to high speed for 30 seconds. Add granulated sugar, brown sugar, baking powder, and baking soda. Beat until combined, scraping sides of bowl occasionally. Beat in egg and vanilla until combined. Beat in as much of the flour as you can with the mixer. Using a wooden spoon, stir in any remaining flour.

2 Divide dough into three portions. On a lightly floured surface, shape each portion into an 8-inch log. Wrap each log in plastic wrap or waxed paper. Chill for 1 to 2 hours or until firm enough to slice.

3 Preheat oven to 375°F. Cut logs into ¼-inch slices. Place slices 1 inch apart on an ungreased cookie sheet.

4 Bake about 8 minutes or until edges are lightly browned. Transfer cookies to a wire rack; cool.

5 Spread Peanut Butter-Honey Filling on bottoms of half cookies, using 2 teaspoons for each cookie. Top with the remaining cookies, bottom sides down. If desired, roll edges of cookies in chopped peanuts.

nutrition facts per sandwich cookie: 126 cal., 6 g total fat (2 g sat. fat), 12 mg chol., 77 mg sodium, 16 g carb., 1 g fiber, 2 g pro.

peanut butter-honey filling: In a medium mixing bowl beat 4 oz cream cheese, softened; ⅓ cup peanut butter; and 2 tablespoons honey with an electric mixer on medium speed until combined. Gradually add 2½ to 3 cups powdered sugar, beating until smooth and creamy.

Crush candies (in a plastic bag) with a rolling pin.

lemon-cream icebox cookie sandwiches

prep: 30 minutes **chill:** 1 hour **bake:** 8 minutes at 375°F per batch
makes: 36 cookies

1 cup butter-flavor
   shortening
1 cup granulated sugar
1 teaspoon baking
   powder
¼ teaspoon salt
1 egg
1 teaspoon vanilla
2¼ cups all-purpose flour
2 teaspoons finely
   shredded lemon
   peel
1 recipe Lemon Cream
   Frosting or 1¼ cups
   lemon curd
   Finely crushed lemon
   drop candies or
   yellow decorating
   sugar (optional)

1 In a large bowl beat shortening with an electric mixer on medium to high speed for 30 seconds. Add sugar, baking powder, and salt. Beat until combined, scraping sides of bowl occasionally. Beat in egg and vanilla until combined. Beat in as much flour as you can with the mixer. Using a wooden spoon, stir in any remaining flour and the lemon peel.

2 Divide dough in half. Shape each half into a 10-inch log. Wrap each log in plastic wrap or waxed paper. Chill for 1 to 3 hours or until dough is firm enough to slice.

3 Preheat oven to 375°F. Cut rolls into ¼-inch slices. Place slices about 2 inches apart on an ungreased cookie sheet.

4 Bake for 8 to 10 minutes or until set. Cool on cookie sheet for 1 minute. Transfer cookies to wire racks; cool.

5 Spread Lemon Cream Frosting or lemon curd on the bottom sides of half the cookies, using about 1 tablespoon frosting or 1½ teaspoons lemon curd per cookie. Top with remaining cookies, bottom sides down. If desired, roll edges of sandwich cookies in crushed candy.

nutrition facts per sandwich cookie: 196 cal., 11 g total fat (5 g sat. fat), 21 mg chol., 82 mg sodium, 23 g carb., 0 g fiber, 1 g pro.

lemon-cream frosting: In a large mixing bowl beat one 8-ounce package cream cheese, softened, and ⅔ cup butter, softened, with an electric mixer on medium speed until smooth. Gradually beat in 3⅓ cups powdered sugar until combined. Stir in 1 tablespoon finely shredded lemon peel.

This is simply an updated twist on chocolate chip cookies, but oh-so-delicious.

macadamia nut and white chocolate chip cookies

prep: 40 minutes **bake:** 8 minutes at 375°F per batch
makes: 60 cookies

½   cup butter, softened
½   cup shortening or
      vegetable oil
1   cup packed brown
      sugar
½   cup granulated sugar
½   teaspoon baking soda
½   teaspoon salt
2   eggs
1   teaspoon vanilla
2¾ cups all-purpose flour
1   12-ounce package
      (2 cups) white
      baking pieces
1   3.5-ounce jar
      macadamia nuts,
      chopped

1 Preheat oven to 375°F. In a large mixing bowl beat butter and shortening with an electric mixer on medium to high speed for 30 seconds. Add brown sugar, granulated sugar, baking soda, and salt. Beat until combined, scraping sides of bowl occasionally. Beat in eggs and vanilla until combined. Beat in as much of the flour as you can with the mixer. Using a wooden spoon, stir in any remaining flour, the chocolate pieces, and nuts. Drop dough by rounded teaspoons 2 inches apart onto ungreased cookie sheets.

2 Bake for 8 to 9 minutes or just until edges are lightly browned. Cool on cookie sheets for 2 minutes. Transfer to wire racks; cool.

nutrition facts per macadamia nut and white chocolate chip or candy chip cookie variation:
99 cal., 5 g total fat (2 g sat. fat), 11 mg chol., 45 mg sodium, 13 g carb., 0 g fiber, 1 g pro.

candy chip cookies: Prepare as directed, except substitute miniature candy-coated semisweet chocolate pieces for the white baking pieces; omit macadamia nuts, and, if desired, stir in 1½ cups chopped walnuts, pecans, or hazelnuts (filberts), toasted (see tip, page 70), with the chocolate pieces.

dutch letters

4½ cups all-purpose flour
 1 teaspoon salt
 2 cups cold butter
     (1 pound), cut into
     ½-inch slices
 1 egg, lightly beaten
 1 cup ice water
 1 8-ounce can almond
     paste (made without
     syrup or liquid
     glucose)
½ cup granulated sugar
½ cup packed brown
     sugar
 1 egg white
     Granulated sugar
 3 recipes Powdered Sugar
     Icing (see recipe, page
     18) (optional)

1 In a large bowl stir together flour and salt. Add butter slices and toss until slices are coated and separated. In a small mixing bowl stir together egg and the ice water. Add all at once to flour mixture. Using a spoon, quickly mix (butter will remain in large pieces and flour will not be completely moistened).

2 Turn the dough out onto a lightly floured pastry cloth. Knead the dough 10 times by pressing and pushing dough together to form a rough-looking ball, lifting pastry cloth if necessary to press the dough together. Shape the dough into a rectangle (dough will still have some dry-looking areas). Make corners as square as possible. Slightly flatten dough. Working on a well-floured pastry cloth, roll dough into a 15×10-inch rectangle. Fold two short sides to meet in center; fold in half like a book to form four layers, measuring 7½×5 inches.

3 Repeat the rolling and folding process once more. Wrap dough with plastic wrap. Chill dough for 20 minutes. Repeat rolling and folding process two more times. Chill dough for 20 minutes.

4 For filling, stir together almond paste, the ½ cup granulated sugar, brown sugar, and egg white.

5 Preheat oven to 375°F. Using a sharp knife, cut dough crosswise into four equal parts. Wrap three portions in plastic wrap and return to the refrigerator. On a well-floured surface, roll one portion into a 12½×10-inch rectangle. Cut rectangle into five 10×2½-inch strips.

6 Shape a slightly rounded tablespoon of filling into a 9-inch rope and place it along the center third of one strip. Roll up the strip lengthwise. Brush edge and ends with water; pinch to seal. Place, seam side down, on an ungreased baking sheet, shaping strip into a letter (traditionally an"S"). Brush with water; sprinkle with granulated sugar. Repeat with remaining dough and fillling. Bake for 20 to 25 minutes or until golden. Cool. Spoon icing over, if desired.

nutrition facts per pastry: 362 cal., 23 g total fat (5 g sat. fat), 35 mg chol., 285 mg sodium, 36 g carb., 1 g fiber, 5 g pro.

espresso tarts, page 407

388

cocktail

coo

13

This chapter takes the notion of cookie time far beyond the usual dessert beat. From savory biscuits that are ideal for serving alongside wine to sweet morsels for accompanying after-dinner brandy, enjoy these adult-only treats.

kies

cocktail **cookies**

Finely chop the dried cranberries in a mini food processor. Then serve these with an assortment of sharp cheeses.

cranberry and pepper shortbread bites

prep: 25 minutes **chill:** 30 minutes **bake:** 8 minutes at 350°F per batch
makes: 48 cookies

1 cup slivered almonds, toasted (see tip, page 13)
2 cups all-purpose flour
½ cup granulated sugar
⅓ cup cornstarch
½ teaspoon salt
1 cup cold butter
½ teaspoon vanilla
2 tablespoons pink peppercorns, crushed
2 tablespoons very finely snipped dried cranberries
Coarse salt or pearl decorating sugar (optional)

1 In a food processor process almonds until finely chopped. Add flour, sugar, cornstarch and salt; process with several on/off turns until mixed. Add butter and vanilla; process until slightly crumbly. Place dough on a lightly floured surface and divide in half. Add peppercorns to one half and knead until smooth. Add cranberries to other half and knead until smooth. Wrap each portion in plastic wrap; chill for 30 minutes.

2 Preheat oven to 350°F. On a lightly floured surface, roll one portion of dough at a time to ¼-inch thickness. Using a 2-inch round cutter, cut out dough. Place cutouts 1 inch apart on an ungreased cookie sheet. Sprinkle with coarse salt or pearl decorating sugar, if desired.

3 Bake for 8 to 10 minutes or until edges and bottoms start to brown. Transfer cookies to wire rack; cool.

nutrition facts per cookie: 78 cal., 5 g total fat (3 g sat. fat), 10 mg chol., 58 mg sodium, 8 g carb., 0 g fiber, 1 g pro.

pesto and cheese shortbread spirals

prep: 30 minutes **chill:** 1 hour **bake:** 11 minutes at 375°F per batch
makes: 40 cookies

⅓   cup butter, softened
½   cup finely shredded
     Asiago cheese
     (2 ounces)
1   cup all-purpose flour
1   to 2 tablespoons cold
     water
3   tablespoons butter,
     softened
⅓   cup purchased dried-
     tomato pesto
1   cup all-purpose flour

1 In a medium mixing bowl beat the ⅓ cup butter with an electric mixer on medium speed for 30 seconds. Beat in cheese until combined. Beat in as much of 1 cup flour as you can with the mixer. Using a wooden spoon, stir in any remaining flour. If necessary, add the cold water and gently knead dough until it holds together. Place dough between two sheets of waxed paper; roll dough into a 12×10-inch rectangle. Set aside.

2 In a clean medium mixing bowl beat the 3 tablespoons butter with an electric mixer on medium speed for 30 seconds. Beat in pesto until combined. Beat in as much of the remaining 1 cup flour as you can with the mixer. Using a wooden spoon, stir in any remaining flour. If necessary, gently knead dough until it holds together. Place dough between two sheets of waxed paper; roll dough into a 12×10-inch rectangle.

3 Remove top sheets of waxed paper. Invert the pesto dough rectangle on the cheese dough rectangle, lining up the edges of the two. Remove top layer of waxed paper. Roll up dough into a spiral, starting from a long side and using bottom layer of waxed paper to lift and roll dough. Discard waxed paper. Pinch edges to seal. Wrap roll in plastic wrap or waxed paper. Chill for 1 to 2 hours or until dough is firm enough to slice.

4 Preheat oven to 375°F. Line large baking sheets with parchment paper. Cut roll into ¼-inch slices. Place slices 1 inch apart on prepared cookie sheet.

5 Bake for 11 to 13 minutes or until edges are firm and just starting to brown. Transfer cookies to a wire rack; cool.

nutrition facts per cookie: 58 cal., 4 g total fat (2 g sat. fat), 8 mg chol., 48 mg sodium, 5 g carb., 0 g fiber, 1 g pro.

Serve this appetizer slightly warm with a dry red wine, such as Merlot or Cabernet Sauvignon.

cheddar-blue thumbprints

prep: 30 minutes **bake:** 13 minutes at 350°F per batch **cool:** 15 minutes
makes: 42 cookies

1½   cups shredded white
      cheddar cheese or
      extra-sharp cheddar
      cheese (6 ounces)
½   cup finely shredded
      Parmesan cheese
½   cup butter, softened
1   egg yolk
¼   teaspoon ground
      black pepper
1   cup all-purpose flour
1   egg white
1   tablespoon water
1¼   cups finely chopped
      almonds, lightly
      toasted (see tip,
      page 13)
⅓   cup seedless
      raspberry preserves
4   ounces blue cheese,
      cut into small cubes

1 Preheat oven to 350°F. Line a cookie sheet with parchment paper or lightly grease a cookie sheet; set aside. In a food processor combine cheddar cheese, Parmesan cheese, and butter. Cover and process until well mixed. Add egg yolk and pepper; cover and process until combined. Add flour; cover and process with on/off pulses until a soft dough forms. (Or in a medium mixing bowl beat butter with an electric mixer on medium to high speed for 30 seconds. Beat in cheddar cheese and Parmesan cheese until combined. Beat in egg yolk and pepper. Beat in flour until a soft dough forms.)

2 In a small bowl combine egg white and the water. Place almonds in a shallow dish. Shape dough into ¾-inch balls. Roll balls in egg white mixture, then in almonds to coat. Place 1 inch apart on the prepared cookie sheet. Press your thumb into the center of each ball, reshaping as necessary.

3 Bake about 10 minutes or until edges are firm and cookies are lightly browned. If cookie centers puff during baking, indent with the back of a measuring teaspoon. Spoon preserves into indentations in cookies. Top each cookie with a cube of blue cheese. Bake for 3 to 4 minutes more or until blue cheese is softened.

4 Transfer cookies to a wire rack; cool for 15 minutes. Cover and chill within 2 hours.

to store: Cool cookies completely. Place cookies in a single layer in an airtight container; cover. Store in the refrigerator up to 2 days. To eat leftover cookies warm, place the chilled cookies on a cookie sheet and reheat in a warm oven.

nutrition facts per cookie: 87 cal., 6 g total fat (3 g sat. fat), 17 mg chol., 101 mg sodium, 5 g carb., 1 g fiber, 3 g pro.

Buttery dough flavored with fresh chives wraps around garlicky cream cheese filling studded with pine nuts.

savory cheese swirls

prep: 45 minutes **chill:** 5 hours **bake:** 10 minutes at 375°F per batch
makes: 50 cookies

2 5.2-ounce packages semisoft cheese with garlic and herbs
2 tablespoons grated Romano cheese
¼ cup pine nuts, toasted (see tip, page 13)
½ cup butter, softened
½ cup shortening
½ cup granulated sugar
½ teaspoon baking powder
½ teaspoon salt
2 eggs
3 cups all-purpose flour
Several drops green food coloring
¼ cup snipped fresh chives

1 For filling, in a small bowl combine semisoft cheese and Romano cheese. Stir in pine nuts; cover and chill until needed.

2 For dough, in a large mixing bowl beat butter and shortening with an electric mixer on medium speed for 30 seconds. Add sugar, baking powder, and salt. Beat until combined, scraping sides of bowl occasionally. Beat in eggs until combined. Beat in as much of the flour as you can with the mixer. Add green food coloring, 1 drop at a time, beating until dough is pale green. Stir in any remaining flour and the chives.

3 Divide dough in half. Cover and chill about 1 hour or until dough is easy to handle.

4 Place one portion of the dough at a time between two sheets of waxed paper; roll dough into a 10-inch square. Spread half the filling on dough to within ½ inch of edges; roll up dough. Pinch edges to seal. Wrap in plastic wrap or waxed paper. Chill for 4 to 24 hours or until dough is firm enough to slice.

5 Preheat oven to 375°F. Line a cookie sheet with parchment paper; set aside. Using a sharp knife, cut rolls into ¼-inch slices. Place slices 2 inches apart on prepared cookie sheet. Bake about 10 minutes or until edges and bottoms are lightly browned. Let stand on cookie sheet for 1 minute. Transfer to a wire rack; cool.

to store: Layer cookies between sheets of waxed paper in an airtight storage container; cover. Freeze up to 3 months. Let stand at room temperature about 15 minutes before serving. (Or freeze the dough rolls up to 3 months. Thaw overnight in the refrigerator, then slice and bake as directed in Step 5.)

nutrition facts per cookie: 102 cal., 7 g total fat (3 g sat. fat), 19 mg chol., 87 mg sodium, 8 g carb., 0 g fiber, 2 g pro.

Instead of frosting these rounds, a sweet onion jam is the crowning finish.

smoky shortbread rounds

prep: 25 minutes **stand:** 30 minutes **bake:** 15 minutes at 325°F per batch
makes: 30 cookies

½ cup shredded smoked Gouda or smoked Cheddar cheese (2 ounces)

¼ cup butter

¾ cup all-purpose flour

¼ teaspoon salt

⅛ teaspoon cayenne pepper

⅓ cup slivered almonds, toasted (see tip, page 13)

⅓ cup Roasted Garlic and Sweet Onion Jam, purchased onion jam, or purchased mango chutney

1 Let cheese and butter stand at room temperature for 30 minutes.

2 In a food processor combine cheese, butter, flour, salt, and cayenne pepper. Cover and pulse until mixture resembles coarse crumbs. Add almonds; process just until mixture begins to cling. Shape dough into a ball.

3 Preheat oven to 325°F. Roll dough between two sheets of waxed paper to ¼-inch thickness. Using a 1½-inch round cookie cutter, cut out dough. Place rounds on an ungreased baking sheet.

4 Bake 15 to 18 minutes or until lightly browned. Transfer cookies to wire racks; cool. Serve cookies with Roasted Garlic and Sweet Onion Jam (refrigerate remaining jam for another use).

nutrition facts per cookie: 42 cal., 3 g total fat (1 g sat. fat), 6 mg chol., 60 mg sodium, 4 g carb., 0 g fiber, 1 g pro.

roasted garlic and sweet onion jam: Preheat oven to 350°F. Slice about ¼ inch off the pointed end of one garlic bulb so the individual cloves show. Place the bulb in a small baking dish, cut side up. Drizzle with 1 tablespoon olive oil. Cover and roast for 45 to 60 minutes or until garlic cloves have softened; cool. Gently squeeze the garlic cloves and juices into a saucepan. Stir in 1 cup finely chopped sweet onion (1 large), ½ cup finely chopped Granny Smith apple, ½ cup granulated sugar, and ½ cup balsamic vinegar. Bring to boiling over medium-high heat, stirring occasionally. Reduce heat; simmer about 30 minutes or until onion and apple have softened and the jam has thickened, stirring occasionally. Makes about 1 cup.

Depending on the brand, jalapeño jellly can be red or green.

cheese wafers with pepper jelly

prep: 15 minutes   **chill:** 2 hours   **bake:** 8 minutes at 400°F per batch
makes: 80 cookies

2   cups all-purpose flour
½   cup butter, cut up
1   teaspoon granulated
        sugar
¼   teaspoon salt
¼   teaspoon curry powder
        Dash cayenne pepper
2   cups shredded sharp
        cheddar cheese
        (8 ounces)
3   tablespoons water
        Jalapeño pepper jelly

1 In a food processor combine flour, butter, sugar, salt, curry powder, and cayenne pepper. Cover and process with two or three on-off pulses until mixture has pea-sized pieces. Add cheese. Cover and process with two or three on-off pulses. Add the water, 1 tablespoon at a time, pulsing after each addition just until dough is moistened.

2 Gather dough into a ball; divide in half. Shape each half into a 10-inch log. Wrap in plastic wrap and chill about 2 hours or until firm enough to slice.

3 Preheat oven to 400°F. Grease a large cookie sheet. Cut logs into ¼-inch slices. Place slices 1 inch apart on the prepared cookie sheet. Prick slices with a fork.

4 Bake for 8 to 10 minutes or until wafers start to brown on edges. Transfer to a wire rack; cool. Serve with pepper jelly.

nutrition facts per cookie: 33 cal., 2 g total fat (1 g sat. fat), 6 mg chol., 33 mg sodium, 2 g carb., 0 g fiber, 1 g pro.

to make ahead: Layer wafers between sheets of waxed paper in an airtight container; cover. Freeze up to 3 months. To serve, thaw at room temperature for 30 minutes. Meanwhile, preheat oven to 350°F. Bake wafers about 10 minutes or until heated through.

Pair these savory wedges with a variety of cheeses.

rosemary and cornmeal shortbread

prep: 25 minutes **bake:** 25 minutes at 325°F
makes: 16 cookies

1   cup all-purpose flour
¼   cup yellow cornmeal
3   tablespoons
    granulated sugar
1   teaspoon snipped
    fresh rosemary or
    ¼ teaspoon dried
    rosemary, crushed
    Dash cayenne pepper
½   cup butter
2   tablespoons finely
    snipped dried
    cranberries
⅓   cup powdered sugar
⅛   teaspoon finely
    shredded orange
    peel
2   to 4 teaspoons orange
    juice
    Fresh rosemary sprig
    (optional)

1 Preheat oven to 325°F. In a medium bowl stir together flour, cornmeal, granulated sugar, the 1 teaspoon snipped rosemary, and cayenne pepper. Using a pastry blender, cut in butter until dough resembles fine crumbs and starts to cling. Stir in dried cranberries. Form dough into a ball and knead until smooth.

2 On an ungreased cookie sheet roll or pat dough into an 8-inch circle. Using your fingers, make a scalloped edge. Cut circle into 16 wedges; do not separate wedges.

3 Bake for 25 to 30 minutes or just until bottom starts to brown and center is set. Cut circle into wedges again while warm. Cool on cookie sheet for 5 minutes.

4 Meanwhile, for glaze, in a small bowl stir together powdered sugar, orange peel, and 2 teaspoons of the orange juice. Stir in enough of the remaining orange juice, 1 teaspoon at a time, to reach a thin spreading consistency. Spread or brush warm wedges with glaze. Transfer glazed wedges to a wire rack; cool. If desired, garnish with rosemary sprig.

nutrition facts per cookie: 110 cal., 6 g total fat (4 g sat. fat), 15 mg chol., 51 mg sodium, 13 g carb., 0 g fiber, 1 g pro.

Include these crisp wafers next time you set out a cracker and cheese tray.

parmesan shortbread rounds

prep: 25 minutes **chill:** 3 hours **bake:** 15 minutes at 325°F per batch
makes: 36 cookies

¾   cup butter, softened
2   cups finely shredded
      Parmesan cheese
      (8 ounces)
1¼ cups all-purpose flour
1   tablespoon paprika
¼   teaspoon cayenne
      pepper
1   cup finely chopped
      pecans
2   tablespoons snipped
      fresh chives
      Apple or pear butter
      (optional)

1 In a large mixing bowl beat butter with an electric mixer on medium speed for 1 minute. Using a wooden spoon, stir in cheese. Stir in flour, paprika, and cayenne pepper until combined. Stir in pecans and chives. Dough will be crumbly.

2 Turn dough out onto a lightly floured surface. Gently knead until dough clings. Shape into a 12-inch roll. Wrap log in plastic wrap or waxed paper; chill about 3 hours or until firm enough to slice.

3 Preheat oven to 325°F. Using a serrated knife, cut log into ¼-inch slices. Place slices 1 inch apart on an ungreased cookie sheet.

4 Bake for 15 to 17 minutes or until set. Transfer rounds to a wire rack; cool. If desired, serve with apple or pear butter.

nutrition facts per cookie: 103 cal., 7 g total fat (3 g sat. fat), 13 mg chol., 103 mg sodium, 8 g carb., 1 g fiber, 3 g pro.

Texas meets Italy in this newfangled biscotti.

chile pepper-cheese biscotti

prep: 30 minutes **bake:** 30 minutes at 350°F + 27 minutes at 325°F **cool:** 1 hour
makes: 56 cookies

1   cup shredded white
    cheddar cheese
    (4 ounces)
¼   cup butter, softened
1   4-ounce can diced
    green chile peppers,
    undrained
2½ teaspoons baking
    powder
¼   teaspoon salt
¼   teaspoon ground
    black pepper
2   eggs
½   cup yellow cornmeal
2   cups all-purpose flour
    Sliced Monterey
    Jack cheese with
    jalapeño peppers
    (optional)
    Bottled sliced pickled
    jalapeño chile
    peppers (optional)

1 Preheat oven to 350°F. Lightly grease a cookie sheet; set aside. In a large mixing bowl combine cheddar cheese and butter. Beat with an electric mixer on medium to high speed for 30 seconds. Add diced chile peppers, baking powder, salt, and black pepper. Beat until combined, scraping sides of bowl occasionally. Beat in eggs until combined. Beat in cornmeal. Beat in as much of the flour as you can with the mixer. Using a wooden spoon or your hands, stir or knead in any remaining flour.

2 Divide dough in half. Shape each portion into a 9-inch log. Place logs about 5 inches apart on the prepared cookie sheet; slightly flatten each log to about 3-inch wide loaves.

3 Bake for 30 to 35 minutes or until lightly browned. Cool on cookie sheet for 1 hour.

4 Preheat oven to 325°F. Using a serrated knife, cut each loaf diagonally into ¼-inch slices. Place slices on an ungreased cookie sheet. Bake for 15 minutes. Turn slices over and bake for 12 to 15 minutes more or until biscotti are dry and crisp (do not overbake). Transfer to a wire rack; cool.

5 If desired, serve biscotti with Monterey Jack cheese and pickled jalapeño peppers.

to store: Layer biscotti between sheets of waxed paper in an airtight container; cover. Store in the refrigerator up to 3 days or freeze up to 2 weeks.

nutrition facts per cookie: 40 cal., 2 g total fat (1 g sat. fat), 12 mg chol., 50 mg sodium, 4 g carb., 0 g fiber, 1 g pro.

Serve as part of an antipasti platter with olives, cured meats, and pickled vegetables.

pepperoni biscotti

prep: 30 minutes **bake:** 20 minutes at 350°F + 20 minutes at 325°F **cool:** 1 hour
makes: 24 cookies

⅓   cup butter, softened
¼   cup grated Parmesan cheese
4   cloves garlic, minced
1   tablespoon granulated sugar
1   teaspoon baking powder
1   teaspoon dried Italian seasoning
1   egg
1   tablespoon milk
1½ cups all-purpose flour
½   cup chopped pepperoni
¼   cup finely chopped red sweet pepper
2   tablespoons finely chopped onion
2   tablespoons snipped fresh parsley
2   tablespoons grated Parmesan cheese

1 Preheat oven to 350°F. Lightly grease a cookie sheet; set aside. In a large mixing bowl beat butter with an electric mixer on medium to high speed for 30 seconds. Add the ¼ cup Parmesan cheese, garlic, sugar, baking powder, and Italian seasoning. Beat until combined. Beat in egg and milk. Beat in as much flour as you can with the mixer. Using a wooden spoon, stir in remaining flour, pepperoni, sweet pepper, onion, and parsley.

2 Knead dough gently until it clings together. Divide dough in half. Shape each portion into a 9×1½-inch log. Roll dough logs in the 2 tablespoons Parmesan cheese to coat. Place logs 4 inches apart on the prepared cookie sheet; slightly flatten each log to about 2-inch wide loaves.

3 Bake for 20 to 25 minutes or until a wooden toothpick inserted near the centers comes out clean. Cool on cookie sheet for 1 hour.

4 Preheat oven to 325°F. Using a serrated knife, cut each loaf into ¾-inch slices. Place slices on an ungreased cookie sheet. Bake for 10 minutes. Carefully turn slices over and bake for 10 to 12 minutes more or until dry and crisp. (Do not overbake.) Transfer biscotti to a wire racks; cool.

nutrition facts per cookie: 80 cal., 5 g total fat (3 g sat. fat), 20 mg chol., 140 mg sodium, 7 g carb., 0 g fiber, 2 g pro.

Try this as a savory dipper with creamed soups.

caramelized onion-tarragon biscotti

prep: 30 minutes **bake:** 20 minutes at 350°F + 12 minutes at 325°F **cool:** 1 hour
makes: 40 cookies

1   tablespoon butter
1   cup finely chopped
     onion
1   teaspoon honey
1   teaspoon salt
½   cup butter, softened
1   tablespoon
     granulated sugar
1   teaspoon baking
     powder
2   eggs
2   cups all-purpose flour
2   tablespoons snipped
     fresh tarragon or
     2 teaspoons dried
     tarragon, crushed
1   tablespoon finely
     shredded lemon
     peel
     Goat cheese (chèvre)
     (optional)

1 Preheat oven to 350°F. Lightly grease a cookie sheet; set aside. For caramelized onion, in a medium skillet heat the 1 tablespoon butter over medium heat. Add onion, honey, and ½ teaspoon of the salt. Cook about 10 minutes or until onion is golden brown, stirring occasionally; cool.

2 In a large mixing bowl beat the ½ cup butter with an electric mixer on medium to high speed for 30 seconds. Add sugar, baking powder, and the remaining ½ teaspoon salt. Beat until combined, scraping sides of bowl occasionally. Beat in eggs until combined. Beat in as much of the flour as you can with the mixer. Using a wooden spoon, stir in any remaining flour. Stir in caramelized onion, tarragon, and lemon peel.

3 Divide dough in half. Shape each portion into a 10-inch log. Place logs 4 inches apart on the prepared cookie sheet; slightly flatten each to about 2-inch wide loaves.

4 Bake for 20 to 25 minutes or until a wooden toothpick inserted near the centers comes out clean. Cool on cookie sheet for 1 hour.

5 Preheat oven to 325°F. Using a serrated knife, cut each loaf diagonally into slices, slightly less than ½ inch thick. Place slices on an ungreased cookie sheet. Bake for 6 minutes. Turn slices over; bake for 6 to 8 minutes more or until biscotti are dry and crisp (do not overbake). Transfer to wire racks; cool. If desired, serve biscotti with goat cheese.

to store: Layer biscotti between sheets of waxed paper in an airtight container; cover. Store at room temperature up to 3 days or freeze up to 1 month.

nutrition facts per cookie: 53 cal., 3 g total fat (2 g sat. fat), 17 mg chol., 86 mg sodium, 6 g carb., 0 g fiber, 1 g pro.

Fennel seeds, a common seasoning in Italian cooking, add mild licorice flavor to these crisp wafers.

fennel-asiago biscotti

prep: 30 minutes stand: 15 minutes bake: 25 minutes at 350°F + 14 minutes at 325°F
cool: 25 minutes makes: 80 cookies

2   cups all-purpose flour
¼   cup white cornmeal
1   teaspoon baking
      powder
1   teaspoon salt
½   teaspoon coarsely
      ground black pepper
⅛   teaspoon baking soda
      Cayenne pepper
¾   cup freshly grated
      Asiago cheese
½   cup pine nuts, toasted
      (see tip, page 13) and
      chopped
2   teaspoons fennel seeds
2   eggs, lightly beaten
½   cup buttermilk or sour
      milk (see tip, page 12)
      Parmigiano-Reggiano
      cheese (optional)
      Dried apricots and/or
      dried figs (optional)
      Pear slices (optional)

1 Preheat oven to 350°F. Line a large cookie sheet with parchment paper or foil; set aside. In a medium bowl stir together flour, cornmeal, baking powder, salt, black pepper, baking soda, and cayenne pepper. Stir in Asiago cheese, pine nuts, and fennel seeds.

2 In a small bowl combine eggs and buttermilk. Add egg mixture to flour mixture; stir until dough clings. Turn out onto a lightly floured surface. Gently knead just until dough is smooth (dough may still be slightly sticky). Shape dough into a ball. Wrap in plastic wrap; let stand at room temperature for 15 minutes to make dough easier to shape.

3 Divide dough into three portions. Shape each portion into a 7-inch log. Place logs 2 inches apart on the prepared cookie sheet. Slightly flatten each log.

4 Bake about 25 minutes or until golden brown. (Tops may split as the loaves bake.) Cool on cookie sheet for 5 minutes. Carefully transfer loaves to a wire rack; cool for 20 minutes more.

5 Preheat oven to 325°F. Line another cookie sheet with parchment paper or foil. Using a serrated knife, cut loaves diagonally into ¼-inch slices. Place slices on the prepared cookie sheet. Bake for 6 minutes. Carefully turn slices over; bake about 8 minutes more or until biscotti are dry and crisp (do not overbake). Transfer biscotti to wire racks; cool.

6 If desired, serve biscotti with Parmigiano-Reggino cheese, dried apricots and/or figs, and pear slices.

to store: Layer biscotti between waxed paper in an airtight container; cover. Store in the refrigerator up to 3 days or freeze up to 2 weeks.

nutrition facts per cookie: 25 cal., 1 g total fat (0 g sat. fat), 6 mg chol., 49 mg sodium, 3 g carb., 0 g fiber, 1 g pro.

Plan a two-day process, allowing the biscotti to stand up to 24 hours between initial and final baking.

dried tomato biscotti

prep: 45 minutes **bake:** 18 minutes at 375°F + 15 minutes at 325°F
cool: 30 minutes **stand:** 6 hours
makes: 32 cookies

½ cup butter, softened
½ cup packed brown
    sugar
¼ cup grated Parmesan
    cheese
2 teaspoons baking
    powder
½ teaspoon salt
¼ teaspoon crushed red
    pepper
¼ teaspoon ground
    black pepper
2 eggs
2 cups all-purpose flour
¼ cup snipped dried
    tomatoes
1 egg, lightly beaten
1 recipe Biscotti Butter

biscotti butter: In a small bowl stir together ½ cup olive oil, 2 tablespoons grated Parmesan cheese, 1 teaspoon bottled minced roasted garlic, and ⅛ teaspoon ground black pepper. Serve as a dipping sauce with biscotti.

1 Preheat oven to 375°F. Lightly grease a cookie sheet; set aside. In a large mixing bowl beat butter with an electric mixer on medium to high speed for 30 seconds. Add brown sugar, Parmesan cheese, baking powder, salt, crushed red pepper, and black pepper. Beat until combined, scraping sides of bowl occasionally. Beat in the 2 eggs until combined. Beat in as much of the flour as you can with the mixer. Using a wooden spoon, stir in any remaining flour and the dried tomatoes.

2 Divide dough in half. Shape each portion into a 9-inch log. Place logs 4 inches apart on the prepared cookie sheet; slightly flatten each logs to about 2 inches wide. Brush tops with the lightly beaten egg.

3 Bake for 18 to 20 minutes or until a wooden toothpick inserted near centers comes out clean. Cool on cookie sheet about 30 minutes or until completely cooled. Wrap loaves and let stand at room temperature for 6 to 24 hours.

4 Preheat oven to 325°F. Using a serrated knife, diagonally cut each loaf into ½-inch slices. Place slices on an ungreased cookie sheet. Bake for 8 minutes. Carefully turn biscotti over and bake for 7 to 9 minutes more or until slices are dry and crisp. Transfer to wire racks; cool. Serve with Biscotti Butter for dipping.

to store: Layer biscotti between sheets of waxed paper in an airtight container; cover. Store at room temperature up to 3 days or freeze up to 3 months. Store Biscotti Butter in an airtight container in the refrigerator up to 3 days; bring to room temperature before serving.

nutrition facts per cookie: 109 cal., 7 g total fat (3 g sat. fat), 28 mg chol., 110 mg sodium, 10 g carb., 0 g fiber, 2 g pro.

Serve with prosciutto or thin slices of hard salami.

seeded cheddar biscotti

prep: 30 minutes **bake:** 20 minutes at 375°F + 20 minutes at 325°F **cool:** 1 hour
makes: 50 cookies

2¼ cups all-purpose flour
⅓ cup yellow cornmeal
1½ teaspoons granulated sugar
1½ teaspoons salt
1½ teaspoons baking powder
½ teaspoon baking soda
½ teaspoon dry mustard
½ teaspoon coarsely ground black pepper
Dash cayenne pepper
¾ cup shredded sharp cheddar cheese (3 ounces)
7 teaspoons assorted seeds (such as poppy seeds, dill seeds, celery seeds, sesame seeds, and/ or flaxseeds) or purchased bread topping seed mix
2 eggs, lightly beaten
½ cup buttermilk or sour milk
2 tablespoons butter, melted

1 Preheat oven to 375°F. Line a very large cookie sheet with parchment paper or foil; set aside. In a large bowl combine flour, cornmeal, sugar, salt, baking powder, baking soda, dry mustard, black pepper, and cayenne pepper. Stir in cheese and seeds.

2 In a medium bowl combine eggs, buttermilk, and melted butter. Add egg mixture to flour mixture; stir to form a crumbly dough.

3 Turn dough out onto a lightly floured surface. Gently knead until dough clings together. Divide dough into thirds. Shape each portion into a 10-inch log. Place logs on the prepared cookie sheet; slightly flatten.

4 Bake about 20 minutes or until a wooden toothpick inserted near the centers comes out clean. Cool on cookie sheet for 1 hour.

5 Preheat oven to 325°F. Using a serrated knife, cut each loaf into about ½-inch slices. Place slices on an ungreased cookie sheet. Bake for 10 minutes. Carefully turn slices over and bake for 10 to 12 minutes more or until biscotti are dry and crisp (do not overbake). Transfer biscotti to wire racks; cool.

nutrition facts per cookie: 39 cal., 1 g total fat (1 g sat. fat), 12 mg chol., 109 mg sodium, 5 g carb., 0 g fiber, 1 g pro.

As a party winds down, serve these light bites with coffee for late-night refreshment.

minty brownie bites

prep: 35 minutes **bake:** 30 minutes at 350°F
makes: 64 brownie bites

½   cup butter
3   ounces bittersweet chocolate, coarsely chopped
1   cup granulated sugar
2   eggs
1   tablespoon crème de menthe
1   teaspoon vanilla
⅔   cup all-purpose flour
¼   teaspoon baking soda
⅛   teaspoon salt
1   recipe Crème de Menthe Topping
     Green edible glitter (optional)

1 In a medium saucepan heat and stir butter and chocolate over low heat until melted; cool.

2 Preheat oven to 350°F. Line a 9×9×2-inch baking pan with foil, extending the foil over edges of pan. Grease foil; set pan aside.

3 Stir sugar into chocolate mixture. Add eggs, one at a time, beating with a wooden spoon after each addition just until combined. Stir in crème de menthe and vanilla.

4 In a small bowl stir together flour, baking soda, and salt. Add flour mixture to chocolate mixture, stirring just until combined. Spread batter evenly in the prepared baking pan.

5 Bake for 30 minutes. Cool in pan on a wire rack. Using the edges of the foil, lift uncut brownies out of pan. Cut brownies into 1-inch squares. Spoon Crème de Menthe Topping into a decorating bag fitted with large star tip. Pipe a large star onto each square. If desired, sprinkle with edible glitter.

to store: Place brownie bites in a single layer in an airtight container; cover. Store in the refrigerator up to 3 days or freeze up to 3 months.

nutrition facts per brownie bite: 67 cal., 3 g total fat (2 g sat. fat), 13 mg chol., 36 mg sodium, 9 g carb., 0 g fiber, 0 g pro.

crème de menthe topping: In a large mixing bowl beat 2 ounces cream cheese, softened, and ⅓ cup butter, softened, with an electric mixer for 30 seconds. Gradually beat in 1 cup powdered sugar. Beat in 2 tablespoons crème de menthe. Gradually beat in an additional 1 cup powdered sugar. Beat in green food coloring and up to 1 tablespoon additional milk, if necessary, to make a thick frosting for piping.

Strictly an adult brownie, to pair with the remaining bottle of wine.

cherry-cabernet brownies

prep: 30 minutes **bake:** 30 minutes at 350°F **stand:** 2 hours
makes: 36 brownies

1   cup dried cherries, chopped
½   cup Cabernet Sauvignon wine
¾   cup butter, cut up
4   ounces unsweetened chocolate, chopped
2   cups granulated sugar
3   eggs
1   teaspoon vanilla
1   cup all-purpose flour
½   teaspoon baking powder
¼   teaspoon baking soda
¼   teaspoon salt
1   recipe Red Wine Ganache

1 In a small saucepan combine cherries and wine. Bring just to boiling. Remove from heat; set aside. Preheat oven to 350°F. Line a 13×9×2-inch baking pan with foil, extending foil over edges of pan. Grease and flour foil; set pan aside.

2 In a medium saucepan stir butter and chocolate over low heat until melted and smooth. Whisk in sugar. Add eggs, one at a time, whisking well after each addition. Stir in vanilla. In a small bowl stir together the flour, baking powder, baking soda, and salt; stir into chocolate mixture until combined. Stir in undrained cherries. Spread batter evenly in the prepared pan.

3 Bake about 30 minutes or until sides begin to pull away from pan. Cool in pan on a wire rack.

4 Pour Red Wine Ganache over cooled brownies, spreading evenly. Let stand about 2 hours or until set. Use foil to lift uncut brownies out of pan and onto a cutting board. Cut into bars.

nutrition facts per brownie: 158 cal., 8 g total fat (5 g sat. fat), 28 mg chol., 82 mg sodium, 21 g carb., 1 g fiber, 2 g pro.

red wine ganache: In a small heavy saucepan combine 6 ounces semisweet chocolate, chopped; 3 tablespoons butter, cut up; and 3 tablespoons red wine. Heat and stir over low heat until melted and smooth.

Prepare the cookie dough one day, then bake and fill the tarts the next day. Pictured on page 388.

espresso tarts

prep: 50 minutes **bake:** 15 minutes at 325°F per batch
makes: 36 mini tarts

1   recipe Espresso Cookie Dough
5   ounces semisweet chocolate, chopped
2   tablespoons butter
1   egg
⅓   cup packed brown sugar
1   tablespoon coffee liqueur
2   teaspoons vanilla
½   teaspoon ground cinnamon
¼   teaspoon ground nutmeg
¼   teaspoon ground cardamom
1   recipe Chocolate-Espresso Ganache
     Chocolate-covered coffee beans (optional)

1 Prepare Espresso Cookie Dough. If necessary, cover and chill dough for 30 to 60 minutes or until easy to handle.

2 Preheat oven to 325°F. Shape dough into 36 (about 1¼-inch) balls. Press each ball into the bottoms and up the sides of 36 ungreased 1¾-inch muffin cups.

3 For filling, in a small saucepan heat and stir chocolate and butter over low heat until melted and smooth. Remove from heat. Stir in egg, brown sugar, coffee liqueur, vanilla, cinnamon, nutmeg, and cardamom. Spoon 1 slightly rounded teaspoon of filling into each pastry-lined cup.

4 Bake for 15 to 20 minutes or just until pastry is firm and filling is puffed and set. Cool in pans on wire racks for 5 minutes. Carefully remove tarts from pans; cool completely on wire racks. Spoon Chocolate Ganache onto tarts. If desired, garnish with coffee beans.

to store: Place tarts in a single layer in an airtight container; cover. Store in the refrigerator up to 3 days or freeze up to 3 months.

nutrition facts per mini tart: 143 cal., 7 g total fat (4 g sat. fat), 22 mg chol., 64 mg sodium, 19 g carb., 1 g fiber, 2 g pro.

espresso cookie dough: In a large mixing bowl beat ¼ cup butter, softened; ¼ cup shortening; and 2 ounces cream cheese, softened, with an electric mixer on medium to high speed for 30 seconds. Add 1 cup packed brown sugar, ½ teaspoon baking powder, ½ teaspoon salt, ½ teaspoon ground cinnamon, and ¼ teaspoon ground nutmeg. Beat until combined, scraping sides of bowl occasionally. Beat in 1 egg, 1 tablespoon instant espresso coffee powder, and 2 teaspoons vanilla until combined. Beat in as much of 2½ cups all-purpose flour as you can with the mixer. Using a wooden spoon, stir in any remaining flour.

chocolate-espresso ganache: In a small saucepan combine ⅓ cup whipping cream and 1 teaspoon instant espresso coffee powder. Bring to boiling over medium heat. Remove from heat. Add 3 ounces chopped semisweet chocolate (do not stir). Let stand for 5 minutes. Stir until smooth.

For a tropical treat, serve with banana or coconut ice cream.

banana-rum bars

prep: 35 minutes **bake:** 55 minutes at 350°F
makes: 36 bars

1½	cups butter, softened
½	cup granulated sugar
1½	teaspoons vanilla
4	cups all-purpose flour
1	teaspoon ground cinnamon
¾	teaspoon salt
2	cups packed brown sugar
1	teaspoon baking soda
3	eggs
1⅓	cups mashed bananas (4 medium)
1	tablespoon rum*
1	recipe Cinnamon-Rum Frosting

1 Preheat oven to 350°F. For crust, in a large mixing bowl beat 1 cup of the butter with an electric mixer on medium to high speed for 30 seconds. Add granulated sugar and ½ teaspoon of the vanilla. Beat until combined, scraping sides of bowl occasionally. Beat in 2 cups of the flour, the cinnamon, and ½ teaspoon of the salt. Press dough evenly into an ungreased 13×9×2-inch baking pan. Bake for 15 to 20 minutes or until lightly browned. Cool in pan on a wire rack.

2 In clean large mixing bowl beat the remaining ½ cup butter on medium to high speed for 30 seconds. Add brown sugar, baking soda, and the remaining ¼ teaspoon salt. Beat until combined, scraping sides of bowl occasionally. Beat in eggs, mashed bananas, rum, and the remaining 1 teaspoon vanilla. Beat in the remaining 2 cups flour just until combined. Spread filling over baked crust.

3 Bake for 40 to 45 minutes more or until a wooden toothpick inserted near center comes out clean. Cool in pan on wire rack. Spread Cinnamon-Rum Frosting over uncut bars. Cut into bars.

*tip: If you like, substitute 1 tablespoon milk and ⅛ teaspoon rum extract for the rum.

to store: Place bars in a single layer in an airtight container; cover. Store in the refrigerator up to 3 days.

nutrition facts per bar: 259 cal., 12 g total fat (7 g sat. fat), 47 mg chol., 173 mg sodium, 40 g carb., 1 g fiber, 2 g pro.

cinnamon-rum frosting: In a large mixing bowl combine ½ cup butter, softened, and one 3-ounce package cream cheese, softened. Beat with an electric mixer on medium to high speed until combined and fluffy. Gradually beat in 3 cups powdered sugar and 1 teaspoon ground cinnamon. Beat in 2 tablespoons vanilla and enough rum or milk to make icing of drizzling consistency.

Pipe the mousse-like frosting on the cookies just before serving.

chocolate-hazelnut "mousse" cookies

prep: 40 minutes **freeze:** 30 minutes **bake:** 6 minutes at 375°F per batch
makes: 72 cookies

2   ounces dark chocolate, coarsely chopped
¾   cup all-purpose flour
¼   teaspoon baking soda
⅛   teaspoon salt
¼   cup butter, softened
½   cup packed brown sugar
2   teaspoons vanilla
1   recipe Chocolate-Hazelnut "Mousse"
    Toasted hazelnuts (filberts) (see tip, page 70)

chocolate-hazelnut "mousse": In a medium bowl beat 3 tablespoons butter, softened, and ⅓ cup chocolate hazelnut spread with an electric mixer on medium to high speed until combined. Gradually add 1 cup powdered sugar, beating until smooth. Add enough milk (2 to 3 teaspoons) to reach piping consistency.

1 In a small saucepan heat and stir chocolate over low heat until melted. Remove from heat; cool. In a small bowl stir together flour, baking soda, and salt; set aside.

2 In a large mixing bowl beat butter with an electric mixer on medium to high speed for 30 seconds. Add brown sugar. Beat until combined, scraping sides of bowl occasionally. Beat in melted chocolate and vanilla until combined. Beat in as much of the flour mixture as you can with the mixer. Using a wooden spoon, stir in any remaining flour mixture.

3 Divide dough in half. Shape each half into a 9-inch log. Wrap each log in plastic wrap. Freeze about 30 minutes or until dough is firm enough to slice.

4 Preheat oven to 375°F. Line a large cookie sheet with parchment paper. Cut logs into ¼-inch slices. Place 1 inch apart on the prepared cookie sheet.

5 Bake about 6 minutes or until edges are set. Cool on cookie sheet for 2 minutes. Transfer cookies to a wire rack; cool.

6 Using a decorating bag fitted with a star tip, pipe a small amount of Chocolate-Hazelnut "Mousse" onto each cookie. Top each with a toasted hazelnut.

tip: To make sandwich cookies, pipe "mousse" onto bottoms of half the cookies. Top with the remaining cookies, bottom sides down.

to store: Layer cookies between sheets of waxed paper in an airtight container; cover. Store in the refrigerator up to 3 days or freeze up to 3 months.

nutrition facts per cookie: 38 cal., 2 g total fat (1 g sat. fat), 3 mg chol., 18 mg sodium, 5 g carb., 0 g fiber, 0 g pro.

The ideal dessert to serve at Kentucky Derby parties.

bourbon brownies

prep: 35 minutes **bake:** 20 minutes at 350°F
makes: 16 brownies

½   cup granulated sugar
⅓   cup butter
2   tablespoons water
1   cup semisweet
      chocolate pieces
2   eggs
1   teaspoon vanilla
¾   cup all-purpose flour
¼   teaspoon baking soda
¼   teaspoon salt
½   cup chopped pecans,
      toasted (see tip,
      page 13)
2   to 3 tablespoons
      bourbon
1   recipe Bourbon
      Frosting
2   ounces semisweet
      chocolate, melted
      Pecan halves, toasted
      (optional)

1 Preheat oven to 350°F. Grease an 8×8×2-inch baking pan; set aside. In a medium saucepan combine sugar, butter, and the water. Cook and stir over medium heat just until boiling. Remove from heat.

2 Stir in 1 cup chocolate pieces until melted. Add eggs and vanilla, beating with a wooden spoon just until combined. Stir in flour, baking soda, and salt. Stir in chopped pecans. Pour batter into the prepared baking pan, spreading evenly.

3 Bake for 20 to 25 minutes or until a wooden toothpick inserted near the center comes out clean and edges start to pull away from sides of pan.

4 Place pan on a wire rack. Brush top of hot brownies with bourbon. Cool completely.

5 Spread uncut brownies with Bourbon Frosting. Cut into bars. Top with melted chocolate and, if desired, pecan halves.

nutrition facts per brownie: 244 cal., 13 g total fat (7 g sat. fat), 39 mg chol., 119 mg sodium, 29 g carb., 2 g fiber, 2 g pro.

bourbon frosting: In a medium mixing bowl beat 3 tablespoons butter, softened, with an electric mixer on medium to high speed for 30 seconds. Gradually add 1½ cups powdered sugar, beating well. Beat in 1 to 2 tablespoons bourbon or milk and ¼ teaspoon vanilla. If necessary, beat in enough additional milk, 1 teaspoon at a time, to make frosting spreading consistency.

Look in specialty shops for smoked salt.

dark chocolate and espresso cookie coins with smoked salt

prep: 30 minutes **chill:** 3 hours **bake:** 10 minutes at 325°F per batch
makes: 30 cookies

1 tablespoon hot water
1 tablespoon instant espresso coffee powder
1 cup butter, softened
¾ cup powdered sugar
1 teaspoon vanilla
¼ teaspoon salt
1¾ cups all-purpose flour
4 ounces bittersweet chocolate, finely chopped
4 ounces bittersweet chocolate, chopped
1 tablespoon shortening
Coarse smoked sea salt or sea salt, slightly crushed

1 In a small bowl stir the hot water into coffee powder until dissolved; set aside. In a large mixing bowl beat butter and powdered sugar with an electric mixer on medium speed for 30 seconds. Beat on medium-high speed for 3 minutes more. Beat in coffee mixture, vanilla, and the ¼ teaspoon salt until combined. Gradually add flour, beating on low speed just until combined. Using a wooden spoon, stir in the 4 ounces finely chopped chocolate.

2 Divide dough in half. Shape each portion into a 10-inch log. Wrap each log in plastic wrap or waxed paper. Chill about 3 hours or until dough is firm enough to slice.

3 Preheat oven to 325°F. Line a cookie sheet with parchment paper. Using a serrated knife, cut logs into ¼-inch slices. Place slices 2 inches apart on the prepared cookie sheet.

4 Bake for 10 to 12 minutes or until cookies are set. Transfer to a wire rack; cool.

5 Meanwhile, in a small saucepan melt the 4 ounces chopped chocolate and shortening over low heat. Dip half of each cookie into melted chocolate, allowing excess to drip back into pan. Return cookies to wire rack. Sprinkle lightly with sea salt. Let stand until chocolate is set.

nutrition facts per cookie: 135 cal., 10 g total fat (6 g sat. fat), 16 mg chol., 152 mg sodium, 13 g carb., 1 g fiber, 1 g pro.

14

The winter holiday season is the most popular time of year to make cookies, and this chapter promises to make all your baking wishes come true. From decorated cutouts to ethnic favorites, you'll revisit tried-and-true recipes while discovering new treats for your holiday cookie tray. As a bonus, check out the cookie mixes—perfect for gift-giving.

holiday SW

chocolaty melting
snowmen, page 433

eets

This recipe originally appeared in our sister publication,
Midwest Living, and it's been a regional favorite for
generations.

vienna almond cutouts

prep: 20 minutes **chill:** 2 hours **bake:** 8 minutes at 350°F per batch
makes: 48 cookies

¾   cup slivered almonds,
       toasted (see tip,
       page 13)
2¼ cups all-purpose flour
¼   teaspoon salt
1   cup butter, softened
¾   cup sugar
1   egg
1   teaspoon vanilla
½   teaspoon finely
       shredded lemon
       peel
¼   teaspoon almond
       extract (optional)

1 In a food processor pulse toasted almonds
with on/off turns until finely ground. In a small
bowl combine the ground almonds, the flour, and
salt; set aside.

2 In a large mixing bowl beat butter and sugar
with an electric mixer on medium speed until
light and fluffy. Add egg, vanilla, lemon peel, and,
if desired, almond extract. Beat until combined,
scraping sides of bowl occasionally. Beat in as
much of the flour mixture as you can with the
mixer. Using a wooden spoon, stir in any remaining
flour mixture. Divide dough in half. Cover and chill
for 2 hours or until dough is easy to handle.

3 Preheat oven to 350°F. On a lightly floured
surface, roll half of the dough at a time to ¼-
inch thickness. Using a 2½- to 3-inch cookie cutter,
cut dough into shapes; reroll scraps as necessary
(if necessary, chill scraps before rerolling). Place
cutouts 1 inch apart on an ungreased cookie
sheet.

4 Bake for 8 to 12 minutes or until edges are
lightly browned and centers are set.
Cool on cookie sheet for 1 minute. Transfer to a
wire rack; cool.

to store: Layer cookies between sheets of waxed
paper in an airtight container; cover. Store at
room temperature up to 2 days or freeze up to
3 months.

nutrition facts per cookie: 77 cal., 5 g total fat (3 g sat.
fat), 15 mg chol., 41 mg sodium, 8 g carb., 0 g fiber, 1 g pro.

Ever-popular sugar cookies get updated with the hint of fresh thyme. Also try other herbs—mint, rosemary, or lavendar.

christmas thyme cookies

prep: 35 minutes **bake:** 6 minutes at 350°F per batch
makes: 36 cookies

½   cup butter, softened
¼   cup granulated sugar
1   tablespoon snipped
       fresh thyme
2   teaspoons finely
       shredded lemon peel
1   tablespoon lemon juice
1¼ cups all-purpose flour
       Green sanding sugar

1 Preheat oven to 350°F. In a medium mixing bowl beat butter with an electric mixer on medium to high speed for 30 seconds. Add granulated sugar. Beat until combined, scraping sides of bowl occasionally. Beat in thyme, lemon peel, and lemon juice until combined. Beat in as much of the flour as you can with the mixer. Using a wooden spoon, stir in any remaining flour. Form dough into a ball and knead until smooth.

2 Divide dough into three portions. On a lightly floured surface, roll one portion at a time into a 6x4½-inch rectangle. Using a fluted pastry wheel, cut dough into 1½-inch squares. Place squares 1 inch apart on an ungreased cookie sheet. Sprinkle with sanding sugar.

3 Bake for 6 to 8 minutes or until bottoms are lightly browned. Transfer cookies to a wire rack; cool.

to store: Layer cookies between sheets of waxed paper in an airtight container; cover. Store at room temperature up to 3 days or freeze up to 3 months.

nutrition facts per cookie: 48 cal., 3 g total fat (2 g sat. fat), 7 mg chol., 23 mg sodium, 6 g carb., 0 g fiber, 0 g pro.

The dough is rolled thinly, so you can sandwich two cookies with buttercream filling to make a chunky cookie.

pistachio nut stars

prep: 30 minutes **chill:** 2 hours **bake:** 6 minutes at 375°F per batch
makes: 18 cookies

1	cup butter, softened
½	cup granulated sugar
¼	cup packed brown sugar
1	teaspoon ground cinnamon
½	teaspoon ground cardamom
¼	teaspoon salt
1	egg
2	tablespoons vanilla yogurt
2½	cups all-purpose flour
2	cups finely chopped pistachio nuts
1	egg white, lightly beaten
1	recipe Buttercream Filling
	Chopped pistachio nuts

1 In a large mixing bowl beat butter with an electric mixer on medium to high speed for 30 seconds. Add granulated sugar, brown sugar, cinnamon, cardamom, and salt. Beat until combined, scraping sides of bowl occasionally. Beat in egg and yogurt until combined. Beat in as much of the flour as you can with the mixer. Using a wooden spoon, stir in any remaining flour and the 2 cups chopped pistachios. Divide dough in half. Cover and chill about 2 hours or until dough is easy to handle.

2 Preheat oven to 375°F. Lightly grease a cookie sheet; set aside. On a lightly floured surface, roll one portion of the dough at a time to ⅛-inch thickness. Using a floured 3- to 3½-inch star-shape cookie cutter, cut out dough, rerolling scraps as necessary. Place cutouts on the prepared cookie sheet. Using a small star-shape cookie cutter, cut and remove a star from the center of half the cookies. Brush cutouts with egg white.

3 Bake for 6 to 8 minutes or until edges are light brown. Transfer to a wire rack; cool.

4 Spread Buttercream Filling on bottoms of the cookies without cutout centers. Top with the cookies with cutout centers, bottom sides down. Sprinkle the buttercream showing through the centers with additional pistachios.

to store: Layer unfilled cookies between sheets of waxed paper in an airtight container; cover. Store at room temperature up to 3 days or freeze up to 3 months. Fill and assemble cookies before serving.

buttercream filling: In a medium mixing bowl beat ¼ cup butter, softened, on medium speed until smooth. Add 1 cup powdered sugar, 2 tablespoons milk, and 1 teaspoon vanilla, beating on medium to high speed until smooth and creamy. Beat in enough additional powdered sugar (¾ to 1 cup) for filling to reach spreading consistency.

nutrition facts per cookie: 358 cal., 20 g total fat (9 g sat. fat), 44 mg chol., 222 mg sodium, 40 g carb., 2 g fiber, 6 g pro.

Look no further. We perfected our basic sugar cookie recipe, resulting in a dough that's easy to cut out—with outstanding buttery taste. Decorate as desired, or try the Royal Icing.

sugar cookies

prep: 35 minutes **chill:** 2 hours **bake:** 7 minutes at 375°F per batch
makes: 36 cookies

⅔   cup butter, softened
¾   cup sugar
1   teaspoon baking powder
¼   teaspoon salt
1   egg
1   tablespoon milk
1   teaspoon vanilla
2   cups all-purpose flour
1   recipe Royal Icing (see recipe, page 18)*
    Food coloring (optional)

1 In a large mixing bowl beat butter with an electric mixer on medium to high speed for 30 seconds. Add sugar, baking powder, and salt. Beat until combined, scraping sides of bowl occasionally. Beat in egg, milk, and vanilla until combined. Beat in as much of the flour as you can with the mixer. Using a wooden spoon, stir in any remaining flour. Divide dough in half. Cover and chill dough about 2 hours or until dough is easy to handle.

2 Preheat oven to 375°F. On a lightly floured surface, roll half the dough at a time until ¼-inch thickness. Cut dough with 2½-inch cookie cutters. Place cutouts 1 inch apart on an ungreased cookie sheet.

3 Bake for 7 to 10 minutes or until edges are very lightly browned. Transfer cookies to a wire rack; cool completely.

4 Add enough water to Royal Icing, 1 teaspoon at a time, just until icing is thin enough to flow over cookies. Tint frosting as desired. Pipe thinned Royal Icing along edges of cookie. Pipe more icing onto center of cookie; using a small metal spatula or a knife, spread frosting to outlines. If desired, pipe contrasting color frosting onto wet icing; immediately draw a toothpick through lines of icing to swirl colors. Let dry.

*tip: For other decorating options, sprinkle wet frosting with sanding sugar or decorate with small candies. Or let Royal Icing dry completely then brush with powdered metallic (luster dust) colors.

nutrition facts per cookie: 124 cal., 4 g total fat (2 g sat. fat), 14 mg chol., 63 mg sodium, 22 g carb., 0 g fiber, 1 g pro.

chocolate-peppermint cookies: Prepare as directed, except place 2 ounces chopped unsweetened chocolate in a small microwave-safe bowl. Microwave on high for 30 to 60 seconds or until melted, stirring once. Cool for 5 minutes. In Step 1, beat chocolate into the butter before adding sugar. Add ½ teaspoon peppermint extract with the vanilla. Continue as directed, except bake until edges are firm.

nutrition facts per cookie: 132 cal, 4 g total fat (3 g sat. fat), 14 mg chol., 63 mg sodium, 23 g carb., 0 g fiber, 1 g pro.

Call on a cookie press to shape the delicate wreaths.

cinnamon-spiced wreaths

prep: 40 minutes **bake:** 7 minutes at 375°F per batch
makes: 72 cookies

1½ cups butter, softened
1 cup granulated sugar
1½ teaspoons ground cinnamon
1 teaspoon baking powder
¼ teaspoon salt
1 egg
2 tablespoons milk
1 teaspoon vanilla
3 cups all-purpose flour
Sliced almonds
3 tablespoons granulated sugar
1½ teaspoons ground cinnamon
Canned frosting
Red and/or green miniature candy-coated semisweet chocolate pieces

1 Preheat oven to 375°F. In a large mixing bowl beat butter with an electric mixer on medium to high speed for 30 seconds. Add the 1 cup sugar, 1½ teaspoons cinnamon, the baking powder, and salt. Beat until combined, scraping sides of bowl occasionally. Beat in egg, milk, and vanilla until combined. Beat in as much of the flour as you can with the mixer. Using a wooden spoon, stir in any remaining flour.

2 Pack unchilled dough into a cookie press fitted with a circle plate. Force dough through cookie press into 2-inch circles on an ungreased cookie sheets, spacing 2 inches apart. Arrange sliced almonds on dough circles to resemble bows. In a small bowl stir together the 3 tablespoons sugar and 1½ teaspoons cinnamon. Sprinkle some of the sugar mixture on wreaths .

3 Bake for 7 to 8 minutes or until lightly browned. Transfer cookies to a wire rack set over waxed paper. Immediately sprinkle warm cookies with remaining sugar mixture. Let cool. Use a small amount of canned frosting to add a candy-coated chocolate piece to the center of each almond bow.

nutrition facts per cookie: 75 cal., 5 g total fat (3 g sat. fat), 13 mg chol., 48 mg sodium, 8 g carb., 0 g fiber, 1 g pro.

The fresh rosemary garnish will remind you of pine trees.

rosemary-almond cookies

prep: 1 hour **chill:** 4 hours **bake:** 8 minutes at 350°F per batch
makes: 36 cookies

1½ cups granulated
    sugar
¾ cup slivered almonds
3 tablespoons fresh
    rosemary leaves
1 cup butter, softened
½ teaspoon baking
    powder
½ teaspoon salt
2 eggs
¼ cup milk
2 teaspoons vanilla
    bean paste or
    vanilla
½ teaspoon almond
    extract
3 cups all-purpose flour
    Very small fresh
    rosemary sprigs
    (optional)
1 recipe Almond Glaze

1 In a small food processor or blender combine ½ cup of the sugar, the almonds, and the 3 tablespoons rosemary leaves. Cover and process or blend with on/off pulses until nuts are finely ground (but not oily) and rosemary is pulverized.

2 In a large mixing bowl beat butter with an electric mixer on medium to high speed for 30 seconds. Add the remaining 1 cup sugar, the baking powder, and salt. Beat until combined, scraping sides of bowl occasionally. Beat in eggs, milk, vanilla bean paste, and almond extract until combined. Beat in the ground almond mixture and as much of the flour as you can with the mixer. Using a wooden spoon, stir in any remaining flour. Divide dough in half. Cover and chill for 4 hours or until dough is easy to handle (dough will still be a little soft).

3 Preheat oven to 350°F. On a well-floured surface, roll one portion of dough at a time to ¼-inch thickness. Using a 3- to 4-inch tree-shape or round scalloped-edge cookie cutter, cut out dough. Place cutouts 1 inch apart on an ungreased cookie sheet. If desired, press very small rosemary sprigs onto cutouts.

4 Bake for 8 to 10 minutes or just until edges are light brown. Transfer cookies to a wire rack; cool. Using a pastry brush, brush a thin layer of Almond Glaze over each cookie.

nutrition facts per cookie: 148 cal., 7 g total fat (3 g sat. fat), 24 mg chol., 90 mg sodium, 20 g carb., 1 g fiber, 2 g pro.

almond glaze: In a small bowl stir together 1 cup powdered sugar, 2 tablespoons milk, and ½ teaspoon almond extract. Add additional milk, if necessary, to make a thin glaze.

Double stack the cutouts with fudge filling for an intense chocolate cookie.

dark chocolate stars

prep: 30 minutes **chill:** 1 hour **bake:** 7 minutes at 375°F per batch
makes: 42 cookies

1 cup butter, softened
1½ cups unsweetened cocoa powder
1¼ cups granulated sugar
4 ounces dark chocolate, melted and cooled
½ teaspoon baking powder
½ teaspoon salt
2 eggs
1 tablespoon milk
1½ teaspoons vanilla
1½ cups all-purpose flour
1 recipe Fudge Filling or 1 cup hot fudge- or chocolate-flavor ice cream topping
3 ounces dark chocolate, melted (optional)
Unsweetened cocoa powder (optional)

1 In a large mixing bowl beat butter with an electric mixer on medium to high speed for 30 seconds. Add the 1½ cups cocoa powder, the sugar, the 4 ounces melted chocolate, baking powder, and salt. Beat until combined, scraping sides of bowl occasionally. Beat in eggs, milk, and vanilla until combined. Beat in as much of the flour as you can with the mixer. Using a wooden spoon, stir in any remaining flour. Divide dough in half. Cover and chill about 1 hour or until dough is easy to handle.

2 Preheat oven to 375°F. On a lightly floured surface,* roll one portion of the dough at a time to ⅛-inch thickness. Using a 2½- to 3-inch star-shape cookie cutter, cut out dough. Using a 1-inch star-shape cookie cutter, cut and remove a star from the center of half the cookies.

3 Place large and small cutouts 2 inches apart on an ungreased cookie sheet. Bake for 7 to 8 minutes or until edges are firm. Transfer to a wire rack; cool.

4 Spread Fudge Filling on bottoms of the large cookies without cutout centers. Top with the large cookies with cutout centers, bottom sides down. Spread Fudge Filling on bottoms of half the small cookies. Top with the remaining small cookies, bottom sides down. If desired, drizzle or spread cookies with 3 ounces melted chocolate and sprinkle with cocoa powder.

*tip: If desired, roll dough on a surface lightly coated with a mixture of flour and unsweetened cocoa powder.

nutrition facts per cookie: 128 cal., 8 g total fat (5 g sat. fat), 23 mg chol., 85 mg sodium, 16 g carb., 2 g fiber, 2 g pro.

fudge filling: In a small saucepan cook and stir ½ cup dark chocolate pieces over low heat until melted. Cool slightly. In a small bowl combine one 3-ounce package cream cheese, softened, and ⅓ cup powdered sugar. Stir in the melted chocolate and ¼ teaspoon vanilla. If necessary, stir in 1 to 2 tablespoons hot water, 1 teaspoon at a time, until filling reaches spreading consistency.

This classic recipe, with its signature anise flavor, is a holiday tradition in the Southwestern United States, especially New Mexico.

biscochitos

prep: 30 minutes **chill:** 1 hour **bake:** 8 minutes at 350°F per batch
makes: 60 cookies

¾ cup granulated sugar
1 tablespoon finely shredded lemon peel
3 cups all-purpose flour
1 teaspoon anise seeds, crushed
1 teaspoon baking powder
½ teaspoon salt
1¼ cups butter-flavor shortening
1 egg
3 tablespoons brandy or milk
1 teaspoon vanilla
2 tablespoons granulated sugar
1 teaspoon ground cinnamon

1 Line a large cookie sheet with parchment paper; set aside. In a food processor or blender combine the ¾ cup sugar and the lemon peel. Cover and pulse with on/off turns until mixture is sandy and fragrant; set aside. In a medium bowl stir together the flour, crushed anise seeds, baking powder, and salt; set aside.

2 In a large mixing bowl beat shortening and sugar-lemon mixture with an electric mixer on medium to high speed until light and fluffy, scraping sides of bowl occasionally. Beat in egg, brandy, and vanilla until combined. Beat in as much of the flour mixture as you can with the mixer. Using a wooden spoon, stir in any remaining flour mixture. Divide dough in half. Cover and chill about 1 hour or until dough is easy to handle.

3 Preheat oven to 350°F. On a lightly floured surface, roll one dough portion at a time to ¼-inch thickness. Using 2½-inch moon and star-shape cookie cutters, cut out dough. Place cutouts 1 inch apart on prepared cookie sheet. In a small bowl combine the 2 tablespoons sugar and the cinnamon; sprinkle over cookies.

4 Bake for 8 to 9 minutes or until bottoms are golden brown. Transfer cookies to a wire rack; cool.

nutrition facts per cookie: 74 cal., 4 g total fat (1 g sat. fat), 3 mg chol., 29 mg sodium, 8 g carb., 0 g fiber, 1 g pro.

Look for the tiny fluted madeleine molds in specialty shops.

gingerbread madeleines

prep: 25 minutes **chill:** 2 hours **bake:** 10 minutes at 375°F per batch
makes: 48 cookies

½   cup butter, softened
½   cup granulated sugar
½   cup packed brown
     sugar
4   eggs
¼   cup molasses
1   cup all-purpose flour
½   cup cake flour
1   teaspoon ground
     ginger
1   teaspoon ground
     cinnamon
½   teaspoon baking
     powder
¼   teaspoon salt
¼   teaspoon baking soda
¼   teaspoon ground
     nutmeg
⅛   teaspoon ground
     cloves
     Powdered sugar

1 In a large mixing bowl beat butter with an electric mixer on medium to high speed for 30 seconds. Gradually add the granulated sugar and brown sugar. Beat until light and fluffy, scraping sides of bowl occasionally. Add eggs, one at a time, beating well after each addition. Beat in the molasses until combined.

2 In a small bowl stir together the all-purpose flour, cake flour, ginger, cinnamon, baking powder, salt, baking soda, nutmeg, and cloves. Sprinkle about half the flour mixture over the butter mixture; fold in until combined. Repeat with the remaining flour mixture. Cover and chill batter for 2 to 4 hours.

3 Preheat oven to 375°F. Grease and flour twenty-four 3-inch madeleine molds. Spoon batter into prepared molds, filling each about half full.*

4 Bake for 10 to 12 minutes or until edges are golden and tops spring back when lightly touched. Cool in molds for 1 minute. Using the point of a knife, loosen each madeleine from the mold; invert mold over a wire rack to release madeleines. Let cool. Dust with powdered sugar before serving.

*tip: Let molds cool completely between baking batches of madeleines. Grease and flour molds for each batch.

nutrition facts per cookie: 61 cal., 2 g total fat (1 g sat. fat), 21 mg chol., 48 mg sodium, 9 g carb., 0 g fiber, 1 g pro.

A cookie press can be a baker's best friend because it shapes dozens of delicate cookies in little time.

vanilla spritz

prep: 25 minutes bake: 8 minutes at 375°F per batch
makes: 84 cookies

1½ cups butter, softened
1 cup granulated sugar
1 teaspoon baking powder
1 egg
1 tablespoon vanilla bean paste
3½ cups all-purpose flour
1 recipe Quick Vanilla Sugar

1 Preheat oven to 375°F. In a large mixing bowl beat butter with an electric mixer on medium to high speed for 30 seconds. Add granulated sugar and baking powder. Beat until combined, scraping sides of bowl occasionally. Beat in egg and vanilla bean paste until combined. Beat in as much of the flour as you can with the mixer. Using a wooden spoon, stir in any remaining flour.

2 Pack unchilled dough into a cookie press fitted with a star plate or other plate. Force dough through the cookie press onto an ungreased cookie sheet. Sprinkle cookies with Quick Vanilla Sugar.

3 Bake about 8 minutes or until edges are firm but not brown. Transfer cookies to a wire rack; cool.

nutrition facts per cookie: 60 cal., 3 g total fat (2 g sat. fat), 11 mg chol., 36 mg sodium, 7 g carb., 0 g fiber, 1 g pro.

quick vanilla sugar: Split 1 vanilla bean in half lengthwise with a small sharp knife (see page 12). Using the tip of the knife, scrape seeds from vanilla bean. Working in batches, in a food processor combine 4 cups granulated sugar and the vanilla seeds. Cover and process until combined. Transfer to a sterilized 1-quart jar; fasten lid. Use immediately or store in a cool dry place indefinitely.

Only paste food coloring will provide intense red color; liquid red coloring tends to tint dough pink.

cherry-almond spritz sandwich cookies

prep: 20 minutes **bake:** 6 minutes at 350°F per batch
makes: 52 sandwich cookies

1   cup granulated sugar
⅓   cup almond paste, crumbled
¾   cup butter, softened
¾   cup shortening
4   egg whites
1   teaspoon vanilla
¼   teaspoon salt
     Red paste food coloring
4   cups all-purpose flour
     Sanding sugar
1   recipe Cherry-Almond Filling

1 Preheat oven to 350°F. In a large mixing bowl beat granulated sugar and almond paste with an electric mixer on medium to high speed until smooth. Add butter and shortening. Beat until fluffy, scraping sides of bowl occasionally. Beat in egg whites, vanilla, and salt until combined. Gradually beat in enough food coloring until dough reaches desired shade of red. Beat in as much of the flour as you can with the mixer. Using a wooden spoon, stir in any remaining flour.

2 Pack unchilled dough into a cookie press fitted with a ribbon plate. Force dough through the cookie press into 2-inch-long strips onto an ungreased cookie sheet, cutting dough from press with a small knife or metal spatula and spacing strips about 1 inch apart. Sprinkle lightly with sanding sugar.

3 Bake for 6 to 8 minutes or until edges are firm but not brown. Transfer cookies to a wire rack; cool.

4 Spread Cherry-Almond Filling on the bottoms of half of the cookies. Top with the remaining cookies, bottom sides down.

nutrition facts per sandwich cookie: 163 cal., 10 g total fat (5 g sat. fat), 16 mg chol., 71 mg sodium, 18 g carb., 0 g fiber, 1 g pro.

cherry-almond filling: Drain ¼ cup finely chopped maraschino cherries on paper towels. Pat cherries dry; set aside. In a medium mixing bowl beat 1 cup butter, softened, with an electric mixer on medium speed for 30 seconds. Gradually beat in 2 cups powdered sugar until combined. Beat in 1 teaspoon cherry liqueur or cherry juice and ¼ teaspoon almond extract. Gently stir in cherries. Makes 2 cups.

A sprinkle of coarse sea salt intensifies the sweetness of the creamy caramel filling.

salted caramel-ginger macaroons

prep: 45 minutes **stand:** 30 minutes **bake:** 9 minutes at 325°F per batch
makes: 30 cookies

1½ cups finely ground almonds
1¼ cups powdered sugar
1½ teaspoons ground ginger
3 egg whites
½ teaspoon vanilla
Dash salt
¼ cup granulated sugar
6 drops yellow food coloring (optional)
½ of a 14-ounce package vanilla caramels, unwrapped
2 tablespoons whipping cream
Coarse sea salt

1 Line three large cookie sheets with parchment paper; set aside. In a medium bowl stir together ground almonds, powdered sugar, and ginger; set aside.

2 In a large mixing bowl beat egg whites, vanilla, and salt with an electric mixer on medium speed until frothy. Gradually add granulated sugar, about 1 tablespoon at a time, beating on high speed just until soft peaks form (tips curl). Stir in nut mixture and, if desired, food coloring.

3 Spoon mixture into a large decorating bag fitted with a large (about ½-inch) round tip.* Pipe 1½-inch circles 1 inch apart onto the prepared cookie sheets. Let stand for 30 minutes before baking.

4 Preheat oven to 325°F. Bake for 9 to 10 minutes or until set. Cool on cookie sheet on a wire rack. Carefully peel cookies off parchment paper.

5 In a small saucepan cook and stir caramels and whipping cream over low heat until melted and smooth. Spread caramel mixture on bottoms of half the cookies; immediately sprinkle each with a little coarse sea salt. Top with the remaining cookies, bottom sides down.

*tip: If you don't have a decorating bag, spoon egg white mixture into a large resealable plastic bag and snip a ½-inch hole in one corner.

to store: Layer unfilled cookies between sheets of waxed paper in an airtight container; cover. Store in the refrigerator up to 3 days or freeze up to 3 months. To serve, thaw cookies, if frozen. Fill as directed in Step 5.

nutrition facts per cookie: 85 cal., 3 g total fat (1 g sat. fat), 1 mg chol., 40 mg sodium, 12 g carb., 1 g fiber, 2 g pro.

Macaroons

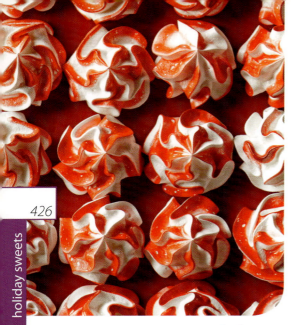

Long baking in a low-temperature oven makes these cookies extra crisp.

peppermint-stripe meringues

prep: 20 minutes **bake:** 1 hour 30 minutes at 200°F per batch
makes: 24 cookies

3 egg whites
¼ teaspoon cream of tartar
¼ teaspoon peppermint extract
⅛ teaspoon salt
¾ cup sugar
   Red paste food coloring

1 Preheat oven to 200°F. Line a cookie sheet with parchment paper; set aside. In a large mixing bowl beat egg whites, cream of tartar, peppermint extract, and salt with an electric mixer on medium speed until soft peaks form (tips curl). Gradually add sugar, about 1 tablespoon at a time, beating on high speed until stiff peaks form (tips stand straight).

2 Using a new small paintbrush, brush stripes of red food coloring on the inside of a decorating bag fitted with a ½-inch open-star tip. Carefully spoon egg white mixture into decorating bag. Pipe 2-inch stars 1 inch apart onto the prepared cookie sheet.

3 Bake about 1½ hours or until meringues appear dry and are firm when lightly touched. Transfer cookies to a wire rack; cool.

nutrition facts per cookie: 27 cal., 0 g total fat, 0 mg chol., 20 mg sodium, 6 g carb., 0 g fiber, 0 g pro.

For another recipe idea using a rosette iron, see page 225.

chocolate rosettes

prep: 20 minutes
makes: 30 cookies

½ cup all-purpose flour
1 tablespoon
     granulated sugar
1 tablespoon
     unsweetened cocoa
     powder
⅛ teaspoon salt
1 egg, lightly beaten
½ cup milk
1 tablespoon coffee
     liqueur or strong
     coffee, cooled
½ teaspoon vanilla
     Vegetable oil for
        deep-fat frying
     Powdered sugar
     Unsweetened cocoa
        powder

1 In a small bowl stir together flour, granulated sugar, the 1 tablespoon cocoa powder, and the salt. Add egg, milk, coffee liqueur, and vanilla. Whisk until batter is smooth. For easy dipping of a rosette iron, pour batter into a shallow 9-inch cake pan or pie plate.

2 In a 3-quart heavy saucepan or deep-fat fryer heat 2 inches of oil to 365°F.* Submerge a rosette iron in hot oil for 10 to 20 seconds. Lift out iron, allowing excess oil to drip back into saucepan (if iron has too much oil on it, the batter won't stick). Quickly dip hot iron into batter to reach three-fourths the way up sides of iron. Return batter-coated rosette iron to hot oil. Fry for 20 to 30 seconds or until cookie is light brown. Lift out iron and tip slightly to allow excess oil to drip back into saucepan. Using the tines of a fork, push rosette off iron onto a wire rack set over paper towels; cool. (If rosette comes off the iron inot the oil, use a slotted spoon to turn the rosette in the hot oil. Remove rosette, allow excess oil to drain, and cool on wire rack set over paper towels.)

3 Repeat with the remaining batter, reheating rosette iron in hot oil each time before dipping it into batter. Stir batter occasionally. Sift powdered sugar over rosettes, then lightly sift additional cocoa powder over powdered sugar.

*tip Use a deep-frying thermometer to accurately maintain the correct temperature of the hot oil.

to store: Layer cookies between sheets of waxed paper in an airtight container; cover. Store at room temperature up to 24 hours, refrigerate up to 3 days, or freeze up to 3 months.

nutrition facts per cookie: 49 cal., 4 g total fat (0 g sat fat), 7 mg chol., 14 mg sodium, 3 g carb., 0 g fiber, 1 g pro.

Raisins and dates keep these oatmeal cookies moist.

cinnamon and fruit cookies

prep: 30 minutes bake: 15 minutes at 350°F per batch
makes: 25 cookies

½   cup butter, softened
½   cup shortening
1½ cups packed brown
     sugar
2   teaspoons ground
     cinnamon
¾   teaspoon baking
     powder
½   teaspoon salt
¼   teaspoon baking soda
2   eggs
1   tablespoon vanilla
1¾ cups all-purpose flour
3   cups regular rolled
     oats
1   cup raisins
½   cup chopped pitted
     dates

1 Preheat oven to 350°F. Line cookie sheets with parchment paper; set aside. In a an extra large mixing bowl beat butter and shortening with an electric mixer on medium to high speed for 30 seconds. Add the brown sugar, cinnamon, baking powder, salt, and baking soda. Beat until combined, scraping sides of bowl occasionally. Beat in eggs and vanilla until combined. Beat in the flour. Stir in the oats, raisins, and dates.

2 Using a 3-tablespoon scoop or a scant ¼-cup measure, drop mounds of dough about 3 inches apart onto the prepared cookie sheets. Bake for 15 to 17 minutes or until edges are set and centers appear dry. Cool on cookie sheets for 3 minutes. Transfer cookies to a wire rack; cool.

tip: To gift these cookies, line the inside of a small burlap gift bag with brown parchment paper. Place desired number of cookies in bag. Tie closed with ribbon.

nutrition facts per cookie: 258 cal., 9 g total fat (4 g sat. fat), 27 mg chol., 107 mg sodium, 40 g carb., 3 g fiber, 5 g pro.

Germany's famous cherry torte inspired these brandy-laced cookies.

kirschtorte cookies (black forest cookies)

prep: 40 minutes **stand:** 15 minutes **bake:** 8 minutes at 350°F per batch
makes: 42 cookies

1½ cups dried tart cherries, halved
3 tablespoons kirsch (cherry brandy) or frozen cherry juice blend concentrate, thawed
½ cup butter, softened
1 cup packed brown sugar
½ teaspoon baking soda
¼ teaspoon salt
1 egg
1 teaspoon vanilla
2 ounces unsweetened chocolate, melted and cooled
1 8-ounce carton sour cream
2 cups all-purpose flour
1 recipe Chocolate Cherry Buttercream

1 In a small saucepan combine cherries and kirsch. Heat just until bubbles begin to form; remove from heat. Cover and let stand for 15 minutes. Preheat oven to 350°F. Line cookie sheets with parchment paper; set aside.

2 In a large mixing bowl beat butter with an electric mixer on medium speed for 30 seconds. Add brown sugar, baking soda, and salt. Beat until combined, scraping sides of bowl occasionally. Beat in egg and vanilla until combined. Add melted chocolate; beat until combined. Beat in sour cream. Beat in as much of the flour as you can with the mixer. Using a wooden spoon, stir in any remaining flour. If necessary, drain cherries. Stir cherries into dough. Drop dough by rounded teaspoons 2 inches apart onto the prepared cookie sheets.

3 Bake for 8 to 10 minutes or until edges are firm. Transfer cookies to a wire rack; cool. Frost cooled cookies with Chocolate Cherry Buttercream.

nutrition facts per cookie: 137 cal., 5 g total fat (3 g sat. fat), 16 mg chol., 68 mg sodium, 22 g carb., 1 g fiber, 1 g pro.

chocolate cherry buttercream: In a large mixing bowl beat ¼ cup butter, softened, with an electric mixer on medium speed until fluffy. Gradually add 1 cup powdered sugar and ⅓ cup unsweetened cocoa powder, beating until combined. Slowly beat in 2 tablespoons kirsch (cherry brandy) or frozen cherry juice blend concentrate, thawed; 1 tablespoon milk; and 1 teaspoon vanilla. Gradually beat in 1 to 1½ cups powdered sugar until frosting reaches spreading consistency.

be merry!

peppermint penguins

prep: 40 minutes bake: 11 minutes at 325°F per batch
makes: 14 cookies

1   cup butter, softened
½   cup granulated sugar
1   tablespoon milk
1   teaspoon peppermint
      extract
¼   teaspoon salt
2¼ cups all-purpose flour
      Orange and black paste
        food colorings
      White decorating icing*

1 Preheat oven to 325°F. Line a cookie sheet with parchment paper; set aside. In a large mixing bowl beat butter with an electric mixer on medium to high speed for 30 seconds. Add sugar, milk, peppermint extract, and salt. Beat until combined, scraping sides of bowl occasionally. Beat in as much of the flour as you can with the mixer. Using a wooden spoon, stir in any remaining flour.

2 Remove ¾ cup of the dough; set aside. Remove ⅓ cup of the dough and tint with orange food coloring; set aside. Tint remaining dough with black food coloring.

3 For each penguin, shape black dough into one 1¼-inch ball and two ¼-inch balls. Shape plain dough into one ¾-inch ball. Shape orange dough into two ¼-inch balls and one ⅛-inch ball. On the prepared cookie sheet, flatten the 1¼-inch black ball into a ¼-inch-thick oval to make the body. For white tummy, flatten the ¾-inch plain ball into a ¼-inch-thick oval. Place the tummy on the body so the bottoms of the ovals align. For wings, flatten the two ¼-inch black balls to make teardrop shapes. Position the wings, rounded sides up, on each side of the body above tummy. For feet, shape the two ¼-inch orange balls into squares. Using the handle of a spoon, make small indentations in one side of squares for webbed toes. Attach feet to the bottom of body. For beak, shape the ⅛-inch orange ball into a triangle and position on body.

4 Bake for 11 to 13 minutes or until edges are set. Cool on cookie sheet for 2 minutes. Carefully transfer to a wire rack; cool. Make eyes with dots of white icing, adding dots of black food coloring for pupils. Let stand until set.

*tip: Use purchased decorating icing, or in a small bowl stir together ½ cup powdered sugar and 1 to 3 teaspoons of water to reach piping consistency.

nutrition facts per cookie: 240 cal., 13 g total fat (8 g sat. fat), 35 mg chol., 159 mg sodium, 28 g carb., 1 g fiber, 2 g pro.

holiday sweets

Like a sweet pretzel, kringla is a Norwegian specialty.

eggnog kringla

prep: 45 minutes **chill:** 1 hour **bake:** 5 minutes at 425°F per batch
makes: 40 cookies

½ cup butter, softened
¾ cup granulated sugar
1 teaspoon baking powder
1 teaspoon baking soda
1 teaspoon grated whole nutmeg or ½ teaspoon ground nutmeg
¼ teaspoon salt
¼ teaspoon ground cardamom (optional)
1 egg
½ teaspoon vanilla
½ teaspoon rum extract
3 cups all-purpose flour
¾ cup dairy eggnog
1 recipe Eggnog Icing
Grated whole nutmeg or ground nutmeg (optional)

1 In a large mixing bowl beat butter with an electric mixer on medium to high speed for 30 seconds. Add sugar, baking powder, baking soda, the 1 teaspoon grated nutmeg, the salt, and, if desired, cardamom. Beat until combined, scraping sides of bowl occasionally. Beat in egg, vanilla, and rum extract until combined. Alternately add flour and eggnog to butter mixture, beating after each addition until combined. Divide dough in half. Cover and chill for 1 to 2 hours or until dough is easy to handle.

2 Preheat oven to 425°F. On a well-floured surface, roll one dough portion at a time into a 10×5-inch rectangle. Using a sharp knife, cut each rectangle crosswise into twenty 5×½-inch strips. Roll each strip into a 10-inch rope. Shape each cookie by crossing one end over the other to form a circle, overlapping about 1½ inches from each end. Take one end of dough in each hand and twist once at the point where the dough overlaps. Carefully lift each end across to the edge of the circle opposite it. Place cookies 1 inch apart on an ungreased cookie sheet.

3 Bake about 5 minutes or until tops are light brown. Transfer to a wire rack; cool. Drizzle cookies with Eggnog Icing. If desired, sprinkle with additional nutmeg.

eggnog icing: In a medium bowl stir together 3 cups powdered sugar and ½ teaspoon vanilla. Stir in 3 to 4 tablespoons dairy eggnog or milk for icing to reach spreading consistency.

to store: Layer cookies between sheets of waxed paper in an airtight container; cover. Store in the refrigerator up to 3 days or freeze up to 3 months.

nutrition facts per cookie: 112 cal., 3 g total fat (2 g sat. fat), 14 mg chol., 84 mg sodium, 20 g carb., 0 g fiber, 1 g pro.

See the photo on page 413 for decorating inspiration.

chocolaty melting snowmen

prep: 50 minutes **bake:** 9 minutes at 350°F per batch
makes: 20 cookies

½ cup shortening
½ cup peanut butter
½ cup granulated sugar
½ cup packed brown
    sugar
1 teaspoon baking
    powder
¼ teaspoon salt
⅛ teaspoon baking soda
1 egg
3 tablespoons milk
½ teaspoon vanilla
¼ cup unsweetened
    cocoa powder
1½ cups all-purpose flour
1 pound vanilla-flavor
    candy coating,
    coarsely chopped
20 bite-size chocolate-
    covered peanut butter
    cups, unwrapped
    Brown and orange
    sprinkles or other
    candies and/or tinted
    frosting

1 Preheat oven to 350°F. In a large mixing bowl beat shortening and peanut butter with an electric mixer on medium to high speed for 30 seconds. Add the granulated sugar, brown sugar, baking powder, salt, and baking soda. Beat until combined, scraping sides of bowl occasionally. Beat in egg, milk, and vanilla. Beat in the cocoa powder and as much of the flour as you can with the mixer. Using a wooden spoon, stir in any remaining flour.

2 Shape dough into twenty 1¾-inch balls. Place balls 2 inches apart on ungreased cookie sheets.

3 Bake for 9 to 11 minutes or just until edges are firm. Cool on cookie sheet for 2 minutes. Transfer cookies to a wire rack; cool.

4 Line a baking sheet with waxed paper. Place cooled cookies on prepared baking sheet. Place candy coating in a medium microwave-safe bowl. Microwave on 50 percent power (medium) for 2½ to 3 minutes or until melted and smooth, stirring every 30 seconds. Spoon melted coating over each cookie to cover. While coating is still tacky, add a peanut butter cup for a top hat and decorate with sprinkles or other candies to resemble snowman faces. (If using frosting to make snowman faces, add it when the candy coating is dry.) Let stand until set.

nutrition facts per cookie: 315 cal., 17 g total fat (9 g sat. fat), 10 mg chol., 101 mg sodium, 38 g carb., 1 g fiber, 3 g pro.

make-ahead tip: Dough may be shaped into balls and then frozen until solid on parchment- or foil-lined cookie sheets. When frozen, transfer balls to an airtight container; cover. Store in the freezer. When ready to bake, arrange frozen balls on cookie sheets and bake as directed for 12 to 14 minutes.

Rolling the dough balls in spiced sugar before baking adds an extra dose of festive cinnamon.

cinnamon-coffee cookies

prep: 35 minutes **chill:** 1 hour **bake:** 10 minutes at 325°F per batch
makes: 36 cookies

2   teaspoons instant coffee crystals
1   tablespoon hot water
½   cup butter, softened
½   cup shortening
¾   cup granulated sugar
¾   cup packed brown sugar
2   teaspoons ground cinnamon
1   teaspoon baking powder
½   teaspoon ground nutmeg
¼   teaspoon baking soda
¼   teaspoon salt
¼   teaspoon ground cloves
2   eggs
1   teaspoon vanilla
2¼ cups all-purpose flour
¼   cup granulated sugar
1   teaspoon ground cinnamon

1 In a small bowl stir coffee crystals into the hot water until dissolved; set aside.

2 In a large mixing bowl beat butter and shortening with an electric mixer on medium to high speed for 30 seconds. Add the ¾ cup granulated sugar, brown sugar, the 2 teaspoons cinnamon, baking powder, nutmeg, baking soda, salt, and cloves. Beat until combined, scraping sides of bowl occasionally. Beat in eggs, vanilla, and coffee mixture until combined. Beat in flour on low speed until combined. Cover and chill for 1 to 2 hours or until dough is easy to handle.

3 Preheat oven to 325°F. Lightly grease a cookie sheet or line the cookie sheet with parchment paper; set aside.

4 In a small bowl combine the ¼ cup granulated sugar and the 1 teaspoon cinnamon. For each cookie, shape 1 tablespoon of the dough into a ball. Roll ball in sugar mixture to coat. Place balls 2 inches apart on the prepared cookie sheet.

5 Bake for 10 to 12 minutes or until edges are set. Cool cookies on cookie sheet for 2 minutes. Transfer to a wire rack; cool.

to store: Layer cookies between sheets of waxed paper in an airtight container; cover. Store at room temperature up to 3 days or freeze up to 3 months.

nutrition facts per cookie: 121 cal., 6 g total fat (2 g sat. fat), 17 mg chol., 67 mg sodium, 16 g carb., 0 g fiber, 1 g pro.

cinnamon ice cream sandwiches: Prepare and bake cookies as directed. Spread cinnamon ice cream on bottoms of half the cookies, using 3 tablespoons ice cream for each cookie. Top with the remaining cookies, bottom sides down. Press together lightly. Wrap each sandwich cookie in plastic wrap. Freeze for at least 2 hours or until firm. Store in the freezer up to 1 month. To serve, let stand at room temperature for 5 minutes. Makes about 18 sandwich cookies.

nutrition facts per sandwich: 292 cal., 14 g total fat (8 g sat. fat), 48 mg chol, 150 mg sodium, 39 g carb, 1 g fiber, 3 g pro.

Lemon cake mix plus fresh lemon-infused olive oil. and lemon extract provide intense citrus taste.

lovely lemon crinkles

prep: 25 minutes **bake:** 7 minutes at 375°F per batch
makes: 36 cookies

1	15.25-ounce package lemon cake mix (for moist cake)
2	eggs
⅓	cup all-purpose flour
⅓	cup lemon-infused olive oil
2	tablespoons finely shredded lemon peel
2	tablespoons lemon juice
1	teaspoon lemon extract
½	teaspoon vanilla
	Granulated sugar
	Powdered sugar

1 Preheat oven to 375°F. Line a cookie sheet with parchment paper; set aside. In a large bowl stir together cake mix, eggs, flour, oil, lemon peel, lemon juice, lemon extract, and vanilla until combined. (Dough will be soft.)

2 Place granulated sugar in one bowl and powdered sugar in another bowl. For each cookie, drop 1 tablespoon of the dough into the granulated sugar; toss to coat with sugar (dough will have a soft ball shape). Toss dough in the powdered sugar to coat. Place balls 2 inches apart on the prepared cookie sheet.

3 Bake for 7 to 9 minutes or until edges are light brown. Cool on cookie sheet for 2 minutes. Transfer cookies to a wire rack; cool.

to store: Layer cookies between sheets of waxed paper in an airtight container; cover. Store at room temperature up to 3 days or freeze up to 3 months.

nutrition facts per cookie: 86 cal., 3 g total fat (1 g sat. fat), 10 mg chol., 82 mg sodium, 14 g carb., 0 g fiber, 1 g pro.

These charming Santa-shape sweets are almost too cute to eat—almost!

roly-poly santas

prep: 50 minutes bake: 12 minutes at 325°F per batch
makes: 12 cookies

1   cup butter, softened
½   cup sugar
1   tablespoon milk
1   teaspoon vanilla
2¼ cups all-purpose flour
    Red paste food
        coloring
    Miniature semisweet
        chocolate pieces
1   recipe Snow Frosting
    Red cinnamon
        candies

snow frosting: In a small mixing bowl beat ½ cup shortening and ½ teaspoon vanilla with an electric mixer on medium speed for 30 seconds. Gradually beat in 1⅓ cups powdered sugar and 1 tablespoon milk until smooth. Gradually beat in an additional 1 cup powdered sugar and enough milk (3 to 4 teaspoons) to make frosting piping consistency.

1 Preheat oven to 325°F. In a large mixing bowl beat butter with an electric mixer on medium to high speed for 30 seconds. Beat in sugar until combined, scraping sides of bowl occasionally. Beat in milk and vanilla until combined. Beat in as much of the flour as you can with the mixer. Using a wooden spoon, stir in any remaining flour.

2 Remove 1 cup of the dough. Tint the remaining dough with red food coloring.

3 For each cookie, shape red dough into one 1-inch ball and five ½-inch balls, Shape plain dough into one ¾-inch ball and four ¼-inch balls. Place the red 1-inch ball on an ungreased cookie sheet; flatten until ½ inch thick. Attach the plain ¾-inch ball for head; flatten until ½ inch thick. Attach four of the red ½-inch balls for arms and legs; attach the plain ¼-inch balls for hands and feet. Shape and attach the remaining red ½-inch ball for a hat. Place cookies 2 inches apart. Add chocolate pieces for eyes and buttons.

4 Bake for 12 to 15 minutes or until edges are lightly browned. Cool on cookie sheet for 2 minutes. Carefully transfer to a wire rack; cool.

5 Decorate cookies with Snow Frosting as desired. Attach cinnamon candies with small dabs of frosting for noses. Let stand until frosting is set.

to store: Place cookies (do not decorate if freezing) in layers separated by waxed paper in an airtight container; cover. Store at room temperature up to 3 days or freeze up to 3 months. If frozen, thaw before decorating.

nutrition facts per cookie: 431 cal., 24 g total fat (12 g sat. fat), 41 mg chol., 138 mg sodium, 52 g carb., 1 g fiber, 3 g pro.

To crush the mint candies, place them a resealable plastic bag and use a rolling pin to pulverize.

peppermint snowballs

prep: 20 minutes **bake:** 9 minutes at 350°F per batch
makes: 36 cookies

1   cup butter, softened
⅔   cup powdered sugar
½   cup crushed
       peppermint candies
       (20)
1   teaspoon vanilla
½   teaspoon salt
2   cups all-purpose flour
1   cup powdered sugar
       Very finely crushed
       peppermint candies
       (optional)

1 Preheat oven to 350°F. Line cookie sheets with parchment paper; set aside. In a large mixing bowl beat butter with an electric mixer on medium to high speed for 30 seconds. Add the ⅔ cup powdered sugar, ½ cup crushed peppermint candies, the vanilla, and salt. Beat until combined, scraping sides of bowl occasionally. Beat in as much of the flour as you can with the mixer. Using a wooden spoon, stir in any remaining flour.

2 Shape dough into 1-inch balls. Place balls 2 inches apart on the prepared cookie sheets. Bake for 9 to 11 minutes or until cookies are set and bottoms are light golden. Cool on cookie sheets for 1 minute. Transfer to a wire rack, cool for 5 minutes. Roll warm cookies in the 1 cup powdered sugar. Cool cookies completely on a wire rack. Roll cooled cookies in powdered sugar again. If desired, dust cookies lightly with very finely crushed peppermint candies.

nutrition facts per cookie: 103 cal., 5 g total fat (3 g sat. fat), 14 mg chol., 79 mg sodium, 14 g carb., 0 g fiber, 1 g pro.

make-ahead directions: Dough may be shaped into balls, then frozen on parchment- or foil-lined cookie sheets. Transfer frozen balls to an airtight container; cover. Freeze for up to 3 months. When ready to bake, arrange frozen balls on cookie sheets. Let stand at room temperature while the oven preheats. Bake for 10 to 12 minutes or until set and light golden on the bottom.

438

Each cookie comes out of the oven with a unique red-and-white design.

candy cane sandwich cookies

prep: 45 minutes **chill:** 1 hour **bake:** 8 minutes at 375°F per batch
makes: 20 sandwich cookies

⅔	cup butter, softened
½	cup granulated sugar
¼	teaspoon salt
1	egg
1	teaspoon vanilla
1½	cups all-purpose flour
	Red paste food coloring
1	recipe Peppermint Filling
	Granulated sugar

1 In a large mixing bowl beat butter with an electric mixer on medium to high speed for 30 seconds. Add the ½ cup sugar and the salt. Beat until combined, scraping sides of bowl occasionally. Beat in egg and vanilla until combined. Beat in as much of the flour as you can with the mixer. Using a wooden spoon, stir in any remaining flour.

2 Divide dough in half. Leave one half plain. Tint the remaining half with desired amount of food coloring. Cover each portion and chill about 1 hour or until dough is easy to handle.

3 Preheat oven to 375°F. Shape each portion of dough into ½-inch balls. Roll together one plain ball and one red ball. Place on an ungreased cookie sheet. Press with the bottom of a sugared glass to about ¼-inch thickness. Place balls 2 inches apart on cookie sheet. Bake for 8 to 10 minutes or until edges are light brown. Transfer cookies to wire racks; cool.

4 Spread Peppermint Filling on bottoms of half the cookies, using 2 teaspoons for each cookie. Top with the remaining cookies, bottom sides down.

nutrition facts per sandwich cookie: 187 cal., 10 g total fat (6 g sat. fat), 34 mg chol., 115 mg sodium, 24 g carb., 0 g fiber, 1 g pro.

peppermint filling: In a medium mixing bowl beat ⅓ cup butter, softened, with an electric mixer on medium to high speed for 30 seconds. Beat in ¼ teaspoon peppermint extract. Gradually beat in 2 cups powdered sugar. Beat in enough milk (2 to 3 tablespoons) to make a filling of piping consistency.

Fun to make without cookie cutters!

lime twist trees

prep: 1 hour chill: 1 hour bake: 10 minutes at 350°F per batch
makes: 24 cookies

½   cup butter, softened
1   3-ounce package
      cream cheese,
      softened
1½ cups powdered sugar
¼   teaspoon baking
      powder
¼   teaspoon salt
1   egg
1   teaspoon vanilla
2¼ cups all-purpose flour
2   teaspoons finely
      shredded lime peel
      Green and yellow
      liquid food coloring
1   recipe Lime Glaze
      Star sprinkles
      (optional)

1 In a large mixing bowl beat butter and cream cheese with an electric mixer on medium to high speed for 30 seconds. Add powdered sugar, baking powder, and salt. Beat until combined, scraping sides of bowl occasionally. Beat in egg and vanilla until combined. Beat in as much of the flour as you can with the mixer. Using a wooden spoon, stir in lime peel, 4 to 5 drops each green and yellow food coloring, and any remaining flour. Cover and chill dough about 1 hour or until easy to handle.

2 Preheat oven to 350°F. Place a rounded tablespoon of dough on a lightly floured surface. Roll dough into a 10- to 12-inch-long rope. On an ungreased cookie sheet, bend rope back and forth into a tree shape, pinching the end at the top into a star shape. Roll a ½-inch ball of dough and gently press against bottom of tree for a trunk. Space trees about 2 inches apart.

3 Bake for 10 to 12 minutes or until edges are light brown. Transfer cookies to a wire rack. While cookies are still warm, brush with Lime Glaze. If desired, decorate trees with star sprinkles. Cool completely on wire rack.

nutrition facts per cookie: 155 cal., 6 g total fat (4 g sat. fat), 24 mg chol., 73 mg sodium, 24 g carb., 0 g fiber, 2 g pro.

lime glaze: In a small bowl stir together 1½ cups powdered sugar, ½ teaspoon finely shredded lime peel, 2 tablespoons lime juice, and 1 tablespoon butter, melted. Add enough water (1 to 3 teaspoons) to make a thin glaze.

mint chocolate trees

prep: 40 minutes **chill:** 2 hours **freeze:** 1 hour **bake:** 6 minutes at 375°F per batch
makes: 72 cookies

¾ cup butter, softened
1 cup granulated sugar
½ teaspoon baking powder
¼ teaspoon salt
1 egg
1 teaspoon mint extract
2 cups all-purpose flour
2 ounces semisweet chocolate, melted
Green paste food coloring
1 cup pecan halves

1 In a large mixing bowl beat butter with an electric mixer on medium speed for 30 seconds. Add the sugar, baking powder, and salt. Beat until combined, scraping sides of bowl occasionally. Beat in egg and mint extract until combined. Beat in as much of the flour as you can with the mixer. Stir in any remaining flour. Divide dough in half. Stir melted chocolate into half the dough. Knead the green food coloring into the remaining half. Cover and chill dough about 1 hour or until easy to handle.

2 Divide the green dough in half. Shape each dough half into a 10-inch log. Flatten the sides of the logs so they have three flat sides and are triangular. Wrap each triangular log in plastic wrap. Chill about 1 hour or until firm.

3 Divide the chocolate dough in half. Between two sheets of waxed paper, roll half the dough into a 10×4-inch rectangle. Remove top sheet of waxed paper. Place one chilled green log in the center of the chocolate rectangle. Using the waxed paper, bring the sides of the chocolate rectangle up over the green log to enclose; press sides to seal. Repeat with the remaining chocolate dough and green log. Wrap logs in plastic wrap and freeze at least 1 hour or overnight.

4 Preheat oven to 375°F. Line a cookie sheet with parchment paper. Using a sharp knife, cut logs into ¼-inch slices. If necessary, rotate log every few slices to keep its triangular shape. Place slices 2 inches apart on the prepared cookie sheet. Press a pecan half into the bottom edge of each triangle slice as a tree trunk.

5 Bake for 6 to 8 minutes or until tops are set. Transfer to a wire rack; cool.

nutrition facts per cookie: 56 cal., 3 g total fat (1 g sat. fat), 8 mg chol., 25 mg sodium, 6 g carb., 0 g fiber, 1 g pro.

The French liqueur, Chambord, intensifies the berry flavor.

sandwich cookie pops

prep: 1 hour **chill:** 4 hours **bake:** 6 minutes at 375°F per batch
makes: 50 cookies

1¼   cups all-purpose flour
1   teaspoon cream of tartar
½   teaspoon baking soda
½   teaspoon salt
½   cup butter, softened
¾   cup sugar
1   tablespoon Chambord or milk
1   teaspoon vanilla
1   recipe Raspberry Buttercream
1½   pounds white baking chocolate with cocoa butter or vanilla-flavor candy coating, chopped
White nonpareils (optional)

raspberry buttercream:
In a large mixing bowl beat ½ cup butter, softened, for 30 seconds. Beat in 1 cup powdered sugar, 1 tablespoon Chambord or milk, and 2 tablespoons seedless raspberry preserves. Beat in 1½ cups additional powdered sugar to make buttercream spreading consistency.

1 In a medium bowl stir together flour, cream of tartar, baking soda, and salt; set aside.

2 In a large mixing bowl beat butter with an electric mixer on medium to high speed for 30 seconds. Add sugar. Beat until creamy and smooth, scraping sides of bowl occasionally. Beat in Chambord and vanilla. Beat in flour mixture until combined. If necessary, cover and chill about 30 minutes or until dough is easy to handle.

3 Divide dough in half. Shape each half into a 12-inch log. Wrap each log in plastic wrap and chill for 4 to 24 hours.

4 Preheat oven to 375°F. Cut rolls into ⅛-inch slices. Place 50 lollipop sticks 1½ inches apart on ungreased cookie sheets. Place a dough slice on the top portion of each stick. Bake for 6 to 7 minutes or until edges are light brown. Bake the remaining cookie slices without sticks. Cool on cookie sheets for 1 minute. Transfer to wire racks; cool completely.

5 Spread a slightly rounded teaspoon of the Raspberry Buttercream on bottoms of cookies with sticks. Top with the remaining cookies, bottom sides down.

6 Place white chocolate in a microwave-safe bowl. Microwave on 100 percent power (high) about 3 minutes or just until melted, stirring after every minute; cool slightly. Holding each pop by the stick, carefully dip and spoon melted chocolate over sandwich cookie to coat, letting excess chocolate drip off. If desired, gently swirl chocolate with back of spoon. Place on waxed paper or parchment paper. If desired, sprinkle with nonpareils. Let stand until chocolate is set.

to store: Layer cookie pops between sheets of waxed paper in an airtight container; cover. Store in the refrigerator up to 1 week or freeze up to 1 month. Let stand at room temperature before serving.

nutrition facts per cookie: 163 cal., 8 g total fat (5 g sat. fat), 12 mg chol., 77 mg sodium, 20 g carb., 0 g fiber, 1 g pro.

For gift giving, nestle cookies in a box lined with shredded brown craft paper, as shown in the photo below.

mint chocolate chip-vanilla wreaths

prep: 45 minutes **chill:** 2 hours **bake:** 10 minutes at 375°F per batch
makes: 16 cookies

1   cup butter, softened
½   cup granulated sugar
⅛   teaspoon salt
2   cups all-purpose flour
⅓   cup miniature
       semisweet
       chocolate pieces
½   teaspoon mint extract
       Green food coloring
1   teaspoon vanilla
1   cup semisweet
       chocolate pieces
       (optional)
¼   teaspoon shortening
       (optional)

1 In a medium mixing bowl beat butter with an electric mixer on medium to high speed for 30 seconds. Add sugar and salt. Beat until combined, scraping sides of bowl occasionally. Beat in as much of the flour as you can with the mixer. Using a wooden spoon, stir in any remaining flour. Divide the dough in half.

2 Add the ⅓ cup miniature semisweet chocolate pieces, mint extract, and a few drops green food coloring to one dough portion; stir until combined. Add the vanilla to the remaining dough portion; stir until combined.

3 Divide each portion in half. Shape each dough half into an 8-inch log. Wrap logs in plastic wrap. Chill logs about 2 hours or until very firm.

4 Preheat oven to 375°F. Line cookie sheets with parchment paper. Using a serrated knife, cut logs crosswise into ¼-inch slices. For each wreath, alternate four slices of green dough and four slices white dough to form a circle, slightly overlapping slices. Leave a 1-inch circle in the middle. Space cookies 2 inches apart on the prepared cookie sheets.

5 Bake for 10 to 12 minutes or until edges are firm but not brown. Cool on cookie sheet for 5 minutes. Transfer to a wire rack; cool.

6 If desired, in a small saucepan melt 1 cup semisweet chocolate and the shortening over low heat. Transfer chocolate to a small resealable plastic bag. Snip off a small corner of the bag. Pipe a bow onto each cookie wreath. Let stand until set.

nutrition facts per cookie: 176 cal., 11 g total fat (7 g sat. fat), 20 mg chol., 81 mg sodium, 19 g carb., 1 g fiber, 2 g pro.

These crunchy cookies are made for dipping in coffee or tea.

cranberry-pistachio biscotti

prep: 40 minutes **chill:** 1 hour **bake:** 30 minutes + 20 minutes at 325°F **cool:** 1 hour
makes: 60 biscotti

4¾ cups all-purpose flour
1 tablespoon baking powder
¼ teaspoon salt
1¼ cups butter, softened
1¼ cups granulated sugar
3 eggs
½ cup orange juice
2 teaspoons vanilla
1½ cups coarsely chopped pistachio nuts
1 cup coarsely chopped dried cranberries
1 egg
2 tablespoons water

1 In a medium bowl stir together the flour, baking powder, and salt; set aside. In a large mixing bowl beat butter with an electric mixer on medium to high speed for 30 seconds. Add sugar. Beat for 3 to 4 minutes or until light and fluffy. Add the 3 eggs, one at a time, beating well after each addition. Alternately beat in the flour mixture and the orange juice and vanilla. Stir in nuts and cranberries. Cover and chill dough about 1 hour or until easy to handle.

2 Preheat oven to 325°F. Line two cookie sheets with parchment paper; set aside. On a lightly floured surface, divide dough into four equal portions. Shape each portion into an 11×2-inch log. Place logs 2 inches apart on the prepared cookie sheets. In a small bowl whisk together the 1 egg and the water until frothy. Brush egg mixture evenly over loaves. Bake for 30 to 35 minutes or until golden and a wooden toothpick inserted near the centers comes out clean. Place cookie sheets on wire racks; cool for 1 hour.

3 Preheat oven to 325°F. Transfer loaves to a cutting board. Using a serrated knife, cut diagonally into ½-inch slices. Place slices, cut sides down, on ungreased cookie sheets. Bake for 10 minutes. Turn slices over; bake about 10 minutes more or until dry and crisp. Transfer to a wire rack; cool.

nutrition facts per biscotti: 116 cal., 6 g total fat (3 g sat. fat), 23 mg chol., 73 mg sodium, 15 g carb., 1 g fiber, 2 g pro.

For extra pizzazz, dip one end of each baked cookie into melted dark chocolate. Let stand on a wire rack until set.

bittersweet chocolate biscotti

prep: 25 minutes **bake:** 20 minutes at 375°F + 15 minutes at 325°F
cool: 45 minutes
makes: 24 biscotti

⅓ cup butter, softened
⅔ cup packed brown
　　sugar
2 teaspoons baking
　　powder
½ teaspoon salt
2 eggs
¼ cup unsweetened
　　cocoa powder
1⅔ cups all-purpose flour
1 cup hazelnuts
　　(filberts), toasted*
　　and chopped
4 ounces bittersweet
　　chocolate, chopped

1 Preheat oven to 375°F. Lightly grease a cookie sheet; set aside. In a large mixing bowl beat butter with an electric mixer on medium speed for 30 seconds. Add brown sugar, baking powder, and salt. Beat until combined, scraping sides of bowl occasionally. Beat in eggs and cocoa powder. Beat in as much of the flour as you can with the mixer. Stir in any remaining flour, the hazelnuts, and the 4 ounces bittersweet chocolate.

2 Divide dough in half. Shape each portion into a 9-inch log. Place logs 4 inches apart on the prepared cookie sheet; slightly flatten each to about 2 inches wide.

3 Bake for 20 to 25 minutes or until a wooden toothpick inserted near the centers comes out clean. Cool on cookie sheet for 45 minutes.

4 Preheat oven to 325°F. Using a serrated knife, cut each loaf diagonally into ½-inch slices. Place slices on an ungreased cookie sheet. Bake for 8 minutes. Carefully turn slices over and bake for 7 to 9 minutes more or until biscotti are dry and crisp. Transfer to wire racks; cool for at least 1 hour.

*tip: To toast hazelnuts, preheat oven to 375°F. Spread nuts in a single layer in a shallow baking pan. Bake for 4 to 5 minutes or until nuts are light golden brown, stirring once or twice. Wrap warm nuts in a clean kitchen towel. Rub nuts in towel to remove any loose skins; cool completely. Chop nuts and set aside.

nutrition facts per biscotti: 140 cal., 8 g total fat (3 g sat. fat), 22 mg chol., 120 mg sodium, 17 g carb., 1 g fiber, 3 g pro.

Crush the gingersnaps in a resealable plastic bag using a rolling pin.

orange-ginger baby cheesecakes

prep: 45 minutes **bake:** 20 minutes at 350°F per batch
makes: 16 mini cakes

¾   cup finely crushed gingersnaps
1   tablespoon packed brown sugar
3   tablespoons butter, melted
1   8-ounce package cream cheese, softened
½   cup orange marmalade
1   egg yolk
1   tablespoon all-purpose flour
    Sliced kumquats (optional)

1 Preheat oven to 350°F. For crust, in a small bowl stir together crushed gingersnaps and brown sugar. Stir in melted butter until combined. Press mixture evenly onto the bottoms and up the sides of 16 ungreased 1¾-inch muffin cups. Bake for 5 minutes.

2 Meanwhile, for filling, in a medium mixing bowl beat cream cheese, ¼ cup of the marmalade, the egg yolk, and flour with an electric mixer on medium speed until combined. Spoon filling into crust-lined muffin cups.

3 Bake about 15 minutes or until a knife inserted in the centers comes out clean. Cool completely in muffin cups on a wire rack (centers will dip slightly). Remove from muffin cups. Top each mini cheesecake with ¾ teaspoon of the remaining marmalade. Serve immediately or cover and chill for up to 24 hours. If desired, garnish with kumquats before serving.

nutrition facts per mini cake: 127 cal., 8 g total fat (5 g sat. fat), 34 mg chol., 104 mg sodium, 13 g carb., 0 g fiber, 2 g pro.

make-ahead directions:
Prepare, bake, and cool mini cheesecakes as directed, except do not top with the remaining marmalade. Place in a single layer in an airtight container; cover. Freeze for up to 3 months. To serve, thaw overnight in the refrigerator. Top with the remaining marmalade.

Savor the flavors of the legendary Lady Baltimore Cake—pecans, figs, and a fluffy frosting—in a bite-size portion.

lady baltimore tassies

prep: 30 minutes **bake:** 25 minutes at 325°F per batch **stand:** 10 minutes
makes: 24 tassies

½   cup butter, softened
1   3-ounce package cream cheese, softened
¾   cup all-purpose flour
¼   cup ground pecans or walnuts
¼   cup orange juice
2   tablespoons orange liqueur (such as Grand Marnier) or orange juice
3   tablespoons finely chopped dried Calimyrna (light) figs
2   tablespoons golden raisins, finely chopped
1   egg, lightly beaten
¾   cup packed brown sugar
      Dash salt
⅓   cup chopped pecans or walnuts
1   recipe Meringue Frosting
      Finely chopped pecans or walnuts

1 Preheat oven to 325°F. For pastry, in a small mixing bowl beat butter and cream cheese with an electric mixer on medium speed until combined. Stir in the flour and the ¼ cup ground nuts. If necessary, cover and chill dough for 30 minutes or until easy to handle. Shape dough into 24 balls. Press each ball into the bottoms and up the sides of 24 ungreased 1¾-inch muffin cups.

2 For filling, in a small saucepan combine orange juice, orange liqueur, figs, and raisins. Bring just to boiling; remove from heat. Let stand for 10 minutes to soften figs and raisins. Drain and discard off any liquid. In a small bowl stir together the egg, brown sugar, and salt. Stir in the ⅓ cup chopped nuts and drained figs and raisins. Spoon a heaping teaspoon of filling into each pastry-lined cup.

3 Bake for 25 to 30 minutes or until pastry is golden. Cool tassies in pan on a wire rack for 5 minutes. Loosen tassies from muffin cups by running a knife around edges. Carefully transfer to a wire rack; cool.

4 Just before serving, prepare Meringue Frosting. Spoon frosting into a pastry bag fitted with a ½-inch round tip. Pipe frosting onto tassies. Sprinkle with finely chopped nuts. Serve immediately.

to store: Layer unfrosted tassies between sheets of waxed paper in an airtight container; cover. Store in the refrigerator up to 3 days or freeze up to 3 months. Frost just before serving.

nutrition facts per tassie: 136 cal., 8 g total fat (3 g sat. fat), 22 mg chol., 58 mg sodium, 15 g carb., 1 g fiber, 1 g pro.

meringue frosting: In a small mixing bowl beat ¼ cup granulated sugar, 2 tablespoons water, 1 tablespoon pasteurized liquid egg whites or 1 teaspoon meringue powder, ½ teaspoon vanilla, and ⅛ teaspoon cream of tartar with an electric mixer on high speed for 3 to 5 minutes until stiff peaks form (tips stand straight).

After piping the filling, serve these within an hour or two.

malted milk chocolate tassies

prep: 30 minutes chill: 30 minutes bake: 8 minutes at 375°F per batch
makes: 24 tassies

1   cup all-purpose flour
¼   cup granulated sugar
¼   cup malted milk
        powder
¼   cup unsweetened
        cocoa powder
½   cup butter
1   egg yolk, lightly
        beaten
2   tablespoons cold water
1   recipe Cream Filling
        Chopped malted milk
        balls

1 In a medium bowl stir together flour, sugar, malted milk powder, and cocoa powder. Using a pastry blender, cut in butter until mixture is crumbly. In a small bowl combine egg yolk and the cold water. Gradually stir egg yolk mixture into flour mixture. Gently knead dough just until a ball forms. Cover and chill for 30 to 60 minutes or until dough is easy to handle.

2 Preheat oven to 375°F. Shape dough into 24 balls. Press balls onto the bottoms and up the sides of 24 ungreased 1¾-inch muffin cups. Bake for 8 to 10 minutes or until pastry is firm. If the centers puff during baking, press with the back of a measuring teaspoon while tassies are still warm. Cool in muffin cups on a wire rack for 5 minutes. Remove tassies from muffin cups. Cool completely on wire rack.

3 Spoon Cream Filling into a decorating bag fitted with an open star tip. Pipe filling into tassies (you will have more filling than you need). Sprinkle with chopped malted milk balls.

nutrition facts per tassie: 197 cal., 7 g total fat (4 g sat. fat), 24 mg chol., 76 mg sodium, 34 g carb., 0 g fiber, 1 g pro.

cream filling: In a medium mixing bowl beat ¼ cup butter with an electric mixer on medium to high speed for 30 seconds. Add one 7-ounce jar marshmallow creme and 1 teaspoon vanilla; beat on medium speed until smooth. Beat in 1½ cups powdered sugar and 1 tablespoon milk. Gradually beat in the 2 cups powdered sugar and enough additional milk to reach piping consistency.

Bake the pecan pastry crust before filling.

caramel-pecan pumpkin cheesecake bites

prep: 35 minutes **bake:** 25 minutes at 350°F **cool:** 5 minutes
makes: 24 cheesecake bites

1 cup all-purpose flour
¼ cup ground toasted pecans
2 tablespoons granulated sugar
½ cup butter
1 egg yolk, lightly beaten
1 3-ounce package cream cheese, softened
¼ cup butter, softened
¼ cup canned pumpkin
2 tablespoons packed brown sugar
1 egg
¼ teaspoon pumpkin pie spice
½ cup caramel-flavor ice cream topping
¼ cup chopped toasted pecans

1 Preheat oven to 350°F. Grease twenty-four 1¾-inch muffin cups; set aside.

2 In a medium bowl stir together flour, ground pecans, and granulated sugar. Using a pastry blender, cut in the ½ cup butter until pieces are pea size. Stir in egg yolk until combined. Shape dough into 24 balls. Press balls evenly onto the bottoms and up the sides of the prepared muffin cups. Bake for 10 minutes.

3 Meanwhile, for filling, in a medium mixing bowl beat cream cheese, ¼ cup butter, the pumpkin, and brown sugar with an electric mixer on medium speed until light and fluffy. Beat in egg and pumpkin pie spice until combined, scraping sides of bowl occasionally.

4 Spoon filling into partially baked crusts. Bake about 15 minutes or until filling is set. Cool in muffin cups on a wire rack for 5 minutes. Carefully remove from muffin cups; cool completely on wire rack. Cover and chill.

5 Before serving, in a small bowl stir together caramel topping and chopped pecans. Spoon about 1 teaspoon of the mixture on each cheesecake bite.

to store: Cool as directed. Place cookies in a single layer in an airtight container; cover. Store in the refrigerator up to 2 days or freeze up to 1 month. To serve, thaw cheesecake bites, if frozen. Top with caramel-pecan mixture as directed in Step 5.

nutrition facts per cheesecake bite: 130 cal., 9 g total fat (5 g sat. fat), 35 mg chol., 90 mg sodium, 11 g carb., 0 g fiber, 2 g pro.

A tender, rich macadamia-studded cream cheese-crust is a perfect fit with the sweet-tart lime filling.

key lime pie tassies

prep: 25 minutes **chill:** 30 minutes + 2 hours **bake:** 30 minutes at 325°F per batch
makes: 24 tassies

- ½ cup butter, softened
- 1 3-ounce package cream cheese, softened
- 1 cup all-purpose flour
- ¼ cup finely chopped macadamia nuts
- 2 egg yolks
- ½ of a 14-ounce can (⅔ cup) sweetened condensed milk
- ½ teaspoon finely shredded lime peel
- ¼ cup fresh-squeezed lime juice (5 to 6 Key limes or 2 to 3 Persian limes)
- 1 to 2 drops green food coloring (optional)
- 1 recipe Sweetened Whipped Cream (optional)

1 In a medium mixing bowl beat butter and cream cheese with an electric mixer on medium to high speed until combined. Add flour and macadamia nuts. Beat on low speed just until combined. Cover and chill for 30 to 60 minutes or until dough is easy to handle.

2 Preheat oven to 325°F. Shape dough into 24 balls. Press each ball onto the bottom and up the sides of an ungreased 1¾-inch muffin cups. Bake for 20 to 25 minutes or until edges are golden. Cool slightly in pan on a wire rack.

3 Meanwhile, for filling, in a medium bowl beat egg yolks with a whisk. Gradually whisk in sweetened condensed milk. Add lime peel, lime juice, and, if desired, food coloring. Stir just until combined (mixture will thicken slightly).

4 Spoon about 1 tablespoon of the filling into each pastry cup. Bake about 10 minutes or until centers are set. Cool tassies in muffin cups on a wire rack for 10 minutes. Remove tassies from muffin cups. Cool completely on wire rack. Chill for 2 to 3 hours or until completely chilled. If desired, before serving, top tassies with Sweetened Whipped Cream.

to store: Place tassies in a single layer in an airtight container; cover. Store in the refrigerator up to 2 days.

nutrition facts per tassie: 103 cal., 7 g total fat (4 g sat. fat), 32 mg chol., 55 mg sodium, 8 g carb., 0 g fiber, 2 g pro.

make-ahead directions: Prepare as directed through Step 1. Wrap dough in plastic wrap and freeze for up to 1 month. Thaw dough in the refrigerator for 24 hours. Continue as directed in Step 2.

sweetened whipped cream: In a medium mixing bowl combine ½ cup whipping cream, 1 tablespoon granulated sugar, and ¼ teaspoon vanilla. Beat with an electric mixer on medium speed just until soft peaks form (tips curl).

Softly melted marshmallows on top make for delicious, sticky fun!

butterscotch-marshmallow tassies

prep: 40 minutes **bake:** 20 minutes at 325°F per batch **broil:** 1 minute
makes: 24 tassies

½   cup butter, softened
1   3-ounce package cream cheese, softened
1   cup all-purpose flour
⅔   cup butterscotch-flavor pieces
½   cup miniature semisweet chocolate pieces
¼   cup butter
2   eggs, lightly beaten
2   tablespoons sugar
12 large marshmallows, halved

1 Preheat oven to 325°F. For pastry, in a medium mixing bowl beat the ½ cup butter and cream cheese with an electric mixer on medium speed until smooth. Beat in flour on low speed just until combined. If necessary, cover and chill for 30 to 60 minutes or until pastry is easy to handle.

2 Divide pastry into 24 portions; shape into balls. Press balls onto the bottoms and up the sides of 24 ungreased 1¾-inch muffin cups.

3 For filling, in a small saucepan heat and stir butterscotch pieces, chocolate pieces, and the ¼ cup butter over low heat until melted. Remove from heat. Stir in eggs and sugar. Spoon filling into pastry-lined muffin cups.

4 Bake for 20 to 25 minutes or until pastry is golden and filling is puffed. Cool in muffin cups on a wire rack for 5 minutes (centers will dip slightly). Remove tassies from muffin cups. Cool completely on wire rack.

5 Preheat broiler. Top tassies with marshmallow halves. Arrange in a 15×10×1-inch baking pan. Broil about 4 inches from the heat for 1 to 2 minutes or until marshmallows are toasted.

to store: Place tassies in a single layer in an airtight container; cover. Store in the refrigerator up to 3 days. To serve, if desired, microwave tassies, two at a time, on 100 percent power (high) for 10 to 15 seconds or until marshmallows are softened.

nutrition facts per tassie: 164 cal., 10 g total fat (7 g sat. fat), 35 mg chol., 76 mg sodium, 16 g carb., 0 g fiber, 2 g pro.

For a whimsical presentation, cut a snowman silhouette out of holiday wrapping paper, and layer the cutout over the pan of brownies. Use ribbon for the snowman's scarf.

white chocolate and cherry brownies

prep: 25 minutes **bake:** 35 minutes at 350°F
makes: 20 bars

1	cup butter
4	ounces white baking chocolate, chopped
4	eggs
1⅓	cups granulated sugar
2	teaspoons vanilla
1	teaspoon almond extract
2	cups all-purpose flour
1½	cups snipped dried cherries
1	cup chopped sliced almonds
1	teaspoon baking powder
⅛	teaspoon salt
6	ounces white baking chocolate, chopped

1 Preheat oven to 350°F. Lightly grease 13×9×2-inch baking pan; set pan aside.

2 In a large saucepan heat and stir butter and the 4 ounces chopped white chocolate over low heat until melted and smooth. Remove from heat; cool slightly. Stir in eggs, one at a time; stir in granulated sugar, vanilla, and almond extract. Using a wooden spoon, beat just until combined. Add flour, 1 cup of the cherries, the almonds, baking powder, and salt; stir just until combined. Spread the batter evenly in the prepared pan. Sprinkle with the 6 ounces chopped white chocolate and the remaining ½ cup dried cherries.

3 Bake for 35 to 40 minutes or just until golden brown and set in the center. Cool completely in pan on a wire rack. Cut into bars.

tip: To give as a gift, bake brownies in a disposable 13½ x 9½-inch foil baking pan.

nutrition facts per bar: 333 cal., 17 g total fat (9 g sat. fat), 69 mg chol., 129 mg sodium, 41 g carb., 1 g fiber, 5 g pro.

Blood oranges derive their name from the intense red flesh.

blood orange bars

prep: 30 minutes **bake:** 35 minutes at 350°F
makes: 16 bars

1 cup all-purpose flour
3 tablespoons powdered sugar
¼ teaspoon salt
⅓ cup butter
1 cup granulated sugar
2 eggs
2 teaspoons finely shredded blood orange peel or orange peel
⅔ cup blood orange juice or orange juice
2 drops red food coloring (optional)
2 tablespoons all-purpose flour
¼ teaspoon salt
Powdered sugar

1 Preheat oven to 350°F. Line an 8×8×2-inch baking pan with foil, extending the foil over edges of pan. Grease foil; set pan aside.

2 For crust, in a large bowl stir together 1 cup flour, 3 tablespoons powdered sugar, and ¼ teaspoon salt. Using a pastry blender, cut in butter until mixture resembles coarse crumbs. Press mixture evenly onto the bottom of the prepared baking pan. Bake about 15 minutes or until light brown around the edges.

3 For fillin in a medium bowl whisk together granulated sugar, eggs, orange peel, orange juice, and, if desired, food coloring until smooth. Stir in 2 tablespoons flour and ¼ teaspoon salt. Pour filling over hot crust.

4 Bake for 20 to 25 minutes or until filling is set. Cool in pan on a wire rack. Using the foil edges, lift uncut bars out of pan. Cut into bars. Sprinkle lightly with additional powdered sugar.*

*tip: For a decorative finish, place a snowflake- or other-shape stencil on each bar before dusting with powdered sugar.

nutrition facts per bar: 138 cal., 5 g total fat (3 g sat. fat), 33 mg chol., 116 mg sodium, 23 g carb., 0 g fiber, 2 g pro.

Sweetened condensed milk is the foundation for a variety of seasonal ingredients.

holiday 7-layer bars

prep: 15 minutes **bake:** 25 minutes at 350°F
makes: 22 bars

1½ cups finely crushed graham crackers (about 21)
½ cup butter, melted
1 teaspoon finely shredded orange peel
1 14-ounce can sweetened condensed milk
2 cups white baking pieces
1 cup flaked coconut
1 cup dried cranberries or dried cherries
1 cup chopped walnuts
½ cup diced Candied Orange Peel (recipe on page 194), or purchased candied orange peel

1 Preheat oven to 350°F. Line a 13×9×2-inch baking pan with foil, extending the foil over edges of pan. Lightly grease the foil; set pan aside.

2 In a large bowl stir together the crushed graham crackers, melted butter, and the orange peel. Press crumb mixture firmly into the bottom of the prepared pan. Pour the sweetened condensed milk evenly over the crust. Sprinkle the white baking pieces, coconut, cranberries, walnuts, and candied orange peel over the condensed milk. Lightly press the layers into the condensed milk.

3 Bake for 25 to 30 minutes or until edges are lightly browned. Use a sharp knife to loosen the edges of the bars from the pan. Cool in pan on a wire rack. Use foil to lift uncut bars out of pan. Transfer to a cutting board. Cut into bars.

to store: Place bars in a single layer in an airtight container; cover. Store at room temperature up to 3 days or freeze up to 1 month.

nutrition facts per bar: 301 cal., 16 g total fat (9 g sat. fat), 16 mg chol., 131 mg sodium, 36 g carb., 1 g fiber, 3 g pro.

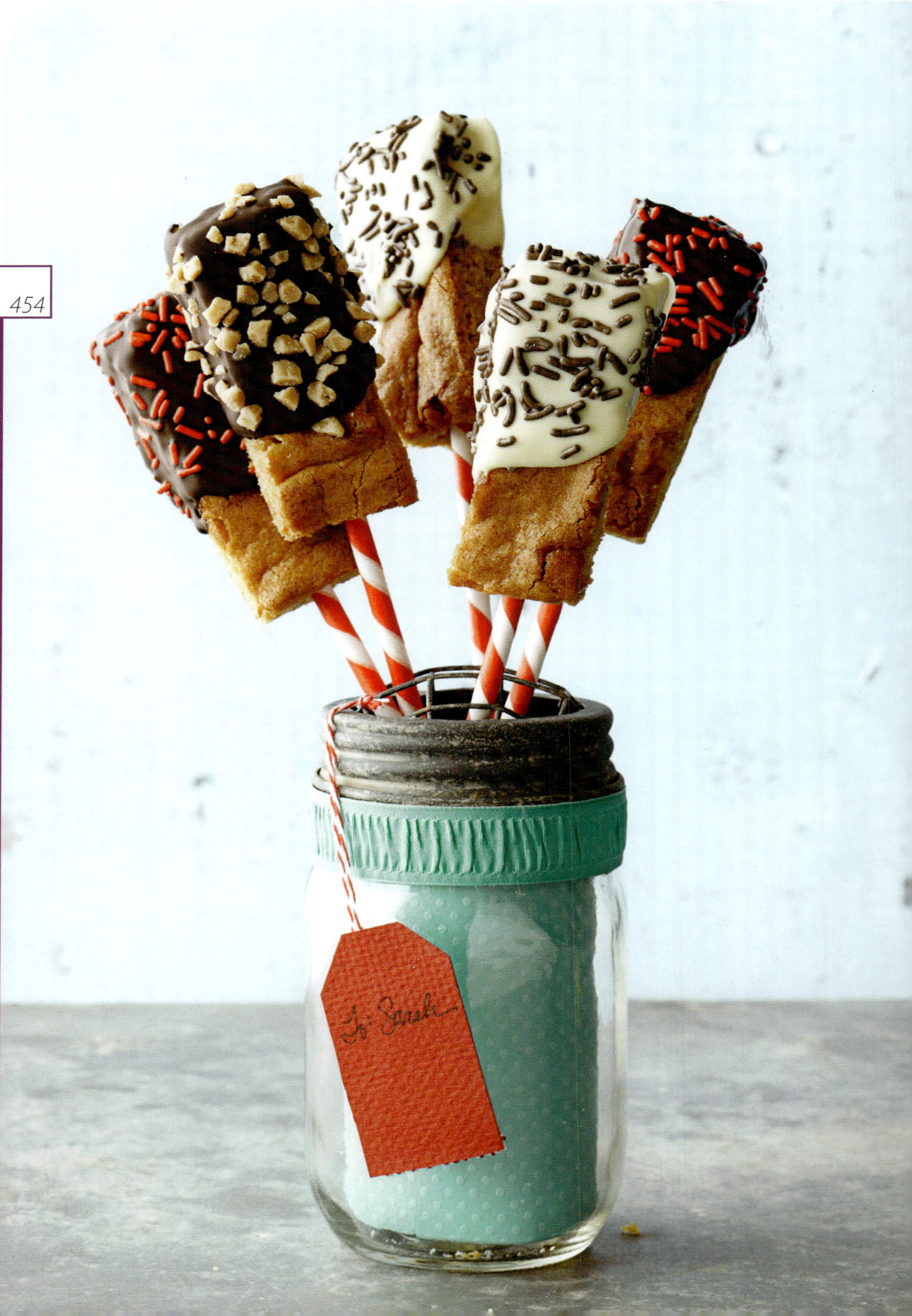
To Sarah

Chocolate-dipped blondies on a stick are special enough for any holiday gathering!

blondie stix

prep: 1 hour bake: 30 minutes at 350°F freeze: 30 minutes stand: 1 hour
makes: 32 cookies

2	cups all-purpose flour
2½	teaspoons baking powder
½	teaspoon salt
2	cups packed brown sugar
¾	cup butter, softened
1	teaspoon vanilla
3	eggs
1	cup tiny marshmallows
32	lollipop sticks or 6-inch wooden skewers
1	cup chopped unsalted cashews, toffee pieces, and/or jimmies
1	11.5-ounce package bittersweet chocolate pieces or white baking pieces

*make-ahead directions:
At this point, you can cover and chill the dough for up to 3 days. For easier spreading, bring to room temperature before using. Or transfer the dough to a freezer bag and freeze for up to 1 month. Thaw in the refrigerator, then bring to room temperature before using.

1 Preheat oven to 350°F. Line a 13×9×2-inch baking pan with foil, extending the foil over edges of pan. Grease foil; set pan aside. In a small bowl combine flour, baking powder, and salt; set aside.

2 In a large mixing bowl beat brown sugar, butter, and vanilla with an electric mixer on medium to high speed until combined. Add eggs, one at a time, beating well after each addition. Gradually beat in flour mixture. Stir in marshmallows.* Spread dough evenly in the prepared baking pan.

3 Bake about 30 minutes or until top is golden and edges are firm. Cool on a wire rack. Using the edges of the foil, lift uncut bars out of the pan. Invert onto a cutting board; remove foil. Trim edges of uncut bars to a 12×8-inch rectangle. Cut rectangle into thirty-two 3×1-inch sticks. Cover and freeze about 30 minutes or until firm.

4 Insert a lollipop stick or skewer into an end of each blondie stick and place on a waxed paper-lined baking sheet. Place cashews, nuts, toffee or candies in a small shallow bowl. In a small saucepan heat and stir chocolate pieces over low heat until melted and smooth.

5 Dip half of each blondie stick into melted chocolate, allowing excess chocolate to drip back into saucepan. Immediately sprinkle with cashews, nuts, toffee or candies. Place on prepared baking sheet. Let stand about 1 hour or until set.

to store: Layer Blondie Stixs between sheets of waxed paper in an airtight container; cover. Store in the refrigerator up to 24 hours or freeze up to 1 month.

nutrition facts per cookie: 211 cal., 11 g total fat (6 g sat. fat), 32 mg chol., 109 mg sodium, 28 g carb., 1 g fiber, 3 g pro.

For breakfast, serve with butter-flavor maple syrup.

maple cookie sticks

prep: 30 minutes **bake:** 25 minutes at 375°F + 12 minutes at 325°F **cool:** 1 hour
makes: about 52 cookies

½ cup butter, softened
½ cup shortening
1 cup packed brown
   sugar
½ cup pure maple syrup
½ teaspoon baking soda
½ teaspoon salt
2 eggs
1 teaspoon maple
   flavoring
1 teaspoon vanilla
2 cups all-purpose flour
¾ cup finely ground
   pecans
1 cup miniature white
   baking pieces
   or regular white
   baking pieces
   Chopped pecans
   (optional)

1 Preheat oven to 375°F. Line a 13×9×2-inch baking pan with foil, extending the foil over edges of pan. Set pan aside.

2 In a large mixing bowl beat beat butter and shortening with an electric mixer on medium to high speed for 30 seconds. Add brown sugar, maple syrup, baking soda, and salt. Beat until combined, scraping sides of bowl occasionally. Beat in the eggs, maple flavoring, and vanilla until combined. Beat in as much of the flour as you can with the mixer. Using a wooden spoon, stir in any remaining flour and the ground pecans. Stir in white baking pieces. Press dough evenly into prepared baking pan. If desired, sprinkle with additional chopped pecans.

3 Bake for 25 to 28 minutes or until golden brown and center is set. Cool in pan on a wire rack for 1 hour.

4 Preheat oven to 325°F. Using foil edges, lift uncut cookies out of pan and place on a cutting board, leaving cookies on foil. Cut cookies crosswise into 4½×½-inch slices. Place slices, cut sides down, about 1 inch apart on an ungreased cookie sheet.

5 Bake about 12 minutes or until cut edges are crisp. Carefully transfer cookies to wire rack (cookies will be tender); cool.

to store: Layer cookies between sheets of waxed paper in an airtight container; cover. Store at room temperature up to 3 days or freeze up to 3 months.

nutrition facts per cookie: 113 cal., 6 g total fat (3 g sat. fat), 13 mg chol., 57 mg sodium, 13 g carb., 0 g fiber, 1 g pro.

Layer the ingredients for one or more cookie mixes in decorative jars then include the baking instructions.

toffee-pecan cookie mix

start to finish: 15 minutes
makes: 30 cookies

1⅓ cups all-purpose flour
⅓ cup packed brown sugar
⅓ cup granulated sugar
½ teaspoon baking soda
½ teaspoon cream of tartar
¼ teaspoon salt
⅔ cup bittersweet or semisweet chocolate pieces
½ cup toffee pieces
½ cup coconut
⅓ cup chopped pecans, toasted (see tip, page 13)

1 In a 1-quart canning jar or other glass jar layer ingredients in the following order: flour, brown sugar, granulated sugar, baking soda, cream of tartar, salt, chocolate pieces, toffee pieces, coconut, and pecans. Fasten lid. Attach directions for making cookies.

to store: Store jar of mix in a cool, dry place up to 1 month.

to make cookies: Preheat oven to 350°F. Empty the contents of the jar into a large bowl. In a small bowl whisk together 1 egg; ¼ cup butter, softened; and ¼ cup vegetable oil. Add egg mixture to flour mixture; stir until combined. Drop dough by rounded teaspoons 2 inches apart onto an ungreased cookie sheet. Bake for 8 to 10 minutes or until edges are very light brown. Cool on cookie sheet for 1 minute. Transfer cookies to a wire rack; cool. Makes 30 cookies.

nutrition facts per cookie (all variations): 123 cal., 7 g total fat (3 g sat. fat), 12 mg chol., 74 mg sodium, 14 g carb., 1 g fiber, 1 g pro.

milk chocolate-cherry cookie mix: Prepare as directed, except use milk chocolate pieces in place of the bittersweet chocolate pieces and snipped dried cherries or cranberries in place of the toffee pieces.

tropical white chocolate cookie mix: Prepare as directed, except substitute white baking pieces for the bittersweet chocolate pieces, snipped dried apricots for the toffee pieces, and toasted chopped macadamia nuts for the pecans.

toffee-peanut cookie mix: Prepare as directed, except use candy-coated chocolate pieces instead of the bittersweet chocolate pieces and salted, roasted peanuts instead of the pecans.

Make edible gifts like cookie mixes for a fraction of the cost of similar store-bought mixes.

peanut butter cup cookie mix

prep: 20 minutes
makes: 40 large cookies

1¼ cups rolled oats
¾ cup all-purpose flour
½ cup packed brown sugar
¼ cup granulated sugar
½ teaspoon baking powder
⅛ teaspoon baking soda
½ cup coarsely chopped dry-roasted peanuts
1 cup miniature chocolate-covered peanut butter cups, halved

1 In a 1-quart jar layer oats, flour, brown sugar, granulated sugar, baking powder, baking soda, and peanuts. Place peanut butter cups in a plastic bag. Set on top of peanuts in jar. Fasten lid; attach directions for making cookies.

to make large cookies: Preheat oven to 350°F. Line a cookie sheet with parchment paper or foil. Remove peanut butter cups from jar; set aside. Empty the remaining contents of the jar into a large bowl. In another bowl whisk together ½ cup creamy peanut butter, ¼ cup softened butter, 2 eggs, and ½ teaspoon vanilla. Add to flour mixture; stir until combined. Gently stir in peanut butter cups. Using a ¼-cup measure or scoop, drop mounds of dough about 4 inches apart onto prepared cookie sheet. Flatten dough mounds to about ¾ inch. Bake for 12 to 14 minutes or until edges are brown. Cool on cookie sheet for 1 minute. Transfer to a wire rack; cool. (For small cookies, drop dough by rounded teaspoons 2 inches apart on cookie sheet. Bake for 9 to 11 minutes.)

nutrition facts per large cookie: 364 cal., 19 g total fat (6 g sat. fat), 45 mg chol., 210 mg sodium, 41 g carb., 3 g fiber, 10 g pro.

Peanut Butter Cup
Cookie Mix

When wrapping your gift, include jar of chocolate-hazelnut spread that can be used for the frosting.

hazelnut rocky road brownie mix

prep: 15 minutes
makes: 16 brownies

1¼ cups granulated sugar

⅔ cup unsweetened cocoa powder

2 ounces milk or dark chocolate, chopped (optional)

1 cup all-purpose flour

¼ teaspoon baking soda

⅛ teaspoon salt

¼ cup chopped, toasted hazelnuts (filberts) (see tip, page 444)

⅓ cup tiny marshmallows

½ cup purchased chocolate-hazelnut spread

1 In a 1-quart jar layer sugar, cocoa powder, and chopped chocolate (if using). In a small bowl stir together flour, baking soda, and salt. Spoon over chocolate in jar. Top with hazelnuts and marshmallows; fasten lid. Attach directions for making brownies. Spoon chocolate-hazelnut spread into a 4-ounce jar or a small resealable container to give with brownie mix.

to make brownies: Preheat oven to 325°F. Line a 9×9×2-inch baking pan with foil, extending the foil over edges of pan. Grease the foil; set pan aside. Set aside the chocolate-hazelnut spread for the frosting. In a large bowl whisk together ⅔ cup melted butter and 3 eggs until well combined. Add the contents of the jar to the butter mixture; stir until well combined. Spread batter evenly in the prepared pan. Bake for 35 minutes. (Moist crumbs will remain attached to wooden toothpick inserted near center of brownies). Cool brownies in pan on a wire rack. For frosting, in a medium mixing bowl beat ¼ cup softened butter with an electric mixer on low speed for 30 seconds. Add ½ cup powdered sugar and beat until smooth. Beat in chocolate-hazelnut spread until smooth. If necessary, beat in 1 to 2 teaspoons milk to make frosting spreading consistency. Spread frosting over cooled brownies. Using foil edges, lift uncut brownies out of pan. Place on cutting board. Cut into bars. Makes 16 brownies.

to store: Store jar of mix in a cool, dry place up to 1 month.

nutrition facts per brownie: 302 cal., 17 g total fat (9 g sat. fat), 63 mg chol., 152 mg sodium, 36 g carb., 2 g fiber, 4 g pro.

Just combine the mix with three beaten egg whites and bake—dessert is served!

christmas macaroon mix

start to finish: 15 minutes
makes: 30 cookies

1   7-ounce package
    flaked coconut
    (2⅔ cups)
⅔   cup granulated sugar
½   cup chopped
    almonds, toasted
    (see tip, page 13)
¼   cup all-purpose flour
¼   teaspoon salt
¼   cup chopped candied
    red and/or green
    cherries
2   tablespoons finely
    chopped purchased
    candied orange peel

1 In a 1-quart jar layer the coconut, sugar, almonds, flour, salt, candied cherries, and candied orange peel; fasten lid. Include directions for making macaroons.

to make macaroons: Preheat oven to 325°F. Line cookie sheets with parchment paper. In a large bowl stir together the contents of the jar. Add 3 lightly beaten egg whites, stirring well to combine. Drop dough by teaspoons 2 inches apart onto prepared cookie sheets. Bake for 15 to 18 minutes or until cookies are light brown. Transfer to a wire rack; cool. Makes 30 cookies.

to store: Store mix in jar in a cool, dry place up to 1 month.

nutrition facts per cookie: 83 cal., 5 g total fat (4 g sat. fat), 0 g chol., 57 mg sodium, 9 g carb., 1 g fiber, 2 g pro.

index

A

index

index

index

index

index

metric information

The charts on this page provide a guide for converting measurements from the U.S. customary system, which is used throughout this book, to the metric system.

Product Differences

Most of the ingredients called for in the recipes in this book are available in most countries. However, some are known by different names. Here are some common American ingredients and their possible counterparts:

- All-purpose flour is enriched, bleached or unbleached white household flour. When self-rising flour is used in place of all-purpose flour in a recipe that calls for leavening, omit the leavening agent (baking soda or baking powder) and salt.
- Baking soda is bicarbonate of soda.
- Cornstarch is cornflour.
- Golden raisins are sultanas.
- Light-color corn syrup is golden syrup.
- Powdered sugar is icing sugar.
- Sugar (white) is granulated, fine granulated, or castor sugar.
- Vanilla or vanilla extract is vanilla essence.

Volume and Weight

The United States traditionally uses cup measures for liquid and solid ingredients. The chart below shows the approximate imperial and metric equivalents. If you are accustomed to weighing solid ingredients, the following approximate equivalents will be helpful:

- 1 cup butter, castor sugar, or rice = 8 ounces = ½ pound = 250 grams
- 1 cup flour = 4 ounces = ¼ pound = 125 grams
- 1 cup icing sugar = 5 ounces = 150 grams

Canadian and U.S. volume for a cup measure is 8 fluid ounces (237 ml); the standard metric equivalent is 250 ml.

1 British imperial cup is 10 fluid ounces.

In Australia, 1 tablespoon equals 20 ml, and there are 4 teaspoons in the Australian tablespoon.

Spoon measures are used for smaller amounts of ingredients. Although the size of the tablespoon varies slightly in different countries, for practical purposes and for recipes in this book, a straight substitution is all that's necessary. Measurements made using cups or spoons should always be level unless stated otherwise.

Common Weight Range Replacements

Imperial / U.S.	Metric
½ ounce	15 g
1 ounce	25 g or 30 g
4 ounces (¼ pound)	115 g or 125 g
8 ounces (½ pound)	225 g or 250 g
16 ounces (1 pound)	450 g or 500 g
1¼ pounds	625 g
1½ pounds	750 g
2 pounds or 2¼ pounds	1,000 g or 1 Kg

Oven Temperature Equivalents

Fahrenheit Setting	Celsius Setting*	Gas Setting
300°F	150°C	Gas Mark 2 (very low)
325°F	160°C	Gas Mark 3 (low)
350°F	180°C	Gas Mark 4 (moderate)
375°F	190°C	Gas Mark 5 (moderate)
400°F	200°C	Gas Mark 6 (hot)
425°F	220°C	Gas Mark 7 (hot)
450°F	230°C	Gas Mark 8 (very hot)
475°F	240°C	Gas Mark 9 (very hot)
500°F	260°C	Gas Mark 10 (extremely hot)
Broil	Broil	Grill

Electric and gas ovens may be calibrated using celsius. However, for an electric oven, increase celsius setting 10 to 20 degrees when cooking above 160°C. For convection or forced air ovens (gas or electric), lower the temperature setting 25°F/10°C when cooking at all heat levels.

Baking Pan Sizes

Imperial / U.S.	Metric
9×1½-inch round cake pan	22- or 23×4-cm (1.5 L)
9×1½-inch pie plate	22- or 23×4-cm (1 L)
8×8×2-inch square cake pan	20×5-cm (2 L)
9×9×2-inch square cake pan	22- or 23×4.5-cm (2.5 L)
11×7×1½-inch baking pan	28×17×4-cm (2 L)
2-quart rectangular baking pan	30×19×4.5-cm (3 L)
13×9×2-inch baking pan	34×22×4.5-cm (3.5 L)
15×10×1-inch jelly roll pan	40×25×2-cm
9×5×3-inch loaf pan	23×13×8-cm (2 L)
2-quart casserole	2 L

U.S. / Standard Metric Equivalents

¼ teaspoon	= 0.5 ml
¼ teaspoon	= 1 ml
½ teaspoon	= 2 ml
1 teaspoon	= 5 ml
1 tablespoon	= 15 ml
2 tablespoons	= 25 ml
¼ cup = 2 fluid ounces	= 50 ml
⅓ cup = 3 fluid ounces	= 75 ml
½ cup = 4 fluid ounces	= 125 ml
⅔ cup = 5 fluid ounces	= 150 ml
¾ cup = 6 fluid ounces	= 175 ml
1 cup = 8 fluid ounces	= 250 ml
2 cups = 1 pint	= 500 ml
1 quart	= 1 litre

emergency baking substitutions

Use substitutions only when necessary because they may affect the flavor or texture of the recipe.

If you don't have:	Substitute:
Apple pie spice, 1 teaspoon	½ teaspoon ground cinnamon plus ¼ teaspoon ground nutmeg, ⅛ teaspoon ground allspice, and dash ground cloves
Baking Powder, 1 teaspoon	½ teaspoon cream of tartar plus ¼ teaspoon baking soda
Buttermilk, 1 cup	Sour milk: 1 tablespoon lemon juice or vinegar plus enough milk to equal 1 cup (let stand 5 minutes before using); or 1 cup plain yogurt
Chocolate, semisweet, 1 ounce	3 tablespoons semisweet chocolate pieces; or 1 ounce unsweetened chocolate plus 1 tablespoon sugar
Chocolate, sweet baking, 4 ounces	¼ cup unsweetened cocoa powder plus ⅓ cup sugar and 3 tablespoons shortening
Chocolate, unsweetened, 1 ounce	3 tablespoons unsweetened cocoa powder plus 1 tablespoon cooking oil or shortening
Cornstarch, 1 tablespoon (for thickening)	2 tablespoons all-purpose flour
Corn syrup, 1 cup	1 cup granulated sugar plus ¼ cup water
Egg, 1 whole large	2 egg whites; 2 egg yolks; or ¼ cup frozen egg product, thawed
Fruit liqueur, 1 tablespoon	1 tablespoon fruit juice
Ginger, grated fresh, 1 teaspoon	¼ teaspoon ground ginger
Half-and-half or light cream, 1 cup	1 tablespoon melted butter or margarine plus enough whole milk to equal 1 cup
Honey, 1 cup	1¼ cup granulated sugar plus ¼ cup water
Milk, 1 cup	½ cup evaporated milk plus ½ cup water; or 1 cup water plus ⅓ cup nonfat dry milk powder
Molasses, 1 cup	1 cup honey
Pumpkin pie spice, 1 teaspoon	½ teaspoon ground cinnamon, plus ¼ teaspoon ground ginger, ¼ teaspoon ground allspice, and ⅛ teaspoon ground nutmeg
Sour cream, dairy, 1 cup	1 cup plain yogurt
Sugar, granulated, 1 cup	1 cup packed brown sugar

Weights and Measures

3 teaspoons = 1 tablespoon	1 tablespoon = ½ fluid ounce	1 teaspoon = 5 milliliters
4 tablespoons = ¼ cup	1 cup = 8 fluid ounces	1 tablespoon = 15 milliliters
5⅓ tablespoons = ⅓ cup	1 cup = ½ pint	1 cup = 240 milliliters
8 tablespoons = ½ cup	2 cups = 1 pint	1 quart = 1 liter
10⅔ tablespoons = ⅔ cup	4 cups = 1 quart	1 ounce = 28 grams
12 tablespoons = ¾ cup	2 pints = 1 quart	1 pounds = 454 grams
16 tablespoons = 1 cup	4 quarts = 1 gallon	